STRANGER AMERICA

Cultural Frames, Framing Culture

Robert Newman, *Editor*

STRANGER AMERICA

A Narrative Ethics of Exclusion

JOSH TOTH

University of Virginia Press
CHARLOTTESVILLE AND LONDON

University of Virginia Press
© 2018 by the Rector and Visitors of the University of Virginia
All rights reserved

First published 2018

ISBN 978-0-8139-4110-3 (cloth)
ISBN 978-0-8139-4111-0 (paper)
ISBN 978-0-8139-4112-7 (ebook)

9 8 7 6 5 4 3 2 1

LIBRARY OF CONGRESS CATALOGING-IN-PUBLICATION DATA IS AVAILABLE FOR THIS TITLE.

Cover art: Both Members of This Club, George Bellows, 1909. (Courtesy National Gallery of Art, Washington, DC)

For Maude,
who's Real strange
(and because she wasn't around for the last one)

Insofar as human beings want to be actual, they must exist [muß dasein] and to this end they must limit themselves. Those who are too dismayed at the finite do not accomplish anything actual, but instead remain trapped in the abstract and fade away into themselves.

—G. W. F. HEGEL, *ENCYCLOPEDIA*

CONTENTS

Acknowledgments — xi

Introduction: *Both Members of This Club* — 1

PART I. BEING WITHDRAWN

1 Melancholics and Specters: Between James Weldon Johnson and Alan Crosland — 13

2 Promising Intrusion in Nella Larsen's *Passing* — 39

3 Articulations of Ambiguity: William Faulkner, Toni Morrison, and James McBride — 63

PART II. BEING EATEN

4 Touching Herman Melville's "Bartleby" (and Other Zombie Narratives) — 93

5 Consuming Androids in the Work of Philip K. Dick — 111

6 The Chameleon and the Dictator in Woody Allen's *Zelig* — 136

PART III. BEING GIVEN

7 The Autonarratives of Ernest Hemingway (and Others) — 159

8	The Divinely Unshareable Self: From Edward Albee to Larry David	183
9	Bob Dylan's Autoplasticity	210
	Notes	235
	Works Cited	263
	Index	275

ACKNOWLEDGMENTS

There are a number of others without whom this book would have remained an unshareable secret: the great students at MacEwan University who, over the years, have challenged and pointed out errors in my thinking (especially Samantha Massey, who forced me to endure zombie literature); an accommodating and very helpful department chair (Jillian Skeffington); the brilliant colleagues who read and offered generous critiques of early drafts, or who let me intrude upon their space and hospitably entertained my arguments (Matthew Mullins, David Rudrum, Marco Katz, Paul Lumsden, Alex Feldman, and David Reddall); a fantastic RA, who caught more errors than I'll ever admit (Victoria Throckmorton); an encouraging and thoughtful editor (Angie Hogan). I must thank, too, Jack Skeffington: a great friend who listened and advised through it all and who supplied the good spirits. And, of course, I am eternally indebted to my children (Maude and Marlow) and my wife (Danica): the former, for forgiving my necessary absences; the latter, for not (yet) divorcing me.

Some of the following chapters develop or recontextualize earlier publications: "'What Miserable Friendlessness and Loneliness Are Here Revealed': Touching Democracy in Melville's 'Bartleby, the Scrivener'" (in the essay collection *Facing Melville, Facing Italy: Democracy, Cosmopolitanism, Translation* [U of Rome (Sapienza) P]); "Do Androids Eat Electric Sheep? Egotism, Empathy, and the Ethics of Eating in the Work of

Philip K. Dick" (in *Lit: Literature Interpretation Theory*); "Deauthenticating Community: The Passing Intrusion of Clare Kendry in Nella Larsen's *Passing*" (in *MELUS*); and "'A Constantly Renewed Obligation to Remake the Self': Ernest Hemingway, *A Moveable Feast* and Autonarration" (in *North Dakota Quarterly*).

STRANGER AMERICA

Introduction: *Both Members of This Club*

I'm not a numerologist. I don't know why the number 3 is more metaphysically powerful than the number 2, but it is.

—BOB DYLAN, *CHRONICLES*

The American nightmare is on full display in George Bellows's famous painting of an interracial boxing match, *Both Members of This Club*. Completed in 1909, the ostensibly "realist" painting depicts violence and voyeurism at a private boxing club while allegorizing its specific subject matter via the deployment of certain protomodernist techniques. As Joyce Carol Oates puts it, the painting is "realistic in conception . . . [but] dreamlike in execution; poetic rather than naturalistic" (297). As do all Bellows's boxing paintings, *Both Members* largely forgoes mimetic accuracy and "depicts . . . men as wholly physical beings in extremis, killer brothers, or twins, trapped in the madness of mutual destruction" (Oates 297). On a certain level, in fact, and as Oates suggests, the painting implies or provokes bewildering uncertainty: "Is this murder, or suicide? Is there any distinction?" (297). Such uncertainty is surely implied by the paradoxical subject—two men exposing and mixing viscera in an effort to assert dominance *as* abject independence; but it is also and just as surely an effect of Bellows's willingness to traverse and exploit an ambiguous line between "Ashcan" realism and expressionistic modernism.[1] The painting's troubling depiction of an impending and irreparable confusion of self and other is conveyed via an equally troubling collapse of structure and line, a blurring of form and color, black and white. The painting asserts its subject by risking its loss to pure form. Were this painting any "truer" (in a distinctly modernist sense) it would have to forgo the distinctive coherence of the two fighters altogether; the form would *become* the subject. In threatening such dissolution, the painting draws our attention to the fantasmatic

Both Members of This Club, George Bellows, 1909. (Courtesy National Gallery of Art, Washington, DC)

nature of identity. More specifically (if more simply), the painting's formal composition and protomodernist style draws our attention to the fantasy that buttresses American conceptions of nationhood and democracy: the fantasy of pure inclusion and, therefore, pure exclusion.

Racial conflict is presented less as subject than as symptom. And yet we must attend to the painting's very specific historical context if we are to track the pathology it denotes. Bellows was working at a time when the veiled problems of a "Gilded Age" were beginning to effect very specific and very conflicting notions of individuality, national identity, and racial purity. Such conflicts accentuated the growing tension between the normative forces of democracy, technology, and social welfare and an equally American effort to retain and valorize the possibility of independence and self-reliance.[2] The fear of disability, social entropy, and the collapse of overt racial demarcations provoked a renewed investment in individualism; but the effort to sustain the individual in the face of egalitarian indifference could do little more than expose the abjectly independent self as paradoxically dependent upon a sustained relation to otherness. To remain identifiably distinct the self must maintain its relation to a whole, relation made possible by communal and regulatory norms. Consequently, the adamantly self-reliant individual invariably faces the terrifying truth that he or she cannot, in Jean-Luc Nancy's terms (and as we'll see in the following chapters), "be alone being alone" ("Inoperative" 4). Bellows lays bare this terror of relational dependence *and* corruption by evoking the very specific threat of Jack Johnson and the erosion of racial difference.

In 1908, Johnson became the first black heavyweight boxer to win the world title. Johnson's various successes against white men stoked racial tensions across the nation, tensions that ran parallel to America's increasingly vehement nativism. Johnson's dominance in the ring became particularly terrifying when, in 1910, the most hopeful in a string of "great white hopes" (the retired Jim Jeffries) was soundly defeated. Such victories, which Bellows's painting both reflects upon and anticipates, openly mocked American appeals to white supremacy and induced a type of racial hysteria. So great was the fear that, in the months leading up to the bout between Johnson and Jeffries, the *New York Times* found itself suggesting that the boxing ring was no place for a white man to assert his true superiority: "While the sort of efficiency which avails in pugilism is in itself a valuable asset for the members of a dominant race, it is perilous to risk even nominally the right of that race to exercise dominance in a conflict which brings so few of its higher superiorities into play" (qtd. in Doezema 107).[3] By providing a space for black men to "face off" against white men, boxing openly flouted the tenuous divide between American whiteness and un-American blackness—and, in turn, risked exposing their troubling interdependence. The danger and terror was therefore double: an interracial bout implied the illusory nature of such distinctions even as it exposed the impossibility of having the one without the other. This is the horrifying paradox that lurks in the shadows of Bellows's painting and that finally undermines the very possibility of the immanently American individual. The painting invokes the troubling racial politics of early twentieth-century boxing *so as* to expose more generally the terrifying and corruptive necessity of otherness (racial or otherwise), the inescapable necessity of supplementary relations. To assert the self by destroying what is other is, finally, to experience the confusing absence of all such relations. Murder becomes suicide.

It is of some significance, then, that Bellows is careful to maintain a distinction between *what* is depicted and *how* it is depicted. The painting is of two boxers (one black and one white), a ring, a jeering crowd. As they do in the earlier *Stag at Sharkey's* (1909), which depicts two white boxers, the opposed bodies in *Both Members* form (along with a third body) a triangular object. However: while the third body in *Stag* is obviously the referee to the right of the opponents, the third body in *Both Members* is easy to miss, a figure to the left who is crouched and obscured by shadows. If we focus on this indefinite figure, the triangular form—which Marianne Doezema sees beginning on the right (where the black fighter's foot pushes against the ground) and then climaxing in the confusion of fists at the top of the frame—concludes by running (equilaterally) down his back. If we fail to see him, the triangular form ends abruptly at the white fighter's shoulder blade and warps inward under the force of the black man's aggression and terrifying independence. While Doezema mentions the former possibility, she maintains a focus on "the ultimate open-endedness of the left side of the triangle" (101). She thus overlooks the fact that the painting encourages two opposed views: the collapse *and* the affirmation of its governing shape. These two possibilities signal the painting's profound undecidability. What will be the outcome? Who will win? These are the obvious questions. More implicitly, though (and given Bellows's decision to move away from more traditional forms of realism), the painting leaves us wondering if the structure itself will prevail. Will the lines of (racial, national, individual) demarcation hold? Everything, it would seem, depends upon the presence or the absence of what Hegel calls a mediating "third term"—or, for Bellows, a referee.

To be clear: the painting does not present its central figures as three equal sides of a triangle—though, of course, two fighters and a referee could form such an image (as they do in Bellows's 1907 pastel, *The Knock Out*).[4] Instead, the painting's triangular composition suggests, more radically, that a third figure is necessary if two opposing forces are to remain in balanced opposition, or communication. The possibility of sustaining two subjects in opposition *or* empathy necessarily entails proximity *as relation.* And yet, in *Both Members,* this third figure is less present than implied. He could be a spectator (as Doezema assumes), a coach, or even the referee. But the latter is unlikely. He appears to be rising out of the crowd, and his hand is holding a rope on the back side of the ring. Or maybe it isn't? It's hard to say with certainty—especially since "the ropes in the foreground inexplicably disappear to the right and the left of the boxers" (Doezema 103),[5] oddly merging with the ropes in the back. To a certain extent, the curious indefiniteness of the figure simply highlights the manner in which the difference between spectacle and spectator is beginning to dissolve. Or rather, if the referee is absent, the figure in his place merely prompts us to see the afterimage of a once stable structure.

Both Members therefore evokes, without actually or simply repeating, Bellows's typical arrangement of boxing's most essential components (i.e., two fighters and a referee). At the same time, it stresses the metonymical function of that arrangement. The triangular shape becomes a mise en abyme, echoing or reduplicating the depiction of a crowd, a structuring or mediating ring, and the spectacle of a fight. Taken further outward, the three-part structure mirrors or implicates the viewer, the painting itself, and the subject depicted. The horror of *Both Members* is, in this sense, tied to the implication that mediation and relation are no longer in play, that the victory of the self or subject has come at the cost of all distinction. In the absence of a referee, the oppositional structure is bound to collapse, and the seemingly inevitable merging of opposed figures will reach its terrifying completion (inside and outside the ring). On a literal level, of course, the referee in boxing ensures a "fair" fight. He insists upon the established order of things, standing in the way of any untoward excess. He is, by metaphoric extension, the physical embodiment of a certain masculine code of ethics. (Boxing is "a gentleman's sport.") But we should not forget, either, that in the era of Jack Johnson, the referee was invariably white, the emissary of a *white* establishment (inclusive of big business, discursive norms, etc.). His ostensible absence in *Both Members* thus points to the potential collapse of the ring and the loss of the white fighter—especially if we take "loss" to mean disappearance, or the utter confusion of self and other. The paradox is that the victory of whiteness requires the supplementary support of an "establishment" that brings it into relation with its "negative." To claim its purity and independence the self must enter a ring of corruption and dependence, a formal setting of shared codes and distressing equivalences. The deck might be stacked in the white fighter's favor, but the promise of his true victory is sustained by its impossibility—that is, a mediating point of relation, the implication of sameness, the very thing he surely wishes he could be without.[6]

Without an officiating relation to sustain difference (while paradoxically frustrating a desire for immanence), white and black, self and other, will become indistinguishable. This threat is signaled in every aspect of the painting: the forceful brushstrokes and thick paint, the grotesque and almost indistinguishable faces, the disappearing ropes. As Oates suggests, there is something Goyaesque about the proceedings (297). We might even hazard the claim that *Both Members* is an American adaptation of any one of Goya's *Los disparates*.[7] Consider, especially, *Disparate matrimonial* (i.e., *Matrimonial Folly,* or *Matrimonial Madness*).[8] In this print, two bodies (one male, the other female) have inexplicably converged, though their bodies continue to assert some semblance of an oppositional or triangular relationship. The male figure—whose face is no less animalistic and contorted than the woman's—points outward (accusingly?) at a ring of spectators. Like Bellows's spectators, these spectators have "ringside" seats; yet their own contorted and distorted faces, along with the fact that their ostensible "ring" is clearly beginning to dissolve, implicates them in the very confusion or madness they have come to witness. The utter absence of an officiating or mediating figure—referee or priest—is undeniable.

In Goya, the subject is presumably a wedding; in Bellows, an interracial bout. We might say this is only a difference in degree—but, really, it is only a difference in kind. The male victory of acquiring and subjecting a female partner is surely and only an effort to actualize the same fantasy that animates an individual's desire to assert and maintain dominance over a racialized other. And let's not overlook the suggestion (overt in Goya but certainly implied in Bellows) that the fantasy in question is also and always the fantasy of sustaining a tenuous line between human and animal. The point in either work is that any such struggle is doomed to fail, that the struggle itself threatens to erode the very ground or mediating point that makes it possible. What we see in *Both Members* is the manner in which this terrifying possibility of dissolution—as in the confusion of self and other, viewer and viewed, form and content—is paradoxically effected by a violent effort to assert the self *absolutely*. Boxing is, after all, an effort to master the other completely, an overt and ritualized staging of Hegel's "life-and-death struggle" (*Phenomenology* 114). Fighters must stake their lives in an effort to assert independence from that which is wholly external, from all that is not *purely* the self. The problem, as Hegel assures us (and as Bellows intimates), is that "this trial by death . . . does away with the truth which was supposed to issue from it, and so, too, with the certainty of self generally. For just as life is the *natural* setting of consciousness, independence without absolute negativity, so death is the *natural* negation of consciousness, negation without independence, which thus remains without the required significance of recognition" (114). While the defeated dead achieves a type of victory by forgoing any stakes in the game, the victorious living succeeds *only* by "put[ting] an end to their consciousness in its alien setting of natural existence[;] . . . they put an end to themselves, and are done away with as *extremes* wanting to be *for themselves*, or to have an existence of their own. But with this there vanishes from their interplay the essential moment of splitting into extremes with opposite characteristics; and the middle term collapses into a lifeless unity" (114).

The struggle for pure independence must necessarily entail a struggle against that which defines and sustains selfhood. Any effort to escape by defeating the other will erode the space of relation that makes the articulation of difference possible. That an *actual* boxing match never results in the horror of true ontological nullity is simply testament to the fact that boxing is a spectacle, a type of tragic (if all too real) play, a performative instance of an all-pervasive repetition compulsion. The obvious response to (yet mere obverse of) such compulsion is abject withdrawal, a distinctly Emersonian form of friendship, or communion—a complete refusal to step into the ring. Significantly, this ideal of withdrawn friendship serves as foundation for any number of more recent efforts to theorize a finally ethical and truly democratic community. From Blanchot to Derrida to Agamben to Žižek (and others) we have seen in the past several decades a clear tendency in theoretical discourse to valorize a certain withholding of the self, the willingness and ability to sustain one's reservoir of *unique* or *monstrous* potential—and, in so doing, sustain the other's. This tendency in contemporary theoretical discourse, which almost invariably runs alongside a critique of America's fraught democratic ideals, surely points to the fact that early twentieth-century anxieties about individualism, egalitarianism, and race persist today. For proof we need look no further than "the great white hope" of Donald Trump's presidential campaign and victory in 2016.[9] Is not the appeal of an "antiestablishment" politician—a politician who "says it like it is," who takes what he wants, who promises freedom and deregulation (economically and politically), who fights while refusing to be "reffed"—tied directly to a desire for immanence, the purity of (a national) identity? That such a politician would manage his affairs via a Twitter account is hardly surprising; the alluring promise of Twitter is the promise of impossible transparency, a finally and truly *im*-mediate exchange.

But if Emerson (in the nineteenth century) naïvely assumes the possibility of finally *and ethically* "put[ting] [one]self out of the reach of false relations" ("Friendship" 353)—of escaping "rash and foolish alliances which no God attends" (353), of sustaining in its purity the godlike mystery of the unique self—contemporary theorists have tended to be (at their most nuanced) more radical. Contemporary efforts to theorize the possibility of sustaining an ideal of communal belonging while forgoing communally mandated acts of exclusion and dominance go beyond Emersonian naïveté whenever they open us to the fact that we must endure "a certain confusion" (Blanchot 22), that we cannot be alone without sharing our aloneness, that the preservation of selfhood is never "a question of withdrawing incognito or in secret" (25). Overly simplistic appeals to ethical withdrawal (even post-Emersonian ones) refuse the necessity of enduring this paradox. For this reason, they tend to be no less futile than the "life-and-death struggle" Bellows appears to critique and that the nationalist and populist movements of today seem to embrace. Nor do they tend to be any less tied to melancholic anxieties about faltering ontological distinctions and hierarchies (between races, genders, or species). Any effort to assert the self as wholly anterior to corruptive and supplementary relations—to mediating and equalizing norms, to relational points of negation, loss and confusion—must entail the self-defeating sacrifice of otherness.

Bellows's painting is an exemplary depiction of this dilemma insofar as it exposes an indissoluble connection between ontological and representational uncertainty. The possibility that the self is bound to dissolve in the moment of its most profound victory (or articulation) is echoed in the possibility that the painting's subject will only appear *in truth* the moment it is no longer opposed to or corrupted by the supplement of its form, the moment when the indecipherability of an ambiguous form finally makes possible our apprehension of the Real. In either case, the subject is only gained in the moment of its loss—when a middle term, an interfering mediator or referee, a ring or a frame, vanishes altogether. But the latent realism of Bellows's painting suggests an alternative. It points to the absolute necessity of representational form, the necessity of an understandable and always corruptive point of communal sharing, while simultaneously signaling (and therefore preserving some sense of) what is lost. While depicting one of the most overt and futile efforts to assert independence (or impossible racial purity *as* ontological immanence), Bellows's painting shares *while preserving* an infinitely plastic subject. It opens us to the possibility of (what I come to call in the following chapters) an autoplastic act. Such an act would entail a profoundly ethical commitment to Hegelian sublation: the possibility of giving a subject by signaling the impossibility of containing its divine truth. To perform an autoplastic act we must "tarry[] with the negative" (Hegel, *Phenomenology* 19). We must endure an ethical imperative to respect and protect that which we can neither defeat nor bring into equivalence with any given form of understanding—even as we question and challenge the efficacy and ethical limitations of such forms (such as, for instance, white patriarchal discourse). Faced with this imperative, our only recourse is to engage in acts of representational concealment that paradoxically smuggle in, by outlining the constituent absence of, a core opacity. Only in this way might we sustain the self while enduring the corruptive necessity of relation, of what sustains an unknowable otherness that is nevertheless the constituent ground of selfhood. This is precisely what the following chapters attempt to demonstrate.

Or rather, *Stranger America* is an effort to track and delineate in America's narrative media the anxieties Bellows's painting provokes. The goal is to intervene in an ongoing theoretical debate about community formation and the ideal of American democracy so as to identify a specific and efficacious modality of democratic self-sharing—one that might allow us to endure and sustain "a certain confusion" while perpetually forestalling the ontological dissolution that threatens Bellows's fighters, their audience, and the representative act that relates them. To that end, the book is divided into three distinct but interrelated parts, each of which contains three chapters. Part I focuses on America's racial anxieties, especially as they are reflected in the narrative forms of the early twentieth century. But race is not the subject per se. In America, as Bellows's works suggests, the phenomena of racial conflict is tightly knotted to the impossibility of fully harmonizing an ideal of democratic equality with a will toward abject self-reliance and individuality. Narrative efforts to negotiate this aporetic knotting tend to be particularly attuned to transhistorical and transnational theories of selfhood and otherness. When placed in direct dialogue with these theories, they have the potential to *attune us* to the possibility of a narrative ethics—the possibility of sustaining otherness in the face of its necessary and corruptive expressions. To approach this possibility, part I follows the thread of racial anxiety, specifically the connection between racial ambiguity and literary acts of obfuscation (both modern and postmodern). But this particular thread necessarily gives way to a larger problem, or knot. The issue of race and racial conflict in part I functions, in other words, as an exemplary access point to the more general issue of communal belonging and identificatory processes: the risk of losing oneself to communal norms and the irresponsibility of preserving one's truth via alienating modes of withdrawal. The necessity of negotiating these extremes—of communal entropy (on the one hand) and feckless egotism (on the other)—is then reapproached in part II. Here the focus is on the politics of eating, on the problem of consuming otherness and of being consumed. What motivates the (physical, economic, ideological) consumption of others? How do we justify it? How might we begin to consume ethically while giving ourselves to be taken in, shared, interiorized? While the specific issue of race is moved to the background, part II nevertheless moves (via this new angle of approach) toward the same conclusion as part I: the necessity and possibility of a narrative form that can "give" a subject (to be consumed) while respecting and preserving the profound unknowability of that which is abjectly other. The specific qualities of this form are finally tracked and defined in part III.

In all three parts, the artifacts considered are strategically diverse. They represent (as much as possible) a broad cross section of narrative genres and historical periods. This diversity highlights the ubiquity of the problem discussed, but it also functions to show how different narrative modalities at different times have been employed (successfully or not) to make sense of and manage that problem. What holds these artifacts together is the manner in which they expose the significance and radical potential of strangeness. On the one hand, they tend to concern characters (like Herman Melville's Bartleby or Nella Larsen's Clare) who adamantly resist being fixed in any given category or performance of identity; on the other, they tend to employ narrative techniques that disrupt the inertia of normative sense making. Often the disruptive nature of the narrative form goes hand in hand with the strangeness of the character(s) depicted. In such cases, the intrusive nature of the text takes on a dual function: (1) it evokes while challenging the very promise that ostensibly defines, even as it necessarily opposes the possibility of sustaining, American identity—that is, the end of exclusionary identity politics; (2) it accentuates the ethical responsibility or promise of narrative representation. Like Bellows's painting, it opens us to the possibility that certain narrative acts can "give" a subject while respecting the profound unknowability of that which is abjectly other. By tracking the varied expressions of such a possibility, *Stranger America* attempts to apprehend a new narrative approach to American democracy ("autoplasticity") and to offer it as a way of resisting America's exclusionary and melancholic tendencies—as a way (perhaps) to realize a truly democratic form of community, or as a way (perhaps) to realize "a relation without relation or without relation other than the incommensurable" (Blanchot 25).

PART I

BEING WITHDRAWN

You are the only one to understand why it really was necessary that I write exactly the opposite, as concerns axiomatics, of what I desire, what I know my desire to be, in other words you: living speech, presence itself, proximity, the proper, the guard, etc. I have necessarily written upside down—and in order to surrender to Necessity.

—JACQUES DERRIDA, *ENVOIS*

1 / Melancholics and Specters: Between James Weldon Johnson and Alan Crosland

> *I'll go along with the charade*
> *Until I can think my way out*
> —~~JAMES T. KIRK~~ BOB DYLAN, "TIGHT CONNECTION
> TO MY HEART (HAS ANYBODY SEEN MY LOVE)"

A Hippopotamus Is Not a Ghost

The American dream is a melancholic's fantasy.[1] Unwilling to forgo the promise of ontological immanence (in the form of solipsistic self-creation), America's melancholic nevertheless dreams of democratic egalitarianism, assimilation, and communal wholeness. Such a dreamer denies the impossibility of reconciling his or her paradoxical desires. Instead of mourning for its loss, the melancholic sustains the possibility of an impossible object of desire. The moment exclusion is required to buttress a sense of selfhood (as defined by communal membership), we are witness to claims and promises of inclusivity and wholeness. These melancholic fantasies reify the abject otherness of the excluded subject/group while simultaneously maintaining the myth of pure inclusion—and thus, through a somewhat bewildering inversion, the myth of the autonomous (or finally immanent) self. The self, after all, is only ever revealed *in* relation. I am who and what I am because I am a member of one group and not a member of another. Yet my *relation* to the same necessarily entails difference, just as my *relation* to the different necessarily entails sameness. The melancholic (as national) idealist denies the impossibility of escaping the supplementary and corruptive nature of relation, the fact that (as Jean-Luc Nancy insists) "presence is impossible except as copresence" ("Being Singular" 62). I necessarily find myself *in* the whole, but that whole (like the individual) is defined by and determined through relation—inclusion *and* exclusion. I am never fully included, and the other is never fully excluded. I am, for instance, white because I am not black. However, my whiteness is never the same as another's whiteness, and blackness is never exclusive of features with which I might otherwise identify.[2] In this sense, we cannot have inclusion without its opposite, and the self never appears anterior to the communal relations that never fully define it. The purity of the self is always corrupted by the very thing that makes it possible. Relation is always (in Derrida's terms) a supplement, a pharmakon,[3] a corruptive necessity. There are no clean cuts. Appeals to selfhood and autonomy are undermined by the self's dependence upon group identification, and a group is only ever the tenuous delineation of what it refuses. The nationalist (or racist, or sexist) melancholic refuses this paradox, insisting instead upon the possibility of the immanent self and pure communal inclusivity. In the national idealist's dream, there is no exclusion because whatever is left out is beyond *or anterior to* relation (e.g., the slave as wholly other). The myth of the immanent self thus demands a concurrent and equally impossible myth: the myth of the immanent or wholly Other.[4] In her efforts to uncover the melancholic nature "of American national idealism" (10), Anne Anlin Cheng largely overlooks this fact. Consequently, in *The Melancholy of Race*, Cheng fails to explore the paradoxical manner in which appeals to pure inclusivity make possible *while utterly frustrating* appeals to pure individuality. Defined by its inclusion, the individual must risk falling victim to the purity of the group. In this sense, an appeal to pure inclusivity is only nominally opposed to an appeal to pure individualism: either the self is abandoned to the entropy of the group, or the group is solipsistically swallowed up by the conceit of the self. At either pole there is no possibility of difference.

    Nevertheless, Cheng is certainly correct to suggest that the consequences of American national idealism manifest most obviously in (or rather *as*) America's race relations. An instructive point of reference in this regard (given, especially, its overtly infantile nature) is Sandra Boynton's 1982 "board book" for toddlers, *But Not the Hippopotamus*. The book functions as a simplistic allegory of America's exclusionary race politics and the melancholia such politics entail. On each page of the book we are given both a description and an illustration of animals frolicking about. On the first page, for instance (and along with a corresponding illustration), we are told that "a hog and a frog cavort in the bog." On this and every other page, we are also witness to an obviously excluded hippopotamus. In the opening illustration, the hippopotamus lurks behind a tree. And so "a hog and a frog cavort in the bog. But not the hippopotamus." This formula repeats throughout: "A cat and two rats are trying on hats"; "A moose and a goose together have juice"; and so on. But not, *but never,* the hippopotamus. Until, of course, the penultimate page. At this point, all the animals previously described and illustrated come together to play, and (as if—we are surely lead to imagine—*an afterthought*) they finally turn and ask the hippopotamus to join. The hippopotamus quickly considers the invitation, and (when we turn the page) we get the victory line: "But YES the hippopotamus!" The message of inclusion seems for a moment quite clear, but this is not the final page of the book. On the final page, which sits opposite the hippopotamus's victory, we are given an illustration of a solitary and clearly depressed armadillo. Beneath this illustration the celebratory line concludes: "But YES the hippopotamus! But not the armadillo." Given Cheng's discussion of American racial politics, we might very well (if too easily) identify the armadillo's depressed state (and *not* the manifest dream that precedes it) as an expression of American melancholia.

Cheng's conception of (racial) melancholia is further justified by the fact that the penultimate moment of inclusion and communal wholeness is followed (or better, *made possible*) by a moment of exclusion. As Cheng puts it, "Racialization in America may be said to operate through the institutional process of producing a dominant, standard, white national ideal, which is sustained by the exclusion-yet-retention of racialized others" (10). "American national idealism," Cheng goes on to note, "has always been caught in this melancholic bind between incorporation and rejection" (10). Cheng thus stresses the manner in which the acts of exclusion necessary to establish and maintain an American dominant necessarily negate the ideal of democracy and egalitarianism to which such a dominant ostensibly subscribes (and which subsequently provides the central grounding for its formation as an identity category in the first place). Cheng, though, concludes that this seemingly inevitable process of "exclusion-yet-retention" creates a type of spectral figure, a ghostly "other" who is neither included nor excluded, present or absent. And so the resulting melancholia Cheng identifies is always twofold. On the one hand, the dominant's melancholia is an expression of its desire but inability to wholly accept (or include) that which it cannot wholly abandon (or deny). On the other, the racialized other experiences a melancholic desire to belong to that which the marks of "race" bar access—that is, to be what one is not.

So, while Boynton's dominant animals—or rather, the other animals who have been previously and successfully interpellated as dominant—may be having a grand old time outwardly, their fun is certainly marred by the presence of the hippopotamus. For surely, like the reader, they cannot avoid what is in plain sight, always present (if abandoned necessarily as absent other)? And even once this tension is seemingly resolved (and democracy, we might say, properly asserted) the armadillo arrives on the scene—quite necessarily, we should note. The hippopotamus, after all, cannot be "accepted" unless there exists a predefined group that can do the accepting. And, as in all such cases, this particular group is defined by *what it is not:* inclusive of armadillos. (We should note that the animals that make up the group—hogs, frogs, cats, rats, moose, hippopotami, etc.—are certainly no more *like* each other than they are *different from* armadillos.) Used, though, to make sense of Cheng's specific conception of American melancholia, Boyton's book begs a significant if simple question: Where is the ghost? Where is the melancholic specter, the subject who is never entirely present *or* absent? Everything (in infantile, or cartoon, fashion) is defined, almost to the extreme. Ontological stability abounds: "A hog and a frog cavort in the bog. But not the hippopotamus." The racial/speciesist differences, and thus the grounds for inclusion or exclusion, are stressed at every turn. Never are we witness to "a group of hogs cavorting in a bog while what *might be* another hog *may or may* not be sitting alone on a log." The hippopotamus (like, later, the armadillo) is certainly just as *present* as everyone else; she or he is just present as marginalized other, as (therefore, and in the dream that sustains the sense of community enjoyed by the other animals) *wholly* Other. In this way, the book reminds us that melancholia (racial or otherwise) is, as Cheng herself notes (following Freud), an effort to sustain or *conserve* the ego. While it is often associated (by Freud and others) with expressions of self-loathing or guilt, melancholia ultimately functions to resist or deny the ego's potential dissolution. Melancholia functions to resist, in other words, *the possibility of ghosts.*[5]

National or racial melancholia therefore entails an effort to sustain the possibility of radical exclusion as the possibility of pure inclusion. The racial other, as confirmed and *fixed* other (or excluded outsider), is hardly terrifying on an ontological level. It is, we might say, the most comforting thing there can be. It *is* (Other); and so it functions to define and reify (safely and quite comfortably) what it *is not.* The group maintains its purity so long as the ambiguity of a necessary and necessarily corruptive relation is denied. This is, as I suggest above, the paradoxical and melancholic dream of pure inclusion. There is simply no confusion about who is—or who should be—included and who shouldn't. At one point the hippopotamus is overtly Other; at another, unquestionably the Same. Or rather, a clearly defined and clearly *present* hippopotamus or armadillo can exist outside the inclusive community or, if and when we change our mind about what race or species is the same as "us," brought in and assimilated as a member. The myth of immanence—of a self-contained community (and thus self)—is sustained. In this sense, American melancholia can be understood as less a state of depression effected by acts of "exclusion-yet-retention" than the effort to remain blind to the corruptive ambiguity of relation in the face of its ontological necessity, for "the pure outside, like the pure inside, renders all sorts of togetherness impossible" (Nancy, "Being Singular" 60). Identity *as being* is only possible in relation, but relation (*with*) makes impossible its immanence, its finality, its cartoonish solidity. What is truly terrifying, what *cannot* be tolerated (not if this whole system of illusory identity formation—or, rather, inclusionary/exclusionary politics—is to be sustained) is the specter, that which refuses (as Derrida would say) all categorical definition.[6] The specter disrupts a specifically nationalistic and racist brand of melancholia as the insistence upon the hallucinatory possibility of inclusion *or* exclusion. Without accounting for this *threat* of the truly spectral (or relation as ontological cross contamination), Cheng's conception of American melancholia as a type of pervasive and virtually unavoidable social disease can hardly account for the violence that is almost predictably tied to racial politics in America. For what the nationalist melancholic ultimately and violently refuses to accept (and therefore mourn) is the impossibility of the self in its purity, or without the burden of existential freedom. The symptom of self-loathing Freud identifies as characteristic of more traditional states of melancholia—effected, typically, by an effort to sustain an idealized yet failed relationship—is thus likely to manifest (on a national or racial level) as guilt, shame, or pity: the desire to be the other is shameful because it is a categorical impossibility just as the other *as Other* simply and quite unfortunately can't be included. This is the oddly comforting shame of the slave *as well as* the self-satisfying pity, or guilt, of the slaveholder. Faith, after all, in the melancholia-inducing possibility of pure inclusivity *as* pure exclusivity must be understood as faith in the possibility of a fixed identity or "libidinal position"—and, as Freud assures us, "People never willingly abandon a libidinal position" ("Mourning" 244). Moreover, the ensuing "opposition can be so intense that a turning away from reality takes place and a clinging to the object through the medium of a hallucinatory wishful psychosis" (244) ensues. And we certainly see such "turning away" on both sides of inclusion/exclusion boundaries. To interrupt it is, almost invariably, to provoke hostility.

The Lynch Conjurative

The American response to racial instability, and by extension to the experience of communal and ontological instability, is almost predictably violent. Given the above, this violence can be understood as a concerted effort to prolong a state of melancholia—as, that is, a refusal to mourn the impossibility of the self's (racial or national) immanence. The problem of lynching is thus particularly germane to any discussion of racial politics in America. Indeed, one of the most noteworthy scenes in James Weldon Johnson's 1912 *Autobiography of an Ex-Colored Man*—one of the first and most influential "passing" narratives in American literature[7]—is a lynching. While we are left to assume that the man the mixed-race narrator describes (in shocking detail) burning alive is unambiguously "black," we simply cannot be certain—not at first, anyway. The narrator refuses, for one reason or another, to specify the race of the man being lynched, even though meticulous descriptions of skin color can be found on almost every other page of *The Autobiography*. However, the fact that we can safely assume that the man being lynched is black speaks to the very function of a lynching. That the man *is lynched* suggests that he *must be* black. The lynching makes the man black in the same way that the fire that ultimately consumes his living flesh leaves nothing but "blackened bones" (128). And, of course, shortly after describing the lynching, the unnamed narrator validates our likely unconscious assumption, stating that he felt utter "shame at being identified with *a people* that could with impunity be treated worse than animals" (129; my emphasis). As a process of blackening the body, the function of the lynching transcends the *physically* violent act of burning a human alive. Such a scene suggests, therefore, that the concept of "a lynching" (with all its horrific and shock-inspiring connotations in tow) is appropriate for connoting *any* process of racial "fixing." One is lynched, we might say, whenever one is brought to the belief that his or her allegiance to a racial group, or community, is defined by an essential and intransgressible bond. Or, as Nancy suggests, the desire to fix the other as Other is *always* "a desire for murder" ("Being Singular" 20). Obviously, the horror and violence of a physical lynching is hardly comparable to the ubiquitous function of interpellation in day-to-day living, and we surely cannot ignore the fact that (in America) the victim of a physical lynching is almost invariably black—or *made to be* black. At the same time, we should not overlook the ways in which the impulse to lynch transcends the physical act; it is implicit in any effort to defend against infectious boundary crossings or states of ambiguity. The result is always a form of mortification, an ossification of exclusionary boundaries. While the consequences of such ossification varies (empowering some and marginalizing others),[8] its function is always the same—to stabilize a sense of self. It is hardly surprising that in America (where appeals to a "native" whiteness are persistently frustrated), the impulse toward self/communal stability manifests overtly in an outrageously brutal act perpetrated against, and so as to maintain, blackness. In this act we see the focused eruption of an overwhelming yet unutterable ontological anxiety—the fear that the other has begun to contaminate and destabilize the self.

Indeed, the impulse to "fix" the black body as Black is presented by Johnson as a direct response to a necessarily tenuous fantasy, a fantasy that reaches its apotheosis in the abjectly exclusionary act of a physical lynching. A lynching is, in short, a type of cure, a harsh but effective form of social chemotherapy. Whether it be ostentatiously violent or inconspicuously ideological, a lynching works to cure what Derrida calls in *Politics of Friendship* the "pathology of the community," the threat of an internal disease eating away at the stability of communal and therefore individual identity, the sickening impossibility of "a solid friendship founded on *homogeneity*, on *homophilia*, on a solid and firm affinity . . . stemming from birth, from native community" (92). The most obvious symptom of this "pathology"—this disease that requires an endless series of curative lynchings—is that person who resists (because of ambiguous skin tone, or whatever) being fixed as Other or Same. Such a person is nothing but a ghost, an intrusive (because perpetually strange) stranger. By extension, the finally lynched Other (in its confirmed binary opposition to the self) is wholly antithetical to all things spectral. Derrida puts it like this: "Where the principal enemy, the 'structuring' enemy, seems nowhere to be found, where it ceases to be identifiable and thus reliable—that is, where [a] *phobia* projects a mobile multiplicity of potential, interchangeable, metonymic enemies, in secret alliance with one another: conjuration" (*Politics of Friendship* 84). Conjuration: to make present finally; to call back into being as confirmed Other; to erase/exorcise the spectrality that terrifies us; to fix, finally. Or rather, given the above, a lynching is always, in one way or another, a curative or conjurative response to the terrifying implications of the spectral.

It is particularly significant, then, that (after passing as a member of a lynch mob), the narrator of *The Autobiography* decides to embrace his ghostly and frightening potential: "I was not going to be a Negro" (131). He is, though, careful to explain that, while passing, he "would neither disclaim the black race nor claim the white race" (129). At this point, the narrator is, as I note above, motivated primarily by feelings of shame and humiliation: "A great wave of humiliation and shame swept over me. Shame I belonged to a race that could be so dealt with; and shame for my country, that it, the great example of democracy to the world, should be the only civilized, if not the only state on earth, where a human being would be burned alive" (128). As it is tied to the narrator's assumption of absolute belonging, this shame is profoundly melancholic. Not only is the narrator, as racialized other, longing to break his racial bond; he is fully aware of the impossibility (as well as the pointlessness) of becoming a member of a dominant group defined primarily by acts of cruelty. This failure of the American democratic machine inspires his apparent decision to abandon the machine altogether. In a moment of what we might call racial purgation, the narrator refuses to end up like the lynched man, to be (that is) *lynched*. Or rather, this moment, which comes at the end of the penultimate chapter, seemingly indicates that the narrator from this point forward will no longer be subject to—or, better, *subjected by*—what we might begin to call "conjurative" forms of racial lynching. If this is true—if the narrator is indeed embracing a type of ghostly status in a culture compelled to impose upon itself a melancholia-inducing state of racial absolutes—then he is most certainly embracing what Nancy (following Sartre) would call "freedom." For we might in fact say (if only tentatively, at this point) that only a ghost accepts being *as freedom*.

The Ghost of Freedom

In the various essays that make up *The Experience of Freedom,* Nancy is particularly interested in the (existential) freedom that relation necessarily entails. Relation *entails* freedom because relation is the impossibility of a fixed identity. That which is indicative of such freedom is, thus, typically dealt with violently, even if the violence inflicted is not always physical. As Nancy notes, *"Evil is the hatred of existence as such"* (*Freedom* 128). By this Nancy suggests that evil is the activity of denying or refusing existence as freedom, as the constant play of emerging (in) relation: "Wickedness does not hate this or that singularity: it hates singularity as such and the singular relation of singularities. It hates freedom, equality, and fraternity; it hates sharing. This hatred is freedom's own (it is therefore also the hatred that belongs to equality and fraternity; sharing hates itself and is devoted to ruin)" (128). An effect of our freedom tends to be a hatred of that freedom, a need (at the simplest level) to *melancholically* "[*refuse*] *existence*" (129). A lynching is the epitome of such a refusal, the epitome of evil. Lynching works to firm up communal boundaries, to impose the essential bond separating *these* from *those,* blacks from whites (in this particular case). As Nancy insists, "Wickedness does not hate *this* or *that* singularity" (128; my emphasis). It hates, instead, the sense, the implication, that there is no foundational reason for maintaining "this" as opposed to "that," that neither a "black man" nor a "white man" can ever *be* anything but *in relation* to blackness or whiteness. Wickedness hates the implication that melancholia is not an unavoidable disease.

But in neither denying nor accepting his black (or white) heritage, and as critics of the novel (and the phenomenon of passing, generally) tend to suggest,[9] the narrator of *The Autobiography* leads us to assume that he plans to become the most threatening (because free) entity there can be: a ghost. He seemingly rejects the evil of the lynching, and the complicity of both "whites" and "blacks" in that evil, so as to live in a state of perpetual ambiguity, a state in which he will never be *this* or *that,* black or white. He will merely acknowledge the fact that (in terms of his racial allegiances, anyway) he is only ever *becoming*—and always for the first time, as both Nancy and Derrida would insist—in a repetitive series of relations.[10] Or, if we recall Sartre (who haunts Nancy's entire discussion of freedom), the narrator, after witnessing the lynching, outwardly embraces his "constantly renewed obligation to remake the *Self*" (72). But it's not quite as simple as this. In the end, the narrator is unable or unwilling to embrace his ghostly status, his contingently relational (and thus *passing*—in the strictly ontological, or "hauntological,"[11] sense of the word) state. The narrator's autobiography *as confessional* is clearly indicative of this failure. While, in the moments after the lynching, the narrator finds the will to walk away from the evil of the lynch mob, the fact that he eventually feels compelled to tell his racial *truth* points to the fact that his escape is momentary at best. More likely, it is an illusion, a categorical impossibility. That he comes to exclude himself from the black community means relatively little (in terms of freedom, anyway), because he never finally escapes the margins, and thus a melancholic claim to (racial) membership. The narrator never escapes his "bad faith" (in the strictly Sartrean sense of the phrase).[12] Each apparent expression or performance of freedom results in another conjurative lynching, another experience of *becoming* wrenched back into an assumption of *being*. On the one hand, the narrator seems rightly concerned that he is irresponsibly refusing to gamble on any particular aspect of his identity; on the other, he fails to maintain (what I will come to call in later chapters) a sense of his "autoplasticity"—or a sense of self that is not simply or only a reification of prevailing social constructs. By submitting to a traditional autobiographical mode, the narrator imposes upon himself (by shamefully confessing) a finite truth. Paradoxically, this final insistence upon a self that is no different from its graphic representation—upon, that is, a self that can be finally and fully revealed—is no less a betrayal of the self than is a perpetually performative (or "passing") state. Both the autobiographer and the harlequin abandon responsibility for the self. By confessing to a *true* self, the autobiographer denies freedom, or latent (relational) potential; in presenting the self as *nothing but* relation, the harlequin evades the risks of sincerity or ontological fidelity. In either case, the self is utterly and irresponsibly withdrawn, and an *ethical* relation is rendered impossible. A potential solution to this dilemma will, I hope, reveal itself by degrees and in the course of the following chapters. For now, the dilemma itself needs to be drawn out—or, perhaps, *traced* more fully in Johnson's text.

Early on in the novel, the narrator tells his mysterious benefactor—who provides the narrator with the opportunity to "culture" himself in Europe and, thus, to embrace and exploit his racial ambiguity for the first time since childhood (when the narrator was still ignorant of his ostensible blackness)—that he plans to return to America so as to become a type of classically trained ragtime artist. He insists, though, that he must do so as a black man. The benefactor is quick to point out the absurdity of such a desire:

> My boy, you are by blood, by appearance, by education, and by tastes, a white man. Now, why do you want to throw your life away amidst the poverty and ignorance, in the hopeless struggle, of the black people of the United States? . . . I doubt that even a white musician of recognized ability could succeed there by working on the theory that American music should be based on negro themes. Music is a universal art; anybody's music belongs to everybody; you can't limit it to race or country. (104)

There are a number of things worth noting here. (1) The benefactor clearly suggests that the narrator is no more essentially black than he is white and that (given his current social situation) the narrator is more white *in relation* than black. Both categories are presented as contingent, not absolute. As the benefactor puts it, the narrator (in returning to America) will only be "*making* a negro of [himself]" (104; my emphasis). (2) The theme of music (and jazz, specifically) is clearly linked here to identity and the desire for absolutes.[13] The suggestion is that an essentially black music is a fantasy, another concept driven by exclusionary politics. Indeed, if we simply insert the word "self" in place of "music," the benefactor's point about music and identity becomes particularly suggestive, especially in light of Nancy's take on freedom and relation: "[The self] is a universal art; anybody's [self] belongs to everybody; you can't limit [the self] to race or country." In this sense, the novel's stress on the overtly playful, improvisational, and *relational* nature of jazz (along with the suggestion that it could be made to *pass* as the classical music of Europe) functions as a sharp counterpoint to the narrator's various conjurative acts, or racial re-turns. Jazz, after all, organizes itself around yet simultaneously refuses a melancholia-inducing absolute (or reassuring and predictable motif).[14] In jazz, this motif is only ever *Real*, or absolute, insofar as it emerges via the various digressions, or performances, that momentarily delineate (while simultaneously and necessarily effacing) it. There is an essentially *non*-essential plasticity to such motifs.

After hearing his benefactor out, the narrator briefly questions his decision. However, he convinces himself, somewhat sheepishly, that his real reason for wanting to be black (and, one might add, American) is benignly and strategically monetary: "I argued that music offered me a better future than anything else I had knowledge of . . . and . . . that I should have greater chances of attracting attention as a coloured composer than as a white one" (106). While we might, at this point, take him at his word (and thus view his return to blackness as nothing but performance), a later and far more striking conjurative event undermines these earlier excuses. Soon after deciding to pass as white, the narrator falls in love with the "most dazzlingly white thing [he] had ever seen" (133). Whenever in the presence of this "dazzlingly white" woman—a woman, moreover, he soon hopes to marry—the narrator feels compelled to confess. He feels that he cannot possibly "ask her to marry [him] under false colours" (134). Her very presence, in fact—or, more accurately, her gaze—forces him "to wonder if [he] really was like the men [he] associated with; if there was not, after all, an indefinable something which marked a difference" (134). And, after finally confessing his secret (self), he sees her "gazing at [him] with a wild, fixed stare, as though [he] was some object she had never seen. Under the strange light in her eyes [he] felt that [he] was growing black and thick-featured and crimp-haired" (137). In the moments that follow, the narrator finds himself melancholically and shamefully wishing he "were *really* white" (137; my emphasis). There is, we might say, a type of double lynching at work here, a conjurative repetition that ensures the return of an undeniably melancholic state. The narrator's confession as an initial self-lynching is reenacted (or confirmed) in the "dazzlingly white" woman's lynch-effecting gaze. And while the narrator does indeed win this woman's hand in marriage (having with her two children, one dark and one light), this moment of confession and conformational gaze seems to pave the way for the narrator's final and perhaps most effective self-lynching—*The Autobiography* itself.

A (Narrative) Self-Lynching

The confessional nature of *The Autobiography* is strikingly clear at the outset:

> I know that I am playing with fire, and I feel the thrill which accompanies that most fascinating pastime; and, back of it all, I think I find a sort of savage and diabolical desire to gather up all the little tragedies of my life, and turn them into a practical joke on society.
>
> And, too, I suffer a vague feeling of unsatisfaction, of regret, of almost remorse, from which I am seeking relief, and of which I shall speak in the last paragraph of my account. (29)

Tied (as it is) to America's late nineteenth- and early twentieth-century fixation on the "tragic mulatto," the joke in question here is surely the doubt that *The Autobiography* would have induced in the readers of its day. Who is this man? Do I know him? Do I know, or am I friends with, a man who is only pretending to be white, a man who is *really* and *in essence* black? In this sense, *The Autobiography* does indeed function as a mockery of the lynching impulse, an exposition and endorsement of freedom, a ghostly intrusion thrust into the melancholic heart of America. Yet *The Autobiography* seems incapable of sustaining its joke. Or, perhaps, *The Autobiography* suggests that such a joke is, on some level, impossible to sustain. The narrator's confidence in his own blackness—which, it's fair to say, ebbs and flows throughout the novel—cannot but reify a reader's sense of a clearly defined racial (and thus melancholic) order. That a reader might well feel frustrated or terrified by the implication that he or she knows this man does not mean that the fantasy of hierarchal absolutes that provokes such frustration and terror has been undermined. Moreover, the "unsatisfaction" (or, we might say, instability and freedom) that the narrator feels—and that the novel initially points to as its playful effect—is nullified by the narrator's own and seemingly inevitable endorsement of the social structures and assumptions that he so often seems to undermine. So, although the narrator feels "shame at being identified with a people that could with impunity be treated worse than animals" (129), his need to confess speaks to his shameful (or intensely melancholic) need for such an identification. He feels it necessary, after all, to "[play] with fire"—to, we might assume, sacrifice himself to the "blackening" fire of a (self-)lynching. But, as the narrator suggests in his opening lines, we need to return to the end to understand the specifics of this desire and this shame.

The novel famously concludes with the narrator (years after his wife's death in childbirth) remarking that, at times, he feels as though he has "never really been a Negro." Yet, "at other times," he goes on to note, "[he] feel[s] that [he has] been a coward, a deserter, ... possessed by a strange longing for [his] mother's people" (140). This observation of his own conflicting desires—for freedom on the one hand, for a stable and melancholic identity on the other—leads the narrator to recall a talk he recently attended by Booker T. Washington. He notes that such men "are making history and a race" and that "[he], too, might have taken part in a work so glorious" (140). For this reason, and even though the narrator asserts that his love for his children keeps him satisfied with his choice (as well as his decision to write *The Autobiography* anonymously), he concludes with lines of clear regret: "And yet, when I sometimes open a little box in which I still keep my fast yellowing manuscripts, the only tangible remnants of a vanished dream, a dead ambition, a sacrificed talent, I cannot repress the thought that, after all, I have chosen the lesser part, that I have sold my birthright for a mess of pottage" (140). It is, of course, easy to read these lines as indicative of the narrator's belief that he has acted as a deserter, that he has denied and abandoned his true self (as reflected in the race to which he is essentially bound by blood). However, we should not ignore the other possible reading, the reading that the guilt expressed here concerns his inability to endure his freedom, to believe that he has never "*really* been a Negro" (or anything else, for that matter), to truly walk away from the violent melancholia of America's racial politics.[15]

This latter reading is supported by the narrator's reference to his "yellowing manuscripts" (or various musical scores) as well has his articulation, in the opening lines, of "a vague feeling of unsatisfaction" (for which *The Autobiography* is meant to function as a curative/conjurative tool). In other words, this final reminder of the narrator's now broken relationship with a potentially transnational and transracial musical form—tied, as it is here, to his desire to feel finally satisfied *and whole*—opens up the possibility that the regret expressed in these closing lines is the narrator's regret for being unable to persist as an always coming, always passing (always repeating yet always new) ghost. For the reference to jazz evokes a direct link between the narrator's inability or unwillingness to accept/understand his benefactor's claims about music and identity and his final compulsion to enact a final, narrative self-lynching. The novel thus concludes by exposing a type of ontological impasse. On some level, the narrator seems to understand or sense that there is no way to preserve himself in truth: either he remains a hollow performance, or effect of transient relations, or he commits fully to his "truth" by way of an autobiographical confession. The narrator tries to find a middle ground by confessing anonymously, but his need to confess already betrays his faith in a concrete self that is wholly anterior to the relations that define it. In this sense, *The Autobiography* (as novel) ponders the possibility of sustaining the self in the face of its relational plasticity—especially when, at the dawn of the Harlem Renaissance and the Jazz Age, the very limitations of racial identity were beginning to seem increasingly arbitrary and tenuous. Yet the novel, like its narrator, clearly seems to suspect that such a possibility is somehow implied by the nature of jazz performance, in the relationship between motif and improvisation. And is not this relationship, already, the relationship between literacy and orality, silence and sound?

A Jazzed Kol Nidre

If Johnson's novel, in 1912, begins the process of uncovering or entertaining a connection between American jazz forms and a potentially ethical performance of (racial) identity, then surely we can trace a direct line between it and the release of Alan Crosland's 1927 film, *The Jazz Singer*. Starring the already famous Al Jolson—an American Jew who frequently performed in blackface—*The Jazz Singer* is perhaps most famous for pioneering the use of recorded dialogue in American cinema. Yet it is also famous (today) for its troubling and ostensibly naïve use of blackface. What is particularly striking about the film, though (especially in light of the above discussion), is the manner in which its use of sound (and thus silence) is inextricably linked to the process or act of "blacking"—and, in turn, its obvious effort to grapple with America's growing fear (in the 1920s) that the line between racial authenticity and racial masquerade was beginning to erode. By 1927, as John T. Matthews notes (while attempting to trace a link between Faulkner's use of dialect and Crosland's use of blackface), American appeals to nativism were in full swing. Evoking the implications of and support for America's 1924 Immigration Act,[16] Matthews goes on to suggest that "for nativists, American identity came to be understood as something one inherited by blood rather than acquired through citizenship" (70). The necessary consequence of this shift in understanding was a growing fixation on family "as the ultimate ground of national identity" (71).[17]

No wonder, then, that Crosland's film, which details an American Jewish boy's rise to fame as an (assimilated) American jazz singer, is so deeply concerned with family, ethnicity, and national belonging. When the film opens, the central character, Jakie Rabinowitz, is a young boy living in the

"New York Ghetto" with his mother and his father, the local cantor. As we soon learn, Jakie longs to perform contemporary jazz numbers on stage, but his father assumes and later insists that he will use "the voice God gave him" and become the next cantor. These opening scenes are entirely "silent." Information is provided visually or via intertitles; a largely orchestral score plays in the nondiegetic background. The score, of course, also includes a number of Yiddish and contemporary American songs—typically played over scenes depicting New York life or Jakie's experiences as a performer. However, whenever we are witness to Jakie's home or family life, the score is overtly and traditionally "classical"—dominated, specifically, by the work of Tchaikovsky.[18] In this way, the film seems to imply a connection between silence, traditional (or specifically romantic) musical forms, text (in the form of intertitles), and the restrictive law of the father. Or rather, the film positions Jakie's father (and, in turn, the edicts of Jewish tradition) as the antithesis of jazz performance and cultural change. Yet this implication is oddly frustrated when the film finally employs—suddenly and quite unexpectedly—overtly synchronized diegetic sound. The scene occurs *after* a young Jakie is discovered singing and dancing to jazz music at a local saloon. After being introduced by the saloon's piano player as "Ragtime Jakie," young Jakie clearly sings the song we hear ("My Gal Sal"). There is, however, little to no sense of synchronization in the scene; the song we hear, like the orchestral score that proceeds and follows it, seems to originate from *outside* the scene. The film maintains its "silence"; by implication, Jakie remains confined within a space of paternal authority.

However, after the cantor is brought to the saloon to witness Jakie's performance—and after the cantor whips and then disowns his son—we are finally presented with truly synchronized sound. But it is not Jakie's voice we hear; it is the cantor's. As both Jakie and his mother look on, the cantor sings Kol Nidre—a traditional Aramaic chant that, as Joel Rosenberg notes, marks the beginning of Yom Kippur and functions as "a legal declaration limiting the force of one's vows and oaths" (17). In Rosenberg's translation, the chant ends with the following lines: "Our vows shall not be vows, / our oaths shall not be oaths, / our prohibitions not be prohibitions" (18). Rosenberg goes on to suggest that the use of the chant in the film (especially given its placement in this early scene and then again at the end) highlights the problem of assimilation with which the film struggles. The chant, after all, "acquired deeper significance when, during the Spanish Inquisition, many Jews who were forcibly converted to Catholicism continued to practice Judaism in secret and used Kol Nidre as a means of renouncing vows imposed by the Inquisition authorities" (17). Such Jews became known as Marranos—a term that is etymologically linked to pigs and uncleanliness. The problem in this scene, as Rosenberg notes, is that Kol Nidre is recited but not completed; the scene ends before the final request for absolution arrives. Cut off from its concluding lines, the chant seems to insist upon (rather than absolve its listeners from) past vows: "It is as if the recitation, with its cascade of oaths and vows and prohibitions, its parade of I-shall-nots, has been heaped higher and higher upon the already burdened soul of each Rabinowitz. Part 1 of the film's story thus ends with each soul enclosed within itself—within its prescribed social itinerary, its gender, its generation, and its linguistic horizon. Each soul's burdens are unrelieved" (20). This problem of a prescribed—or better, *fixed*—"linguistic horizon" is worth stressing, as the scene clearly highlights the imposition and expectations of cultural allegiance and fixed sociosymbolic identities. From a strictly Lacanian perspective, the scene articulates the reassertion of a fixed symbolic order, an order in which Jakie can no longer be the Jewish son of a cantor if he is also an American jazz singer. The now disowned Jakie must therefore listen (in secret) from outside the synagogue proper; likewise, his distraught mother must listen from the *Ezrat Nashim* (or women's section). In this sense, the scene insists upon a type of silence (or symbolic rigidity)—especially if we associate that silence with the figure of the presiding cantor/father who is frequently presented in wide and medium shots that highlight both his agency and his control. And yet the cantor's voice finally and fully breaks the film's nondiegetic barrier. His song is heartfelt; clearly coming from *within*—or rather, from *outside*—the silent/symbolic construction of the scene. The scene's depiction of a symbolic absolute, or law of the father, is disrupted even as it is reaffirmed. The cantor's passion functions to remind us that, as Jakie's mother has already noted, "[Jakie] knows all the [cantor's songs]—he has them in his head—but not his heart." This display of the cantor's own heart thus establishes the film's tendency to link the voice of the individual with the possibility of an authentic self, the opacity of which remains always anterior to the social structures that necessarily define and confine it. Jakie's heart (recognized by and now associated with his mother) is unable to find satisfactory expression here; to sing at synagogue would be, for young Jakie, an imposition upon the self, a reified performative act, a type of lynching. Pure silence. It would be akin to the narrator of Johnson's *Autobiography* assuming his "blackness."

We should note, too, as Rosenberg does, that this initial performance of Kol Nidre introduces the film's apparent employment or endorsement of a type of Bakhtinian "polyphony." The film weaves together a classical score, English jazz performances, Aramaic chants, and Yiddish songs—all the while combining the visual with the audible. In this way, the film—as representative of a larger move toward cinematic sound in the twenties and thirties—seems to parallel the development of the modern experimental novel: the deployment of narrative ambiguity, linguistic play, and streams of consciousness. Sound in film, like avant-garde literary technique, ostensibly signals and responds to the sterility of those narratives that would have us believe their images or their signifiers are transparent and mimetically fixed. We might in fact say (following Bakhtin) that silence is to the hegemonic poetic tradition what sound is to the heteroglot novel. Not surprisingly, then, the introduction of sound signals, too, the promise as well as the threat of an increasingly diverse American society. The arrival of voice in film "exaggerated difference and singled out the foreigner. It displayed the rich variegation of regional identities, but likewise intensified pressure for conformity and censorship" (Rosenberg 13). The cantor's singing of Kol Nidre seems therefore to have an oddly dual function. On the one hand, it marks the arrival (in *The Jazz Singer* and in film more generally) of the individual voice and, in turn, the apparent impossibility of fixed meaning and directorial (or authorial) control. As Rosenberg puts it, "Sound film exchanged the hegemony of a director's voice for that of the actor's, and traded the intimacy of director-actor communication for the *mise-en-scène,* the staged construction" (29). In terms of the film's depiction of race and familial allegiances, this auditory "rupture" in the film's visual diegesis necessarily undermines its *silent* expression of (racial) melancholia. The cantor's own allegiances and vows (racial, religious, and cultural) are subtly associated with *his* performance of Kol Nidre. The implication is that such allegiances and vows are always already performances—overtly individual, mutable, and unbinding. On the other hand, the truncated nature of the chant closes down, or leaves deferred, the promise its *performance* implies. The first act of the film thus concludes by suggesting that the promise of jazz performance (and cinematic sound) must be denied by—*because it frustrates the very possibility of*—a fixed or mute racial identity.

Mothers, Fathers, and Jazz Singers

If the promise of jazz *as the mutability of sound* is implied yet deferred or repressed in the film's first act, it is fully realized in the second—when, that is, Al Jolson (as Jakie) finally sings *and* talks. The first instance is particularly striking (if not disconcertingly uncanny)—even, I would suggest, for a contemporary audience. After an intertitle informing us that what we are about to see occurs "years later—and three thousand miles from home," a fade out (and then in) brings us to "Coffee Dan's" and an adult Jakie eating and enjoying lively music. Jakie, we are told by intertitle, is now known as the jazz performer "Jack Robin." After being approached by the café's proprietor, Jack agrees to perform "Dirty Hands, Dirty Face." When Jolson begins to sing he is fully synchronized, and it is clearly Jolson's own voice. Yet the score in this scene, as in the earlier instances of synchronization, blends smoothly into the performance. For this reason, Jolson's performance of "Dirty Hands" is hardly "jarring"; it barely disrupts the film's silent inertia, seeming more "classic" than "contemporary." However, as soon as Jolson finishes the song, and the audience roars its approval, Jolson (as if by magic) suddenly speaks: "Wait a minute, wait a minute," he says. "You ain't heard nothin' yet." The line—which Jolson was already famous for uttering during performances—is simply too apropos. He's right; we haven't. Jolson *as Jack,* and after audibly talking to the band behind him, then launches into a swinging version of "Toot, Toot, Tootsie (Goo' Bye)." The entire film seems to change at this point, and sound (at least momentarily) takes over. Yet, at precisely the same time, we get the fairly obvious suggestion that Jakie (now the Americanized and compromised "Jack Robin") is in danger of wholly losing himself to the vagaries of that sound—that, in losing himself to performance *as (only) performance,* he is justifying his father's earlier and silent lament: "We have no son."

If we can indeed trace a connection between the development and use of sound in film, the rise of the modernist avant-garde novel, and the threat of an increasingly pluralized American society, then we must take seriously Crosland's ostensible effort to negotiate the central paradox of the modernist movement—which is, of course, the paradox haunting any effort to valorize or wholly deploy Bakhtinian heteroglossia. As Matthews notes (referencing Michael North's *Dialect of Modernism*), the central "modernist irony . . . rests on the effort to transcend language through language" (74). The modernist's increasingly impenetrable deployment of polyphony or dialogic play can be understood as symptomatic of "a widespread modernist frustration with the limitations of language to deliver the thing itself" (74). No single representational act can lay claim to the truth or opacity of "the thing"; this fact—like the thing itself—entails a virtually endless series of complementary and competing representational acts. A properly dialogic text paradoxically renews the possibility of ontological access by deploying various viewpoints that are always clearly in relation to, or frustrated by, a host of others. Such polyphony is precisely what, according to Bakhtin, the hegemonic (or poetic) text refuses: "The possibility of another vocabulary, another semantics, other syntactic forms and so forth, to the possibility of other linguistic points of view, is . . . foreign to poetic style . . . [T]herefore a critical qualified relationship to one's own language (as merely one of many languages in a heteroglot world) is foreign to poetic style—as is a related phenomenon, the incomplete commitment of oneself, of one's full meaning, to a given language" (285). Bakhtin's effort to valorize an "incomplete commitment" of the self is particularly noteworthy. The sense we get is that a "full commitment of the self"—like any hegemonic act of representation—entails a loss of the self (or thing represented). The self/thing is preserved insofar as it is *only* implied by a series of equally contingent representational acts, or dialogic strands. The problem is that the self/thing becomes increasingly incoherent the more diffuse, the more multiple and plural, such strands become—to the point, obviously, of representational opacity. Consider, as just a single representative instance, Faulkner's most impenetrable works. The arrival of such impenetrability can be viewed, if we return to Nancy, as the moment when the possibility of a self that is anterior to relation and intersubjective definition is entirely lost *to relation*. Such an opacity must surely represent a type of inverted evil. Not an evil that "hates sharing" (if we follow Nancy), but an evil that abandons responsibility for the self/thing to an indecipherable cacophony of arbitrary possibilities. While polyphony implies the self's innate ontological freedom (as well as, then, the illusory nature of racial absolutes), it simultaneously risks becoming the evil of pure and irresponsible performance. While the hegemony of the poetic text certainly silences by closing down the perpetual play of expression, the freedom to speak *only* in tongues entails the troubling possibility and irresponsibility of pure incoherence. At either pole—the absolute materiality of the self *or* its absolute immateriality—the promise of a sustained and democratic hauntology is denied. At either pole a certain sense of melancholia is sustained. Either we succumb to a satisfying sense of guilt (concerning an abject inability to be or include the other) or we concede to an equally satisfying sense of existential despair (concerning the fact that *all* ontological allegiances are illusory).

This brings us back to Jakie/Jack. While the truth of Jakie's self is clearly threatened by the hegemonic imposition of his symbolic role (or cultural obligation), Jack frequently seems to be in danger of losing himself to the arbitrariness of performance. This tension is mirrored throughout the film in the distinction between the home and America's cultural centers. Outside the home, Jakie is no longer himself; at home, Jack is unable to play. The film's effort to negotiate this conflict is announced most overtly when Jack finally returns home to begin rehearsing for his first Broadway revue. Once back in New York, he immediately goes home to see his mother. Her love and support are expressed silently through visuals and intertitles, and Jack decides to sing her "one of the songs [he's] going to try out." He leads her to a chair near the piano and begins to play. Jolson's voice once again ruptures the silence, and we are given an extended and very playful depiction of a son singing to and conversing with his mother. Jolson's flirtatious behavior, though, clearly announces the Oedipal nature of the relationship. He flutters his eyelashes and rolls his eyes. He "steals" a kiss and then promises to "give it back . . . someday." He promises to move her up to the Bronx where a "whole lotta 'bergs" live. He tells her that he'll buy her a "nice pink dress." The entire time Jolson plays the piano, maintaining a jazzy rhythm. The sense we get is that Jack (and not Jakie) has invaded the home with his artifice, that he is simply "playing" his mother—as he would any other woman in an audience. (Jolson, in fact, refers to himself in this scene as "little Jackie," not Jakie.) Moreover, he seems intent on drawing the defining characteristics of Jewish life into his "play." He claims that there are too many "'bergs" to know, and the suggestion that he'll dress the cantor's wife in pink—"You'll wear pink, or else," he says—is simply absurd. The scene carries with it an edge of awkwardness, if not outright tension. This awkwardness effectively foreshadows the arrival of the cantor. As Jack begins playing an even more "jazzy" version of the song he's been singing ("Blue Skies"), his father becomes visible in the background. His authority is signaled by the fact that he is momentarily framed (in full) by the bedroom doorway. He looks on for a minute as Jack continues to play; then, in a rage, he yells, "Stop!" All sound immediately ceases. The film returns abruptly to the silent tradition, and the rest of scene is played out (tragically) through intertitles. The cantor decries Jack's decision to "bring [his] jazz songs . . . into [his] house." But Jack reminds the cantor "that music is the voice of God! It is as honorable to sing in the theatre as in the synagogue!" In saying this, Jack reminds us of the obvious connection between the cantor's synchronized singing (earlier) of Kol Nidre and his own jazz performances. But the cantor remains firm and silent and again casts Jack out.

While the Oedipal implications of this scene cannot be ignored, its role (in the context of the film as a whole) is more Hegelian than Freudian—if, that is, it is possible to sustain such a distinction for any length of time. Once again we get the suggestion that Jakie's mother accepts and represents Jakie's innate self, or "heart"—even if Jakie, *as Jack*, can offer her little more than a performance of that self. Jack's return to his mother and his home signifies his effort to hold to and articulate (as Hegel might say) "the law of the heart," the *notion* of his true or essential self. (It's worth recalling that the narrator of Johnson's *Autobiography* also associates his *true* self with "[his] mother's people" [140].) And yet, as the film repeatedly suggests, that self must find its signification outside the self—outside, that is, its maternal home. Lost somewhere between the ribald sound of his maternal serenade and the hegemony of his father's silence, Jack must struggle to satisfy the mandates of his "heart" while negotiating "the law . . . which confronts the law of [that] heart" (Hegel, *Phenomenology* 222). While the former, for Hegel, is linked to the maternal body, the latter is associated with the mandates of the father and virtuous behavior, the will of the Other (if we follow Lacan's use of the uppercase O). The latter, too (as Hegel frequently suggests), is never more than "the way of the world" (or the law of all other hearts), for "this ordinance is really animated by the consciousness of all, that it is the law of every heart" (224–25). The problem is that any effort to abide by the "law of the heart" necessarily entails activity within and thus acquiescence to that which ostensibly opposes it:

> The individual who seeks the pleasure of *enjoying his individuality*, finds it in the Family, and the necessity in which that pleasure passes away is his own self-consciousness as a citizen of his nation. Or, again, it is in knowing that the law of his own heart is the law of all hearts, in knowing the consciousness of the self as the acknowledged universal order; it is virtue, which enjoys the fruits of its sacrifice, which brings about what it sets out to do, viz. to bring forth the essence into the light of day, and its enjoyment is this universal life. (276–77)

If the enjoyment of one's innate truth is to find its expression, the essential bond of family must give way to social order. In this sense, Jack's maternal serenade signals a futile effort to stay home, to preserve himself *in truth*. The cantor may see in Jack's heartfelt jazz a type of domestic intrusion, but it is clearly Jakie's mother who signifies consanguinity and the divine law of a "true" self. The cantor's "house" is something else; it is the house of law. The cantor functions as a type of cultural guardian, the law of a communal or universal will (in the form of race, gender, religion, etc.) pitted against the individual who refuses to behave with virtue, to abandon his individual aims and (by doing so) rediscover enjoyment as acquiescence to universal law and the common good.[19] At, then, the very moment he finds himself in danger of *over* performing, Jack struggles to bring to the surface "that [self] which belongs to the divine law [and which] sees in the other side only the violence of human caprice" (280); or rather, in singing to his mother and breaking the silence of his father's hegemonic household, Jack resists "that which holds to human law [and sees *in Jack*] only the self-will and disobedience of the individual who insists on being his own authority" (280). Ultimately, though, and quite necessarily, these ostensibly opposed positions fall in on each other: the arbitrary and human laws of the (in this case, Jewish) community become fixed and *silent* absolutes, while the essential and divine law (or "heart") of the self is undermined by its necessary acquiescence to communal and therefore performative modes of expression. Jack defies one father only to risk submission to another (American) one. Instead of being a silent Jew, Jack risks becoming a silent American—with silence, of course, signifying the endpoint of hegemonic representation, the phallogocentric delusion that the self *is* the intersubjective role it plays. While the film obviously struggles with this apparent danger, it struggles too (if more implicitly) with the apparent alternative: preserve the essential opacity of the self by refusing altogether the coherent and thus delimiting codes of an intersubjective order (i.e., the law of all other hearts); this would entail preserving the self within *or as* radical cacophony, endless improvisational play, jazz in the absence of an accessible motif. But such a preservation would be no less an effacement.

And so this collapse of opposing poles brings us back to our starting point—the paradox of community *as* the possibility of the individual. As Hegel puts it, "The community ... can only maintain itself by suppressing [the] spirit of individualism,[20] and, because it is an essential moment, all the same creates it and, moreover, creates it by its repressive attitude towards it as a hostile principle" (288). The self cannot exist outside communal involvement, and the community cannot exist without the individuals who determine while necessarily negating the essential nature of its coherence and its laws. The self (as absolute and moral)[21] is only ever preserved in the moment of its sublation.[22] This is, it would seem, precisely what Jack comes to understand in the end—as, significantly, he "blackens" himself in preparation for his first Broadway performance. Indeed, the film's most famous and troubling scene seemingly confirms Hegel's suggestion that "the ethical consciousness must ... acknowledge its opposite as its own actuality, must acknowledge its guilt" (284).[23] Jack can only sustain his immanent self as a *guilty* self. But surely this guilt is a step beyond the pleasurable guilt of the melancholic? Surely it is not the guilt of pity, or self-gratifying sympathy? It is the guilt that opens up the possibility of (what Hegel understands to be) "conscience"—the guilt of a self that acknowledges and sustains the necessity of an ongoing betrayal or dissemblance of that self. Jack's, then, is the quintessential guilt of the specter, a specter who neither refuses nor assumes its material and wholly anterior immanence.

Passing, Blacking

In her discussion of the film's "blacking" scene—and while referring to Mary Ann Doane's efforts to distinguish between sexual transvestitism (which reifies the difference between the performer and the identity performed) and masquerade (which highlights the performative nature of the mask itself)[24]—Ruth D. Johnston suggests that "Jack's blackface image structurally resembles female masquerade in that it calls into question stable identity" ("Construction" 386). In this way, Johnston resists Michael Rogin's influential suggestion that blackface in *The Jazz Singer* (like all other instances of American blackface) functions to undermine the threat of miscegenation and racial ambiguity in early twentieth-century America.[25] Rogin's point is this: in a time when the racial identity of most immigrants (including Jews) was largely indeterminate, the act of blacking signified the innate whiteness (i.e., Americanism) of the performer. Blackface solidified a white/black binary. Or rather, as a type of racial transvestitism, blacking enacts yet another mode of lynching, an *evil* effort to maintain the melancholic possibility of pure exclusion/inclusion. But as Johnston suggests, and as we've already seen, Crosland's film clearly problematizes just such a possibility.

When we first see Jack blacking he is clearly struggling with—and thus, on some level, confirming—his Jewish identity. The scene plays out in silence. Jack's gentile girlfriend, Mary Dale (May McAvoy) enters Jack's changing room to show off the dress she'll be wearing in the show. Jack compliments her but seems distracted. Mary encourages Jack to reveal his true feelings as he carefully covers his face and hands in cork, slowly (and quite uncannily) transforming his look. When he finally puts on his wig and presents himself in full blackface, Jack insists that "[he's] going to put everything [he's] got into [his] songs." Significantly, Jack seems to speak from *beneath* his mask even as the mask comes to signify what, exactly, he's "got." Jack's blackface is, after all, the blackface we see in minstrelsy; it is not the blackface we see in, say, a film like D. W. Griffith's

The Birth of a Nation (1915).[26] There is no effort to "fool" the viewer here. An overt and comical "white space" remains around Jolson's lips. And while this white space should (following Rogin) signify Jack's whiteness and thus Americanness, it seems instead to signify his Jewishness even as the cork ostensibly links that Jewishness to the most marginalized group in America (and, by implication, the improvisational nature of what was then understood to be "black" music). In other words, Jack's Jewishness is simultaneously maintained even as it is equated with his performance of blackness and jazz. Immediately after we see his "blackface" in close-up, Jack looks wistfully to a picture of his mother. Mary notices and then comments on his gaze. Her comment, though, seems oddly "off topic": "I'm afraid you're worrying—about your father." But she's right, of course. As Jack confirms, "I'd love to sing for *my people*—but *I belong here*" (my emphasis). Once again Jack's mother seems to remind Jack of his true "heart" and (as Mary clearly intuits) his opposition to the paternal community that both opposes and makes possible the expression of that heart. Not surprisingly, then, it is when Jack is at his "blackest" and most performative that we see his most sincere and guilt-ridden expression of his Jewish identity, "the cry of [his] race."[27] Jack's subsequent delivery (in blackface) of "Mother of Mine (I Still Have You)" extends this moment of sincerity while further stressing the necessity of its performance. Or rather, as the film comes to its close, we begin to see that Jack's core opacity, or immanence, is preserved only in those moments when it is expressed as a performance of Hegelian conscience, a resistant acquiescence to the silencing nature of intersubjective, or *paternal,* sense. The film seemingly courts so as to finally subvert the evil of melancholia—a possibility, we should add, Nancy largely overlooks (as does also, of course, the narrator of Johnson's *Autobiography*).

Neither of the film's final two scenes offer us a Jack who is fully anterior to a (relational) performance. And yet both intimate—particularly through the use of diegetic sound—that Jack's heart is on full display. Jack, of course, finally and virtuously decides to risk his career to fulfill his father's dying wishes. This penultimate scene cuts between Jack singing Kol Nidre and his father dying in bed. Yet the final scene finds Jack back on stage and back in blackface, his sacrifice apparently rewarded. However, the blackfaced Jack who sings to his mother (or rather, given the song he sings, his "mammy") in the first row of the Broadway auditorium is no more (or less) a performance than the Jack who finally sings Kol Nidre (in full cantorial garb). Jack's Jewish vestments in this penultimate scene clearly take the place of his cork mask, masking so as to reveal what is preserved beneath. Moreover, Jolson's lamentational and impassioned singing (in cantorial garb) of Kol Nidre resonates with his earlier singing of "Mother of Mine." Even more significantly, as Rosenberg notes, Jolson effectively sings Kol Nidre "as jazz." And, as it is when his father sings it earlier in the film, the chant is oddly truncated; the final appeal for absolution never arrives. Jolson's jazzlike version stresses this truncation; the song begins to break up toward its conclusion as Jolson "riffs" on the central terms of its first clause, its stress on oaths and prohibitions. The chant consequently suggests that "Jack is still caught in the bramble of I-shall-nots that had enmeshed young Jakie and his parents on that night, years before, when he had left home" (Rosenberg 37). Only this time, Rosenberg suggests, Jack has forsaken his allegiance to Broadway and modern jazz culture—*not* his ethnicity or the Jewish culture. However, Jolson's singing of "Mother of Mine" (which tonally parallels his singing of Kol Nidre) seemingly provides the atonement cut from the Kol Nidre. The song opens with an apology to a "Mother divine": "Mother, I'm sorry I've wandered away / Breaking your heart as I did." This apology is then effectively canceled by the song's central refrain: "With your arms about me," the song goes on, "I know I'm not to blame." Back to back, the two performances confirm the film's tendency to link communal oaths with paternal authority, "the law of the heart" with maternal divinity (or immanence). The former must necessarily be lost to the latter *even if* the latter must never wholly subsume the former. Jack absolves himself even as he sustains a sense of conscience through guilt—guilt that signifies his responsibility to an always still anterior self. The success of such absolution is seemingly confirmed by the more upbeat performance of "My Mammy," which closes the film and brings Jack's mother to tears.

As *both* blackfaced jazz musician and Jewish cantor, Jack performs himself so as *to make sense of himself*, to gamble on a relationally coherent version of himself. In this way, the film seemingly confirms Hegel's suggestion that "an individual cannot know what he [really] is until he has made himself a reality" (*Phenomenology* 240). Linked in the film to the performative and improvisationally contingent nature of jazz, this process of "making oneself a reality" is most certainly the effect of relation. Like the improvisations of jazz, "relation happens only in the withdrawal of what would unite or necessarily communicate me to others and to myself, in the withdrawal of the community of the being of existence, without which there would be no singularity but only being's immanence to itself" (Nancy, *Freedom* 69). And yet it is through relation that I am *in any way* understood, or communicated—just as it is by way of improvisation that, in jazz, a central motif is sustained. Paternal silence in *The Jazz Singer* represents, then, the assumption that a given improvisation *is* the motif, that the self *is* its communally understood performance, or utterance. Paternal silence is at the heart of racism, the dream of pure inclusion, melancholia itself. It is akin to the purifying fire of a lynching.

Whenever sound violently ruptures the diegesis of *The Jazz Singer*, we are given the possibility of the immanently divine self. These moments are always paradoxical; the disruption of sound signals the impossibility of any single and final utterance, any pure relation. Sound *reveals* the immanent self while paradoxically signaling the impossibility of its final apprehension. In a certain sense, the film overcomes what we might think of as a Nancyian tendency to fixate on the impossibility of *being* outside relation. Like Johnson's *Autobiography* it points to the potential irresponsibility of such a tendency, the irresponsibility of abandoning the self entirely to the contingency of relations, the cacophony of a purely "heteroglot world." But, unlike Johnson's *Autobiography*, Crosland's film seems to open the way to a possible solution—the possibility, that is, of sublating the immanent self through relation *as performance*. Dressed as cantor, Jack is, after all, as Mary puts it, "a jazz singer—singing to his God." This "statement registers," as Rosenberg suggests, "a kind of simultaneous consternation and admiration—that a jazz singer, the very essence of modernity, would have a God or an ethnically rooted tradition of worship—and, implicitly, a suggestion that the worship is itself a form of jazz, pouring forth in the spontaneity and ecstasy of the jazzmaker's riffs" (38). Taken further, Mary's statement (which can be applied also and equally to Jack's performances in blackface) highlights the film's ostensible affirmation of a type of Hegelian dialectics, its suggestion that the immanent or divine (self) is that "which, in being laid hold of, flees, or . . . has already flown" (*Phenomenology* 131). However, before we can consider the full political efficacy of such a return to Hegel, we must first continue to explore the full extent and full implications of America's melancholic tendencies—racial and otherwise. At the same time, we must consider (as both Johnson and Crosland seem to) the way in which certain forceful denials of melancholia might lead to irresponsible appeals to the contingency of relation, or the absolute withdrawal of the self. As the antithesis of pure inclusion (and therefore nationalist melancholia), such a withdrawal would surely signal the frightening hegemony of cultural and contingent frames of knowledge and the impossibility of a self that is ever anterior to *and thus responsible for* such frames. But this is, of course, a problem for subsequent chapters.

2 / Promising Intrusion in Nella Larsen's *Passing*

You're invisible now, you got no secrets to conceal
How does it feel?
—BOB DYLAN, "LIKE A ROLLING STONE"

Transparent Opacity

Nella Larsen's 1929 account of racial passing—her novel *Passing*—ends with its most troubling character, Clare Kendry, dangerously "framed" by an open window. Of both European and African descent, Clare has "dark, almost black, eyes and [a] wide mouth like a scarlet flower against the ivory of her skin" (177). However, in the novel's final scene, after having passed much of her life as a "white" wife and mother, Clare finds herself passing as "black." She is at a party in Harlem, surrounded by black men and black women. Present also is Irene Redfield, Clare's one-time childhood friend and the woman whose life Clare's return to Harlem has utterly disrupted. Like Clare's, Irene's mixed-race heritage allows her to pass. Yet, unlike Clare, Irene fully assumes a black identity, taking (by implication) America's "one drop" rule as the expression of ontological truth.[1] Focalized through Irene, the entire novel (along with its final climactic moments) is inflected with paranoia, desperation, and misperception. Irene outwardly views Clare as a threat; her mystery, enchanting beauty, and ivory skin are frighteningly attractive. She has no ties, no fixed allegiances. She is utterly, seductively, and dangerously free. Clare thus threatens Irene's sense of (black) bourgeois stability: her marriage to a black doctor (Brian) and her role as mother to two black children. In other words, the novel stages a conflict between two impossible extremes: transience and immanence. And yet, in the novel's final scene, we see these two extremes fold back in on each other; at either pole, responsibility for the self is refused.

The inevitability of this collapse becomes evident the moment Clare finds herself—after spending the night "clinging to Brian's *other* arm" and "looking at him with that provocative upward glance of hers" (269; my emphasis)—in the dangerous vacuum-like space of an open frame, as if her entire being has become the mere effect of relation, the supplementary space between her and the community in which she momentarily finds herself. In this moment, she is in danger of disappearing altogether. Of course, her name foreshadows her potential dissolution. Derived from the Latin *clarus*, "Clare" denotes brightness and clarity, the utter transparency of a window. It is significant, too, that Clare's position "in frame" is effected by the arrival of white, racist husband, John Bellew. Having tracked Clare down through her relationship with Irene, Bellew arrives in full possession of the "truth"; he now knows that his wife and daughter are black. This "fact" is reified by Clare's position in the room. Her blackness (in relation) is now surely, for Bellew, overwhelmingly obvious: she is black because she is *with* other black individuals. Bellew further confirms this relation—and its ontological effect—by uttering an abjectly violent and lynch-like accusation: "So you're a nigger, a damned dirty nigger!" (271). And so, while his aggressive entry into the room literally forces her to "back[] a little" (271) toward the window, it is surely the hegemony of his gaze and the power of his reifying utterance that puts her into frame. The problem, though, especially for Irene, is Clare's reaction to this moment of framing. Rather than assuming the identity implied by her relation to the room and the silencing language of her husband, Clare appears to embrace the contingency of the frame as the contingency of her *self*. She is *nothing* but the frame in which she appears, and the frame in which she appears is merely a passing construct.

In this moment of danger, Irene sees only a threat to herself. Her empathetic perception of Clare's unstable position foregrounds her fear of (the possibility of) Clare's response to that position: "Clare stood at the window, as composed as if everyone were not staring at her in curiosity and wonder, as if the whole structure of her life were not lying in fragments before her. She seemed unaware of any danger or uncaring. There was even a faint smile on her full red lips and in her shining eyes" (271). More than anything else "It was that smile that maddened Irene" (271). Faced with this maddening smile, this utter lack of allegiance to a fixed identity, Irene's one, all-consuming thought is that "she couldn't have her free" (271). The ambiguity of the ensuing moments cannot be overstressed. For one reason or another, Irene "ran across the room, her terror tinged with ferocity, and laid a hand on Clare's bare arm" (271). "What happened next," we are told, "Irene Redfield never afterwards allowed herself to remember. Never clearly" (271). What *is* certain is the fact that Clare finally disappears altogether. On a literal level, Clare simply falls (or is pushed) out the window. Perhaps she jumps. But the overt ambiguity of the scene forestalls our desire for a literal and final reading. While it initially seems obvious that Irene murdered Clare, it is impossible to account for the fact that (in a crowded room of people focused on Clare) no one sees Irene act. No one even seems to suspect her. Yet Irene expresses and displays obvious guilt. We are told that she "wasn't sorry," that she felt "nothing in that sudden moment of action" (272); she even perseverates over the possibility that "Clare was not dead" (273).

In our effort to make sense of Clare's disappearance/death and Irene's sense of guilt, we must not overlook the fact that, at the very moment Clare is lost to the frame of the window, Irene arrives to occupy (and indeed dominate or saturate) its space. While Clare abandons herself wholly to the contingency of relation (identifying *only* as the perpetual mutability of a social frame), Irene struggles to maintain her belief that the identity delineated by the frame is in fact anterior to the frame—that it is a priori and immanent. At the moment Clare becomes the frame, the frame necessarily becomes Irene. Clare's transparency resolves (into) Irene's opacity. The two are, after all, doubles[2]—a fact that is stressed whenever this final scene is itself foreshadowed and thus doubled. Consider, for instance, the earlier scene in which Clare (having been invited by Brian) arrives at a party Irene is hosting in honor of Hugh Wentworth—a famous (white) writer who often plays the role of voyeuristic spectator at "black" parties in Harlem. Unable to stop thinking about the possibility that Brian is attracted to Clare, Irene loses focus and drops her cup of tea. "Dark stains [dot] the bright rug" as Irene's maid begins "gather[ing] up the white fragments" (254). As it does in the final scene, Clare's transient nature clearly disrupts the stability of Irene's world. Moreover, Clare arrives at the precise moment Irene is seemingly tempted to transgress racial and marital lines. This temptation is implied when Hugh suggests that he "must have pushed [her]" (254)—*even though* there is no suggestion he was *physically* involved. His mea culpa signals the possibility that the breaking of her white porcelain is an ostensible effect of Irene's relation to a charming white man. Can we not in fact assume that Irene's fixation on the possibility of Brian's infidelity is merely a displacement of her own wayward desires? Does Hugh *push* her to abandon her blackness—a push she must counter by shattering the appearance of her whiteness? In other words, Irene's moment of vertiginous rage can be read as symptomatic of a momentary inability to maintain the purity of her assumed racial identity. The threat (or *potential*) of this inability is echoed in the finale—when, that is, Irene is witness to "the whole structure of [Clare's] life ... lying in fragments before her." But in light of this earlier scene, might we not view these "fragments" as actually and already Irene's? Read in tandem, the two scenes stress Irene's utter fear of instability—suggesting in turn that Clare's dissolution must necessarily signal Irene's. Clare cannot be free because that would mean, by implication, that Irene is free. And we must of course look beyond the more mundane threat of marital freedom, as the novel clearly employs such freedom in both scenes as a metonym for a far more general and far more threating "experience of [ontological] freedom" (as Nancy might understand it).[3] What happens in the end can in fact be viewed as the ultimate apotheosis of an uncanny experience of doubling. Irene does away with Clare—as, that is, the harbinger of Irene's own innate and infinite potential to be (only) *in relation*—so as to (re)solidify herself as wholly anterior to relation. As a moment that is more psychological than physical, the disappearance of Clare is therefore fated, predictable. It is clearly mirrored (or seen) in the breaking of the white teacup. And it is anticipated (or seen) again when, at the final party, Irene opens the window and discards her cigarette: "Irene finished her cigarette and threw it out, watching the tiny spark drop slowly down to the white ground below" (270). Even more than the shattered cup, this disappearing cigarette prefigures the event toward which Irene is inexorably drawn. When Clare finally disappears altogether, Irene even finds herself recycling her earlier reflection: "One moment Clare had been there, a vital glowing thing, like *a flame* of red and gold. The next she was gone" (271; my emphasis). At the moment Clare is destined to disappear (or to become altogether *clear*), the novel presents us with a series of echoes, an uncanny sense of déjà vu. It positions us, along with Irene, at the end of an ostensibly inescapable cul-de-sac, a somewhat pointless "adventure of experience" (as Emmanuel Levinas might say) "between the clear and the obscure" ("God and Philosophy" 58)—or rather, the transient and the immanent.

Irene's rush toward the framed, window-like Clare signifies the collapse of the double, the vertiginous conflation of the self and its specular image. From this perspective, Clare's death (or disappearance) must be viewed as tantamount to Irene's. As a type of uncanny double, Clare stands in for Irene's potential to become other, to become different than she repeatedly and adamantly insists she *is*. It is this infinite potential (of the self *as other*) that Irene refuses; she refuses "the proximity of the other" (Levinas, "God and Philosophy" 71) *as the very possibility of the self*. This means, also, though, if we follow Levinas, that she is just as *irresponsible* as Clare. Irene desperately eschews her responsibility for the other because such responsibility entails the impossibility of constituting the self "into an *I think*, as substantial as a stone or, like a heart of stone, into an in- and for-oneself" (71). Such responsibility "goes to the point of substitution for the other, up to the condition—or the noncondition—of a hostage" (71). Put differently, Irene cannot abide the manner in which the other (as Clare, as double) holds her hostage to the impossibility of her immanence. And yet, at precisely the same time, Clare is merely Irene's *other* extreme, the abject refusal to assume a fixed or immanent quality of selfhood. Clare, in the end, is only the frame that defines her. For Clare, there is only frame, only relation, only perpetual *becoming*. Clare refuses the responsibility that (if momentarily, yet also perpetually) "binds [her] as irreplaceable and unique" (71). Clare simply and irresponsibly "*slip[s] away* from the face of the other in its nakedness without recourse" (71; my emphasis). No gaze can hold her. And yet Clare's utter withdrawal is finally tied to its opposite: Irene's assumption of complete immanence. Because neither is *willing to persist in opposing it,* both are lost to the frame—the necessarily corruptive supplement of communal relation, of proximity. The difference (if it can be called a difference) is this: Clare announces by abandoning herself to the artifice of the relation that defines her *while* Irene wholly assumes its ontological veritability. The result is that nothing of either woman remains present, not in *truth* anyway.

Or rather, in the specific instance of the final scene, Bellew's racial slur effaces both women.[4] However, while Irene ostensibly allows Bellew's language to fix her completely, Clare's smile utterly mocks its efficacy; it announces the fact that she is coincidently and momentarily in the *position* of "a damned dirty nigger." For Clare, the phrase is simply part of a larger game—and, by implication, an arbitrary and essentially meaningless utterance. It cannot hold her. Any innate connection to the trauma or historical legacy of the phrase is simply denied. It is merely another in an endless chain of potential performatives. Clare, we might say, announces and indeed revels in "the bankruptcy of transcendence [as] a theology that thematizes the *transcending* in the logos, assigns a term to the passing of transcendence, congeals it into a 'world behind the scenes'" (Levinas, *Otherwise* 5). She therefore effectively and radically neuters Bellew's language, exposing it as a futile and violent effort to lynch (her) being. And yet Clare finds herself unable to hold on—*to anything*; she loses any sense of selfhood in "play or detente, without responsibility, where everything possible is permitted" (6). Rather than refusing the ossifying nature of the "said" by enduring the endless work of "saying"—of, that is, perpetually introducing the infinite potential of the exceptional into and by means of the known or symbolically coherent[5]—Clare finally abandons herself to the endless cacophony of play, the thematized manifestations of being. The problem (if we follow Levinas) is that the "fallacious frivolity of [such] play" is never "free of interest" (6). Clare, in other words, abandons the possibility and thus responsibility of dis-inter-*est*; she refuses a position outside the immediacy of being (i.e., *esse*). Clare forgoes her potential to "dissimulate being" (7), to sustain any sense of that which is *otherwise than being*, or radically and perpetually unsaid. In a game that recognizes only the effect of thematizing frames, frames necessarily fill the void of an impossible content. The inverted hegemony of such play is signaled most overtly via the cacophony that immediately precedes Bellew's arrival: "Someone in the room had turned on the phonograph. Or was it the radio? [Irene] didn't know which she disliked more. And nobody was listening to its blare. The talking, the laughter never for a minute ceased. Why must they have more noise?" (270). In the face of this noise—which clearly echoes the "noise" that precedes the cantor's emphatic "Stop!" in *The Jazz Singer*—Bellew's arrival and subsequent slur imposes a type of ontological silence or absoluteness, a silence that Irene desperately desires.

This tension between (and eventual conflation of) noise and silence, play and sense, is in fact echoed in the novel's structure. As Mae Henderson puts it, while considering the linguistic breakdown that occurs as Irene considers (in the opening scene) Clare's "mysterious," "furtive," and "sly" letter (Larsen 171), a "crisis of representation . . . is textually embodied in the form and structure of *Passing*. Through its narrative gaps and repressions, as well as its open-ended resistance to closure and resolution, Larsen's novel performs as an early exemplar of black (post)modernist indeterminacy" (Henderson l). While we should be wary of assuming that such "(post)modernist indeterminacy" signals an allegiance to a potential referent that is (in the end) no different than Clare's, Henderson is certainly correct to suggest that (on some level) the novel mirrors Clare;[6] it is, after all, Clare's fractured "composition" that so frightens Irene. Like Clare, the novel constantly runs the risk of abandoning its meaning to the cacophony of pure and purely arbitrary linguistic play. The reader is therefore cast alongside Irene as she struggles to deny the radically subversive *because intrusive* potential Clare embodies. But we should not overlook the obvious: if Clare is Irene's double, Irene is Clare's. If the novel encourages us (à la postmodernism)[7] to reject as dangerous Irene's desperate assumption of immanence, it exposes us also to the possibility that Clare's inducement of disorder and instability—*as* her irresponsible withdrawal from committed action and communal allegiance—is tantamount to the very thing it exposes as dangerously false. At its extreme, Clare's tendency to revel in or induce cacophony effects a desire for the finally inaudible—"the bad silence that shelters the secret of Gyges" (Levinas, "God and Philosophy" 75). Either the infinite potential of a *true* self is abandoned to the cacophonous silence of its invisibility, or it is lost in the assumption of its silent opacity.

Communities of Paranoia

Let's double back—to Nancy. In "The Inoperative Community," Nancy suggests that the possibility of the individual is necessarily predicated upon the possibility of a stable community, a preexisting totality that encompasses and defines the individual as a coherent "I." In the previous chapter we saw this problem play out in both Johnson's *Autobiography* and Crosland's *Jazz Singer*. We saw, in other words, that *a sense of* individuality is effected by the contingency of communal relations that necessarily precede that sense. We might (now) think of these relations as Levinasian "themes"—as finite representations or categorizations. To say "I am white" or "I am a heterosexual" is to say that I have an essential link to a community of "whites" or a community of "heterosexuals." And yet, by implication and quite paradoxically, I am a singular and coherent entity only insofar as I am (in one way or another) indistinguishable from a certain communal whole, or plurality. If, however, my individuality is ambiguous or unfixed—if I do not clearly belong anywhere—then I disrupt the stability of the communities to which I only *seem* to belong. Such an intrusion would signify the radical promise of a community stripped of its melancholia, or the possibility of pure inclusion and (therefore) exclusion. It would demand the difficult burden of Levinasian responsibility. At the same time, and at its extreme, the ambiguity such an intrusion entails threatens to frustrate the very possibility of recognition—if, that is, we understand recognition as the effect of proximity. Does not the persistent ambiguity of infinite potential entail the impossibility of a meaningful and consistent face, a point of medial relation? On the one hand, the intruder signals the radical and finally egalitarian promise of an*other* community, what for Derrida would entail a "common affirmation of being unbonded, an untimely being-alone and, simultaneously, in joint acquiescence to disjunction" (*Politics* 55). On the other hand, the intruder must necessarily risk dissolving (entirely) the possibility of communication. This promise and this threat are at base the promise and the threat of "passing" (racially or otherwise) in American literature. When, though, it is viewed from within the miasma of America's melancholic fantasy, the promise of the intruder *is* the threat.[8] For now, this is the problem with which we must concern ourselves, for it is the stage upon which the actual danger of intrusion becomes perceptible. But let's try to approach it through a slightly different frame.

Without doubt, the problem of passing is inextricably tied to the issue of community and the (im)possibility of communal stability. Characters who refuse to align or identify themselves with the communities to which their lineage (or gender, class, sexuality, etc.) assigns them deny their origins and the communal stability upon which their coherence as individuals is based. For this reason they disrupt the possibility of sustaining melancholia by challenging the possibility of a communal totality. Given the way in which it stages this challenge, there can be little doubt that Larsen's novel points to the fact that racially or sexually ambiguous characters who embrace the full implications of their marginal status threaten the possibility of totalized, or totalizing, communities *because* they frustrate the validity of the assumptions upon which their failure as individuals is necessarily predicated. Clare's "passing" (non)presence clearly disrupts the illusory possibility that any community can be rigorously defined by an immanent bond. As a type of irritant, Clare can be viewed as an overt symptom of a (Lacanian) Real—especially, that is, if we begin to think of this Real as the inexhaustible site of the unsaid (or better, *unsayable*). Clare, in this sense, frustrates the melancholic compulsion to deny the other *as* the harbinger of the self's infinite potential.

Indeed, as Žižek—or rather, Žižek's Lacan—tends to suggest, our sense of a coherent, stable, and understandable reality is dependent upon our absolute immersion and faith in an all-pervasive symbolic order, a social order of codes and discourses that define and fix the world through which we move. If this symbolic order fails or is disrupted, then we are faced with the "impossible Real"—that which precedes and exceeds symbolization, that which cannot be said. The Real is "impossible" because it cannot *be*; it *is* only insofar as it is *not*. The Real is the essential absence around which the symbolic order is structured. A refusal of meaning, the Real simultaneously and paradoxically makes possible our desire for that which is stable and final. We thus mask, or elide, the frustrating and utterly unfathomable nature of the Real via a process of always inadequate symbolization, a process that, as Žižek suggests, "mortifies, drains off, empties, carves the fullness of the Real" (*Sublime Object* 169). When this process of symbolization fails—when, that is, it stumbles and is unable to mask the impossibility of any final and stable truth—our faith in reality as a stable field of determinable meanings is undermined. This moment of failure is the experience of what has *not been* "said," what remains impossible to know: "the Real is a shock of a contingent encounter which disrupts the automatic circulation of the symbolic mechanism; a grain of sand preventing its smooth functioning; a traumatic encounter which ruins the balance of the symbolic universe of the subject" (171). For this reason, as Brian Carr suggests, the traumatic experience of the Real can be equated to the reader's (and Irene's) experience of Clare. Clare's (passing) presence in *Passing* resists complete apprehension; she disrupts our illusion of a coherent and stable reality because she refuses to be fixed or understood (finally) via a process of symbolization. Clare is therefore a "nonobject" (Carr 283), frustratingly resistant to symbolic apprehension. Faced with Clare, the melancholic is unable to maintain the illusion of authentic communities and immanent identities.

Larsen's text is all the more troubling since its central thematic is not necessarily limited to the problematics of racial transgression. Numerous critics have argued that the novel's focus on race is a deflection of other much more troubling, or "unspeakable," issues. These critics suggest that these issues are encoded in the surface tensions of the text, tensions that we must "decode" if we are to access its "true" implications. The true kernel of the text becomes accessible *if* we shift our focus from race to class, *or if* we uncover its coded exploration of homosexual desire. The overarching suggestion is that "passing" (as an act and as the title of the novel) has multiple implications, implications that encompass race, class, and sexuality. And yet, as Carr notes, such readings also signal a form of critical paranoia, a critical desire to fix the *true* meaning of Larsen's text, to stabilize (our knowledge of) the other, to locate meaning (at last). Such paranoia is surely a side effect of melancholia, compelling us to cure or *subject* the symptoms of a perpetually unsaid to a process of interpretive symbolization. How, though, do we distinguish the paranoiac from the properly critical—especially since *all* interpretative gestures signal a desire to maintain, as Žižek would have it, "the balance of the symbolic universe of the subject" (*Sublime Object* 171)? Is not this process of symbolization impossible to avoid? Larsen's novel seems to answer such questions via the specific way it depicts the uncanny doubling of Irene and Clare: the act of sense making becomes a problem when, on the one hand, it becomes an effort toward reification (as it does with Irene) or when, on the other, it becomes untethered from the possibility of *a* Real (as it does with Clare). Our reading of the novel, then, must avoid approaching its content as Irene approaches Clare's. At the same time, it must avoid mimicking

Clare's own (finally) perverse—or perversely postmodern—attitude toward identity and interpretative closure.[9] While we should certainly avoid reducing the text's themes to a single factor—such as race *or* gender *or* sexuality *or* class—we must also avoid abandoning the possibility of *any* core intent. The best we can do is maintain a focus on the more general ontological dilemma that the act of passing foregrounds throughout the text. *In that sense,* passing, in *Passing* (and as its title), comes to denote the threatening promise of an "in joint acquiescence to disjunction." It exposes identity as the effect of contingent and unstable moments of (dis)location, as the paradoxical effect of our immersion in *and* our complete separation from any number of communal "totalities." Clare's passing challenges the possibility of stable identity by implying that we are never wholly inside nor wholly outside any given community or category of being. For this reason, Clare embodies the threating promise of freedom—just as the novel in which she passes opens up the threatening promise of a perpetually unfixable (i.e., heteroglot) mode of expression.

Threating Promise

As the multiplicity of critical responses to *Passing* suggest, Clare passes *through* a variety of identity categories in which she can, if only temporarily, be placed: as she has African lineage, she passes most obviously as a white woman; as she officially resides in Europe (but was born and raised in America), she passes as an upper-class European; as she has a child (Margery) who attends a boarding school in Europe, she passes as a mother; and, given her sense of marital detachment (and her sexually charged relationship with Irene), she passes as a heterosexual.[10] However, given the arbitrary deferral to blackness that buttresses America's racial politics, as well as the liminal state of becoming passing connotes, Clare is also (and necessarily) passing as the dialectical opposites of these various identity categories: as her easy interactions with Irene's "black" friends indicate, she is passing as black;[11] as a person who now officially resides in Europe (but is visiting America), she is passing as American; because she is oblivious to the welfare of Margery, she is passing as a woman without a child; and, given her apparent attraction to, and possible affair with, Brian,[12] she is passing as homosexual. Clare thus sustains a perpetually tenuous state of *inbetweenness* (or *nowhereness*), a state that points to the impossibility of sustaining a hierarchal relationship between two ostensibly opposite positions, or categories of being. As Claudia Tate suggests, we get the clearest sense of Clare's profoundly destabilizing transience in those moments when Irene tries to describe her: "Irene repeatedly describes Clare in hyperbole—'too vague,' 'too remote,' 'so dark and deep and unfathomable,' 'utterly strange,' 'incredibly beautiful,' 'utterly beyond any experience'" (144).

In stark contrast to Clare's multiple transgressions, Irene is only ever passing (self-admittedly, at least) twice in the novel. Both times she feels compelled to pass. Immediately before reuniting with Clare, Irene passively agrees to the cab driver's suggestion that she go to the Drayton (a posh Chicago establishment for whites); and, during her first meeting with Bellew, his blatantly racist opinions force her to pass for Clare's sake. In these instances, and throughout the novel, Irene abhors *and* entertains the idea of passing. At the Drayton, faced with the immediacy of both her and Clare's passing states, Irene is unable to determine how she feels about Clare's blatant willingness to pass: "It was as if the woman sitting on the other side of the table, a girl she had known, who had done this rather dangerous and, to Irene Redfield, abhorrent thing successfully and had announced herself well satisfied, had for her a fascination, strange and compelling" (190). While emphasizing the homosexual undertones that pervade the text, Judith Butler highlights this strange vacillation in Irene's opinion of Clare (and the act of passing): "Irene finds herself drawn by Clare, wanting to be her, but also wanting her. It is this risk-taking, articulated at once as a racial crossing and sexual infidelity, that alternately entrances Irene and fuels her moral condemnation of Clare with renewed ferocity" ("Passing, Queering" 169). Butler's argument easily extends beyond its narrow focus on sexuality, for Irene clearly fears and rejects (but is curiously attracted to) *everything* that is not fixed, constant, or permanent. There is perhaps never a moment when Irene is not also attracted to the promise of Clare's transience—to, that is, the promising impossibility of ever locating and embodying an essential opacity—but Irene's terror of that promise grows distinctly more paranoiac as the novel progresses. The result is the parallel development of two characters who become profoundly more inverted, profoundly more reflective.

At first, Clare's passing state simply and overtly compels Irene to reaffirm her own racial identity (and her responsibility to the community that legitimizes that identity). Reflecting on her own willingness to pass in front of John Bellew, particularly during his racist tirade, Irene chastises herself for betraying the very community to which her blood assigns her: "And mingled with her disbelief and resentment was another feeling, a question. Why hadn't she spoken that day? ... Why, simply because of Clare Kendry, who had exposed her to such torment, had she failed to take up the defense of the race to which she belonged?" (212). But, just as

Clare is passing between more than two dialectally opposed communities of being, Irene's desire for permanence quickly begins to radiate across a multiple range of identity categories—suggesting in turn that America's racial politics are merely symptomatic of a melancholia that demands the violent maintenance of immanence *in general*. For instance, Irene's need to maintain a fixed national (i.e., American) identity compels her to repeatedly resist her husband's desire to move to Brazil: "For she would not go to Brazil. She belonged in this land of rising towers. She was an American. She grew from this soil, and she would not be uprooted" (267). Irene struggles, too, to stress the essential characteristics that define her (and, by implication, every woman's) identity as a mother. And yet she is horrified by *and* self-loathingly curious about Clare's apparent ambivalence to motherhood. When Clare offhandedly remarks that "children aren't everything" (240), Irene reifies her allegiance to the community of mothers: "You know you don't mean that, Clare. You're only trying to tease me. I know very well that I take being a mother rather seriously. I *am* wrapped up in my boys and the running of my house. I can't help it" (240). Presumably, she "can't help it" because, like *being* "black" or *being* "American," Irene can't help *being* a "mother." It is what she *is*.

Even if we bracket the various instances in which Irene appears to be in danger of, and struggling against, becoming unfixed from her heterosexual identity, the disparity between Irene's and Clare's distinct *yet mirrored* approaches to the problem of (racial) ambiguity are readily evident. Unlike Clare, Irene rebels against the larger ontological implications that her ability to pass suggests. While Clare moves toward the irresponsible assumption that *all* identity categories are social constructions, Irene moves toward the equally irresponsible assumption that she *is* those categories. Irene desperately wants *to be* black, *to be* a mother, *to be* an American, *to be* heterosexual, etc. Clare, then, both allures and repels Irene, for her passing state implies that every seemingly stable identity category is merely (a) performative, a script that always precedes its enactment. Always less than authentic, such performatives make possible an "I" who speaks and who interacts from a certain subject position with an identifiable world of things. It matters little if the identity performed is perceived as negative or positive. As Butler suggests, a term like "'queer' has operated as one linguistic practice whose purpose has been the shaming of the subject it names or, rather, the producing of a subject *through* that shaming interpellation" ("Critically Queer" 226). Just as a marriage ceremony culminates in a performative—"I pronounce you . . ." (224)—that discursively produces a "married" couple who then proceed to live out, or perform, a married existence, so too does the invocation of "queer" function to produce "a queer" (with all the negative and positive attributes that come with that particular subject position). However, the interpellative process that the performative works on the subject is never complete; I am always in excess of the label that seems to fix my identity once and for all. This is what Butler calls "the impossibility of a full recognition, that is, of ever fully inhabiting the name by which one's social identity is inaugurated and mobilized" (226). Clare's passing announces, confirms, and ostentatiously embraces "the instability and incompleteness of subject-formation" (226). But Irene strives to blind herself, or refuses to acknowledge, the impossibility of being "self-identical" (230)—of, that is, *being* a subject that is absolutely and without exception the labels that define it. Tentatively, then, we might understand the performative—as Butler theorizes it, anyway, and as it plays out in *Passing*—as an effect of thematization. By means of a performative I am capable of locating the other, of *facing otherness*. But it is then also and paradoxically through this performative that I am necessarily faced with and responsible for that other's "forsaken nakedness, which glimmers through the fissures that crack the mask of the personage or his wrinkled skin, in his 'without recourse,' . . . without voice or thematization. There the resonance of silence—the *Geläut der Stille*—certainly resounds" (Levinas, "God and Philosophy" 71–72). Can we not in fact say, following these threads, that "performative noise" makes possible my confrontation with the infinite (and therefore *total*) silence of the other? By implication, the silence of the self cannot be heard or known *in* silence (as Irene would have it); and yet, at the same time, this fact does not justify recourse to *or irresponsible revelry in* the purity of unrecognizable and wholly unpredictable noise (as Clare seems to assume). At either pole we are lost to "bad silence."

This problem of performativity returns us to both the dangers and the necessity of bad faith *as bad silence*.[13] While Clare finally seems to have no faith whatsoever, Irene succumbs to a faith in that which is necessarily impossible. Or as Žižek might say, Irene works desperately to deny "a certain limit, a pure negativity, a traumatic limit which prevents the final totalization of the social-ideological field" (*Sublime Object* 164). Irene struggles to accept the impossibility of her identity/identities, the impossibility of the Real (or social bond) that, if apprehended, would finally fix the symbolic order that determines her (self). Clare frustrates this struggle because she represents the ultimate terror and allurement of freedom, the freedom suggested by the fact that the self *as* "Real" always and necessarily escapes complete symbolization: "There is always a leftover which opens the space for desire and makes the Other (the symbolic order) inconsistent, with fantasy as an attempt to overcome, to conceal this inconsistency, this gap in the Other" (Žižek, *Sublime Object* 124). Since no fantasy (no matter how paranoiac, no matter how complex) can hold Clare together, Irene is forced to recognize her various failed fantasies *as fantasies*. The irony is that at the very moment Clare must be expelled *or lynched* if any fantasy is to sustain its illusory efficacy, Clare has already brought herself to the outside edge of (Irene's, or anyone else's) apperception.

The Communal Lie of the Individual

Even Sartre suggests that it is impossible to escape bad faith—or, in Žižek's terms, the need for fantasy. Regardless of what a critic like Carr might think, there is simply no (responsible) way to avoid "substantializ[ing] everything as if there were no nothing" (283). Without bad faith, without fantasy, without a willingness to accept the potential efficacy of symbolization, without an assumption of the possibility of performative veracity, even a temporary subject position would be impossible. For Sartre, bad faith can only be *and must be* acknowledged; it must be perpetually exposed *as* bad faith. And to expose one's own faith in immanence as "bad" is to expose (by implication) the impossibility of *any* authentic community of being. This is the problem around which we've been circling since chapter 1. Irene is able to view herself as black because she shares certain characteristics with the black community. The authenticity of her blackness, or the possibility that she is a self-identical (black) subject, is legitimated by the fact—or rather, *the faith*—that something essential or immanent unites *all* people who are considered, or consider themselves *to be*, black. But this is a paradox. Irene can never be self-identically black insofar as *to be* black she must be able to recognize herself (at a distance) as black, or as *a* part of / apart from a black community. Her sense of individuality as a black heterosexual woman remains contingent upon her ability to distinguish herself within, and therefore against, the communities that define what it means to be a black heterosexual woman. In other words, Irene's ability to identify with the communities that define her paradoxically depends upon her difference from those communities. She can be absolutely black *only if* her blackness is no longer defined *in relation* to other blacks. In "The Inoperative Community," Nancy puts it like this:

> The absolute must be the absolute of its own absoluteness, or not be at all. In other words: to be absolutely alone, it is not enough

that I be so; I must also be alone being alone—and this of course is contradictory. The logic of the absolute violates the absolute. It implicates it in a relation that it refuses and precludes by its essence. This relation tears and forces open, from within and from without at the same time, and from an outside that is nothing other than the rejection of an impossible interiority, the 'without relation' from which the absolute would constitute itself. (4)

Without relation (as the effect of difference, or proximity) there can be no possibility of identification. By extension, the possibility of being the same as others—the possibility, that is, of a communal totality, or immanence—is ultimately and paradoxically a condition of its impossibility. More simply, individual identity is made possible through relation, through community; but the differences that make those relations possible rule out the possibility of a stable and fixed communal bond, of *a being* that is without recourse to the infinite potential of otherness.

For Nancy, then, community is only ever a state of "ecstasy," a state (if we consider the etymology of the term) of "standing outside one's self": "Ecstasy . . . defines the impossibility, both ontological and gnosological, of absolute immanence (or of the absolute, and therefore of immanence) and consequently the impossibility either of an individuality, in the precise sense of the term, or of a pure collective totality" ("Inoperative" 6). However, a character like Irene is bound to "the theme of the individual and that of communism" by her "denial of ecstasy" (6)—that is, by her nostalgia for a state (both communal and individual, for the two are inseparable) of immanence. Irene is convinced that she has a "duty" to Clare: "She was *bound* to her by those very ties of race which, for all her repudiation of them, Clare had been unable to completely sever" (213; my emphasis). In these moments when she nostalgically appeals to unbreakable and absolute bonds, Irene actively represses "that fear which crouched, always, deep down within her, stealing away the sense of security, the feeling of permanence, from the life which she had so admirably arranged for [her family], and desired so ardently to have remain as it was" (217). Given her inability to shake her doubts, though, Irene's "feeling of permanence" is presented to the reader as a fantasy, a tenuous but outright denial of the necessary disjunction between a Real and its symbolization, the refusal to accept the impossibility of an essential social bond and, thus, the impossibility of a stable (or finally and accurately symbolized) self. As Žižek suggests, "The Social is always an inconsistent field structured around a constitutive impossibility, traversed by a central 'antagonism'—this thesis implies that every process of identification conferring on us a fixed socio-symbolic identity is ultimately doomed to fail. The function of ideological fantasy is to mask this inconsistency, the fact that 'Society doesn't exist,' and thus to compensate us for the failed identification" (*Sublime Object* 127). By exposing "the menace of impermanence" (Larsen 262), Clare effectively disrupts this ideological fantasy and forces Irene (if not the reader) to acknowledge the fundamental impossibility of the social bond, of the "fixed socio-symbolic identity." This is Clare's radical promise—even if the profoundly melancholic Irene must perceive it as a threat. For Clare, at least initially, does not threaten community *as such*; she does not simply eviscerate the potential veracity of the performatives she momentarily takes as her own. At her most promising, Clare embraces a "passing" state that exploits "*the being-ecstatic of Being-itself*" (Nancy, "Inoperative" 6) and exposes "community as neither a work to be produced, nor a lost communion, but rather as space itself, and the spacing of the experience of the outside, of the outside-of-self" (19). Clare's "ability for a quality of feeling that was to [Irene] strange and even repugnant" (Larsen 226) exposes the social bond as only the mediatory point of ineffaceable and infinite difference—as, therefore, the very possibility of community and identity.

Clare's sustained passing speaks to what remains (in her *and in Irene*) perpetually anterior to whatever is or can be *said*. Clare compels Irene (along with the reader) to acknowledge absence as the constitutive factor in any process of symbolization or thematization—*constitutive* because, as both Nancy and Žižek insist, it is the distance, the barrier, or the spacing, between identity and self, between a community and its individual, between the same and the other; it is the infinite remainder of who I might (still) say I am. In the light of Levinasian ethics, we might view this lack as the paradoxical site of infinite plenitude, the always still to be said, still to be known. Implicated via Clare's sustained state of passing (at its most promising), this lack *as infinite potential or plenitude* is the "negative, disruptive power, menacing our identity" (Žižek, *Sublime Object* 176); but it is *also* "a positive condition of it" (176). With this paradox in mind, we might then reapproach the manner in which Clare's inexhaustible state of becoming parallels the novel's own tendency to refuse interpretative closure. Like Clare's refusal to succumb to the identities she only ever performs, the novel's overtly *novelistic* (or Bakhtinian) gestures signal the impossibility of a coherent intention anterior to (or wholly aligned with) its expression. The novel, though, simultaneously and consistently sustains the echo of such an intention, a truth that governs the veracity of its expression—*even if* it must necessarily remain anterior to that expression. It is not quite correct to say (as Henderson does) that the novel is simply or only "(post)modernist." It never abandons its referent to endless and perverse play. We are persistently reminded of a space *beyond articulation* whenever we are reminded of Irene's tendency to misperceive—whenever, that is, we are encouraged to question (and thus look beyond) the focalized perspective that restricts our access to that which *is* perceived, or intended. The narrator constantly reminds us that what we know is only ever what Irene "remembered," or what she "let herself remember." The novel's narrative body sustains its secret, its promise of an opacity anterior to its always necessarily inadequate expressions; *Larsen's* body of text therefore diverges from and contrasts itself with Clare's—the tentative or always passing solidity of which finally dissolves altogether.

It is the novel, then, and not Clare, that finally reveals the possibility of sustaining a *sense* of what is unsaid. It persists in "saying" the unsaid because it refuses to abandon its potential to be said (in an infinite number of ways). The intrusiveness of the novel is equatable to an overt "signifying [of] the uncontained *par excellence*" (Levinas, "God and Philosophy" 63). And for Levinas, this "uncontained" is precisely "God in us," or "the infinite in me" (63)—but only insofar as "the *in* of the Infinite signifie[s] at once the *non*-and the *within*" (63). We will return to this idea of the self as God in part III. For now, the implication is that Larsen's novel works to sustain a certain "exceptional relation," constantly opening or "awakening" us to the possibility that "the difference between the Infinite and that which [has] to encompass and comprehend it [*can be*] a non-indifference of the Infinite to this impossible encompassing, a non-indifference of the Infinite for thought: the placing of the Infinite in thought, but wholly other than the thought" (63). Clare, like the novel in which she is cast, has this intrusive potential to "awaken" consciousness. At its most efficacious such an awakening would be a "sobering or a waking up [*réveil*] that shakes the 'dogmatic slumber' that sleeps at the bottom of all consciousness resting upon [an] object" (63). But if Irene's paranoiac trajectory entails "a repression into the unconscious" (63), Clare's abject "breakup of consciousness" leaves nothing *before* its wake. Clare forgoes the strenuous effort of her potential intrusiveness by conceding a type of ontological defeat. She finally assumes nothing but what *is* said, and what is said is (for Clare) *only* ever a performative artifice.

And yet, at her most promising (and therefore terrifying), Clare signals the radically democratic possibility of the perpetual intruder—or what (more specifically) Nancy calls "*l'intrus*": "Once [the *intrus*] has arrived, if he remains foreign, and for as long as he does so—rather than simply 'becoming naturalized'—his coming will not cease; nor will it cease being in some respect an intrusion: ... that is to say, being without right, familiarity, accustomedness, or habit, the stranger's coming will not cease being a disturbance and perturbation of intimacy" ("L'Intrus" 1-2). Clare intrudes upon Irene's—along with the reader's—fantasy of a stable social order, a stable and therefore melancholic communal bond. Since she "steal[s] away [a] sense of security, [a] feeling of permanence" (Larsen 217), we long desperately for her departure if not her destruction. And yet the novel itself finally refuses this destruction, or "naturalization." By the time we arrive at the finale, Clare's passing state has certainly come to signify (if only unconsciously) the particular "truths" the novel leaves unsaid. Who or what is Clare, really? Is she having, or intending to have, an affair with Brian? Who is finally responsible for her death? What, *exactly*, is Irene refusing to remember or see? Is her problem racial or sexual? The irony, of course, is that these questions remain unanswered— or *unanswerable*—even after Clare finally disappears. But this is not to suggest that, when Clare disappears, she takes her secrets with her. Clare disappears because no secret can hold her; she refuses the possibility of a secret, the possibility of a truth anterior to what is articulated *as* that truth. The secrets that remain are the novel's, not Clare's. Yet it is Clare whom we come to associate with those secrets. Her disappearance simply coincides with Irene's (*and the reader's*) desire. But this co-incidence is hardly coincidental. At the very moment Clare finally abandons her potential as an *intrus* who remains perpetually "foreign" (by remaining intrusively present), at the very moment Clare becomes *too clear to see*, Irene acts "to restore order, stability and identity" (Žižek, *Sublime Object* 128). The two extremes or desires—Clare's irresponsible refusal *to be* anything and Irene's desperate insistence that she *is* a definable something—collapse in on each other. In this moment of collapse, the novel undoes the possibility of simply countering Irene's paranoia with Clare's promise of perpetual passing. Instead, and while exposing us to our own violent tendency to impose a sense of familiarity upon the other, to eliminate the intrusive, the novel refuses (itself) to be naturalized, to cease being intrusive. But this refusal functions as a critique of *both* Irene and Clare. The novel counters its own heteroglot polyphony with Irene's fantasy of immanence *and* Clare's refusal to commit to a self that precedes and is therefore *responsible for* the roles she performs. The novel therefore resists by finally conflating as equally problematic (if not unethical) Irene's hysteria and Clare's perversity.

Perversity/Hysteria

Read retrospectively, the opening passages of Larsen's novel function to frame its contents, setting up a type of figure or motif that is then reflected in Clare's climactic disappearance. Like the finale, then, the opening passages have been the subject of innumerable critical readings. Henderson's is, however, one of the more concise and compelling. It is difficult to dispute Henderson's suggestion that, in these opening passages, Larsen establishes the possibility that "Clare as text—as performative text—[is] a work of art . . . and, as such, an object of *desire* and *knowing* for Irene and the spectatorial reader" (Henderson xlvii–xlviii). But how, *specifically,* is this parallel between the novel's "textual performance" and Clare's established? And how is it maintained through to the end? Or, in light of the novel's finale, what are the full implications of its beginning? To move toward some sense of a conclusion we must, in other words, return to the beginning. The novel opens with a letter—"the last letter in Irene Redfield's little pile of morning mail" (171). This letter, we are told, is "out of place and alien" in relation to "[Irene's] other ordinary and clearly directed letters." There is something "furtive" but also "sly" about it, something (even) "flaunting." Perhaps most significantly, this "thin sly thing," this "almost illegible" letter written in "purple ink" on "foreign paper of extraordinary size," arrives without any "return address to betray the sender." The letter literally intrudes; it arrives even though it cannot be (re)addressed or redressed. It can't be sent away, for there is no place to put it, nowhere to return it. It is therefore, on some level, just as "purloined" as Poe's infamous letter. We might in fact say—following Lacan's reading of Poe—that Clare's letter has fallen outside the symbolic circuit. It is the ultimate "disturbance and perturbation of intimacy." And yet, unlike Poe's letter, Clare's letter seems to find its place *even as* it frustrates the possibility of placing it. It is a "perturbation"—or a proper *intrus*—because it arrives *without arriving;* it presents itself only to expose its absence—the absence of what it cannot express. The letter therefore signals Clare's intrusive potential, but it does not necessarily prefigure her final disappearance—as, that is, the final evacuation of anything resembling a content, or graspable meaning. We must then be cautious when comparing the letter to Clare, Clare to the novel, Irene to the reader. Moreover, we should not necessarily assume that, in being "mindful that the challenge in reading the text is prefigured by Irene's encounter with Clare's letter, the reader/critic, *like Irene,* must attempt to elicit the mystery of its meaning—to uncover the secret of the text (figured in some respects by the secrecy of Clare's passing)" (Henderson li;

my emphasis). Irene most certainly feels that she *must* do this, and the novel most certainly works to provoke a similar response in the reader. But Irene's reaction to Clare's "*almost* illegible scrawl" (171; my emphasis) is presented, even at the outset, as hysterical.

Irene's response to the letter is to *impose* sense upon it. Her first impulse is to retreat into memory, memory that is overtly "constructed" in nature. After "reflect[ing]" on the fact that the letter is "a piece with all that she knew of Clare Kendry," Irene "*seem[s]* to see a pale small girl sitting on a ragged blue sofa, sewing pieces of bright red cloth together, while her drunken father, a tall, powerfully built man, raged threateningly up and down the shabby room, bellowing curses and making spasmodic lunges at her which were not the less frightening because they were, for the most part, ineffectual" (172; my emphasis). Unable, finally, to account for (by reconstructing a memory of) Clare's abject indifference—indifference, we should note, that she links to performativity and "theatrical heroics" (172)—Irene finally reads the letter. But her reading is questionable (at best); she merely "[runs] through the letter, puzzling out, as best she [can], the carelessly formed words or making instinctive guesses at them" (174). Larsen then presents us with the text *as Irene reads it,* full of ellipses and overtly suggestive of *a* desire that (given the reading strategy employed) is far more a construction of Irene's than an articulation of Clare's. Irene clearly overlooks any number of words and passages to fixate on Clare's evocation of some "terrible, . . . wild desire" provoked by "that time in Chicago" (174). This latter phrase even causes "brilliant red patches" to appear in "Irene Redfield's warm olive cheeks" (174). The suggestion we get—especially given the overt claim that these *particular* "words stood out from among the many paragraphs of other words" (174)—is that Irene reads only what makes sense to her, that she struggles to fill up (with *imposed* sense) any intimations of otherness, or sites of *in*finite absence, that might remain within the text. But the letter, like Clare, frustrates her efforts—as the novel frustrates ours. Yet it is this very frustration that signals our traumatizing responsibility for infinity *in* the *finite,* a responsibility (moreover) that entails the impossibility of finalizing *an in*finite (self). The more Irene's efforts at sense making are faced with this responsibility to an impossibility, the more hysterical they become. Hysteria, after all, tends to occur at the moment the subject is no longer capable of believing in his or her identity; it is a response to the realization that I am always in excess of a given performative, or set of performatives. As Žižek puts it, hysteria responds to a traumatic moment of "self-" doubt: "What is hysteria if not precisely the effect and testimony of a failed interpellation;

what is the hysterical question if not an articulation of the incapacity of the subject to fulfil the symbolic identification, to assume fully and without restraint the symbolic mandate?" (*Sublime Object* 113). Irene's hysteria, though, tends to manifest as or become confused with a type of paranoia, a terrifying suspicion and doubt about what the other might want or think or do. Such paranoia—which aims to make sense of everything, to apprehend the other's secret, to impose order—simply reflects a hysterical fear of incompleteness, of transience.

Nevertheless, and despite Irene's hysterical response to its ambiguity, the letter (and therefore Clare) seems intent on saying some*thing*. It apparently says quite a lot, in fact—"many paragraphs of other words." There is no reason to assume that these words are simply random either, or a *postmodern* series of signifiers functioning (merely and only) to corrode the possibility of meaningful signification. Clare *intends* (to say something about) herself; the problem for Irene is that this intent seems to exceed the series of "norms" in which it is cast; it refuses the comfort Irene finds in those "other ordinary and clearly directed letters." Instead, Clare's letter—like the book itself—employs coherent language and clearly directed grammar only to the point of absolute necessity. Its intent or secret is left discoverable as the *infinite*. Is this not what is implied by the fact that Clare's letter is "*almost* illegible," that it signals "the *edge* of danger" (172; my emphasis)? Like the letter, then—or rather, *at her most promising*—Clare sustains an opacity while *and by* exposing the inadequacy of the performative "norms" that make the sharing of such an opacity possible. It is only in the coherence of sense that *some sense* of the "infinite in me" can be smuggled across the border. Norms of understanding limit the self; but this means, too, that they are points of in-betweenness. In exposing us to this paradox, the novel offers a radical alternative to Irene's hysterical demand for immanence, or a fixed social bond that would validate claims of understanding or communal experience. The passing nature of the novel's content disrupts the fantasy of communion by exploiting the infinite potential of (what Nancy understand as) "compearance," which "consists in the appearance of the *between* as such: you *and* I (between us)—a formula in which the *and* does not imply juxtaposition, but exposition" ("Inoperative" 29). The finitude of singular beings compears, or co-appears, through communication, the *between*. The possibility of finitude (which we might understand as the possibility of an *articulated* individual) demands a limit, an *other*, a point of contact. This "between," for Nancy, is the antithesis of an immanent social bond, entropic communion, or total understanding. Communication is in fact an obstacle to communion, yet it makes sharing possible. My individual finiteness entails absolute otherness, but it also (then) entails relation, a point of contact, a common and therefore limited tongue. For this precise reason, "Sharing is always incomplete, or it is beyond completion and incompletion. For a complete sharing implies the disappearance of what is shared" (35). How, though, might we square this necessary articulation of finitude with Levinasian ethics—except to say that I cannot share the "infinite in me" if there is no point of finitude, no contact (as in *proximity*) between the self and the other? Surely this is why, as Butler puts it (in her own effort to negotiate the tension between "norms" of linguistic coherence and the *in*finite "opacity" of the self), any effort to articulate the self must deploy a certain "suspect coherence ... an acceptance of *the limits* of knowability in oneself and others" (*Giving an Account* 63, my emphasis). And yet, as Butler assures us, this in no way suggests that "radical fragmentation" is somehow more ethical or efficacious than "hyper-mastery" (52).

We might then say that Clare's letter signifies the promise of Clare's passing state, but it does not establish a one-to-one equivalence between Clare and the textual strategies of the novel itself. The novel, like the letter—like, again, Clare *at her most promising*—sustains the possibility of an unsaid that is more or less (but never fully) implied by the text that necessarily effaces its potential. The novel is internally focalized through Irene's paranoiac perceptions and constructions of reality, but there remains a space of distance between these perceptions and constructions and the narrative voice that translates them. Like Crosland's *Jazz Singer*, the novel carefully maintains a space between the diegetic and the nondiegetic, the idiosyncratic heart of the matter and "the way of the world." While we are left to wonder what *really* happened, we are never given to doubt that *something* (akin to Irene's perception of it) happened. The focalization never reaches a zero point (as it were)—which is to say that the narrator never reveals something that Irene does not or cannot know; yet the narrator frequently reminds us that there is a reality anterior to Irene's perception of it. There are also moments when Irene's perception is ostensibly confirmed—such as "It *was* the last letter" (171; my emphasis), etc. While we surely have to concede that our knowledge of Clare is restricted by the limits of Irene's understanding, we can nevertheless assume that Clare's actions and behaviors are more than mere fantasies or projections. On the one hand, this suggests that the novel is never interested in enacting (simply) a "(post)modern" evisceration of phenomenal knowledge; the novel, in some respects, seems to exceed or go beyond (what we might think of as) postmodern indeterminacy, or perversity.[14]

On the other, it means that we are *allowed* to assess the trajectory of Clare's behavior—a trajectory toward "radical fragmentation" and thus an abject resistance to sharing.

After all, the Clare *of the letter* is subtly different from the Clare of the finale—if only because (we might say) there is *no* Clare in the finale. The phrasing in the two scenes implies this difference. When, in response to the letter's intrusion, Irene struggles to re-member Clare, she sees Clare's white father "bellowing" at his indifferent daughter. The memory is problematic for Irene because these angry and violent outbursts "were not the less frightening because they were, for the most part, ineffectual." What makes these outburst frightening *for Irene* is the fact that they are "ineffectual"—but only, we must not forget, *"for the most part."* Clare's resistance to "symbolic inertia" (Lacan, *Seminar* 190)[15] is terrifying and radically subversive: she does not behave (entirely) as she should. She frustrates the fantasy of essential norms of behavior while, on some level, remaining present or recognizable within the socially constructed scene of action. Something about these norms still applies to her. It might be impossible to readdress/redress her with any sense of certainty; like the letter she sends years later, she is already without a fixed or fixable address. But she remains (to some degree) *in* place—just as her letter is *still* "postmarked in New York the day before" (171–72). In the beginning, Clare signals the novel's limited allegiance to the perversely postmodern subject—insofar as she exemplifies the manner in which a *"self . . . exists in a fabric of relations" while or by* remaining "located [*or still locatable*] at a post through which various kinds of messages pass" (Lyotard 15). However, when this memory repeats in the finale, there is no sense of "for the most part"; Clare simply disappears altogether. There is not even any longer a "postmark," or contingent point of coherent focus—only the cacophonous messages that mean to locate it. All such messages become—if we can anticipate our discussion of Bartleby in chapter 4—*dead* letters. Or more specifically, her bellowing father becomes her husband (Bellew), but what *he* bellows utterly misses its mark.

We likely miss the mark (too) if we assume, along with a critic like Neil Sullivan, that Irene and Clare (as mirror images of each other) are simply *overtaken* by the racial signifier Bellew uses to define them during the finale.[16] The word itself does not cause Clare's fall, nor does it necessitate (what Sullivan understands as) Irene's final exclusion from the world. While, as Butler puts it, Clare "represents the specter of a racial ambiguity that must be conquered" ("Passing, Queering" 172), we should not reduce the finale to the moment in which we see the stabilization of Bellew's identity as a "white" hinging upon the stabilization of Clare's identity as a "nigger." We must take the implications of Bellew's outburst a few steps further—especially in light of the fact that it repeats *while failing to repeat* Irene's initial memory of Clare. To begin with, we must entertain the possibility that Bellew's deployment of the most racist of performatives functions (on some level) as an almost calming reification of the essential self to which Irene so desperately clings. For Irene, the scene begins to play out precisely as it should, as it *must*, as it is *fated to*. It is, therefore, Clare's response to Bellew's outburst—and not the outburst itself—that causes all the problems. Clare, of course, as we've seen, merely smiles as her life falls to pieces, leaving nothing but (what we might now understand to be, following Butler) "radical fragments." Clare's (non)response is simply perverse, a complete refusal of anything *in*finite that might be in line with *or radically in excess of* the symbolic mandates that define the scene. Clare's indifference to the implications of identity categories (in this case, the category of "nigger") and her (non)position in a room that is now filled with both "whites" and "blacks" thrust Irene into a state of pure hysteria. In this moment, though, Irene's hysterical demands for "hyper-mastery" become inextricably confused with Clare's perverse withdrawal in "radical fragmentation." Or rather, both women are, as Sullivan rightly suggests, lost—for at either extreme the ordeal of the *in*finite is abandoned; only the finite norms of communication remain. But all of this is finally framed by the novel itself, which therefore critiques both Clare's irresponsible withdrawal and Irene's fantasy of immanence by expressing and sustaining its own *in*finite content. In the end, it is the novel *itself* that exploits and sustains the promise of passing—a fact that certainly seems to imply that the potential of a specter (that would threaten to *undo* melancholia) is intimately tied to the possibility of *a type of* narrative form. Larsen's novel *passes* as a coherent and recognizable frame so as to *pass on* what it preserves as always in excess of that frame; it works to preserve *and* share its content by signaling the incessant and intrusive incompletion of that which is shared. It opens us to the possibility of sustaining a finally ethical relation between self and other.

3 / Articulations of Ambiguity: William Faulkner, Toni Morrison, and James McBride

> *Put your heart on a platter and see who will bite*
> *See who'll hold you and kiss you good night*
> —BOB DYLAN, "SCARLET TOWN"

Poetics of Disgust

Certain threads have begun to converge: the rise of nativism at the turn of the century, the rupture of voice in (silent) film, the heteroglot polyphony of the modern novel. At the intersection is the promise and the threat of the intruder, of *l'intrus*. But let's continue to follow, for now, the political role of modernist discourse in the early twentieth century—in particular, the relationship between the melancholic desire for immanence (communal and individual) and the possibility of its complete or coherent expression. To do so, we need to perseverate a while longer on America's fixation with race and the terror of racial ambiguity. The obfuscations of the modernist novel surely parallel the rising threat of a racially confused America—an America with increasingly porous racial and ontological boundaries. We traced this parallel in chapter 1, especially as it related to the codification of whiteness and the growing polarization of black Americans and other (nonblack) minorities. This effort toward racial regimentation is signaled by the rising popularity of blackface minstrelsy in the twenties and thirties—*insofar as* such performances functioned to reify a difference between the *authentically* "black" and those "nonblacks" who might assert their whiteness by donning a mask so as to *perform* blackness. But the minstrelsy was just one of America's more subtle (if paradoxical) efforts to confront its specter of ambiguity, the threat of its dissolving communal boundaries. Nativist immigration acts and Jim Crow laws were far more overt efforts to manage the fact that intrusions of the unrecognizable were proliferating exponentially. And of course much of America's anxiety was exasperated—if not *caused*—by the proliferation of mechanized and rapid transit (of both people and ideas). Reflecting and responding to new media and new forms of transportation, modern art was increasingly produced, as Raymond Williams notes, in "transnational capitals . . . by the restlessly mobile emigré or exile, the internationally anti-bourgeois" (34). And since, as Williams goes on to point out, "Such endless border-crossing at a time when frontiers were starting to become much more strictly policed . . . worked to naturalize the thesis of the *non-natural* status of language," modernism finds itself inextricably tied to "the experience of visual and linguistic strangeness, the broken narrative of the journey and its inevitable accompaniment of transient encounters with characters whose self-presentation was bafflingly unfamiliar" (34).[1] But if it is possible to read the modern American novel—its move toward abstraction, lacunae, and heteroglossia—as an effort to take up the promising threat of intrusive transience (racial, national, sexual, etc.), to endorse its democratic potential and strengthen its resolve, then surely we must evaluate the ethics of the modern novel in the same way we might evaluate the social responsibility of a character like Clare Kendry. How do such novels struggle to *give* their subject—in relation (as the language of the Lacanian Other)—while *or by* withholding that subject, while *or by* sustaining a remainder that is always coming but never arriving? More importantly, how does this struggle reflect on the promising threat of the intrusive stranger? How might writing and reading imply a strategy for democratic giving and understanding?[2]

At stake is the *way in which* the modern American novel risks obfuscation in an effort to express that which goes beyond the obvious—or that which cannot be held (in full) by common language or "usage" (as the narrator of Melville's "Bartleby" might say). In America—especially in the early twentieth century—this risk of obfuscation (in the form of what Julia Kristeva might call "poetic language" or Roland Barthes might call a "writerly text")[3] exasperates while highlighting an already profound melancholic sensibility. The indecipherability of the textual body signals the indecipherability of the human body. Identity becomes text—which is precisely Barthes's point in his famous essay "The Death of the Author." Alongside the risk of elitist and exclusionary difficulty, the modern danger is the danger of the abjectly unreadable, the utterly withdrawn. As Pamela L. Caughie puts it, "Writing [becomes] a matter of effacing—not expressing—the self" (404). This is why, Caughie insists, modernism is far more tied to an "ethics of concealment"—to themes of absence, performance, and passing—than is postmodernism, which tends to parallel and buttress a contemporary investment in "getting personal, breaking silence, coming out" (404). Caughie certainly overlooks or downplays the complexities of postmodernism by confusing its development in the latter half of the century with a far more contemporary moral imperative (one that more clearly parallels the post-postmodern rise of social media and the popularity of "reality TV" in the late twentieth and early twenty-first centuries); but her point is not without merit. If modernism engages in a viable ethics it is most certainly an "ethics of concealment."[4] But if that ethics is to sustain its efficacy, if it is to oppose *perverse* acts of "passing" (which we might also call *post*modern), if it is to circumvent the irresponsibility of assuming "an autonomous subject without heritage, family, or history" (Caughie 389), modernist writing must necessarily eschew simple acts of effacement. Such effacement or withdrawal would surely signal the preservation of the truth, the secret (self) maintaining absolutely its divinely unknowable secrecy. But it would entail (also) the utter refusal to share, to relate at all, "to confront and to struggle with one's own historically constituted identity" (389).

In this specific sense, and as we already started to see in the previous chapter, the problem and promise of the modern novel in America is impossible to disentangle from the problem and promise of racial passing.[5] The passing subject (like "novelistic" content or meaning) is a transient target, an unassimilable object of disgust, that which refuses to be consumed or understood. The ethics of passing—like the ethics of the modern novel—is therefore tied to the possibility of fomenting and sustaining *manageable* disgust. But how? How might we sustain a modality of disgust that is also, somehow, palatable? What form of *dis*-gust might we employ so as to forestall a simplistic and irresponsible effacement of the self and of meaning? If we are to answer such questions, we must first take a moment to consider the way in which disgust is always already supplemental to the possibility of (mimetic) authenticity. As Derrida assures us in "Economimesis," disgust is the very thing that frustrates the aesthetic economy of beauty, the mimetic articulation of *authentic* genius. Following Derrida (*following Kant*), the goal of art is the goal of "the free man" ("Economimesis" 6): "Genius, as an instance of the Fine-Arts ('Fine-Arts must necessarily be considered arts of *genius*,' §46) carries freedom of play and the pure productivity of the imagination to its highest point" (6). Fine art—the peak of which for Kant would be (spoken) poetry—manages to escape any economic or coercive forces, producing independently (and never *actually* imitating) via an insistence upon *naturally* original "play." The truly mimetic (for Kant) only imitates insofar as it imitates the production of divinity, of nature's playful spontaneity: "Art is beautiful to the degree that it is productive *like* productive nature, that it reproduces the production and not the product of nature" ("Economimesis" 10). Derrida's point is that this escape—in the form of production *ex nihilo*—is wholly and dangerously illusory, another effect of economic exchange or circulation. Such art seems to confirm the divine status of humanity (in opposition to all other being[s]); it replicates a universally communicable nature that is also and nevertheless anterior to preexisting "concepts," or free from mechanistic mandates. It eschews the excesses and corruptive nature of "enjoyment" (which, in Derrida, is the English translation for "*jouissance*") in favor of purely disinterested pleasure: "The Fine-Arts seek pleasure [*Lust*] without enjoyment" (8). What Derrida demonstrates, then, differs little from what Levinas shows (and, therefore, from what we saw already during our discussion of Clare)—that the "fallacious frivolity of [such] play" is never "free of interest" (Levinas, *Otherwise* 6).[6] As Derrida asserts,

> in the exercise of a liberal art (of the free spirit) a certain constraint must be at work. Something compulsory ('*zwangmässiges*' is also the word used to designate the constraint imposed on handicraft) must intervene as a 'mechanism' [*Mechanismus*]. Without this coercive constriction, this tight corset [*corsage*], the spirit which must be free in art 'would have no body and would evaporate altogether.' The body, constraint, or mechanism, for example, of poetry, the highest of the liberal arts, would be lexical accuracy or richness [*Sprachrichtigkeit, Sprachreichtum*], prosody or metrics. ("Economimesis" 7)

If we follow and extend Derrida's economic puns, the genius of poetry can never articulate its purely pleasurable disinterest without accruing interest, without the corruptive supplement of the frame. The problem is that this necessarily corruptive supplement is masked as the "rule" of God, the play of genius *as* the divinely natural—as, that is, *not* a rule anterior to the subject in question. Surely this is the precise reason Bakhtin sees in poetry the threat of hegemony, or the *impossibility* of expressing "the incomplete commitment of oneself, of one's full meaning, to a given language" (285).

We have not strayed as far from a focus on race and racial ambiguity as it might seem. The problem we are circling around is the problem of an art—or mode of expression—that would strive to be an expression of a *naturalized* freedom, a "pleasure [*Lust*] which alone is universally communicable, without being based on concepts" (Kant, qtd. in Derrida, "Economimesis" 9). But the effort toward such naturalization is surely melancholic, and thus the antithesis or disavowal of freedom. Kantian poetics are, in other words, the poetics of an abject and exclusionary humanism—which is to say that they are also and necessarily a *melancholic* poetics of race and immanence. They assume the dream of a "[silent] . . . language between nature and man" (15). Such poetics blind us, or *allow us to remain blind,* to the fact that freedom is always only in excess, that which cannot be assimilated or naturalized. It is only ever that which must be endured. For this reason, "The beautiful would always be the work [*l'oeuvre*] (as much the act as the object), the art whose signature remains marked at the limit of the work, neither in nor out, out and in, in the parergonal thickness of the frame" (7). Freedom as supplement, as relation,[7] is therefore marked (within the anthropocentric economy of mimesis) by disgust: "While the beautiful is a name for the balanced and harmonious metabolism, the closed economy remains threatened from within by disgust, and this analytic of the beautiful falls apart when it reaches the point of disgust and vomiting—a point at which the economy reaches its limit in terms of what is absolutely inassimilable" (Derrida, "Interview"). What, then, we might say the modern American novel struggles to "foreclose" (while *or by* exemplifying the performative potential of the racially ambiguous) is a certain "vicariousness of vomit . . . [of] some other unrepresentable, unnameable, unintelligible, insensible, unassimilable, obscene other which forces enjoyment and whose irrepressible violence would undo the hierarchizing authority of logocentric analogy—its power of *identification*" (Derrida, "Economimesis" 25). This is the violence that undoes or forestalls melancholia—the ability to hold to an impossible dream of naturalization, of racial or communal purity, of the immanent individual—while simultaneously *persisting* (or forever *coming*) as "what one cannot resign oneself to mourn" (23). We cannot "get over" (or forget) such violence because it refuses "idealisation" (22).[8] The disgusting can only be consumed ad nauseam; it can never be interiorized, or made "auto-affect[ive]" (18). It always only *passes* right through me. In both the passing subject and the passing text (as we saw in our discussion of *Passing*), we are faced with a disgusting demand to "respect . . . [what] cannot be assimilated . . . a remainder that cannot be read, that must remain alien. This residue can never be interrogated as the same, but must be constantly sought out anew, and must continue to be written" (Derrida, "Interview").

But if it "must be constantly sought out anew, and must continue to be written," the disgusting must also attach itself (at least momentarily) with what *can* be taken in, with what *can* be understood. We must, at the very least, *understand* that we are disgusted. We must be given to recognize our disgust via the picture or meal it corrupts. Could we not in fact infer from this that only what is *not* disgusting can (in the end) effect disgust? Such a claim would, though, imply a type of Hegelian sublation—a sublation that (at least before the late 1990s) Derrida would certainly reject as *all-consuming*.[9] And yet an ethics of sharing, of friendship and of democracy, must surely entail sustaining *a type* of disgust that would risk its sublimation—risk, even, entering an economy of "coercive constriction" in the form of a sublimely "*negative* pleasure." Some work of mourning must be permitted if we are to avoid swinging simply and pointlessly from one mode of silence (i.e., the universal and naturalized communion of the human, or *racialized*, genius at play) to another (i.e., the "in-sensible and un-intelligible, irrepresentable and unnameable, the absolute other of the system" [Derrida, "Economimesis" 22]).

At its extreme, and if we recall our discussion of jazz in chapter 1, we might align our understanding of the disgusting—of what induces only endless vomit, the antithesis of what is representable, or sharable—as the repulsive silence (or nonmeaning) of maddening cacophony. And yet even cacophony would have to be understood as other to a truly disgusting Thing (in the Lacanian sense of *das Ding*); it would merely signal the absence of pattern, coherence, or recognizable modality. Such cacophony would be the silence of innumerable performative frames announcing their inability to hold a content, or subject. This would be or would signal the outside limit of modern experimentation. At the other extreme, though—at, that is, the extreme of a logocentric poetics—we have only the silent law of the father, the framing corset *as body* (with no space left over for disgust). This corset (pulled too tight) puts an end to sound—just as the cantor in *The Jazz Singer* does when he shouts "Stop!" Poetic silence works to stabilize our sense of the other as wholly definable, as wholly Other (in the sense that Nancy uses the capitalized form).[10] Or rather, it does the work of a lynching, reinvigorating our melancholic faith in an immanent self. A lynching, as we've seen, responds to the fear that a melancholic state of pure inclusion/exclusion will no longer be possible, the fear that the other will no longer be definable, or locatable, that we might have to accept instability, disorder, disconnection, transience, disgust, the impossibility of an idealizable subject position. But the passing subject, as *l'intrus,* ruptures this silence, disturbs its sustainment: for "if he remains foreign, and for as long as he does so—rather than simply 'becoming naturalized'—his coming will not cease; nor will it cease being in some respect an intrusion: . . . a disturbance and perturbation of intimacy" (Nancy, "L'Intrus" 1–2). But this leads us, again, to our earlier question: How does such an intruder, such an object of disgust, *begin* to come? What carries him or her (or it) *through* the door?

Or at least up to the threshold? What signals its coming in the absence of its arrival? On some level, the radically intrusive must "perform" an arrival if the possibility of that arrival as an idealization or naturalization of the other is to be negated. Some meaningful enunciation or utterance is required *even if* the "enunciating subject ... [is] [a]lways foreign to the subject of its own utterance; necessarily intruding upon it" (Nancy, "L'Intrus" 2). But in the moment of utterance so many things can go wrong. If the performative that opens the door to the subject's potential arrival is offered as the subject au natural then the subject is lost to its conjuration, to logocentric mimesis: a lynching. If, on the other hand, the performative vehicle is too *authentically* disgusting or cacophonous to recognize, then nothing (or no one) can begin to come. The door would open to the silence of unintelligible noise. And if, finally, the performative is given perversely as *only* its arbitrary self, as wholly exchangeable for any other mode of communal understanding, then the door would open to a subject in irresponsible (or *post*modern) flight.

The ambiguously passing subject must risk, always, the latter two dangers. And because we might define the modern novel—at, that is, its most "novelistic"—as that which increasingly risks the second of the three, we might say (at the risk of oversimplification) that the modern novel *at its most efficacious* is always a novel of and about passing. At its best, it frustrates by exasperating a lynching impulse.[11] It disentangles freedom from themes of naturalization and exposes it as a condition of relation, of that which "happens only in the withdrawal of what would unite or necessarily communicate me to others and to myself, in the withdrawal of the community of the being of my existence, without which there would be no singularity but only being's immanence to itself" (Nancy, *Freedom* 69). By struggling to *give* a passing subject, the modern novelistic project works to expose *freedom* as the withdrawal of the essential (or naturalized, or idealized) bond—as that which "would unite or necessarily communicate me to others" (69). And yet the success of such polyphonic textual strategies (which must always risk becoming cacophonic) must nevertheless entail opening the door to communication. We cannot, after all, "*receive*[] the stranger by effacing his strangeness at the threshold" ("L'Intrus" 2; my emphasis). The goal must remain a form of reception.

Novelistic Passing

Faulkner's are, perhaps, the most exemplary of passing modern novels—especially those novels that deal explicitly with the literal implications and effects of racial passing. *Light in August* (1932), *Go Down, Moses* (1942), and

Intruder in the Dust (1948) come to mind. All three novels deal directly with the problem of racial disgust as racial ambiguity. All three novels also exemplify Faulkner's move from what Carl J. Dimitri terms "a [strictly] modernist aesthetic to an aesthetic of engagement" (12).[12] But let's focus primarily on *Intruder*—if only because one of its most striking moments clearly associates the spacing of a doorway with the ethical problem of understanding, of fully *interiorizing* a situation or person.

Early on in the novel, the central character—a sixteen-year-old boy named Charles "Chick" Mallison—returns home to seek out the aid of his lawyer uncle (Gavin Stevens). After finding the door to the room Gavin uses as an office closed, Chick "hear[s] the murmur of the man's voice beyond it during the second in which without even stopping he rapped twice and at the same time opened the door and entered" (74). But in the moment of entering—of *intruding*, in fact—Chick fails to enter. His inertia (which is already signaled in the inertia of Faulkner's cascading language), is interrupted by his sudden awareness of the woman sitting opposite his uncle. In the space of the next several pages and via an inexorable piling up of interconnected images, Faulkner details almost all Chick knows about the woman he has stumbled upon: the elderly Miss Habersham. The flood of largely unconscious memory is finally reduced to a single conscious and *graspable* fact: Chick can and should overlook her presence. While she bears a noble southern name (and thus descends from a noble southern bloodline), Miss Habersham is "a kinless spinster of seventy living in the columned colonial house on the edge of town which had not been painted since her father died" (75–76); she drives a "pick-up truck" (75) and wears a "gold brooch on her flat bosom" (74–75). She's an odd but unimportant woman. She is *just* a woman. Thus, in the mere seconds immediately following the momentary disturbance of his inertia—his headlong rush into his uncle's office, or "world"—Chick "had already forgotten Miss Habersham, even her presence" (77). And so he begins moving forward again, begins talking: "I've got to speak to you" (77). But Faulkner is careful to have the scene play out in extreme slow motion. Chick lingers in the doorway for seven pages. As a result, a strange anticipation, or sense of dread, is provoked. Chick's arrival remains in doubt; he keeps entering, always *seeming* to move forward yet still "at the door and still holding it, half in the room which he had never actually entered and shouldn't have come even that far and half already back out of it in the hall where he should never have wasted time passing to begin with" (77–78).

Are we not lead to sense that Chick's *moral* success hinges utterly on his ability to stay outside this office—or better, to remain in some space between the inside and the outside of his uncle's world? The novel is, after all, a type of bildungsroman. So it is difficult to view the space of Gavin's office—located, in turn, within the space of Chick's paternal home—as anything but the space of manhood. That Miss Habersham's (non)presence disrupts Chick's movement (in that it must be overcome or ignored or reified if Chick is to continue moving in his destined direction) is, then, all the more significant. Miss Habersham is not *just* a woman. She is old yet independent. She drives a truck and has a "flat bosom." She wears nice yet practical clothes—"the clean print dresses which you could see in the Sears Roebuck catalogues for two dollars and ninety-eight cents" (76). She's never been married. She is no one's mother. Within the symbolic mandates of the adult world, Habersham is *barely* a woman. She might only be *passing* as one. Or worse, she may be passing—with her independence and her truck and her house on the "edge of town" and her lack of a man or a child—*as* a man. It should come as no surprise that Chick finally responds to her as a type of ghost. Without the concepts necessary to make sense of her, his mind is forced to dismiss (or overlook) her: "At the moment he was neither rediscovering her presence in the room nor even discovering it; he didn't even remember that she had already long since ceased to exist" (79–80). And yet Faulkner makes it clear that her (non) presence is working on him, forestalling or checking his *proper* movement forward, keeping him (like her) in a state of in-betweenness.[13] His unconscious mind remains flooded with images of her. He is particularly fixated on, or *disgusted* by, her "flat unmammary front" (76).

The scene functions as a type of mise en abyme. Chick has come seeking aid for Lucas Beauchamp—an irascible mixed-race man who has been accused of shooting a "white" man in the back. The man he ostensibly shot and killed (Vinson Gowrie) belongs to one of the most racist families in Yoknapatawpha County. As Chick lingers in his uncle's doorway, the Gowries (and with the full support, or at least indifference, of the townspeople of Jackson) are preparing to lynch Lucas. Worried such violence may be unjustified (or even unjustifiable), Chick finds himself in a state of profound uncertainty, haunting the threshold of adulthood and hoping his wise uncle will be of some assistance. But Lucas (after having earlier compelled Chick to bring him to the jailhouse) has already meet with Gavin. During this first meeting, Lucas refuses to tell Gavin anything that might help his case. He simply manipulates Gavin into agreeing to represent him and then dismisses him. But before Gavin and Chick can leave the jail, Lucas asks for some tobacco. The request is another manipulation, as it allows Lucas to get Chick alone—at which point he tells Chick that, if he digs up Vinson's body, he will see "He wasn't shot with no fawty-one Colt" (68). The scene of this revelation sets up the scene of Chick's nonentry at his uncle's door: "'Come here.' Lucas did so, approaching, taking hold of the two bars as a child stands inside a fence. Nor did he remember doing so but looking down he saw his own hands holding to two of the bars, the two pairs of hands, the black ones and the white ones, grasping the bars while they faced one another above them" (67). Here Faulkner suggests that liminality is always somehow childlike, a refusal or an innocence in the face of "symbolic inertia": "as a child stands inside a fence." This theme or representation of liminality is buttressed by the ontological ambiguity of the moment. As he does throughout, Faulkner employs the pronoun "he" while or by ignoring all grammatical rules of antecedence. "He" always refers to Chick, no matter the subject that precedes its usage in a given phrase or clause. And since our inertia as readers resists these pronoun slips, we end up with a series of "double" readings.[14] We must force ourselves to insert Chick "in place" at the very moment we have already (on some level) conflated "him" with another. Chick is therefore also Lucas when "he [sees] his own hands holding to two of the bars, ... the black ones *and* the white ones." The certainty of Chick's identity or societal role is therefore always slipping, always still between possibilities—but also, as Dimitri suggests, always also in danger of becoming "enslaved" (19). Faulkner's typical deployment of meandering and at times untrackable streams of consciousness signals precisely this slipping. Chick's thoughts and memories and impulses constantly intrude unannounced and even (at times) unrecognized or unfathomed. "Smell[s]" that might "[mean] nothing now or yet" have lasting "ramifications" (11) and memories of stories affect his momentary perceptions even if Chick has "forgot[ten] that he had remembered even the having been told" (10–11). Motivations and subjects always seem in excess of a given vocabulary or effort to account for them—even if most of what happens and most of who Chick might become is mandated by the terms he must use to make sense of and move through the world. Destiny is always likely to lynch us, to imprison us in our role(s), and to determine what power (or lack of power) we might exert on the other. As we'll see, the potential and the threat of Chick's own indeterminability (as a resistance to lynching) is paralleled with and highlighted by Lucas's. But let's stay focused (for now) on the problem of language Faulkner both articulates and exploits—especially as it relates to Chick's development in the face of characters like Lucas and Miss Habersham.

 Chick comes to occupy his uncle's doorway because he wants Gavin to assist in exhuming Vinson's body. But before he can even make his request (or enter the room in full), his uncle anticipates and refuses his request: "So you took it to him yourself. Or maybe you didn't even bother with tobacco. And he told you a tale. I hope it was a good one" (77). Even before he hears it, Gavin refuses to accept the tale that was told. And once he does hear it, he asserts that he'd rather tell Vinson Gowrie's father (Nub) that he "wanted to exhume [the body] to dig the gold out of its teeth than to tell him the reason was to save a nigger from being lynched" (79). Gavin—who has been educated at Harvard and Heidelberg—ameliorates his ostensible racism by telling (so as to comfort) Chick that he "dont believe there are that many people in this county who really want to hang Lucas to a telephone pole and set fire to him with gasoline" (79). But Gavin is surely incorrect—and just as surely unable to perceive a possibility outside his restricted expectations (or the "rich and immanent destiny" [5] he *assumes* of racial and social types). Chick, though, while coming through (but never fully crossing) the doorway, begins to glean the problem: "And he marvelled again at the paucity, the really almost standardised meagerness not of individual vocabularies but of Vocabulary itself, by means of which even man can live in vast droves and herds even in concrete warrens in comparative amity: even his uncle too" (79). And with this truth in mind—but with, also, "the significantless speciosity of his uncle's voice" (80) working to pull him in—Chick resists his inertia and finally "close[s] the door, who had heard it all before" (80).

Back outside, Chick enlists the aid of Aleck Sander, his childhood friend and the son of his parents' black cook. And again Faulkner confronts us with a moment of liminality. In their teens, Chick and Aleck seem to be lingering "inside a fence"—with the destined and finally entrenched roles of master and servant beckoning on either side. Aleck clearly feels free to argue with and to question Chick's plan, but that freedom is obviously tenuous, something made possible by childhood. Aleck, after all, perceives the destiny of adulthood lynchings (figuratively and literally) on the horizon: "Me? Go out there and dig that dead white man up?" (85). And if Chick and Aleck do indeed find themselves occupying a fleeting moment of in-betweenness, that moment is once again drawn out or sustained by the intrusion of Miss Habersham—who we learn has followed Chick outside to escape (also) the hegemony of Gavin's professional male space. To Chick's surprise, Habersham offers to help with the exhumation, explaining that Lucas did not tell Gavin the truth because "he's a Negro and [Gavin's] a man" (88). Chick cannot help but notice that, in saying this, Habersham is "in her turn repeating and paraphrasing." But this time he understands that what seems like "a paucity a meagreness of vocabulary" effectively signals the fact that "the deliberate violent blotting out obliteration of a human life was itself so simple and so final that the verbiage which surrounded it enclosed it insulated it intact into the chronicle of man had of necessity to be simple and uncomplex too, repetitive, almost monotonous even" (88). In this sense, he comes to realize that "what Miss Habersham paraphrased was simple truth, not even fact and so there was not needed a great deal of diversification and originality to express it because truth was universal, it had to be universal to be truth and so . . . anybody could know truth; all they had to do was just to pause, just to stop, just to wait" (88).[15] Chick thus comes to perceive the "truth" as a type of universal, a symbolic mandate disguised as that which is always a priori to such a mandate—like Kant's *play* of genius. The silent hegemony of such law is (for Faulkner) represented in the blind inertia of adult masculinity, the blindness (as Lacan would say) of a king who "knows nothing" (Lacan, *Seminar* 199) beyond the symbolic mandates he is destined to maintain. This is why Lacan insists that "only in the dimension of truth can something be hidden" (201–2); for "the dimension of truth," or the realm of the symbolic, operates according to law and expectation, according to destiny. In this realm we play the role we are lead to assume (as adults) we were always destined to play—at which point, of course, the distinction between play and reality vanishes altogether.[16] But it is precisely such law that Lucas (and, to a lesser degree, Habersham) is able to perceive and thus flout[17]—very much *like* Poe's Dupin (or *maybe* even Poe's minister). "Lucas knew," Habersham explains, "it would take a child—or an old woman *like me:* someone not concerned with probability, with evidence. Men like your uncle and [the sheriff] have had to be men too long, busy too long" (88; my emphasis).

Lucas thus comes to embody Faulkner's own textual strategies—or rather the inevitable failure of any "Vocabulary" so standardized and so meager. Lucas, like Faulkner's streams of consciousness and disruptive pronoun play, interrupts "truth" *as* symbolic inertia. Lucas not only performs a whiteness that mocks the "essence" of his blackness, he actively manipulates (and exposes as contingent and predictable) the linguistic/symbolic laws that govern white masculine identity.[18] Lucas maintains a space of possibility by securing Gavin as his lawyer while "refus[ing] to make any statement at all" (79)—that is, any account that could be immediately reified as the lies of a desperate "nigger." He then "positions" Chick so as to ensure that action is taken in spite of the assumptions that would typically forestall it. After closing the door to his uncle's office and reflecting on the fact that he now has to go back to Lucas and ask for directions, Chick realizes that "Lucas had already taken care of that too, foreseen that too;

remembering not with relief but rather with a new burst of rage and fury beyond even his own concept of his capacity how Lucas had not only told him what he wanted but exactly where it was and even how to get there and only then as afterthought asked him if he would" (80). These grand manipulations—along with his overt performances of both whiteness *and* blackness—make Lucas an object of disgust, a nausea-inducing disruption of the South's socio-economimesis. But just how disgusting is Lucas? Does his disgustingness exceed the possibility of an ethical relation, or moment of democratic equivalence—as Clare's seems to? Lucas *does* bring Chick (and many others) to a point of rage "beyond even [a] *concept* of ... capacity"; but surely this is Chick's problem, not Lucas's? For all his disruptions, for all his refusals to play by the rules, Lucas (like, we might say, Faulkner's later narrative voice) never abandons the possibility of operational valuations for himself or for others. He simply refuses to acquiesce to any preestablished assignment of (fixed) value—or even, perhaps, the possibility that he can be wholly located within any given economy of representation. We might say that, like the novel that depicts him—a novel that begins to risk more overt yet still ambiguous claims—Lucas works to sustain a type of engaged or articulate silence.

Racial Debts

Like Gavin and Chick, Lucas appears in more than one Faulkner story. He "first" appears in the interconnected stories that make up *Go Down, Moses*—as a main character in "The Fire and the Hearth" and then tangentially in "Pantaloon in Black" and "The Bear."[19] As we are told throughout *Intruder in the Dust* and *Go Down, Moses*, Lucas has a "strain" of white McCaslin blood. Yet even Lucas seems to accept that (in terms of his visual identity) he *is* black. The problem—*the problem with Lucas*—is that his willingness to accept his inherent "blackness" (or, that is, the labels of "negro" and "nigger") is not accompanied by a consistent willingness to *act* "black," or to take up permanent membership in the black community. Even more troubling is the fact that Lucas does not simply reject a black community in favor of a white one; rather, he seems to sustain a certain state of communal intrusiveness, a certain state of passing.[20] But Lucas's ability to pass must be viewed as even more disconcerting than (say) Clare's. Because Lucas *looks* black while acting white, his performance must always seem overtly performative. Such overtness could, of course, be comforting—or laughed off in the same way one laughs off the adult gestures of a small and precocious child or animal—but Lucas frequently shifts or slides between overt performances of whiteness and equally overt performances of blackness. His ability and willingness to switch between such roles undermines the assumption that either is less performative than the other. Consider, for instance, the moment in *Go Down, Moses* when Lucas manipulates Carothers (Roth) Edmonds into telling the sheriff about an illegal whiskey still (which is, of course, a threat to Lucas's own illegal still): "Without changing the inflection of his voice and apparently without effort or even design Lucas became not Negro but nigger, not secret so much as impenetrable, not servile and not effacing, but enveloping himself in an aura of timeless and stupid impassivity almost like a smell" (58). The profoundly intrusive nature of such (disgusting) performativity is highlighted every time Lucas's face is described. As we are told again and again (in both *Go Down, Moses* and *Intruder*), Lucas's face—which is "the color of a used saddle" (*Moses* 104), which seems "Syriac" and "heir to ten centuries of desert horsemen" (104), which is "the composite tintype . . . of ten thousand undefeated Confederate soldiers" (104)—is always "impenetrable" (68), or "absolutely blank" (69). Even his "eyes [appear] to have nothing behind them" (69). And, as Chick is shocked to realize, what *does* at times look out from behind Lucas's "composite" face has "no pigment at all, not even the white man's lack of it, not arrogant, not scornful: just intractable and composed" (*Intruder* 7).

Lucas's intractability, his lack of a definitive subject position, frustrates the majority (if not all) of those who encounter him and experience his intrusiveness.[21] After Lucas (in *Intruder*) saves a twelve-year-old Chick from drowning, Chick finds himself being sheltered and fed by a "black" man. While Chick finds the situation intolerable (for he cannot accept being dependent upon or in debt to a "black" man's charity), Lucas seemingly refuses to acknowledge (via his posture, his inscrutable face, etc.) any abnormality. Chick attempts to rectify the situation—to reaffirm or restabilize his subject position, his identity as a white male—by forcing Lucas to accept payment. But Lucas's refusal to acknowledge a "reason" for the payment frustrates Chick to the point of (almost violent) rage:

> "What's that for?" the man said, not even moving, not even tilting his face downward to look at what was on his palm: for another eternity and only the hot dead moveless blood until at last it ran to rage so that at least he could bear the shame: and watched his palm turn over not flinging the coins but spurning them downward ringing onto the bare floor . . . : and then his voice:
> "Pick it up!" (15)

Can we not read Chick's futile command—"Pick it up!"—as a desperate plea, a plea for Lucas to fall in line, to assume a stable black identity and, in turn, to allow Chick to stabilize his own "white/male" identity? His plea, in this sense, is a plea for common or universal understanding, or (again) "common usage." But Lucas refuses his place—or, as Doreen Fowler suggests, he refuses to take up his supposedly *natural* position of subservience within a "dialectics of domination" (797). Lucas is for a time utterly silent and wholly indifferent, speaking finally and only to instruct Aleck to retrieve the money and give it back to Chick. And yet, even in the moment of speaking, Lucas seems to transcend any specific position or determinable identity. It is not a definable *Lucas* that speaks, but an indefinable "voice": "The man didn't move, hands clasped behind him, looking at nothing; only the rush of the hot dead heavy blood out of which the voice spoke, addressing nobody: 'Pick up his money'" (16). Lucas looks at "nothing" and his voice speaks to "nobody"—*as if* his own inexplicable absence (within an economy of delimiting terms of reference) entail's Chick's. And so Chick, utterly disgusted "and writhing with impotent fury" (18), begins to think of Lucas in the same way that "every white man in that whole section of the country had been thinking about him for years" (18). Chick thinks this: "*We got to make him be a nigger first. He's got to admit he's a nigger. Then maybe we will accept him as he seems to intend to be accepted*" (18). In this moment, we are given to understand the real motivation behind the community's desire to "lynch" Lucas: that Lucas may have murdered Vinson has far less to do with the mob's mobilization than does his refusal to be "black" *as* a "nigger." Only by making Lucas "admit" to *being* a "nigger" can the South sustain (undisturbed) the melancholic illusion of universal and natural representation.

But Lucas's figurative and literal silence (here as elsewhere) is not *just* silence, or the silence of *the* (Lacanian) father.[22] Nor is it merely and only freedom in the guise of apolitical and irresponsible withdrawal. Lucas has and uses *a* voice; that voice simply cannot be contained or understood by any one (racial) form or mode of characterization. This is why, according to Dimitri, Lucas (like Faulkner's later novels) represents the possibility or potential of a "positive liberty" (19), or the "virtues of engagement" (20). Rather than simply and stoically withdrawing (as does a character like Ike McCaslin in "The Bear"),[23] Lucas (according to Dimitri) opens Chick (and readers) to an idea of freedom as "self-creation" (18). To make his point, Dimitri quotes a passage from "The Bear" (in which the narrator explains Lucas's decision to change his name from "Lucius"): "Not refusing to be called Lucius, because he simply eliminated that word from the name; not denying, declining the name itself, because he used three quarters of it; but simply taking the name and changing, altering it, making it no longer the white man's but his own, by himself composed, himself selfprogenitive and nominate, by himself ancestored" (Faulkner, "The Bear" 269). Lucas articulates himself within a preexisting circuit of exchange and valuation; at the same time, he frustrates the naturalness of this system so as to maintain control over his own valuation (which is, moreover, always given as inadequate, or never fully determinable). Even as he asserts a "selfprogenitive" identity, he acquiesces to the name he was given. He acquiesces, also (and on some level), to his blackness, or at least his nonwhiteness: his new name is *"no longer the white man's* but his own." Lucas, in this sense, pays his debts while simultaneously exposing the impossibility of a full account. He refuses Chick's handful of coins because it signals the value of servitude. He refuses, also, Gavin's offer to work pro bono and he insists on paying Chick and Aleck for their work. And, even in the end, when Gavin forces him to act like a "nigger" and count out the bag of pennies he uses to pay his two-dollar fee (itself an effort at reifying mockery), Lucas plays his role while simultaneously refusing to let the signification of blackness *as debt* overtake him.[24] The last words of the book are, after all, Lucas's response to Gavin's irritable need to know "what [Lucas is] waiting for"—as Lucas says, "My receipt" (241). The humor such a line might generate is surely an effect, or defense against, disgust. In letting Lucas pay an overtly farcical bill (while also making him count his pennies), Gavin smugly assumes that he has put Lucas in his place; all accounts are finally paid up *insofar* as Lucas's race is finally confirmed via his indebtedness to a white man. However, Lucas's overtly conscious decision to pay in pennies and then ask for a receipt radically undermines this assumption. Not only does it signal the fact that Lucas is still "owed" an account of services rendered, it stresses, as Masami Sugimori suggests, the irreducible difference between a receipt for two dollars and a two-dollar pile of pennies (71). This irreducible remainder, or debt of signification, is utterly unaccountable and (so) utterly disgusting. It (and *not* the free acquiescence to the illusion of natural law) is the ground of freedom, the possibility of self-(re)creation.

This link between freedom and a certain type of *nonsignifying* debt is made overt in the passages that link Chick's memory of trying to pay Lucas to the opening scene of the novel (in which Chick finds himself loitering outside the jailhouse as the sheriff brings in Lucas). Chick spent the intervening four years trying to escape his debt. At first it haunts him in the material form of the coins he still possesses and which end up (in his child's imagination) "transposed and translated . . . into the one coin one integer in mass and weight out of all proportion to its mere convertible value" (20–21). Eventually this single unaccountable "coin swelled to its gigantic maximum, to hang fixed at last forever in the black vault of his anguish like the last dead and waneless moon and himself, his own puny shadow gesticulant and tiny against it in frantic and vain eclipse: frantic and vain yet indefatigable too because he would never stop, he could never give up now who had debased not merely his manhood but his whole race too" (21). But no coin, no matter how big, can match his debt—which is to say that Chick necessarily fails to bring Lucas's race (along with his own) back into circulation via preexisting and fixed equivalents of representation. Were he to do so—were he to manage the "reequalization, reaffirmation of his masculinity and his white blood" (26)—he would (Chick assumes) be "free" (23). And on numerous occasions—after, for instance, sending Lucas's wife (Molly) a dress—he assumes he has attained his liberation. But Lucas always rebalances the books (so as, paradoxically, to leave exposed a wound of representational debt): for Molly's dress he sends "a white boy ... on a mule" to give Chick "homemade sorghum molasses" (23). Nevertheless, and after finally assuming that "whatever would or could set him free was beyond not merely his reach but his ken" (23), Chick comes to believe that he has accidently stumbled upon it when (in the wake of Molly's death) a mourning Lucas ignores him in the town square. After Lucas fails to address or seemingly recognize him a second time, Chick tells himself that "he was free" (27). But Faulkner ultimately turns Chick's presumption of freedom into an anxiety-ridden refrain, a mantra he repeats even as he finds himself waiting outside the courthouse, still clearly hoping to erase his debt. This refrain highlights (also) the fact that, even when Lucas first ignored him in the square, a sense of debt grew. Chick realizes that "[Molly] *had just died then. That was why he didn't see me ... :* thinking with a kind of amazement: *He was grieving. You dont have to not be a nigger in order to grieve*" (25). This revelation further confirms and accentuates Lucas's ghostlike status and, in turn, leaves Chick "*haunting the square*" (25; my emphasis). It also leaves Chick open, later, to the disconcerting realization that even a racist "violent foulmouthed godless old man" (158) like Nub Gowrie can grieve.

Ultimately, Chick's four-year struggle to be "free" suggests that what Chick aims desperately to be free of is freedom itself—the freedom signified by the failure (or inescapable debts or reminders) of signification, "a leftover which opens the space for desire and makes the Other (the symbolic order) inconsistent" (Žižek, *Sublime Object* 124). And it is precisely between these two freedoms that Chick finds himself pulled, or finds himself "haunting." And if, as Nancy suggests, "wickedness" can be defined as that which "hates singularity as such and the singular relation of singularities . . . [and therefore] freedom" (*Freedom* 128), then Chick is surely pulled inexorably toward wickedness. But we can now begin to understand such wickedness, also, as a form of consumption, a form of consumption that aims to interiorize everything by mandating fixed (because *natural*) representational equivalences. Lucas mirrors Faulkner's textual strategies by sustaining himself within *or as* the liminal (or ghostly) space between the irresponsible freedom of utter inexpressibility and the illusory freedom of acquiescing to (or aligning with) the natural and divine rules of representation. Lucas allows himself to be consumed or understood even as he utterly resists being swallowed *in full*. In this sense he forestalls the ultimate danger of disgust—which would be to effect easy exclusion and therefore to perpetuate (paradoxically) the melancholic illusion of pure inclusion, or communal and individual wholeness. As Fowler suggests, *Intruder in the Dust* can be described (itself) as a concerted effort to "expose and question a system of signification that exalts exclusionary tactics—like the lynching of Lucas Beauchamp—as the foundation of meaning and identity" (788–89). By balancing the possibility of sharing and the radical effects of disgust, Faulkner's novel (like the character of Lucas it represents while failing to capture) opposes both the silencing and indisputable law of the father *and* the feckless cacophony of strategically obfuscating rhetoric.

The latter ends up being satirized in the form of Gavin's various "liberal" speeches. As critics frequently (and anxiously) point out, these speeches (which Gavin presents as enlightened yet conservative approaches to the problem of southern autonomy and the fraught livelihood of "Sambo") echo Faulkner's own tendency to promote a "go slow" approach to racial inequality in the South. But there is a certain metafictional quality to Gavin's various efforts to extemporize (poetically) about southern "homogeneity" (150) and the moral necessity of maintaining the "privilege of setting [Sambo] free ourselves" (151). Unlike most of Faulkner's character's, Gavin's dialogue (in these meandering and self-aggrandizing diatribes) clearly replicates and satirizes Faulkner's own narrative voice (*along with* Faulkner's own problematic statements about southern independence). As a result, Gavin's overtly "significantless speciosity" exposes the danger always lurking at the heart of Faulkner's own rhetorical moves, even finally undermining Faulkner's earlier tendency to engage (simply and only) in the "Great [modernist] Refusal—the protest against that which is" (Herbert Marcuse qtd. in Dimitri 12). Tied as it is to his inability to act (or to act effectively), Gavin's digressive, fragmentary and inconsistent speeches finally expose the troubling possibility that obfuscation can itself become a way of appealing to the illusion of authenticity that invariably buttresses hierarchal social structures. Does not Gavin, after all, present himself in these moments of intellectual (yet *natural*) "free play" as the Kantian poet par excellence? And yet what motivates ethical action in the novel is never his words; it is only ever Lucas's simplistic statements and communicative refusals to enter fully into the economy that propels and defines Gavin's supposed "free play."

Perverse (Post)modern Authenticity

The ridiculous and even dangerous nature of Gavin might in fact signal Faulkner's efforts to avoid slipping into a certain kind of (post)modern trap—not the trap of eviscerating utterly the possibility of accessible content or engaged meaning, but rather the trap of aligning and finally confusing fragmentation and intertextual play with (a type of backdoor, or inverted) authenticity, of enacting a resumption of divinely *natural* free play. Such would be, according to Žižek, the postmodern "illusion that we live in [or can bring about] a 'post-ideological' condition" (*Sublime Object* 7). The effects of this "trap" certainly echo appeals to postmodern perversity. While the pervert par excellence escapes responsibility by succumbing to a symbolic universe "running its course" (Žižek, *Ridiculous* 36), a writer might very well present such an escape (into the unrestricted play of narrative form and self-construction) as an *authentic* and radically informed choice, something mandated by the "law of the heart" (as Hegel might say). A certain bifurcation of postmodern perversity thus leads us (on the one hand) to the trap of relocating authenticity in its deconstruction and (on the other) to the trap of reveling in discursive play *so as* to construct freely and then impose an idealized and singular version of reality. With this in mind, and by way of a somewhat extended conclusion, let's move past Faulkner to look at how these two (post)modern traps manifest in narrative *as* symptoms of America's melancholic dilemma—even if they are also, in certain ways, the same.

Consider, in terms of the former trap, Toni Morrison's *Tar Baby* (1981). One of the two central characters of the novel (Jadine Childs), a light-skinned "black" woman who works as a model in Paris, clearly echoes Faulkner's depiction of Lucas. She tends to identify more readily with white culture than black culture, and her relatively pale skin frustrates blind assumptions about her race and background. Morrison, though, almost ostentatiously positions her as the "tar baby" in question—a dangerous lure, a "white" construction *of blackness* designed to lead members of the black community astray. For this reason, Jadine is an obvious threat to the novel's other central character (Son), a black man who is on the run for killing his wife. It is therefore Son, and *not* Jadine, who is aligned with Morrison's early efforts[25] to deploy a "fragmented and highly subjective narrative structure" (Moffitt 12)—that is, to shift from perspective to perspective while deploying and (re)inventing western and African myth. From the outset, Son's mobility and authentic fluidity highlights the novel's. The novel begins and ends with Son fleeing a dangerous situation. First he is fleeing the law (and murder charges) and then he is fleeing Jadine—who threatens to seduce him away from the "true and ancient properties" first referenced in the novel's epigraph. A central and recurring problem is Son's desire for "safety," a desire that is implied in the first line of the novel: "He believed he was safe" (3). However, after he is caught hiding in Valerian and Margaret Street's Caribbean home, the home in which Jadine was raised by her "black" aunt and uncle—Ondine and Sydney Childs, the Streets' housekeepers—Son meets and, it would seem, falls in love with, Jadine (who has returned home for Christmas). Almost immediately, then (and as most critics suggest), Son's temporary safety is endangered. The "threat" is a dangerously beautiful lure, a lure that could lead him away from his black community and his authentic identity as a black man.

While we might say, following a critic like Marilyn E. Mobley, that Jadine is a threat because her "sense of self is based upon a denial of her own cultural heritage and an identification with one that is not her own" (761), to do so would mean overlooking the fact that Jadine never overtly or simply identifies as white, or with "white culture." We would have to overlook, too, the fact that Jadine tends to represent two inherently opposed threats. She frustrates the possibility of Son's safety, but that "safety" is aligned with a type of impossible sterility, a lack of movement or vitality. Son's lively manliness, his "black" authenticity, is tied (after all) to his transience, his mobility, and his potential fluidity. As a threat to this potential, Jadine should *ensure* his safety—if, that is, "safety" is antithetical to "black" virility and mobility. And yet Jadine threatens Son's safety even as her refusal to align (clearly or fully) with "her own" heritage is presented as a dangerously corrosive influence. The novel thus aligns the authentic with the mutable and the living while simultaneously (and necessarily) assuming a hierarchy in which Jadine's radically disgusting transience is rejected as both unnatural and corruptive. Safety—which comes to imply the assumption of a final or fixed resting place—is most certainly the problem, as Son's authenticity is tied to his potential for change and growth; yet Jadine (who is *no less* a threat to that authenticity) threatens such "safety" insofar as she frustrates or refuses the possibility of assuming an authentic identity. Son's desire for safety (in the form of social or ontological certainty) is therefore problematized *even as* the authentic fluidity it opposes comes to represent a form of delimiting coherence, or satisfaction.

This problem becomes all the more salient if we consider the fact that Mobley's condemnation of Jadine is typical. As Letitia Moffitt notes, critics tend to assume that Son "represents values endorsed in the novel by Morrison herself. Specifically, Son is often credited with being connected to African American ideals of community and nature, whereas Jadine is criticized for abandoning these" (13). Such claims are hard to refute. Jadine's refusal (or inability) to embrace or embody her authentic identity repeatedly implies a type of spiritual or moral bankruptcy. She even revels in wearing "the hides of ninety baby seals" (87). Her dangerously seductive inauthenticity is repeatedly highlighted via references to her fair (or ambiguous) features, features that have allowed her to achieve success as a model in a predominantly "white" fashion industry. While Jadine never needs "to straighten [her] hair" (48), Son's hair tends to "spread like layer upon layer of wings from his head, more alive than the sealskin. It made him doubt that hair was in fact dead cells. Black people's hair, in any case, was definitely alive. Left alone and untended it was like foliage and from a distance it looked like nothing less than the crown of a deciduous tree" (132). Not only does Jadine lack "living" (black) hair, her skin tone is (as Gideon, one of the Street's other "hands," assures Son) "yalla" (155). This remark about skin tone is, from the *authentically black* Gideon, a warning: "Don't fool yourself. You should have seen her two months ago. What you see is tanning from the sun. Yallas don't come to being black natural-like. They have to choose it and most don't choose it. Be careful of the stuff they put down" (155). Even though (for whatever reason) Jadine doesn't come by her blackness "natural-like," her refusal or inability to embrace it fully makes her, as Eleanor W. Traylor puts it, "an unwilling Delilah sucking at the Samson strength of Son . . . [and thus] the embodiment in language of the carcinogenic disease eating away at the ancestral spirit of the race at the present time" (146). Or, more pointedly, she is "the disease of disconnection, whose malignancy causes a slaughter of reality" (146). Traylor, of course, is absolutely correct—*if only* because her almost violent response to this "disease" points directly to the dangerous melancholia we have been tracing since chapter 1. Such melancholia can in no way abide the "pathology of the community," which (as we've seen) invariably eats away at "friendship founded on *homogeneity,* on *homophilia,* on a solid and firm affinity . . . stemming from birth, from native community" (Derrida, *Politics* 92).

While, then, Son is literarily the intruder, it is Jadine's pathological intrusiveness that the novel opposes, or refuses. Son's transience is somehow authentic and grounded, while Jadine's is somehow constructed and sterile. While he ends the novel escaping into the woods (like the folk hero Brer Rabbit) "lickety-split" (306), she ends the novel on a plane back to Paris—having "forgotten her ancient proprieties" (305). She has refused the bare-breasted shadow women that haunt her (and thus the societal pressure to be a nurturing, feminine and life-giving black woman); or, from Jadine's perspective, she has refused "that black-woman-white-woman shit" (121) and any person who might claim to know "what a black woman is or ought to be" (121). This refusal of clear communal boundaries, or natural rules of blood and representation, utterly frustrates Son—even if "in those eight homeless years [after he killed his wife] he had joined that great underclass of undocumented men" (168). The problem is that Son's own efforts to find (and sustain) "some other way of being in the world" (166) are undermined by his unwillingness to "give up the last thing left to him—fraternity" (168). And since she undermines the possibility of such fraternity (or safety), Jadine threatens and confounds. She must be "fixed" (in place). She must be made *safe.* She must be cured or conjured. Son thus finds himself resorting to forms of violence. That he does so certainly suggests a tendency on the novel's part to present his own melancholic assumptions about race as no less artificial and corrupted than Jadine's unnatural "whiteness." Yet Son's violent efforts "to initiate [Jadine's] struggle to attain an authentic racialized and gendered identity" (Duvall 346) tend to be overlooked or even endorsed by critics of the novel. While this tendency surely speaks to the melancholia lurking in the machinery of American academia, it speaks also (in this case) to the types of readings the novel itself encourages.

After failing "to insert his own dreams" (119) of stereotypical black life *into* Jadine, he resorts (in desperation) to physical rape.[26] What is so odd and so striking about this moment of violation—especially if we consider Morrison's other novels, in which violent acts are typically described in startling clarity—is its ambiguity. The act itself is almost wholly masked behind (or even made *palatable by*) Morrison's fragmentary prose. At the same time, the rape cannot be denied. Jadine's dialogue, immediately after Son "[tears] open his shirt" (270) and begins retelling the story of the "Tar

Baby," includes the following lines: "Don't touch me"; "Quit! Leave me *alone!*"; "You better kill me. Because if you don't, when you're through, I'm going to kill you"; etc. (270). And afterward Son leaves her "[lying] . . . slippery, gutted, not thinking of killing him" (271). Significantly, Son's *need* to rape Jadine occurs precisely at the moment when he feels that his identity (as a black man) is most in jeopardy. Immediately before he performs a type of sexual lynching, he chastises her (and her "kind") for corrupting the black community, or "brotherhood": "You turn little black babies into little white ones; you turn your black brothers into white brothers; you turn your men into white men and when a black woman treats me like what I am, what I really am, you say she's spoiling me" (270). What truly frustrates him, though—that is, what drives him (like Irene in Larsen's *Passing*) to a point of violent hysteria—is the fact that she responds to his lecture with a "mouth fat with disgust" (270). It is certainly Jadine who is, in the moment, disgusted; but it is also surely Jadine who is most profoundly disgusting. She will not let Son "insert his dreams" (and thus interiorize her dreams *as naturally his own*). In this sense, her "mouth fat with disgust" exhibits an object that resists being consumed *by refusing to consume*. Rape is therefore the violence necessary to force an insertion—and by implication, the possibility of interiorization and ownership, the process by which "the other becomes the Other according to the mode of desire or hatred. . . . This desire is the desire to fix the origin, . . . once and for all, and in one place for all, that is, always outside the world" (Nancy, "Being Singular" 20).

However, Jadine's is not the suffering we are left to consider; Son's is. After leaving her "gutted" and oddly indifferent, Son returns hours later (now "repentant"). He finds her still naked from the waist down. While at first she speaks "quietly"—"I can't let you hurt me again" (271)—the power dynamic quickly shifts. An argument about money and the misguided sacrifices Jadine has made to earn it ensues. Eventually, and in a manner that almost perfectly echoes Chick's effort's to buy back Lucas's racial indebtedness, Jadine throws a dime on the floor and tells Son to "pick it up": "She said it again and didn't even sit up. She just lay there, stroking her raw silk thighs the color of natural honey" (272). Whatever violence may have been in evidence earlier is here suddenly placed under erasure, for it is clearly Jadine's honey-like or Delilah-esque seductiveness that threatens to place Son within a white economy of racial signification. And when he bends finally (unlike Lucas) to pick up his "payment," Jadine's racial villainy is clearly cast as the *cause* of the rape. The implication of rape is then almost entirely abolished—just as Jadine's dangerously unmanageable seductiveness is further foregrounded—when Jadine finds herself siting on the plane to Paris and reflecting upon the mating rituals of ants. While likening herself to a queen ant who sacrifices the male in the moment of copulation, Jadine realizes that "it would be hard. So very hard to forget the man who fucked like a star" (292).

Quiet simply, or *too simply*, Jadine becomes a "honey-pot," a "tar baby" made by an artificial white culture to ensnare and corrupt the cultural authenticity of *living* and *fluid* blackness. We should not forget that Valerian Street—the white man who helped raise Jadine and then sent her to the Sorbonne to study—made his riches by manufacturing candy. But if we are led to understand that any desire to interiorize Jadine is always only a desire for the artificial and the unwholesome, we are simultaneously shown that she is too disgusting to ever really swallow in full. The narrative thus presents itself, in opposition, as a type of whole food—one in which, for all his faults (including his dangerous and finally unnatural fixation on "safety"), Son is more naturally aligned. The novel's "movement toward ambiguity" (Moffitt 23)—or rather, its use of "conflicting narratives and definitions of race [to] show how no one can truly be representative of his or her race" (Heinert 50)—becomes, in the end, a move toward the naturalized *as* the palatable. Such a move is reflected in the critical tendency to suggest (paradoxically) that the novel represents Morrison's effort to show how "African Americans [can] forge an authentic identity for themselves" (Duvall 329), or how certain "cultural constructions of race and mothering... [can] heal and transform [black female] consciousness" (Mobley 763). Somehow a postmodern awareness and interrogation of what is "forged" and what is culturally "constructed" signals an escape *out of* ideological networks and *into* something recognizably anterior—as if, again, the corset of form has (in the free play of racially defined genius) become no longer *imitative of* but *productive like* nature. It *shapes* the body in its truth. In opposition to the false system of exchange signaled by Jadine's dime, the novel presents a naturalized system of representation that leaves no traces of debt—because, we might say, it overtly recognizes and manages (à la postmodernism) such traces. The novel therefore gives us to believe that it has finally circumvented or escaped the economimesis of race it interrogates. And yet, by interrogating the lure of narrative and ontological safety, the novel finally valorizes an authentic form of fluid vitality, a fragile form of refuge that must remain closed to the intrusive transience of *a* Jadine—of, that is, any figure who might corrupt such a refuge by exposing the uncertainty of an "unlimited 'deficit'" (Levinas, *Otherwise* 125).

Faulkner's work surely runs similar risks—and it certainly at times falls prey to those risks—but Morrison's novel (when read alongside a text like *Intruder*) allows us to ponder the potential pitfalls of moving from a modern form of indeterminacy (still somehow grounded in the possibility of nebulous truth claims) and a postmodern form of indeterminacy (which tends toward self-congratulatory authenticity by rejecting its very possibility). Moreover, the novel suggests that, in the movement out of late modernism—signaled by an almost obsessional fixation on intertextuality and cultural relativism—racialized communities in America tended to reject white male culture as false and oppressive ideology while seeking to preserve or rediscover some sense of racial authenticity anterior to that ideology. Finally seeing in the 1960s and 1970s the real possibility of self-making narrative acts, America's minorities were understandably reticent about identifying those acts as no less constructed than the grand narratives of the dominant culture. There is, after all, little or no political efficacy in postmodernism *at its extreme*—which is, to a certain extent, bell hooks's point in "Postmodern Blackness." While Morrison might (in this early novel) stumble into a postmodern cul-de-sac, she reminds us to question the radical subjectlessness implied by figures like Barthes, or even Louis Gates Jr. If the self is only a "ready-formed dictionary" (Barthes, "Death" 146) and if "race is a text (an array of discursive practices)" (Gates, "Talking Black" 79), *who* could possibly take responsibility for such dictionaries/texts and to *whom* should such an entity be responsible? How do we articulate *yet sustain* our disgust? This is in essence the question Nancy asks Derrida in the interview "Eating Well, or the Calculation of the Subject"—that is, "Who comes *after* the subject?" (255; my emphasis). This interview will, therefore, need to inform our discussion in part II. However, let us consider first (and briefly) the *other* postmodern "trap" in question here—if only because such a consideration will bring us finally and head on to the central aporia of part II: eating and being eaten.

As an example—and so as to maintain (for a while longer) our focus on race—let's consider James McBride's 1995 autobiography, *The Color of Water: A Black Man's Tribute to His White Mother*. The book was a *New York Times* best seller for over two years and, as the tenth anniversary edition makes abundantly clear, a favorite of critics. But the very title signals something troubling and overtly paradoxical about the text itself. On the one hand, the main title—*The Color of Water*, which evokes (as we come to discover) the moment when McBride's mother told McBride that God is the "color of water"—suggests a commitment to color blindness, to an indifference to racial categories as such. On the other hand, the almost stringent reaffirmation of defined and absolute racial groups ("black man" and "white mother") signals the novel's central task: to conjure McBride's mother into a coherent and racialized *presence*—that is, "to fix" and therefore interiorize Ruth McBride Jordan. This task is outlined in the preface:

> As a boy, I never knew where my mother was from—where she was born, who her parents were. When I asked she'd say, "God made me." When I asked if she was white, she'd say, "I'm light-skinned," and change the subject. She raised twelve black children . . . yet none of us even knew her maiden name until we were grown. It took me fourteen years to unearth her remarkable story—the daughter of an Orthodox Jewish rabbi, she married a black man in 1942—and she revealed it more as a favor to me than out of any desire to revisit her past. Here is her life as she told it to me, and betwixt and between the pages of her life you will find mine as well. (xix)

The language is striking. McBride and his siblings are *simply* "black." And in the text that follows they are never described as white or Jewish, and only rarely as "mixed race." McBride, as the title almost ostentatiously confirms, is a *black* man—even though he is (as he discovers, and according to the categories of race he himself relies upon throughout) just as white as he is black. The same goes for all his siblings, as both of Ruth's husbands were "black." Also worth noting is the ambiguity concerning what, exactly, we will be reading in the following pages. This is, apparently, Ruth's life "as she told it to [McBride]," but are the Ruth chapters (which appear in italics) straightforward transcriptions of a recorded conversation? It's unclear, but it seems unlikely; Ruth's language only occasionally seems spontaneous, oral (or transcribed) in nature. It is also very similar to McBride's in the way it yields to poetic tropes and romanticized cadences. Is this a simple appropriation of his mother's life? This is *her* story, but it is also a story McBride is both telling and desperate to hear.

While McBride dedicates the book to his "mother, and her mother, and mothers everywhere," the entire text reads (as McBride almost admits outright in the preface) like a forced confession, a repudiation by Ruth (instigated by McBride) of the very things she tried to teach McBride as he was growing up. Take, for instance, the scene in which Ruth tells a young McBride to never use the phrase "tragic mulatto":

> "Don't ever use that term."
> "Am I black or white?"

"You're a human being," she snapped. "Educate yourself or you'll be a nobody!"

"Will I be a black nobody or just a nobody?"

"If you're a nobody," she said dryly, "it doesn't matter what color you are."

"That doesn't make sense," I said. (92)

Frustrated, McBride goes to his brother (David) with the same question, and gets a much more satisfactory (because unequivocal) answer: "'*I'm* black,' said David, sporting a freshly grown Afro the size of Milwaukee" (93). There is obviously something infantile about all this. And one imagines, as the text suggests, that this is simply a young McBride's problem, that an older McBride will come to respect his mother's and his own spectrality. But the fact that this book was written at all suggests something different. As the text unfolds we see McBride grow more determined, finally unearthing or uncloseting his mother's traumatic past (a past she clearly wishes to conceal) and convincing her (when she is much older—and, one presumes, worn to exhaustion in the same way a character like Joe Christmas finally seems worn) to abandon her raceless (non)identity and *disgusting* potential by admitting to what she truly *is*: a "white" Jewish woman who married black men and, thus, had quantifiably black children.

And yet—and as a product of its time—the text ends up presenting these appeals to authentic selfhood and true histories as self-made constructions. The memoir is offered as a construction of the self, one that is made possible by the almost *violent* reconstruction—or rather, conjuration—of an intrusive other. McBride admits this outright, as would almost any writer during the watershed years of postmodernism: "I felt like a Tinkertoy kid building my own self out of one of those toy building sets; for as she laid her life before me, I reassembled the tableau of her words like a picture puzzle, and as I did, so my own life was rebuilt" (270). As we will see in part II, it would be a mistake to take such lines as evidence of actual or sustained perversity. McBride's autobiographical universe is in no way "the universe of the pure symbolic order . . . unencumbered by the Real of human finitude" (Žižek, *Ridiculous* 36). But a type of (postmodern) perversity is nevertheless deployed or hijacked in the above passage so as to justify what is actually an overt form of self-defining consumption. While McBride claims to be simply and freely constructing himself—as if to suggest that all such constructions are just *that*—the text (as a whole) undermines this claim in two startling ways: (1) it stabilizes his construction of self by ensuring that his identificatory *relations* are constructed likewise; and (2) it implies that his decision to take up such constructions, and to narrate his life in such terms, is a natural consequence of his "free play." He therefore undermines the more mendacious tactics of autobiography and documentary—tactics (like verbatim dialogue) which we will need to address more fully in the following chapters—so as to employ them as *natural* supplements to his (mother's) story. Asserting, then, less a type of postmodern perversity than a problematic form of "positive liberty," McBride finds himself (as Berlin warns such a person might) "in a position to ignore the actual wishes of men or societies, to bully, oppress, torture them in the name, and on behalf, of their 'real' selves" (133). Ruth may very well be the "only individual [McBride] has ever known who has been in the process of moving for ten years straight" (268), but this novel (in the name of McBride's own need for stable selfhood, the need to make possible and perpetuate his own ego-forming racial melancholia) seems to put an end to any future movement/uncertainty. Ruth, in these pages, is effectively "fixed," or swallowed whole. After all, if his memoir expresses anything (in the sense of an *in*finite truth) it is the fact that there has always been something about his mother—and therefore, if we recall our discussion of motherhood in chapter 1, something about himself—that McBride has never been able to hold down, to swallow completely. While McBride exposes us to the potential and even the necessity of literary self-invention, he exposes us also to its dangers (or the ease with which it can serve distinctly melancholic ends). He reminds us that every effort to express the self must risk effacing the other as *in*finite. To conclude with his memoir is therefore to begin on a path of inquiry that leads directly to the concerns of part III—the problem and possibility of giving (while sustaining) *in*finite otherness. However, between here and there we must address (more fully) the way in which the desire for self-articulation is almost invariably a desire to consume the other whole and without reserve, without disgust. This means addressing the problem or paradox of eating *as self-preservation*. For if the ego must consume the other in order to sustain and delimit itself, it must *at the same time* risk losing itself to a state of entropy, an all-consuming reality—a state in which *all* otherness has been rendered the same.

PART II
BEING EATEN

(and who can be made to believe that our cultures are carnivorous because animal proteins are irreplaceable?)
—JACQUES DERRIDA, "EATING WELL"

4 / Touching Herman Melville's "Bartleby" (and Other Zombie Narratives)

> *I ain't lookin' for you to feel like me*
> *See like me or be like me*
> —BOB DYLAN, "ALL I REALLY WANT TO DO"

Zombies, Cowboys, and Quislings

As we have seen, the theme of passing announces both the promise and the threat of the empathic other. Perhaps more than any other example of *l'intrus*, the passing subject is inextricably tied to America's dream *as well as* America's nightmare of a finally egalitarian society. It is therefore hardly surprising that the theme of passing reemerges in Max Brooks's best-selling zombie novel, *World War Z*. The fantasy of a zombie apocalypse is undoubtedly effected by America's conflicted dream of a finally egalitarian state. A cursory look at the zombie narrative's more striking characteristics is, then, oddly instructive, especially since those characteristics speak to a collusion of desires that (in retrospect) preoccupies a striking proportion of American literature since before the Revolution—including, of course, Melville's "Bartleby."

As every child knows, the typical zombie narrative (in film, novel, comic, or video game) is a thinly veiled critique of capitalism; for confirmation, we need only recall the various shots of the undead wandering aimlessly about a suburban mall in George A. Romero's *Dawn of the Dead*. Zack Snyder's remake of Romero's film (more than twenty-five years later) does little (if anything) to redirect this critique, the particulars of which are plainly outlined on the back covers of the various "collected volumes" of Robert Kirkman's ongoing *Walking Dead* comics: "The world of commerce and frivolous necessity has been replaced by a world of survival and responsibility. / An epidemic of apocalyptic proportions has swept the globe causing the dead to rise and feed on the living, / In a matter of months society has crumbled, / no government, / no grocery stores, / no mail delivery, / no cable TV. / In a world ruled by the dead, / we are forced to finally start living" (Kirkman). Capitalism has made zombies of us all! And, in the wake of a zombie apocalypse, we have but two options: (1) succumb to the zombie horde and become mindless automatons without thought or identity, walking corpses who only consume, endlessly feeding (without conscience or consciousness) on the body of the other; or (2) resist the horde and "*finally* start living."

But what, exactly, in a zombie narrative, does "living" entail? Certainly it means liberating ourselves from all things "frivolous": grocery stores, cable TV, technology in general. (Kirkman's comics begin with a community of survivors reestablishing themselves in the wilderness outside Atlanta; the men begin to hunt while the women cook over a campfire and clean clothes in the river.) But this "liberation" also and necessarily implies a return to a more true because more basic social order—a social order free of political correctness, a social order that sees men killing (zombies, animals, other humans) with impunity and women (like children) in need of protection. Clearly, the zombie narrative is far less horror than fantasy, for the rise of the zombie heralds a return to a time of concrete differences and stable hierarchies. Consider the initial pages of Kirkman's inaugural issue, in which illustrator Tony Moore provides several frames of Rick Grimes (the comics' principal character) riding toward Atlanta on a deserted highway. He is on horseback, wearing a lawman's uniform (Stetson included), and carrying a shotgun. His plan is to find and rescue his wife and son.[1] He brings law and order with him, but (in the wake of society's demise) it is *his* law and order. Grimes is the quintessence of America's autonomous male hero. In contrast, his zombie foe clearly replaces—even as it transgresses the line between living and dead—the concrete and definable other America lost during the schizophrenic breakdown of late capitalism. We should not overlook the fact that the first real depiction of a mindless and homogenous zombie horde (in Romero's *Night of the Living Dead*) occurs in 1968,[2] the peak of the civil rights movement and the ostensible watershed year of American postmodernism. Is not the zombie simply a response to the societal entropy of equal rights and the postmodern deconstruction of binary absolutes? Is not the zombie simply that thing with which we cannot empathize, that thing we can kill—and, in killing, define our*selves* against? Is not the zombie, and however odd it might initially seem, the last "thing" we're allowed to consume without experiencing a type of melancholia, the guilt effected by empathy?

The zombie narrative's critique of capitalism veils while paradoxically buttressing the fantasy of the autonomous self. If the zombie is the inevitable result of unfettered consumer culture, then (according to Kirkman, and in line with his predecessors) consumer culture effaces the individual in favor of irresistible social homogeneity. The zombie horde is marked by its profound loss of difference, its utter rejection of individuality; in (un)death, even the lowest of us trudge along with "kings and counsellors" (Melville, "Bartleby" 45). But the paradox is this: the zombie horde—an all-consuming and empathically indifferent mass—is offered as a critique of an economic system that both requires and makes possible the illusion of the self-governing individual. At the very moment the zombie horde arrives on the scene we get the simultaneous arrival of its ostensible cause: the heroic outlaw whose autonomy borders on abject solipsism. The zombie narrative repeatedly exposes us to the fact that the possibility of the autonomous self necessarily implies (or makes possible) its antithesis. The fantasy of the zombie is the fantasy of distinguishing between the dream of the autonomous self and the nightmare of the undifferentiated mass. The effort (and impossibility) of maintaining such a distinction is played out yet again in Brooks's novel—in both the novel's form and its striking redeployment of a passing thematic.

In *World War Z: An Oral History of the Zombie War*, Brooks presents the story of the zombie apocalypse via a series of interviews conducted and recorded (by an unnamed protagonist) in the wake of humanity's marginal victory over the undead. This collection of unique voices comes together to explain how humanity survived the threat of its complete zombification. Like other zombie narratives, Brooks's novel suggests that, for all the horror and trauma, the apocalypse allowed humans to return to a more natural mode of being. Numerous interviewees hint at a new (and better) postwar economy, and even more suggest that (since the war) they have become better (because more authentic) human beings. Take, for instance, the story of Kondo Tatsumi, a Japanese computer nerd. Tatsumi is (at the outbreak of the zombie infection) "a skinny, acne-faced teenager with dull red eyes and bleached blond highlights streaking his unkempt hair" (204). After his obsession with using his computer to track the progress of the apocalypse prevents him from realizing that his entire city, his apartment, and even his parents (with whom he still lives) have been taken by the zombie horde, Tatsumi is forced to flee into the wilderness. There he becomes a lean and disciplined swordsman. When he meets the novel's unnamed interviewer, he is "clean-shaven, tanned and toned"; he has "the composure of a predatory animal at rest" (204). Like Kirkman's comics, Brooks's novel repeatedly celebrates the (re)emergence of the autonomous self in the face of what largely amounts to fraternal entropy, or undifferentiated communal wholeness.[3] Zombieism (at least initially) represents the threat of empathic schizophrenia, the self perpetually becoming by indiscriminately consuming the other. Hence the novel's form: a series of individual voices relating multiple perspectives of the same event. The novel (as a cohesive collection of "unique" narratives) confirms the possibility of humanity's salvation, the possibility of both an in-divisible ego *and* an egalitarian whole. At the same time, the novel (like, again, Kirkman's comics) cannot help but open up the possibility that, at its extreme, the latter is indistinguishable from the former.

In the end, the zombiefied mass effected by the breakdown of self and other is tantamount to the monolingualism of the abject solipsist; the more I extract myself from the all-consuming whole, the more I consume the whole within a singular vision of the world—as does Hegel's adamantly virtuous consciousness or Berlin's self-abnegating stoic.[4] And so, not surprisingly, Brooks's various "unique" voices are noticeably uniform. Consider a short passage from an interview with Philip Adler, a German soldier forced to accept the strategic sacrifice of civilians: "I asked for confirmation. I got it. I asked again. . . . This isn't happening, I told myself. Funny, eh? I could accept everything else that was happening, the fact that dead bodies were rising to consume the world, but this . . . following orders that would indirectly cause a mass murder" (113). This apparently German voice is virtually indistinguishable from the voice of the Samurai-sword-wielding Tatsumi. The conflation of the two voices is particularly obvious when Tatsumi is asked if he tried to contact his neighbors before fleeing his apartment: "No. Isn't that odd? Even at the height of my breakdown, my social anxiety was so great that actually risking personal contact was still taboo. I took a few steps, slipped, and fell into something soft. It was cold and slimy, all over my hands, my clothes. It stank" (209). This repetition of speaking patterns is typical throughout; in the wake of the war, the earth's entire population seems to think and speak in the same controlled, active voice—a voice that employs sardonic (American) humor with clipped (American) efficiency.

Obviously, Brooks is not Faulkner. But in casting aside his prose as simply careless, we risk missing the larger implications of the novel's narrative collapse. For surely the novel's strange monolingualism functions as a type of shorthand, a way of easily representing (to a general readership) the "postzombie" ideal it necessarily controverts: a finally egalitarian community of autonomous and unique individuals. The interviewees all seem like (finally) real, concrete individuals because they all sound like real, concrete individuals; they all sound *the same*. In this way, the possibility of a post-zombie humanity is paradoxically tied to the possibility of its performance, the playing out of one man's ideal of American self-reliance. In contrast, the zombie appears "in-itself," the concrete body without supplementary[5] (or performative) frame. The novel therefore enacts an uncomfortable if unsurprising inversion: the zombie (initially defined by its nonstatus within an indifferent horde) emerges as singular, inert, without relation; and the supposedly authentic human emerges as frame, supplement, performance (only). Yet this is less an inversion than a mirroring; for at their extremes both solipsistic autonomy and communal wholeness imply a type of entropy, a homogeneity that is antithetical to the possibility of a finally democratic state—the possibility of sustaining both equality *and* individuality.

However, this paradoxical and problematic conflation of zombie and human is largely obscured via Brooks's introduction of World War Z "quislings":[6] "You know, the people that went nutballs and started *acting* like zombies" (155; my emphasis). As we saw in part I, the representation of characters who pass almost invariably speaks to America's anxiety about the possibility of maintaining fixed categories of identity (white and black, male and female, etc.). Brooks's quislings are no different in this regard. Traitorous and ostentatiously performative, the quislings of World War Z begin to figure prominently just as the novel's monolingualism becomes undeniable. They betray a certain anxiety on Brooks's part, functioning to solidify the line between zombie and human (or autonomous subjects). The quisling, not the human, is guilty of inauthenticity. Even more so than the zombie (who does not choose its homogenous state), the quisling abandons the responsibility of his or her individuality to the inertia of the indifferent mass. The World War Z quisling is therefore presented as a type of pervert, a subject who performs whatever the fantasy of the other demands.[7] Because they "just can't deal with a fight-or-die situation[,] [quislings are] always drawn to what they're afraid of. Instead of resisting it, they want to please it, join it, try to be like it" (156). What the quisling doesn't understand is that there is "no gray area in this fight, no in between" (156). There is no room for performance; either you are or you are not (human). The quisling fails to see or honor the absoluteness of this line. But we should not overlook the way in which this failure functions as a type of reification; it reasserts the essential difference between authenticity and performance. The quisling, like any other passer, forsakes the possibility of a real (self) in favor of endless and irresponsible "play." To focus on the fecklessness of such play is to restabilize the increasingly questionable individuality of the interviewees. The temptation, in other words, is to focus exclusively on the suggestion that the quisling yields to the will of the zombie horde. But the truly perverse nature of the quisling is to be found elsewhere, for the quisling actually confirms the fantasy of the interviewees (as well as, one must assume, the fantasy of both reader and author). Its intrusive arrival dispels while simultaneously mimicking the zombiesque homogeneity of the novel's "unique" human voices.

The Prudence of Self-Reliance

Simply put, the contemporary zombie narrative—since, at least, Romero—is simultaneously nightmare and fantasy. Its function is to circumvent (and, in circumventing, alleviate a certain persistent anxiety about) the more terrifying implications of the American Dream. However, in attempting to do so, the zombie narrative must necessarily expose America's democratic dream as the dream of resolving a monumental paradox. On the one hand, the democratic promise entails the possibility of the truly autonomous individual, the self before or above all others. On the other, it guarantees egalitarian fraternity and communal wholeness. The problem, as we've seen, is this: the identity of an individual is necessarily contingent upon that individual's ability to identify with a communal whole, but the very idea of the whole undermines the self as unique, as in-divisible. Or, if we recall Nancy,[8] progress toward an ideal egalitarian community of individuals will invariably see us marooned between a rock and a hard place; either we are left with "lost totality, or totality accomplished in the lie of the individual: there is no way out of this circle of disenchantment" ("Inoperative" 38). The move toward egalitarian sympathy and fraternity threatens the individual's claim to self-contained "totality," yet the process of self-definition requires the possibility of communion, the possibility of shared—as in identifiable—characteristics. This is most certainly the paradox that effectively disrupts the zombie nightmare/fantasy (and the concomitant nightmare/fantasy of a self that is finally resistant to the possibility of ontological confusion), but it is in no way unique to the mid-twentieth century.

In America, the paradox first emerges as a glaring and problematic obstacle in the mid-nineteenth century, when, for instance (as John Matteson notes), Massachusetts chief justice (and Herman Melville's father-in-law) Lemuel Shaw begins to seek "standards of behavior on which all persons could agree" (36). Shaw's various efforts to establish "prudence" (in favor of politically awkward appeals to Christian morality) as an all-encompassing human quality—or rather, a foundation for national consensus and rational behavior—necessarily run parallel to the emergence of equally vehement efforts to privilege individual desire above all such imposed "absolutes." Matteson puts it like this: "While the great judge was writing reasonableness into the case reports, Emerson was writing 'whim' on his door post and, along with the other New England literati, trying to vindicate a self-legitimating, self-defining 'I.' . . . Apollonian law contended with Dionysian art, and their contradictions became a recurrent theme for Melville" (36).[9] For Matteson, a character like the "eminently *safe*" (Melville 14), or "prudent," lawyer in "Bartleby" functions on a certain level as a stand-in for Shaw, while Bartleby comes to represent the vehemently autonomous yet increasingly threatened man of letters—Emerson, Thoreau, Poe, Melville.

Yet this conflict between objective and sympathetic prudence on the one hand and autonomous and virtually solipsistic subjectivity on the other becomes all the more complicated if we view it through a much wider lens—a lens, for instance, capable of encompassing objects as seemingly disconnected from Melville and "Bartleby" as the contemporary zombie narrative. In many respects, this is precisely what some of the most famous and influential critics of "Bartleby" attempt to do. For instance, theorists such as Deleuze, Derrida, and Agamben open up the possibility that Melville's stress on the tensions between sympathy (or prudence) and egotism (or autonomy) exposes a much larger democratic, or ontological, problem.[10] But, as does Matteson, these theorists invariably privilege the autonomous artist, the *one* who isolates himself from all communion and thus preserves his *self*, or his "heart," from dissolution and corruption. As a result, these theorists risk celebrating Bartleby as the heroic "man without particularities, the Original Man" (Deleuze 85), an "angel that writes nothing but its potentiality to not-write" (Agamben, *Community* 36), the defender of an eternal secret who "responds without responding" (Derrida, *Gift* 74). Or rather, they risk celebrating Bartleby as a prototypical Rick Grimes, a truly autonomous hero battling the inertia of a zombie horde. The problem is that Melville ties Bartleby's heroic autonomy to his ostensible zombification, his increasingly corpse-like demeanor and behavior.[11] Melville thus exposes and negotiates the paradox that both defines and frustrates the contemporary fantasy of the zombie apocalypse. To celebrate Bartleby's abject refusal to "relate" is to overlook the implications of this negotiation.

Put differently, these readings all stumble as a result of a persistent impulse (in Melvillian criticism generally) to approach Bartleby as (1) a pitiable misfit, or outcast, or (2) a heroic, if tragic, Christ figure. Instead of looking at the way in which Melville works to move beyond America's democratic paradox, such readings simply take a side, doing more to highlight than critique the seemingly irresolvable tension that pervades the story and America as a whole. They fail to consider the manner in which the narrator's struggle with Bartleby mirrors the conflict as well as the inevitable conflation of the whole and the individual, the ideal of entropic empathy and the desire for abject egotism. At either pole, the self is at risk. Either the individual is lost in the homogenizing "sympathy" of the whole or is left to wither in isolation, utterly alone and without the "references" necessary for self-identification.[12] If we are to untangle Melville's critique of America's idealistic dream of reconciling the individual with a state of fraternal egalitarianism and his ostensible outline for a radical order to come, we must be open to the possibility that Bartleby is no less complicit in a failed (or failing) democratic order than is his employer. Just as the narrator comes to represent the dangerous inertia of entropic and homogenizing sympathy, Bartleby comes to represent the threat of rigid and ultimately self-defeating solipsism. That these two opposed positions ultimately and necessarily conflate is highlighted whenever Melville exposes an uncanny resemblance between Bartleby and the narrator. In such moments of uncanny doubling (which surely anticipate the moments of doubling we see in Larsen's *Passing*), these two extremes are represented as two different points on a single Möbius strip. Both are governed by a desire for totality or wholeness; both invariably necessitate the dissolution of the individual. Upon neither can democracy or friendship be found.

Natural Expectancy

We get the most humorous and disconcerting moments in "Bartleby" whenever the natural expectations of the "eminently *safe*" (14) narrator are utterly thwarted. The first of these moments occurs when the narrator suddenly decides to "call upon" the newly hired Bartleby—a "motionless young man" who is "pallidly neat, pitiably respectful, incurably forlorn" (19)—to examine some documents: "In my haste and *natural expectancy of instant compliance,* I sat with my head bent over the original on my desk, and my right hand sideways, and somewhat nervously extended with the copy, so that immediately upon emerging from his retreat, Bartleby might snatch it and proceed to business without the least delay" (20; my emphasis). But the narrator's "natural expectancy" is left nauseatingly[13] unjustified. Met with Bartleby's utterly unpredictable and unfathomable formula—"I would prefer not to" (20)—the narrator's faith in the "symbolic inertia" of convention is suddenly and disconcertingly shattered.[14] His expectancy is replaced by internal doubt bordering on existential nausea: "Immediately it occurred to me that my ears had deceived me, or Bartleby had entirely misunderstood my meaning" (20). The disconcerting effect of Bartleby's absence is comparable to the nauseating effect of the absent yet expected Pierre in Jean Paul Sartre's *Being and Nothingness:* "I myself expected to see Pierre, and my expectation has caused the absence of Pierre" (42). That is, Sartre's expectation that his acquaintance will emerge as a "solid" figure against the undifferentiated "ground" of a café results in a feeling of nausea, a recognition of the ground as nothing: "This figure which slips constantly between my look and the solid, real objects of the café is precisely a perpetual disappearance.... So that what is offered to intuition is a flickering of nothingness" (42). In a similar sense, Bartleby's disruption of the narrator's expectation simultaneously undermines his faith in a fixed division between ground and figure, social whole and individual identity. Bartleby's unexpected absence disturbs the narrator's faith in his own relationally determined identity. The scrivener's refusal to give himself over to the identity prescribed by his social order threatens the possibility of identity. Indeed, as the story progresses, versions of Bartleby's phrase—"I would prefer not to"—begin to slip from the mouths of the lawyer and his other subordinates (Turkey and Nippers), revealing a problematic conflation, or doubling, of identity within the office.

Bartleby's passive refusal is fundamentally uncanny, provoking (in Freud's words) an "ego disturbance" ("Uncanny" 236), a "feeling of helplessness" (237). And from this point on, the narrator must contend with a troubling "conflict of judgement" as to what is "possible" (Freud, "Uncanny" 250). Bartleby repeatedly and violently[15] forces the narrator to "stagger in his own plainest faith," forcing him (again and again) to reestablish a predetermined order and stable ontological roles by appealing to "disinterested persons ... for some reinforcement of his own faltering mind" (22). In other words, Bartleby's uncanny "disturbances" of the "ego" are relieved (if only momentarily) via appeals to consensus, or the possibility of empathic communion—as the narrator puts it, "common usage and common sense" (22). Yet the narrator's various appeals fail to make sense of Bartleby's uncanny disruptions, or the experiences of doubling they tend to effect.

For instance: while on his way to hear a "celebrated preacher" one Sunday morning, the narrator makes the impromptu decision to stop in at his office. To his surprise, his key is "resisted by something inserted from the inside" (26). His surprise is only exacerbated by the fact that the key is being resisted by a matching key somehow obtained by Bartleby—who has, it would seem, taken up residence in the narrator's office. The scene is simply fantastic in its improbability. How did Bartleby get a key? Of course, the narrator admits that there are (according to the custom of New York law offices) many keys. And while he can account for three, he cannot account for the fourth. That this fourth key should have somehow fallen into the hands of Bartleby seems, though, highly unlikely—especially if we consider the fact that Bartleby must have gained possession of the key at the outset. (The narrator notes that he has never seen him leave the office and there is certainly no evidence that Bartleby has some other place of residence.) In other words, if Bartleby has been living in the narrator's office since the beginning, then he most likely acquired a key during his first few days of employment. For although the narrator has not (until this point in the story) known him to leave the office, Bartleby most certainly must and does. Are we to assume that the "eminently *safe*" narrator has simply left a key lying around, or that the "eminently decorous" (27) Bartleby has stolen one from someone else? However we try to square it, Bartleby's serendipitous discovery of the very thing his residence requires is (like his "wonderful mildness" [27]) largely inexplicable, if not simply absurd. And it is this sense of absurdity that is so disconcertingly humorous.

This later scene of thwarted expectations thus highlights and compounds the uncanny nature of those that come before, including the first. Not only does the narrator's key literally encounter its exact counterpart in the keyhole, Bartleby's almost mystical discovery of the narrator's fourth key opens up the possibility that Bartleby somehow knows that which the narrator has forgotten, or repressed.[16] There is a suggestion of "mental processes leaping from one of these characters to another," a strange "doubling, dividing and interchanging of the self" (Freud, "Uncanny" 234). And so it is hardly surprising that this "utterly unsurmised appearance of Bartleby" (26) on a Sunday morning "disarm[s]" and "unman[s]" the narrator (27). When Bartleby suggests that he "preferred not admitting [the narrator] at present" (26), the narrator "*incontinently* . . . [slinks] away from [his] own door" (27; my emphasis). No longer capable of *holding himself together*,[17] the narrator does "as desired" (27). But, at this point, it is hardly clear who (precisely) is doing the "desiring"; we are left with the possibility that Bartleby's desire has suddenly and inexplicably become the desire of the now unmanned and incontinent narrator. This ostensible dissolution of the narrator's identity, or sense of determinate selfhood— his "doubt as to which his self is" (Freud, "Uncanny" 234)—is finally announced outright when he reflects upon the feelings of "melancholy" he experienced upon returning to a suddenly empty office. His musings are worth quoting at some length:

> What miserable friendlessness and loneliness are here revealed! His poverty is great; but his solitude, how horrible! Think of it. Of a Sunday, Wall-street is deserted as Petra; and every night of every day it is an emptiness. This building too, which of week-days hums with industry and life, at nightfall echoes with sheer vacancy, and all through Sunday is forlorn. And here Bartleby makes his home; sole spectator of a solitude which he has seen all populous—a sort of innocent and transformed Marius brooding among the ruins of Carthage!
>
> For the first time in my life a feeling of overpowering stinging melancholy seized me. Before, I had never experienced aught but a not-unpleasing sadness. The bond of a common humanity now drew me irresistibly to gloom. A fraternal melancholy! For both I and Bartleby were sons of Adam. (27–28)

There are several points of note here: (1) The narrator refers to Bartleby as a "sole spectator of a solitude"; yet, at this particular moment, it is the narrator (not Bartleby) who is a "sole spectator." (2) Friendlessness is an attribute the narrator clearly shares with Bartleby. He is, after all, walking to church alone when he decides (in light of having nothing better to do) to stop in at his place of work. (There is little indication that the narrator has any friends or family; he only has employees and fellow lawyers whom he occasionally refers to as "*professional* friends" [37; my emphasis].) (3) The narrator's acute "fraternal melancholy" is tied directly to his (and, no doubt, the reader's) troubling and uncanny inability to disassociate his sense of self from Bartleby and Bartleby's increasingly pronounced immobility and solitude. As Elizabeth Barnes suggests, the narrator's final decision to abandon Bartleby by abandoning his own office building—and, in turn, passively permitting Bartleby's eventual imprisonment for (ironically) the crime of vagrancy—is ultimately effected by the terrifying possibility of "his complete identification with Bartleby, and the risk to self that it portends" (240). Pointing specifically to the narrator's earlier fear that Bartleby will "in the end perhaps outlive [him], and claim possession of [his] office by right of his perpetual occupancy" (38), Barnes highlights the way in which the narrator's frequent experiences of self-effacement result in his various efforts to "gather [his] faculties together" (38). The narrator experiences a profound feeling of "fraternal melancholy" at the precise moment his experience of empathetic pity is terrifyingly obstructed by the dissolution of identity such empathy risks; the narrator cannot hold on to his conscience-satisfying pity without simultaneously *and melancholically* distancing himself from the object of that pity.

Melancholia and Monomania

This brings us back to Cheng's conception of racial melancholia. According to Cheng, as we saw in chapter 1, "Racialization in America may be said to operate through the institutional process of producing a dominant, standard, white national ideal, which is sustained by the exclusion-yet-retention of racialized others" (10). The result is a type of spectral figure, a ghostly "other" whose "exclusion-yet-retention" ultimately results in a troubling lack of inclusion or exclusion, presence or absence. Cheng's thinking clearly extends beyond race to all manner of estranged others—from homosexuals to scriveners who refuse to move, write, or consume. But in the light of a text such as "Bartleby," we are yet again exposed to the possibility (explored in part I) that the melancholia Cheng outlines is in fact a reassuring if problematic evasion of the self's perpetual lack of stability, its always already inherent and ineffaceable spectrality. By ostentatiously announcing this spectrality via his increasingly self-willed exclusion,[18] Bartleby exposes melancholia as the necessary effect and foundation of a democratic social order that hopes to maintain its faith in the promise of inclusion while simultaneously practicing exclusion. As the narrator happily admits, he has always experienced a "not-unpleasing sadness" with regard to forlorn and strange creatures like Bartleby. He goes on to explain: "My first emotions had been those of pure melancholy and sincerest pity; but just in proportion as the forlornness of Bartleby grew and grew to my imagination, did that same melancholy merge into fear, that pity into repulsion" (29). The problem here is that the narrator is no longer capable of sustaining his reassuring and "not-unpleasant sadness," his "pure melancholy," his "sincerest pity." And it is everywhere apparent that the narrator is very much invested in establishing, maintaining, and *finally forgetting* a distinctly melancholic relationship with Bartleby. Consider the narrator's "resol[ution] to assign Bartleby a corner by the folding-doors, but on [his] side of them" while simultaneously setting up a "high green folding screen, which might entirely isolate Bartleby from [his] sight, though not remove him from [his] voice" (19). Turkey, Nippers, and Ginger Nut are similarly deployed: they work outside of the narrator's "ground glass folding-doors," which he opens or closes "according to [his] humor" (19). The narrator "resolves," in short, to organize his office as a space of "exclusion-yet-retention," as a space of pity, empathy, or melancholy—the function of which certainly extends beyond and predates the overtly strange Bartleby. Bartleby frustrates the "natural expectancy" of this setup, rending the illusory veil of difference (and thus the possibility of self-gratifying empathy and pity) it assumes and perpetuates.

The narrator's office space (tied, as it is, to the manner in which he would like to relate to his employees) exposes the condition of pity as the self's separation from the other who is being pitied—excluded yet happily and self-gratifyingly retained.[19] On the one hand, melancholia assures me of a sense of determinate selfhood by confirming the boundary (glass doors or folding screen) between self and other; on the other, it allows me to "retain" the other via those expressions of pity and empathy that belie my selfishness and egotism. Melancholia is, in this sense, a persistent effect and condition of the American democratic ideal insofar as it is a refusal to abandon the very thing that ideal necessarily and paradoxically threatens at its extreme: a sense of determinate selfhood, of autonomy and individuality. The narrator's "sincerest pity" springs back into pure repulsion because it begins to liquidate (in its purity as unconditional empathy) the repulsion (or grounds for rejection) it ultimately demands and sustains. Or again, as Barnes puts it, "one of the problems with empathy [in 'Bartleby'] is the threat it holds to the empathizer's sense of self" (241).

Read alongside the story's various moments of uncanny doubling and sociosymbolical disruption, the narrator's sudden shift from "sincerest pity" to "repulsion" explicitly stresses the profound tension between the American desire for autonomous selfhood (or determinate identity) and the democratic promise of egalitarian inclusion and universal empathy. However, Melville is careful to avoid endorsing either alternative; instead, his story carefully navigates the ontological implications of American's struggle toward two conflicting ideals: extreme empathy (represented by the narrator) and impossible self-reliance (represented by Bartleby). The narrator and Bartleby are doubles only insofar as they are opposites: two matching keys pushing against each other in an office door. There are three significant points of difference: (1) Bartleby moves less and less (of his own volition, anyway) as the story progresses, while the narrator becomes increasingly transient, eventually living in his rockaway; (2) Bartleby neither laments nor attempts to remedy his lack of companionship, while the narrator seems desperate for yet wary or incapable of friendship; (3) Bartleby does not eat, while the narrator (we are lead to assume) most certainly does—albeit without the apparent excess of his other employees.[20] The issue of eating or consumption is, of course, paramount, but let's continue to bracket it for the moment. For now, I'd like to stress the way in which these differences echo two extreme ends of an American democratic spectrum, or paradox. Bartleby's anorexia and immobility come to represent the extremes of concrete and determinate egotism—or, in typical Melvillean terms (and in opposition to Deleuze), "monomania"; he is a rock or ontological island, a singularity that desires only nothing, a self whose idée fixe is to be anterior to all relation. This brings us to Deleuze.

In paraphrasing "Knights and Squires," chapter 26 of *Moby-Dick*, Deleuze asserts that "America is the potential of the man without particularities, the Original Man" (85). Melville's texts thus reveal, according to Deleuze, the *promise* of America, the promise of a radical democracy *to come*: "In the society of brothers, alliance replaces filiation and the blood pact replaces consanguinity . . . : according to Melville this is the *community of celibates,* drawing its members into an unlimited becoming. A brother, *a* sister, all the more true for no longer being 'his' or 'hers,' since all 'property,' all 'proprietorship,' has disappeared" (84). And Bartleby is, as Deleuze asserts, "the man without references, without possessions, without properties, without qualities, without particularities: he is too smooth for anyone to be able to hang any particularity on him" (74). For this reason, Bartleby is, "even in his catatonic or anorexic state, . . . not the patient, but the doctor of a sick America, the *Medicine-Man,* the new Christ or brother to us all" (90). This reading is dependent upon Deleuze's assumption that Melville tends to cast three main types, or "great characters" (79): "At one pole, there are those monomaniacs or demons who, driven by the will to nothingness, make a monstrous choice. . . . But at the other pole are those angels or saintly hypochondriacs, almost stupid, creatures of innocence and purity, stricken with a constitutive weakness but also with a strange beauty" (79–80). Between these two extremes is the figure of law, "the prophet" who has "the power to 'See'" (80). Deleuze locates Bartleby in the position of "angel" or "saintly hypochondriac." But surely there is a problem with such an exuberant reading of Bartleby. While little suggests that Bartleby is demonic (as is, more certainly, Ahab), his impenetrable singularity of purposelessness makes him far less a "saintly hypochondriac" (79) than it makes him a monomaniacal "organ," a Sartrean being "in-itself." For that matter, the narrator's untenable empathy and Christian guilt puts him increasingly in danger of merging with the other, of finally dissolving in a state of social entropy. He is hardly a Melvillean "prophet," as Deleuze would have it.

Bartleby and the narrator are clearly opposed yet conflated; they are not, as Deleuze's reading seems to suggests, two unequal pieces in a common Melvillean triad. As Deleuze himself notes, it is Bartleby's "*relation with the attorney* ... [that] mark[s] the possibility of a becoming, of a new man" (74; my emphasis). The between, then, is the space of promise—not *the one or the other*. Bartleby and the narrator are, for this reason, better understood as the two fronts Deleuze identifies with the "battle" of American pragmatism, a battle "against the particularities that pit man against man and nourish an irremediable mistrust; but also against the Universal or the Whole, the fusion of souls in the name of great love or charity" (87). It is therefore surely a mistake to view Bartleby as "the new Christ"—never mind the ideal (because heroically resistant, noncommunicative, and self-martyring) artist. He offers little but the possibility of abject isolation, the self's utter dissolution via complete withdrawal from the other, or social whole. And in the end this dissolution is hardly discernible from the dissolution that continually threatens the narrator, redoubling his uncanny collusion with Bartleby.[21]

On the one hand, Bartleby's death is the inevitable effect of his "forlorn immobility"—his increasingly adamant refusal to offer and define himself *in relation*; on the other, the narrator's tendency to empathic hypermobility—his incessant need to temper his own egotism with guilty appeals to "common usage and common sense" (22), to find ways to "befriend" or "humor" (23)—risks his own self's dissolution *in relation*.[22] But either trajectory leads to the same inorganic state. As Freud might have it, the narrator's pleasure principle and Bartleby's death drive become conflated in a compulsion to repeat that links the desire for satisfaction in the fulfilment of selfhood with the desire for the dissolution of selfhood in the experience of satisfaction. Both signal a desire "to return to the quiescence of the inorganic world" (Freud, *Beyond* 62). And it is in those moments when the narrator comes to suspect (or experience) this collusion or dissolution of a stable social order that he suddenly experiences profound "repulsion" (29), a desire to "turn [Bartleby] away" (23), a desire for "actual thrusting" (35), "the irritable [and murderous] desperation of the hapless [John C.] Colt" (36). The narrator must, as a result, repeatedly recuperate his sense of self (along with his Christian, prudent, and contradictory ability to empathically "love thy neighbor as thyself")[23] by reasserting the possibility of his melancholic relation to the stranger, his "exclusion yet retention" of the other. He thus seems to regain his earlier melancholic contentment at the very moment he visits *so as to pity* Bartleby in prison. His final words—"Ah Bartleby, Ah Humanity!"—do little more, after all, than mark his utter failure to escape the melancholic double bind that structures and sustains the American democratic ideal. His pity simply spreads outward to every other who is both outside the self and yet utterly and comfortably reducible to a common humanity that justifies his need for empathic connection. What the narrator cannot seem to do—and what the story therefore presents as the answer to this melancholic double bind—is *relate* to the other *without empathy*. He cannot relate without violently reducing the other's *otherness* (in all its intrusiveness) to a reductive "sameness," a sympathetic quality of shared "humanity." And, I think, we hardly need to enumerate the various moments when the narrator struggles to do just this. Nevertheless, we should be wary of seeing in the narrator's failure Bartleby's success.

Sharing an Unshareable Secret

Like Deleuze and (in turn) Agamben, Derrida oddly attempts to position Bartleby as a type of poetic hero. In *The Gift of Death*, Derrida briefly compares Bartleby to the biblical Abraham. Like Abraham, Derrida argues, Bartley "responds without responding" (60). When Isaac asks—during their ascent up Mount Moriah—"where the lamb is to be found for the sacrifice" (*Gift* 59), Abraham replies while maintaining his "secret" and (in turn) his divine responsibility: "God will provide a lamb for the holocaust" (qtd. in Derrida, *Gift* 59). In a similar manner, Bartleby responds without responding whenever he offers his "formula": "I would prefer not to." As does Agamben when he argues that this phrase sustains Bartleby as pure potentiality—repeatedly reminding the narrator and the reader that the eternal possibility of being sustains itself upon the "threshold between Being and non-Being" (Agamben, "On Contingency" 257)[24]—Derrida suggests that this "response without response" preserves Bartleby's unassimilateable otherness. For "if the other were to share his reasons with us by explaining them to us, if he were to speak to us all the time without any secrets, he wouldn't be the other, we would share a type of homogeneity" (58). And, no doubt, Bartleby's "I would prefer not to" frustrates every effort (on the part of the narrator or the reader) to empathize with Bartleby, preserving otherness on both sides of the equation. But Bartleby's "I prefer not to" is certainly far less giving than Abraham's "God will provide"—and, as a consequence, simply ends up demonstrating that the dissolution of the self (as the effect of homogenizing entropy) is as much an effect of an utterly egotistical withholding of self as it is the effect of an utterly empathic giving of the self. Derrida's brief reading of "Bartleby" is, in this sense, problematic, especially given the fact that it is largely contradicted by claims he makes in his (earlier) interview with Nancy ("Eating Well").

For Derrida, "eating well"—a literal and metaphoric reference to the way in which we treat others—is only possible when we accept the fact that the "obligation to protect the other's otherness is not merely a theoretical imperative" ("Eating Well," 276). This is because the perpetual ascendency of the self toward determinate subjectivity is contingent upon the very thing that makes it impossible to complete—an ineffaceable relation to the other, the necessary and constant projection of the self *out of* the other, the incessant cutting off of the self (as a "subjectile" [275]) *from the other*. Thus: "as concerns the 'good' [*Bien*] of every morality, the question will come back to determining the best, most respectful, most grateful, and also most giving way of relating to the other and of relating the other to the self" (281–82). But this question is not (or at least not simply) a question of becoming more empathic, which would be tantamount to liquidating the self's otherness in a state of entropic homogeneity, effectively putting an end to the possibility of relation as perpetual consumption. Nor is it a question of refusing to consume or be consumed, to withhold one's secret absolutely, to (simply) "prefer not to." This is, as we saw in part I, a matter of artistic practice as much as it is a matter of day-to-day living. (It is hardly a coincidence that both *The Gift of Death* and "Bartleby, the Scrivener"—later works of famously and impenetrably secretive authors—work to retain a certain secret in the most giving, *as in the most accessible*, of ways.) As Derrida puts it, "One must eat well [implies] . . . respect for the other at the very moment when, in experience (I am speaking here of metonymical 'eating' as well as the very concept of experience), one must begin to identify with the other, who is to be assimilated, interiorized, understood ideally" (282–83). Democratic melancholia—or rather, the diseased effort to deny or avoid this aporia—can be surmounted only if we forgo the violent dream of Christian and self-gratifying inclusion. In its place, we must embrace and endure (at least, *to a certain extent*) the rigor of perpetual and radical exclusion. Or, if I can anticipate Žižek's phrasing, we must insist upon the relentless enmity of the neighbor as *monstrous other* and, thus, true friend.[25] What such enmity might ultimately entail *in practice* is, in fact, the central concern of the following chapters. For now, though, let's simply note that the exclusionary process to which Melville points is not the self-willed exclusion of a Bartleby—"'the silent man' . . . huddled at the base of the wall" (44) who refuses to eat while abjectly refusing to be consumed by others—and it certainly is not the violence of forced exclusion (which we saw represented again and again in the passing narratives discussed in part I). The exclusion in question perpetually gives while withholding all promise of final comprehension, or consumption.

It leaves us open to being touched and to touching the other. At the same time, the touching it both prompts and makes possible is not motivated by any desire for final and empathic understanding, as is (we must assume) the narrator's final effort to "touch" Bartleby: "Something prompted me to touch him. I felt his hand, when a tingling shiver ran up my arm and down my spine to my feet" (45). The effect of this final touch on the narrator is left unstated. But we might wonder if it opens him momentarily to the possibility of a new and far more radical democratic state, a state in which there is little reason to be shocked or dismayed if, in our sincere efforts to touch the other, we are inhibited by "a tingling shiver."

5 / Consuming Androids in the Work of Philip K. Dick

> ... *he not busy being born is busy dying*
> —BOB DYLAN, "IT'S ALRIGHT, MA (I'M ONLY BLEEDING)"

Overpopulated LA or Desolate San Francisco?

By the time the first iteration of *Blade Runner* found its way to theaters (in 1982), neither director Ridley Scott nor screenwriter David W. Peoples—who inherited an already well-doctored script from a relatively long line of predecessors—had actually read the novel they were adapting: Philip K. Dick's *Do Androids Dream of Electric Sheep?* Or so the story goes.[1] Yet the apparent thematic accuracy of Peoples's script, along with Scott's preliminary productions of that script, transformed Dick's utter contempt for a possible Hollywood adaptation into veritable jubilation. "It's like," Dick asserted in an interview (immediately before his death and well before the completion of the film), "they took my brain out and did sight stimulation on my brain, so it projected an image on the screen" (qtd. in Rickman 103). Such ecstatic praise is far from understandable. The script (which shifts the action from a barren San Francisco to an ostentatiously crowded LA) largely elides one of the novel's central concerns: animals.

In the novel, the majority of animals (as a result of nuclear fallout from World War Terminus) are extinct; the ones that remain are regarded with utter reverence. The very worst thing a human can do is harm, or feel nothing at the idea of harming, an animal. Conversely, caring for an animal is the best and perhaps *only* sign of one's humanity—so much so that an entire line of electric animals has been created to provide less affluent citizens the opportunity to display their ostensible humanity. This human-animal relationship is particularly germane to the novel since it is empathy for animal life that distinguishes humanity from the androids Rick Deckard, a bounty hunter of "escaped" androids, is tasked to "retire." The Voigt-Kampff[2] test, which Deckard must administer before retiring a suspected android, works by provoking empathic responses to descriptions of animal suffering or death. If suitable (as in "instinctive") empathy is not garnered, the subject is identified as an android and summarily retired. The fact that the issue of animals is not overtly addressed in *Blade Runner* is thus striking—and, one would think, reason (alone) for Dick to have maintained his contempt for Hollywood adaptations.

Dick, of course, only ever saw one short scene, a scene in which Harrison Ford (as Deckard) jumps down onto a crowded postapocalyptic LA sidewalk. The focus of the scene is LA itself. As we are reminded throughout Scott's film, LA is crowded to the point of absurdity. It's dark, dirty, and chaotic. Yet, as Dick's comments intimate, the idiosyncratic peculiarity of the various "weirded-out" individuals is effectively lost to the homogenous density of the crowd: "It takes a long time for [Ford] to find an empty spot amongst [the] milling throng to hop down" (qtd. in Rickman 106). Like Dick's barren and empty San Francisco in *Do Androids Dream,* Scott's crowded and confused LA functions (cinematically) to stress a future struggle to assert and maintain individuality while simultaneously experiencing the entropic confusion of identity *as such*. Moreover, Scott's mise en scène links this futile struggle for selfhood in the face of entropy to pervasive consumerism. As Dick is quick to note, "There's millions of signs, information everywhere, do this, buy that" (qtd. in Rickman 106). But this connection between entropic confusion and consumerism is not simply (or only) a critique of late-stage capitalism. The film subtly links the problem of entropy (as it relates to identity politics) to consumption *as eating,* to the human desire (or need) to violate and "take in" the body of an "other."

After an opening interview scene in which we see Deckard's predecessor administer a Voight-Kampff test (and thus raise, however indirectly, the problem of animals and empathy), we are introduced to Deckard. Scott follows the interview sequence with several establishing shots of LA (including one of a giant billboard depicting a geisha-esque woman happily swallowing some sort of food or pill); the camera then slowly tracks (or pierces) through a crowded and chaotic street (like, we can assume, the one Dick saw) to eventually locate and frame Deckard reading a newspaper. Deckard closes the paper he is reading and moves through the throng to order food at a street vendor. After pointing at some unidentified food item (and struggling to indicate that he'd like four of whatever he is pointing at), Deckard adds that he'll have "it" with noodles. Deckard is soon approached by two men who tell him that the chief of police needs him for a new job. Deckard, who has (in the film) retired from bounty hunting, sees no reason to obey; and we should not overlook the manner in which he asserts his independence: "Tell him," he says contemptuously (through a mouthful of noodles and *whatever else he ordered*), "I'm eating."

It is a logical necessity that the humans in the novel are vegetarian; yet the theme of vegetarianism is strikingly subtle and largely implicit. While the novel necessarily touches upon the practical implications of a world in which vegetarianism has become an ethical imperative—what do these postapocalyptic humans eat?—Dick's interest in vegetarianism and eating is (if I can redeploy Derrida's phrasing)[3] significantly more "metonymic" than literal. The problem of eating is inextricably linked to much larger problems of ontology and, by extension, ethics: How do we maintain a sense of human selfhood if we lose the ability or ground to violate, to impose ourselves upon, others? Significantly, then, in *Blade Runner*, the temporary power Deckard has to deny the men who wish to "bring him *in*" is (however loosely) tied directly to the power, rights, and stability he gets from eating, from overtly violating (and defining himself against) a definable other—animal, vegetable, *or machine. What* he is eating is thus vital—and, for that reason, one imagines, so oddly ambiguous. While the act of eating (along with the biological imperative to eat) is typically reason enough for refusing social engagements or conversation, the scene in question highlights the fact that Deckard's identity (in film and novel) is tied to *what* he is able to (bring himself to) consume, or violate—from the food he is able/willing to place in his mouth to the animals, the people, and the machines he is able/willing to impose himself upon. In other words, *Blade Runner*'s stress on consumption and encroaching entropy foregrounds the novels' more striking critique of America's ongoing appeals to egalitarian (or democratic) empathy.

Indeed, Dick's novel ultimately exposes and critiques the problematic trajectory of human empathy—from the establishment of communities based on race, gender, and class to the end of racism, sexism, and classism to the end of speciesism.[4] The novel's anxiety about this trajectory is all the more apparent if we consider the fact that its publication (in 1968) coincides with the height of the American civil rights movement. The rhetoric of the most prominent American civil rights activists tends to echo, renew, and extend a prerevolutionary democratic ideal based upon fraternal sympathy and the reduction of "essential" human differences[5]—the very ideal that animates the narrator in "Bartleby." The central concern of Dick's novel—reflected (or embodied) in the metonymic particulars of eating *as* violence—*is*, therefore, democracy, or the problem of establishing and maintaining equity between the self and the other (in all the "other's" possible forms). Like Melville's "Bartleby" (and, as we'll see in chapter 6, Woody Allen's *Zelig*), the novel exposes and critiques the central paradox upon which the American democratic dream is founded: the promise of fraternal sympathy and egalitarianism on the one hand and individualism and solipsistic self-reliance on the other. If our sense of self demands that we "consume" others, how can we possibly relate empathically *to others* without risking our ability to assert and maintain our*selves?* Or inversely, how can we hope to eliminate acts of consumption/violence if the dream of a democratic (because universally sympathetic) order must inevitably manifest as ontological entropy?

These questions are implicit throughout, yet particularly apparent whenever the problem of eating is announced outright. Deckard confirms his humanity by appealing to his empathy (which, of course, he associates with vegetarianism); empathy, though, as the dissolution of difference, robs him of the ability to define himself (at least without enduring or acknowledging intense feelings of melancholia) by rejecting others. For this reason, the enslaved androids are—in their initial manifestations, anyway—a type of godsend. They are quite simply a substitute for good "meat"—or, more specifically, a definable and excludable other (in the place of, for instance, African Americans).[6] Humans *can violate* (enslave, exploit, maim, kill) an android *without having to violate* their own identity; a human does not, or *cannot*, share an empathic bond with a lifeless machine. In contradistinction, the android confirms the human *as human*.

However, when the novel opens, the new (Nexus 6) androids look and act like humans; they desire freedom and they often demonstrate concern for the well-being of other androids. Their uncanny *because inhuman* monstrosity—they are human *and* not human, self *and* other—undermines a sociosymbolic order utterly dependent on yet increasingly unable to maintain stable ontological definitions. The implicit threat is this: human empathy will expand outward (à la entropy), eventually coming to encompass even the android (and, by extension, all that is living *and all that is not living*). Such entropic expansion would mark, as Derrida might suggest, the end of the self as a definable subject; it would make impossible any justification for eating, of taking in, or cutting off that which is *not me*.[7] Contrary, then, to the claims of most critics (who tend to assume that Dick is primarily interested in reclaiming a properly human subject),[8] *Do Androids Dream* negotiates the unavoidable problem of eating and, in turn, the possibility of what Derrida understands as "eating well"—a type of "ethical violence," as Žižek might put it, capable of fostering a new and radically just democratic order. The novel critiques the human tendency (so apparent in America's various exclusionary practices) to commodify, exploit, and estrange "others" in the name of humanity and the sustainment of exclusionary identity categories *while simultaneously* exposing the paradoxically self-serving limits of naïve empathy, of the Judeo-Christian call (naïvely echoed by the narrator in "Bartleby" and rigorously critiqued by Freud) to "love thy neighbor as thyself."[9]

The Theology of Empathy

The future society depicted in *Do Androids Dream* is largely defined and sustained by a single hegemonic theology known as Mercerism. At some unspecified time in the past "empathy boxes . . . appeared on Earth" (31). When held, these empathy boxes transport a human's consciousness into a type of virtual reality. In this virtual reality, the subject "fuses" with all others who are also, at any given time, fused. This human collective then *becomes* the messianic Wilbur Mercer as he struggles to climb a seemingly insurmountable hill. This climb satisfies his (or humanity's) overwhelming "need to ascend" (22). During the climb, unidentifiable assailants bombard the fused humans with rocks. The "cycle" ends (and begins again) when the collective "[falls] into the trough of the tomb world" (31). The experience of the Mercer box (and the theology of Mercerism, more generally) mirrors the central tension in the novel—the tension between a need to experience communal empathy (*as* entropy) and the paradoxical desire to assert and maintain a sense of selfhood. The ambiguous "tomb world"—a representation of the "pit of corpses and dead bones" (24) in which the "real" Mercer was cast for reversing time and resurrecting dead animals—is overtly linked to the former; the experience of ascension to the latter. Stripped, it would seem, of individual agency, the "real" Mercer could not ascend out of this tomb until "the bones strewn around him grew back into living [and therefore distinct] creatures" (24). After this mysteriously effected event of revivification occurred, Mercer began to "ascend, along with the others" (25). But, as he ascended, he quickly "lost sight of them. He found himself evidently climbing alone. But they were there. They still accompanied him; he felt them, strangely, *inside him*" (25; my emphasis). All humans who experience fusion undergo this cyclical and perpetual trajectory: (1) Mercer's fall into the entropy of the tomb world; (2) his ascension, while linked to a residual collective, out of the tomb world; (3) his final experience of being utterly alone yet *full of* all "others."

In this way, the Mercer box satisfies a type of repetition compulsion, the "*fort/da*" experience described by Freud in *Beyond the Pleasure Principle*. The experience of the Mercer box is the satisfying experience of the self's "disappearance and return [and disappearance again]" (Freud, *Beyond* 15). The Mercer box fuses humanity in a state of utter empathy *so as to* provide an experience of ascension that culminates when the individual is truly alone and "encompassing every other living thing" (Dick, *Androids* 25). The box moves participants from one extreme (the loss of selfhood in entropic confusion) to another (the solipsistic moment when everything outside the self has been brought inside). Or perhaps, and if we are open to hearing in Freud an echo of Hegel, the box exposes its users to the paradoxical tension between "particular individuality" and "citizenship," or the "extremes of divine and human law" (Hegel, *Phenomenology* 278). In the former, which Hegel associates with the family and maternal consanguinity, the individual's immanence is achieved in death.[10] The latter, however, fosters life by "subduing the natural aspect and separateness of his existence, and training him to be virtuous to a life in and for the universal" (269). There are two paradoxes at play here. First: at the peak of pure (familial) individuality—at the moment the individual has "liberated his *being* from his *action* or his negative unity [with others]"—the finally immanent self is nothing more than "a passive being-for-another, at the mercy of every lower irrational individuality and the forces of abstract material elements, all of which are now more powerful than himself" (271). Immanence is therefore achieved in death, *but only insofar as* it is subsumed within a specific familial community, or entropic whole—one, moreover, that persists in the face of the individual's dissolution and "which prevails over and holds under control the forces of particular material elements and lower forms of life" (271). In other words, pure individuality *is* the utter loss of the self in the immanence of pure communal relations—or, more specifically, blood and the absoluteness of biological determinates. Marked by the self's reduction into "a single completed shape" (270), familial immanence is the end of external activity, the end of being "actual and substantial" (270). To sustain vitality is, then, to forgo determinate selfhood, for citizenship and social engagement necessitates my self-effacement (or departure from the maternal whole) even as it ensures my survival. This is the *other* paradox. To remain self-conscious I must sacrifice myself to the will of the Other; I must endure a type of "negative unity" (or *another kind* of death).[11]

The self is no less at risk in the nation than it is in the family—for surely the extreme of either *association* marks the end of selfhood *as such*. Either can be viewed as comparable to the start point *and* the end point of the Mercerian climb—or, that is, to Thanatos as the necessary conclusion of Eros. The one Mercerian extreme (isolation at the top of the hill) marks the return of the former (the fall into the tomb world); the inability to distinguish oneself from the world outside—tied, as it is, to acute empathy and entropic ruin—is indistinguishable from the solipsistic experience of having swallowed *everything* that formerly defined an outside, a difference. The fused "I" finds itself "alone" (25); all others are now (experienced as) "inside" (25) the self. Thus, while the boxes function to provide increasingly isolated and desperately lonely humans (on a hauntingly empty planet) a sense of communion and social relevance, Dick's depiction of an empty world filled with isolated individuals in need of such boxes functions far less to highlight humanity's *exhaustion*—its desperation to reestablish a sense of communal purpose or direction—than it does to highlight the fact that (at the level of the individual) the experience of abject isolation is little different than the experience of what we might begin to understand as schizophrenic communion. Or rather, like Melville's "Bartleby" (and, as we'll see, Allen's *Zelig*), *Do Androids Dream* presents empathy and egotism, communal belonging, and abject self-assertion as "different" sides of a single Möbius strip.

Dick's descriptions of Mercerian "fusion" highlight (if I can borrow N. Katherine Hayles's phrasing and, in turn, recall Freud) a problematic "pendulum . . . swing between dangerous hyperinflation and excruciating shrinkage of the ego without stabilizing at the middle position of everyday reality" (170). And, as Hayles astutely notes, this tension between consuming everything *or* being consumed by everything is everywhere evident in Dick's oeuvre and biography.[12] In *Do Androids Dream,* though, this "consume or be consumed" aporia is doubly stressed. While the experience of the Mercer box signals the inevitable and paradoxical conflation of egotism and empathy, Dick's refusal to maintain stable boundaries between the various "types" he depicts—from radioactively damaged *sub*humans (caustically labeled "chickenheads") and animals (real or electric) to humans *proper* and Nexus 6 androids—repeatedly highlights the need for *and* the impossibility of sustaining fixed categories of being. Take, for instance, the character of J. R. Isidore, a "chickenhead" who works for a company that repairs electric animals while presenting itself as a *real* veterinarian service for *real* animals. Because he carries "distorted genes" and has "failed to pass the minimum mental faculties test" (19), Isidore is unable to emigrate to an off-world colony. As a further consequence of his "chickenhead" status, and since only emigrants are assigned them, Isidore cannot own an android servant designed specifically "for [his] UNIQUE NEEDS, FOR [him] AND [him] ALONE" (17). The obvious suggestion is that Isidore is not unique. He is not an individual. He no longer belongs to a family of *humans:* "Upon him the contempt of three planets descended" (19). The fact that Isidore does not own an animal—electric or real—simply confirms his utter isolation from a human community:

> Okay, he thought; I'm off to work. He reached for the doorknob that opened the way out into the unlit hall, then shrank back as he glimpsed the vacuity of the rest of the building. It lay in wait for him, out there, the force which he had felt busily penetrating his specific apartment. God, he thought, and reshut the door. He was not ready for the trip up those clanging stairs to the empty roof where he had no animal. The echo of himself ascending: the echo of nothing. (21)

Isidore's failing sense of selfhood is here tied to two distinct factors: (1) his disconnection from humanity (as a result of his inability to *display* human empathy in the form of animal ownership); (2) his sense that, outside the human community, there is only entropic decay. "Eventually," Isidore tells himself, "everything within [his] building would merge, would be faceless and identical, mere pudding-like kipple piled to the ceiling of each apartment" (20). Isidore is in danger of becoming lost to entropic confusion, lost to "the tomb world slough of being a special" (72), lost to an undifferentiated and categorically *not*-human milieu. Yet, at the same time, and quite paradoxically, Isidore is frequently depicted as the *most* human (i.e., empathic) character in the novel.

When he is sent to pick up a malfunctioning electric cat that "really sounds as if it's dying" (70), Isidore chastises himself for becoming emotionally connected to a machine: "Funny, he thought; even though I know rationally it's faked the sound of a false animal, burning out its drive-train and power supply ties my stomach in knots" (72). And since "the synthetic sufferings of false animals [don't] bother [his] . . . boss" (72), Isidore decides that he is simply "declin[ing] in sagacity and vigor. He and the thousands of other specials throughout Terra, all of them moving toward the ash heap. Turning into living kipple" (73). This assumption is only confirmed when, after getting the cat back to the shop, Isidore discovers that the cat is in fact "real." Isidore's confusion does not signify (to Isidore or anyone else) an intuitive and human connection to real animals; his inability to distinguish a real cat from a mechanical cat simply confirms his dissolution as a human subject. As his coworker suggests, "To him they're all alive, false animals included. He probably tried to save it" (77). Isidore's not-human *because unsagacious* empathy is stressed most emphatically when, toward the end of the novel, the androids he has (as a result of misdirected empathy) harbored in his apartment begin to mutilate a spider, cutting off a leg at a time so as to see how many it needs to walk. This moment, which echoes the cold objectivity of scientists engaged in exploratory vivisection, coincides with two other striking events: (1) the revelation, by Buster Friendly (an android variety show host who manages to broadcast forty-six hours a day), that Wilbur Mercer is a fraud, a now out-of-work actor who was hired (by some unknown authority) to *perform* the climb humans experience when fused to an empathy box; and (2) the absolute dissolution of Isidore's sense of distinction, of difference.

Just as Pris and Irmgard (the two female androids Isidore is currently harboring) begin to cut the spider's legs and Friendly begins to lay out the evidence that will ultimately confirm the androids' assumption that "the whole experience of empathy is a swindle" (210), Isidore begins to feel "a weird terror" (206). Thus the androids' distinctly not-human *because unrestrainedly egotistical* effort to demonstrate their mastery over the world outside them—their insistence, in other words, that nothing *is* outside them—is paralleled by Isidore's loss of an "inside," or sense of concrete selfhood, his failing ability to maintain a distinction between inside *and* outside. After he experiences his walls disintegrating into "fragments of plaster resembling... radioactive dust" and chair screws "ripping out and hanging loose" (212), Isidore calls for help: "Mercer, he said aloud. Where are you now? This is the tomb world and I am in it again, but this time you're not here, too" (213). In this moment, Isidore's unrestrained empathy for the least human of creatures (a spider) marks his final schizophrenic dissolution and his complete estrangement from humanity. At the same time, the androids' mutilation of the spider—especially as it is presented from Isidore's unreservedly empathic perspective—confirms their mechanical megalomania. And while Isidore's empathy leads to his isolation—albeit an isolation experienced as schizophrenic confusion with all things (living and not living)—the androids' efforts to assert themselves as above (or against) all others sees them (e)merge as an isolated singularity (as, that is, categorically "android"). Thus, in Dick's own terms, both Isidore and the androids lose themselves to (forms of) "schizophrenia." Or, if we wish to trace out the connection to the previous chapter more clearly, we might (cautiously) assert that both Isidore and the androids undergo a type of zombification. Lost to the entropy of the tomb world, and "too 'nuts' to be much of a threat to anyone *but himself*" (Hayles 176; my emphasis), Isidore succumbs to an extreme form of "psychotic schizophrenia"; and, in their efforts to display "power over others" (176), the androids reveal themselves as "neurotic schizoids" (176).[13] By the end of the scene, neither the androids nor Isidore are identifiable as (in Dick's nominalist[14] terms, "human") subjects. No one is *alive*: "The corpse of the spider has taken over" (Dick, *Androids* 212).

Subjects and Subjectiles

The extremes represented by the androids (on the one hand) and Isidore (on the other)—and, by implication, the "extremes of divine and human law" (Hegel, *Phenomenology* 278)—can be understood as ontological extremes of distance and proximity. This problem of distance versus proximity is expressed by Mercer himself—who, in what may or may not be a hallucination, miraculously appears to Isidore as he struggles to return from the tomb world. Upon recognizing Mercer, Isidore immediately questions him about Friendly's claim that the scene experienced via the empathy box is just an illusion staged on a cheap Hollywood set:

> "Is the sky painted?" Isidore asked. "Are there really brush strokes that show up under magnification?"
> "Yes," Mercer said.
> "I can't see them."
> "You're too close," Mercer said. "You have to be a long way off, the way the androids are. They have a better perspective." (215)

The ontological (and thus ethical) problem of empathy is here brought into sharp relief—particularly since Mercer is now a confirmed fraud (though, at the same time, the fact of his fraudulence is ultimately frustrated when he appears to Isidore and, later, to Deckard). In light of the androids' disconcerting ability and willingness to torture and kill an innocent creature and Isidore's equally troubling inability to realize (while witnessing the mutilation) that, as Irmgard assures him, "[he] didn't lose anything" (210; my emphasis), Mercer's claim that Isidore is "too close" must be considered with some diligence. It suggests that we must work to accept and maintain, in Derrida's terms, "appurtenance, the co-appurtenance of identity" (*Politics* 55). Appurtenance is the "other" *to* and *as* the "self." The other *as appurtenance* must remain infinitely distant *and* impossibly close. Naïve and self-effacing empathy denies the former (by conflating the other and the *self*), while solipsism denies the latter. Understood (here) as a hegemonic imposition of one's self upon all others, or the assumption that one's worldview is indistinguishable from the Real, solipsism violently "subjects" the other as *nothing* but an effect of the self. Yet loving the other *as thyself* is no less violent than solipsistically denying the fact that the other's worldview and, by implication, *civil rights* are always equal to my own. *Do Androids Dream* counters the dream of egalitarian or universal sympathy—*as*, that is, *the answer* to a world in which only the self matters because only the self can be known—with "a politics of separation," a politics that we might very well understand as a new and radical democratic order, a new "social bond, a contemporaneity, but in the common affirmation of being unbounded, an untimely being-alone and, simultaneously, in joint acquiescence to disjunction" (Derrida, *Politics* 55).

This idea of a radically democratic order defined by an "injoint acquiescence to disjunction" is, according to Derrida (and as we began to see via a discussion of "Bartleby"), only possible when we accept the fact that "the determination of [a] singular 'Who?'—or at least its determination as subject—remains forever problematic. And it *should* remain so. This obligation to protect the other's otherness is not merely a theoretical imperative" ("Eating Well" 276). It is "not merely a theoretical imperative" because the perpetual ascendency of the subject toward subjectivity—like the perpetual ascendency of Mercer (as *all others*) up the Mercerian hill—is made possible by an ineffaceable relation to the other, a constant projection of the self (as "subjectile" [275]) *out of* the other. Or rather, the perpetual promise of the subject's subjectivity is, as Nancy puts it, the effect of perpetual birth, but the perpetual birth(ing) of its own difference: "But identity, while pulling itself together, *assumes* and resorbs within itself the differences that constitute it: both its difference from the other, whom it posits as such, and its difference from itself, simultaneously implied and abolished in the movement of 'grasping itself'" ("Identity and Trembling" 10). In this sense, a subjectile is never finally *born*: "It *is* not, in it is born, in the movement, the delay, and the incompletion of being born" (13).

However, the western metaphysical concept of the immanent subject (so overtly exemplified in America's identity politics) is defined by a desire for a birth that is *once and for all*. In *Do Androids Dream*, Dick critiques this view of (and desire for) the immanent subject most blatantly via his depiction of the androids who torture the spider (and thus Isidore). In mutilating the spider, the androids demonstrate an almost maniacal desire to separate, or "distance," themselves from all that is *not* them. This distance, this state of being (as Mercer says) "a long way off," ostensibly ensures their sense of dominance, of individuality—or better, of *in-divisibility*. They are, in this scene, presented as beings who wish to *be* finally outside all relation, without any supplementary excess. And, significantly, the female androids' move toward dominance (via the cutting up of an innocent other) is effectively presided over by the male android Baty—who casually occupies Isidore's "chair as if he intended to remain permanently" (203), who repeatedly demands that the others "stop talking" (204), and who finally holds a match "near the [mutilated] spider, closer and closer, until at last it [creeps] feebly away" (210). In all respects, the scene clearly exposes and critiques a desire for subjectivity that is, in Derrida's terms, symptomatic of "*carno-phallogocentrism*": "Authority and autonomy . . . are through this schema, attributed to the man (*homo* and *vir*) rather than to the woman, and to the woman rather than to the animal. And of course to the adult rather than to the child" ("Eating Well" 280–81). The myth of the immanent subject maintains itself via the delimiting effects of "necessary" sacrifice, the definition and consumption of those others that have *no relation* to my*self*: "The subject does not want just to master and possess nature actively. In our cultures, he accepts sacrifice and eats flesh" (281). To assert the possibility of a final or *determinant* answer to the question of "Who?," the subject eats the other *as other*—never (except in the most nauseatingly uncanny of moments) accepting its consumption of the other as always also the consumption *and thus erosion* of the *self*. The physical and sacrificial act of eating meat is, in this sense, the most human/autonomous of activities; it confirms the reality of a categorically determinant *not me* (i.e., the not-human, not-living, not-autonomous *thing*—animal, machine, woman, child, etc.). The animal's (or, in this case, the spider's) lack of subjectivity/humanity is the natural *and paradoxically foundational* consequence of *carno-phallogocentrism*.

However, if, as an effect of the postmodern, late-capital, or schizophrenic modes of perception simultaneously critiqued and celebrated in Dick's texts,[15]

> the limit between the living and nonliving now seems to be as unsure [as it clearly is for Isidore], at least as an oppositional limit, as that between 'man' and 'animal,' and if, in the (symbolic or real) experience of the 'eat-speak-interiorize,' the ethical frontier no longer rigorously passes between the 'Thou shalt not kill' (man, thy neighbor) and the 'Thou shalt not put to death the living in general,' but rather between several infinitely different modes of the conception-appropriation-assimilation of the other, then, as

concerns the 'good' [*Bien*] of every morality, the question will come back to determining the best, most respectful, most grateful, and also most giving way of relating to the other and of relating the other to the self." (Derrida, "Eating Well" 281–82)

But this question "of relating to the other and of relating the other to the self" is not (or at least not simply) a question of becoming more empathic—a fact that the narrator of "Bartleby" is largely unable to accept. The schizophrenic and entropic empathy experienced by Isidore (and ostensibly sought by Melville's lawyer) marks the end of difference itself—the end, that is, of relation and thus the possibility of *relating,* of the "co-appurtenance of identity." Such empathy marks the *impossibility* of eating: "The moral question is . . . not, nor has it ever been: should one eat or not eat, eat this and not that, the living or the nonliving, man or animal, but since *one must* eat in any case and since it is and tastes good to eat, . . . *how* for goodness' sake should one *eat well* [*bien manger*]?" (282).

The answer, it seems (as *Do Androids Dream* ultimately works to demonstrate), is to respect and preserve (while feeding off of, or relating to) the other's otherness and, in turn, the otherness that is always necessarily supplemental to the self. Or rather, and as I intimated in the previous chapter, the answer is a type of "infinite hospitality" (Derrida, "Eating Well" 282), "respect for the other at the very moment when . . . one must begin to identify with the other" (282–83). Such hospitality or respect is, after all, and if we can return to Hegel, the ground upon which self-consciousness is sustained. For self-consciousness, "through the very contradiction of its pure universality [or immanence], which at the same time still strives against its identity with the other, and cuts itself off from it, *explicitly* supersedes itself within its own self. Through this externalization, this knowledge which in its existence is self-discordant returns into the unity of the *self.* It is the *actual* 'I,' the universal knowledge *of itself* in its *absolute opposite*" (*Phenomenology* 409).[16] But this is not the hospitality Isidore displays—when, that is, he asserts that the androids' status *as androids* "made no difference" (163), or when he finally suffers *as* the spider. Infinite hospitality[17] must surely entail a certain egotistical violence, the violence of cutting oneself (or allowing oneself to remain cut) from the other/Other. Eating well *as* infinite hospitality is in no way accomplished in the moment we *selflessly* refuse to consume (or exploit or disregard) that which we have anthropomorphized, or empathically linked to ourselves— dolphins, kittens, seeing-eye dogs, intelligent monkeys, other humans, etc. Unless our respect is for the other's otherness, it is not respect. The acutely empathic is no more respectful than the acutely egotistical. Both efface/deny the space, or relation, or supplement, that separates (while necessarily making *inseparable*) self and other: "For that relation is a *mediating* one in which the related terms are not one and the same, but each is an other for the other, and only in a third term are they one" (Hegel, *Phenomenology* 398). Only when I accept that whatever I eat is me (empathy) *and* absolutely not me (egotism) can I possibly begin to "eat well." And it is precisely this fact that Rick Deckard must learn to endure.

Uncanny Androids

Immediately after arriving at his office and learning that a fellow bounty hunter (Dave Holden) has been shot by escaped Nexus 6 androids, Deckard reassures himself about the defining characteristics of humanity: "Empathy, evidently, existed only within the human community, whereas intelligence to some degree could be found throughout every phylum and order including arachnida. For one thing, the empathic faculty probably required an unimpaired group instinct; a solitary organism, such as a spider, would have no use for it.... It would make him conscious of the desire to live on the part of his prey. Hence all predators, even highly developed mammals such as cats, would starve" (30–31). Deckard's reference to a spider (occurring as it does long before Pris and Irmgard's ostentatiously mechanical mutilation of Isidore's spider) is notable. In identifying the spider as "a solitary organism," Deckard draws a direct link between spiders (as well as cats) and androids. Like the spider, "the humanoid robot constituted a solitary predator" (31). Neither spider nor android (nor cat) has, or *could have,* empathy; empathy would paralyze it, making it "conscious of the desire to live on the part of [its] prey" (31). For this reason, Deckard assumes, "Empathy... must be limited to herbivores or anyhow omnivores who could depart from a meat diet. Because, ultimately, the empathic gift blurred the boundaries between hunter and victim, between the successful and the defeated" (31). The conclusion that androids lack empathy reassures Deckard: "It made his job palatable. In retiring—i.e., killing—an andy, he did not violate the rule of life laid down by Mercer. *You shall only kill the killers*" (31).[18] But Deckard's logic is necessarily strained and troubling.

If "andys" can be enslaved, marginalized, or retired because they lack empathy as "solitary predators," how is it possible to define the human as that which empathically desires to care for *other* solitary predators (like cats)? What Deckard's musings imply is that the fictional difference between an andy and a cat is tantamount to the very real distinction (we make all the time) between a cat and a spider. The former is worthy of empathy—so much so that I weep when my pet cat (a member of the family, after all) dies; the latter is not—so much so that the collapse of its body under my sole tends to fill me with far more satisfaction than angst. Granted, I may very well, if only for a moment, feel *bad* about the spider— in the same sense that Deckard, even at the outset, hardly feels "good" about his job; it's merely "palatable." However, the reservation I may feel when "retiring" a spider (or andy) is ultimately and simply indicative of persistent and reassuring social melancholia. Like any marginalized because *constituently other* entity (from the African slave of the nineteenth century to the Mexican immigrant or the transgender activist), I egotistically impose myself, my needs, and my worldview upon the spider while simultaneously and melancholically lamenting the necessity of doing so. Like eating meat, as Derrida insists, killing the spider is simply a sacrifice *I am compelled to make*. Feeling bad about the spider makes me feel good about myself. Yet if "the empathic gift blur[s] the boundaries between hunter and victim, between the successful and the defeated," how is it possible for the human *and thus acutely empathic* subject to maintain, while feeling good about, this melancholic double bind? Here (yet again) we are exposed to the tension between egotism and empathy. An android (unlike a cat) is no more a victim than the spider who might unfortunately wind up under my sole. This is because, as Deckard egotistically and quite arbitrarily assures himself, there is nothing human about *it*. The extremely tenuous nature of such a distinction is nowhere more obvious than in the moment when we are encouraged to empathize with Isidore's schizophrenic response to the spider's slow death; but it is also exposed throughout the novel in Deckard's various interactions with the androids he is tasked to retire.

Deckard begins his hunt of escaped androids confident that no *human* "fails to pass" (37) the Voigt-Kampff test. However, and not surprisingly, the line between android and human quickly begins to dissolve—though, at first, this dissolution is only apparent to the reader (if anyone). Take Deckard's first application (in the novel) of the Voigt-Kampff test. Sent to Eldon Rosen of the Rosen Association—the corporation that manufactures Nexus 6 androids—to confirm the Voigt-Kampff's efficacy, Deckard finds himself questioning Rachael Rosen, Eldon Rosen's ostensible niece and a woman who may or may not be an android. At one point, Deckard describes a "chef drop[ing] [a] lobster into [a] tub of boiling water" (50). While Rachael is quick to express disgust—"That's awful! Did they really do that?"—the "[Voigt-Kampff] gauges . . . [do] not respond. Formally, a correct response. But simulated" (50). In this moment, Rachael exposes her lack of humanity; she *is* an android—a physical designation that becomes indisputable as the novel progresses. But Deckard seems to ignore the fact that Rachael's lack of empathy for the lobster must necessarily imply one of two things: (1) either the human of the novel's past (i.e., the reader, who is likely to have eaten lobster) was/is an android *or* (2) Rachael *is not* an android. Or more problematically, Rachael's lack of empathy for the lobster exposes the human *as android* while opening up the possibility that the android *is human*. When Deckard is finally forced to confront this monstrous possibility—or rather, when he confronts the monstrously ambiguous nature of certain Nexus 6 androids—his ability to continue (working, killing, eating, persisting as a concrete subject) is undermined to the point of life-threatening paralysis.

The first indication that Deckard is on the same road to entropic ruin as Isidore comes when he confronts Luba Luft, an android passing as a human opera singer. Not only does Luba's voice and body provoke "real" emotions in Deckard, he comes to view her as further proof that "androids . . . have more vitality and desire to live than [his] wife" (94). Luba's ability to provoke such responses/thoughts at first suggests to him that "the better she functions, the better a singer she is, the more [he is] needed" (99). The more human an android *seems* the more Deckard is needed to confirm (by retiring) the android *as android*. Confronted with the emergence of a seemingly empathetic android—and thus the dissolution of the self/other boundary that buttresses humanity's ability to define itself as an uniquely empathic species—Deckard (as a human subject) feels compelled to reestablish the boundary by egotistically perpetuating and thus justifying violence.[19] As Sherryl Vint notes, Deckard's ultimate realization is that his job "is about making rather than policing a boundary" (116). But the process of establishing such a boundary is oddly and also the process of its destabilization. Empathy can remain the defining characteristic of the human subject *only if* the human subject is willing to engage in the egotistical and self-serving violence that defines the android. If (as Deckard tells Luba) "an android . . . doesn't care what happens to another android," then Deckard (as Luba logically concludes) "must be an android" (101).

As is the narrator's growing sense of dissolution in "Bartleby," the effect (on Deckard) of a clearly untenable and thus eroding human/android boundary is utterly uncanny. Directly linked to Isidore's acutely empathic or schizophrenic "breakdown," Deckard's sense of the uncanny—his sense of a "doubling, dividing and interchanging of the self" (Freud, "Uncanny" 234)—intensifies as his hunt progresses. For instance, while struggling to prove that Luba is an android, Deckard is suddenly arrested. The arresting officer, having arrived in response to a phone call made by Luba, demands that Deckard verify his status as a bounty hunter and, by implication, as a human. Deckard is able to bring his supervisor up on a "vidscreen" (107), but the screen goes strangely blank the moment the arresting officer looks at it. And, en route to the "Hall of Justice" to be "booked," Deckard notices that "Officer Crams had steered the car in the wrong direction" (110). Crams, though, assures him that they are headed in the right direction: "The new [Hall of Justice] is on Mission. That old building, it's disintegrating; it's a ruin. Nobody's used that for years. Has it been that long since you last got booked?" (110). The frightening possibility that the building to which he drives "every morning" (111) has been long abandoned is further exasperated by the fact that, once at the "new" Hall of Justice, Deckard begins to experience a strange feeling of déjà vu:

> "Over here," Officer Crams said to Rick, leading him to a small white table at which a technician operated familiar equipment. "For your cephalic pattern," Crams said. "Ident-purposes."
> Rick said brusquely, "I know." In the old days, when he had been a harness bull himself, he had brought many suspects to a table like this. *Like* this, but not this particular table. (112–13)

This sense of the familiar as unfamiliar, the homely as unhomely, the self *as other* is continually stressed as Deckard's detour to the new Hall of Justice plays out. While the officers he encounters have never heard of the Voigt-Kampff test (or Deckard), many are also in the business of retiring "andys." And, in realizing that Officer Garland, the commanding officer at *this* Hall of Justice, appears on Deckard's list of androids in need of retirement, Deckard suddenly faces the possibility that he too might appear on such a list.

At first glance, this odd and uncanny "detour" simply appears to open up the possibility that Deckard *is* an android—"With [as Officer Crams suggests] a false memory, like they give them" (111). However, since Deckard's status as a physical human is hardly in doubt by the end, the detour functions (more problematically) to further highlight the tenuousness of the boundary separating human and android, self and other. Indeed, after the scene at the (new) Hall of Justice, the possibility that Deckard is an android is largely abandoned. Yet his uncanny sense of "doubling, dividing and interchanging" grows.

With assistance from the cold and cruel Phil Resch (a bounty hunter from the new Hall of Justice), Deckard finally manages to kill Luba. Yet, even as he kills her, he is far less certain of Resch's humanity than he is of Luba's. In an effort, as Resch puts it, to "undergo renewed faith in the human race" (140), Deckard decides to test him. The test simply confirms Resch's status as a human and leaves Deckard feeling "both psychologically and physically weary" (140). Faced with the fact that he is beginning to identify with a determinant other—or rather, to include "androids in [his] range of empathetic identification, as [he] do[es] animals" (141)— Deckard is forced to negotiate the possibility that he is losing his ability to "protect" (141) himself. On the one hand, and quite simply, the suggestion is that he is losing the ability to remain emotionally detached from his prey; on the other, and more problematically, he is in danger (à la acute empathic schizophrenia) of utterly losing his sense of selfhood—his sense of being a concrete subject, of having (in Lacan's terms) an "ideal I."[20] In recognizing his human (and familiar) desires and emotions in the other (and unfamiliar) he is killing, Deckard necessarily undergoes an uncanny experience not unlike the experience we might undergo if we were to suddenly anthropomorphize the animal whose flesh we just ate and enjoyed—if we were, that is, to suddenly view a half-eaten steak as no different than a well-cooked slice of kitten or any other animal we tend to define via references to human emotion and behavior.

This outward-spreading entropic dissolution of all *self preserving* boundaries is brought to a head when Deckard is seduced by the monstrously ambiguous Rachael. Boyish and female, human yet android, Rachael seduces him so as to confirm his empathic link to all other androids: "'No bounty hunter ever has gone on,' Rachael said. 'After being with me. Except one. A very cynical man. Phil Resch. And he's nutty; he works out in left field *on his own*'" (198; my emphasis). This assertion generates a certain amount of suspense. If Deckard is to continue, he will be no better, or *no more human,* than Resch. Isidore confirms this threat when he tells Deckard, who arrives at Isidore's apartment immediately after Mercer's miraculous appearance, that "if you kill [the rest of the androids] you won't be able to fuse with Mercer again" (219). That pulling the trigger means abandoning his humanity is ostensibly confirmed by the fact that the first of the three androids he faces (Pris) is an exact and uncanny replica of Rachael. To kill her is to kill a woman he has come to love—or, at the very least, desire. To kill her is to sacrifice that part of himself he is most desperate to preserve: his humanity. Nevertheless, Deckard "fire[s] at her as, imploringly, she dashe[s] toward him" (221). But the Deckard who kills Pris is not the

Deckard who kills Luba. This Deckard has come, in some respects, to embrace the uncanny crucibles to which he has been subjected throughout. Moreover, this Deckard has come armed with knowledge gleaned from two apparently miraculous encounters with the *real* Mercer.

Immediately before killing Pris, Deckard is told by Mercer that (regardless of Isidore's warning) "what [he is] doing must be done" (220). This apparent justification of murder is foreshadowed when, earlier, Deckard speaks with Mercer while fused to an empathy box. In this earlier conversation, Mercer intimates that he cannot help Deckard to resolve his dissolving sense of identity or stabilize his relationship with the androids. There is, Mercer assures him, "*no salvation*" (178): "It is the basic condition of life, to be required to violate your own identity. At some point, every creature which lives must do so. It is the ultimate shadow, the defeat of creation; this is the curse at work, the curse that *feeds* on all life" (179; my emphasis). Both the naïve push toward universal empathy and the egotistical drive toward concrete selfhood are aligned in the novel as efforts to deny, or circumvent, this torturous reality, to naïvely maintain the illusion of ontological salvation, the possibility of the immanent subject. Both are profoundly unethical. While empathy requires that I arbitrarily deny or efface the other's otherness, the violence of egotism demands and justifies the illusion that the self can be finally determined as inertly *not other*. The otherness of the other—as that which can never be related to or understood *in full*—must be accepted with "infinite hospitality"; simultaneously, the *in*finite other (in all its intrusive and perpetual otherness) must be recognized as an essential condition of the self. Only when treated as such can the other be "eaten well." In other words, eating well—as in feeding and preserving the self by cutting off the other—is only possible when all violations of the other (*any other*) are understood as violations against the other (in all its otherness) *and* the self.

With this in mind, we might very well argue that Deckard kills Pris when he can no longer *rest assured* of the "need, desire, authorization, the justification of putting to death, putting to death [that is] as denegation of murder" (Derrida, "Eating Well" 283). Of course, Deckard's actions are "justified" by the fact that, as the "laser tube" that falls from her hand confirms, Pris and the other androids are intent on killing him. But at this point there can be no real justification for killing; Deckard's reasons for initiating his hunt no longer make sense. What is significant is the implication that Deckard acts while enduring the monstrous and uncanny trauma of undecidability, a trauma effected by his knowledge that the sense of (human) selfhood he wishes to maintain has never been anything but a condition of that which violates it. He is no longer capable *or willing* to fix the other—in this case, Pris—as self (or *subject* of empathy) or other (without the right to autonomy). Deckard recognizes Pris in this final moment as lover *and* enemy, human *and* android, self *and* other: "The clothes, he thought, are wrong. But the eyes, the same eyes. And there are more like this" (221). She is no more nor any less a concrete subject than is Deckard. There is nothing a priori that could justify Deckard's violation of her or her violation of Deckard. Yet to preserve himself—physically (to stay alive) and psychically (to avoid losing himself to entropic ruin)—Deckard makes an impossible decision *in the moment*. He acts without the assurances or irresponsible privilege we grant and paradoxically use to justify ourselves as concrete (human) subjects. He acts without circumventing or denying the fact that to assert and maintain the self is necessarily, as he later laments (à la Hegel), a matter of forever "becom[ing] alien to [that self]" (230). He therefore commits an act of ethical violence.

Violent Ethics

Let's be clear: Deckard's act of ethical violence is not the murder of Pris, or any other android. It's likely that Pris's death could have *and should have* been avoided. But that is, perhaps, *impossible to decide*. Deckard's act of ethical violence is evident in the way in which *he relates* to Pris in the moment he makes the impossible decision to shoot. In this moment, Deckard is no longer willing or able *to reduce* her to the qualities that make her *like him* (and thus worthy of empathy and love); yet, and simultaneously, he is no longer willing or able to regard her otherness as any less or more than his own. Because he neither loves her (as a result of violently consolidating her into a subject *like* himself) nor hates her (because she has come to signify the illusion of such consolidation), he treats her with justice. Or rather, Deckard finally opens himself to the crucible of "*eating well*"—a crucible that necessarily entails some form of (ethical) violence.

While reflecting upon Freud's critique of the Judeo-Christian imperative to "love thy neighbor as thyself"—and while interrogating Judith Butler's opposition to "ethical violence"—Žižek asserts that "justice and love are . . . structurally incompatible" ("Neighbors" 182). On the one hand, "true love"—as in my love for an individual "neighbor"—is always and necessarily dependent upon my "universal indifference: I am indifferent toward All, the totality of the universe, and as such, I actually love *you*, the unique individual who stands/sticks out of this indifferent background" (183). On the other hand, the universal love espoused by Christianity—like, we should note, the ideal of universal empathy espoused by Mercerism—"acquires the level of actual existence only if 'there is at least one whom I hate'—a thesis abundantly confirmed by the fact that universal love for humanity always led to the brutal hatred of the (actually existing) exception, of the enemies of humanity. This hatred of the exception is the 'truth' of universal love" (183). And without doubt the androids (in *Do Androids Dream*) stand in for any number of exceptions that have been historically hated in the name of, and so as to verify, the universal love of the *truly* human subject.[21] More simply, the injunction to "love thy neighbor as thyself" is too often or too easily taken as an injunction to gather up and reserve *all love* for "thyself"—or rather, for only those others in whose face I empathically recognize or imagine myself. From this perspective, empathy is the consequence of imagination, of imagining myself in or as the other. Such empathy is therefore opposed to justice. "In order to practice justice," Žižek insists, "one *has* to suspend one's power of imagination; if hate [according to Graham Greene] is a failure of imagination, then pity is the failure of the power of abstraction" (185). Unlike universal or "true" love, justice is necessarily "blind": "It must disregard the privileged One whom 'I really understand'" (182). In this sense, loving *justly*—and, in turn, in the name of a radical "*democracy* to come" (Derrida, *Politics* 104)—entails never relegating anything or anyone to the indifferent background; but this in turn means never succumbing to the "imaginary lure" of a neighbor's coherent and identifiable face, never reducing the neighbor to the "'inner wealth . . .' displayed through his or her face, reducing him or her to a *pure* [or imaginary because impossibly ideal] *subject*" (Žižek, "Neighbors" 185). Via this distinctly Hegelian take on *just* love, Žižek assumes that it is *only* through "the 'dead letter' of the law" (185) that the absent other is approached *as purely other*, as abjectly *in*human. The coherent and recognizable face of the other—which, Žižek assumes, can only be human, or *a human's*—simply distracts us (perhaps, we might say here, *melancholically*) from his or her or *its* traumatic absence.

But we must be careful here. Žižek wants desperately to move beyond the ethical necessity of a face-to-face encounter. To do so, his reading of Levinas (and even Butler) must remain relatively superficial, or too concerned with *seeming* radical. As we might expect, Žižek presents "the 'dead letter' of law"—or the violent exclusions effected by the intractable mandates of the symbolic—as the only *space* in which the radical absence of the other is preserved, or *left* to be loved. But in doing so he refuses to acknowledge in the face—or, in less strictly "human" terms, the mask of subjectivity or the phenomenal appearance of a Thing—a necessarily uncanny point of recognition, one that points (too) to the unfamiliar, the inscrutable, the constitutively absent. (We might do well to recall here Faulkner's description of Lucas's inscrutable face.) My face, or any *Thing's* surface, is a "said" (in Levinas's terms) that necessarily conceals while pointing us toward a radically "unsaid" otherness, an otherness for which I must bear responsibility. I can never *not* "prepare a face to meet the faces that [I] meet" because a face is what I present to the law—which, surely, is never as blind as it (or Žižek) might claim. Like a postal code, the face is what the law tracks and regulates. This is why, in Levinas, the insistence upon the face-to-face encounter never implies, as Žižek supposes, "the postulate of a final translatability of the Third [or absent other] into a relation to the Other's face" ("Neighbors" 184). It implies, rather, and as we've seen, a profound and traumatic openness to the other's "forsaken nakedness, which glimmers through the fissures that crack the mask of the personage or his wrinkled skin, in his 'with no recourse' ... without voice or thematization" (Levinas, "God and Philosophy" 71–72). The face is what finally faces us with facelessness. In other words (and if we can indeed disentangle the Levinasian "face" from the strictly human), we cannot simply abandon the necessity of the face-to-face when "dealing with" the other, which is to say that we cannot abandon the necessity of assuming or locating some point of spatial or temporal relation, of establishing some form of recognition, of "com-pearing." Surely, as Žižek insists, ethical love entails a type of hate, a commitment to the violence "of separation" ("Neighbors" 186); but is not such "hate" already implied by *or essential to* the face-to-face encounter? Isn't this as much Nancy's point as Levinas's? And is this not in fact what Žižek himself *implies* when he finds himself holding on to "the 'good' Levinasian Judaism of justice" *by* positioning it (ironically) alongside "the 'bad' tradition of Jehovah, his fits of vengeance and genocidal violence against neighboring people" (186)? Must we not retain the Levinasian encounter—and thus the face—as (also) a "positive condition of ethics" (184)? Without a gamble on the face, I cannot know who or what I am missing, and I certainly cannot gamble on one separation over another, one cut and not another. I must face the other in all sincerity if I am to remain open, or if I am to *become open,* to his or her or *its* "faceless monstrosity."

To a certain extent, this is precisely what Žižek presents as his "anti-Levinasian conclusion"—a willingness to endure what is *beyond* the face of the other. We simply must be careful, when considering this conclusion, that we do not lose sight of the responsibility implied in the face-to-face encounter, the responsibility (quite simply) of "facing up" to the other, of being recognizable while somehow always giving and encouraging an acceptance of what *cannot* be recognized, what *cannot* be faced, what is *infinite*. Žižek's position becomes all the more salient if we keep this proviso in mind. For surely we treat the neighbor with "infinite hospitality" *only when* we treat him or her or it as "a *faceless monster*" ("Neighbors" 185), a monster known only via "ethical violence," or the strictures of law—what Butler thinks of as "the demand for self-identity" (*Giving an Account* 42). Instead of a violence that works to effect idealistic and "nonviolent harmony," an "ethical step . . . *beyond* the face of the other" (Žižek, "Neighbors" 183) demands "violence as such (the violent gesture of discarding, of establishing a difference, of drawing a line of separation) which liberates" (186). The "ethical step beyond the face of the other" is then and also the step beyond the two oppressive extremes highlighted throughout *Do Androids Dream*: (1) empathy, which can be conflated with Freud's *Eros* and the inexorable and paradoxical fall into Mercer's tomb world; (2) egotism, which can be conflated with Freud's *Thantos* and the inexorable and paradoxical ascension to Mercer's acutely isolated mountaintop. Or rather: this step *beyond* the face of the consolidated and *imaginary* subject is a violent and persistent insistence upon the *in*human—that which is neither human nor not human, that which is perpetually and violently "being born." This step is a step beyond the desire that animates all manner of *human* atrocities: the *human* desire to consolidate the self *finally* by consuming the other, a desire which is always and also the paradoxical desire to lose the self *finally* in the other. But again, we must nevertheless hold to (on some level) *an ethics of the face*—as in an ethics of sharing and receiving something recognizable. If we do not hold to such an ethics, then (as we'll see in the following chapter) a "plea for ethical violence" could easily justify an egotistical withdrawal of the self, an abject refusal to share the self or to *work* at understanding the other. A willingness to share the self or take in the other must necessarily imply a willingness to offer and to take seriously a certain supplementary excess, a certain effort to communicate. A refusal to endure faceless monstrosity is *no less* ethical than attempting to "cleanse[] the neighbor [or the self] of *all* imaginary lure" (185; my emphasis)—*even if* the latter is far less possible. We will return to this problem more directly in chapter 7.

For now, let's simply follow the manner in which Žižek finally returns us to Derrida—for *if* "this obligation to protect the other's otherness is not merely a theoretical imperative[,] . . . it is perhaps more 'worthy' of humanity to maintain a certain inhumanity, which is to say the rigor of a certain inhumanity" (Derrida, "Eating Well" 276). This is surely what Dick's novel comes to suggest. Once all the androids are dead—and neither the reader nor Deckard can possibly think of them as "retired"—Deckard escapes to the postapocalyptic desert that surrounds San Francisco. He is weary, depressed, and clearly unstable. And while it is easy to view his emotional state as symptomatic of the guilt he feels for killing beings he can no longer simply disregard as determinately other, it seems far more likely that his exhaustion speaks to his now undeniable inability to rest assured in the ideal of his determinant subjecthood. He is in danger of finally repeating Isidore's descent into the tomb world. He is beginning to suspect that "*everything* is true" (227; my emphasis), that all distinctions are simply illusions. With this promise of entropic ruin/comfort filling his mind, he finds himself, "with no notion of how it could be, a step from an almost certainly fatal cliffside fall—falling humiliatingly and helplessly, he thought; on and on, with no one even to witness it. Here there existed no one to record his or anyone else's degradation" (230–31). This hallucinatory revelation—or inevitable confusion of entropic ruin and abject solitude—suddenly transforms into a "real" Mercerian climb, a climb that significantly requires Deckard to endure, without the illusion of empathy provided by the empathy boxes, the pain of stones thrown by a host of faceless others. This experience leads Deckard to lament that he *is* Wilbur Mercer—whose fraudulence, we should note, is now as suspect as his authenticity—and that he will have to climb "forever, as Mercer does . . . trapped by eternity" (234). In this moment, though, Deckard sees a "real" toad on the ground, a supposedly extinct animal and one of Mercer's most treasured creatures.

Deckard assumes his discovery of a real toad must constitute a miracle and happily yields once again to a promise of salvation—the end of a climb that, as he has been forced to accept again and again throughout the novel, is impossible to complete. However, as his wife realizes when he returns home, the toad is actually electric. In this moment, Deckard's sense of salvation is clearly tied to a problematic willingness to give himself over to the comfort of empathic confusion, the very same confusion we witness when Isidore confuses a real cat for a fake one. Yet when Deckard realizes the truth, he heroically manages to accept the electric toad as both electric *and* real (or alive): "But it doesn't matter. The electric things have their lives, too. Paltry as those lives are" (241). We might too easily say that Deckard here merely reasserts his assumption that "electric things" are less vital than humans (or other animals); but such a reading must overlook the emotional state in which Deckard makes his observation.

He is dejected and broken; he has been forced to face the paltriness of his own existence, the fact that his identity is contingent upon its perpetual violation, its "negative unity." Consequently, Deckard's recognition of and respect for the paltry and inhuman life of the toad surely signals a revised understanding of and respect for his own. The toad's life (like Deckard's life) is only and always the *paltry* "incompletion of being born"; it (like Deckard) must incessantly embrace so as to incessantly cut itself off from the other. Such cutting *feeds* any (sense of) self. Resigned to this realization, Deckard goes to sleep no longer desperate for a sense of concrete selfhood—or rather, no longer in need of artificially stimulating a sense of "long deserved peace" (243). His wife, though, decides to stay up and attend to the toad. In doing so, she demonstrates her own understanding and acceptance of "paltry" life. And in a moment that sees her apparently respecting the toad's otherness while simultaneously empathizing with its own desire to assert it*self,* "she wondered what *it* 'ate'" (243; my emphasis).

6 / The Chameleon and the Dictator in Woody Allen's *Zelig*

> *The only thing we knew for sure about Henry Porter is that his name wasn't Henry Porter*
>
> —BOB DYLAN, "BROWNSVILLE GIRL"

Totalitarian Fools

Set in the years leading up to World War II and concerned with the peculiar history of a man whose physical and intellectual identity is wholly contingent upon those who surround him, Woody Allen's 1983 faux documentary *Zelig* culminates at a Nazi rally in Munich. In these final climatic scenes, the Jewish Leonard Zelig (Allen) is discovered performing the role of a high-ranking National Socialist by his psychoanalyst and future wife, Eudora Fletcher (Mia Farrow). The setting is announced by the narrator and confirmed by what seems to be archival footage of Hitler walking toward the camera (through two rows of saluting soldiers) and then standing on a stage with white-draped tables to his left and right. A row of officials stand in the rear. While the film never announces the exact date of the rally, an extremely (if not impossibly) astute viewer might recognize the footage as being from the famous rally in 1933—in Berlin, not Munich—when Hitler first spoke as chancellor. Without recourse to the actual footage, though, it is unlikely that even an astute viewer would or could gamble a claim on its authenticity. As the scene cuts from shots of the audience (in which Fletcher is apparently struggling to locate Zelig) and Hitler delivering his speech—and as the narrator tells us that, "suddenly, a figure flanking the chancellor catches [Fletcher's] attention"—Allen suddenly becomes visible. Allen's appearance is jarring, if not uncanny. Where did he come from? Was he there all along? Absent in all previous shots of Hitler and the stage, he now peeks comically and inexplicably from behind one of the background officials. "Struggling to make contact," Eudora (we are told) finally "manages to catch his eye." Thus, as Hitler continues to speak, Zelig *as Allen* slowly—and "like a man emerging from a dream"—becomes more and more distinct, no longer lost to the anonymity of the background faces.[1] His emergence (and eventual decision to wave ostentatiously back at Fletcher) attracts the attention of his fellow officers and, as a result of the ensuing commotion, Hitler turns to face him.

But just as Hitler turns (and the scene is at its most absurd and inexplicable), the film cuts to the "Hollywood" re-creation of the event—the version in *The Changing Man* (which Allen's film tells us is "the 1935 film based on the life of Zelig"). At this point, the viewer has two options: (1) assume that the archival footage of Hitler is fake and that the entire scene was filmed with and for Allen; (2) assume that Allen (and his cinematographer, Gordon Willis) managed to find archival footage of Hitler turning (for one reason or another) and then inserted Allen via matte photography.[2] But the incredible similitude of the scene to real archival footage and the inertia that is effected by the film's use of more readily verifiable archival footage throughout (along with the sudden and dramatic cut to the obviously fictional Hollywood film) encourages us to assume the latter. Indeed, Allen is mysteriously absent before Fletcher sights him. When he does become visible, his slow emergence appears out of place; oddly noticeable shadows appear as Allen begins to move (particularly when he begins to wave), a likely symptom of matte photography. Yet the utter improbability of Allen and Willis having stumbled upon such perfect (and perfectly rare) footage confounds our ability to make an easy decision about the scene. The scene is therefore defined by a troubling mix of absolutes and undecidables, the fixed and the unfixable. And since the film purports to be a documentary about a man whose excessively protean nature sees him losing himself in a movement defined by its opposition to all things protean, this mix of extremes is hardly coincidental. The scene functions metonymically, reduplicating and stressing the central theme that runs throughout.

The film frequently offers comforting absolutes: Allen and Farrow have never attended a Nazi rally; *The Changing Man* is an obvious fabrication; etc. At precisely the same time, the film repeatedly forces us to endure the trauma of the undecidable: Are we seeing the real Hitler? What footage is authentic? What is faked? Significantly, the elements that tend to provide the comfort of certainty are the elements that are undeniably fictional. The film repeatedly employs and announces its *fictional* elements so as to sustain the possibility of determining the authentic at the very moment it exposes the utter impossibility of such a task. In this sense, the film exposes and critiques the illusions of authenticity that define the documentary or realist mode while simultaneously appealing to a type of Lacanian Real that necessarily effects the contours of its own effacement, or fictionalization. Just as Zelig's ability to pass signals the possibility and promise of an empathic breakdown of self and other, the film's ability to pass signals and even endorses a schizophrenic (or postmodern) breakdown of fact and fiction.[3] However, and regardless of his obvious commitment to the simulation before us, Allen never allows us to forget that *Zelig* is not a *real* documentary. Just as Allen's notoriety anchors the protean character he plays, the employment of sight gags and one-liners disrupts the film's ability (or ostensible desire) to pass *in full*. Consequently, the film cautions against a tendency toward ontological entropy and cultural schizophrenia, pointing toward a need to sustain categorical and ontological differences while simultaneously guarding against the dangers of clinging too rigidly to such differences: solipsism and totalitarian egotism. The film can thus be located on a literary trajectory that includes both Melville's "Bartleby" and Dick's *Androids*. Yet more so than either Melville or Dick, Allen stresses (by ostentatiously embracing) the necessity and the danger of the fictional supplement in any truly democratic effort to share the Real (self) *in truth*.

Consuming Anguish

Leonard Zelig is (as Bruno Bettelheim insists during one of the many contemporary interviews the film presents as authentic) "the ultimate conformist." While the film ultimately and unsurprisingly links this problem of conformity to the rise of fascism in Europe, Zelig's "disease" initially highlights the increasingly fickle demands of a rapidly growing consumer society. In one of the first scenes of the film, we get contemporary (color) footage of Susan Sontag telling us that "[Zelig] was *the* phenomenon of the twenties." A clip of Saul Bellow soon follows; he adds that "it is ironic to see how quickly he has faded from memory." Upbeat jazz music then kicks in and the narrator (over ostensibly archival footage of burlesque shows, dancing chorus girls, and lascivious speakeasies) tells us that "the year is 1928. America, enjoying a decade of unequaled prosperity, has gone wild. The Jazz Age it is called. The rhythms are syncopated. The morals are looser. The liquor is cheaper, when you can get it. It is a time of diverse heroes and madcap stunts, of speakeasies, and flamboyant parties."

It is, in other words, a time of ephemeral desires and fifteen-minute stars. We are told, after all, that the first record of Leonard Zelig can be found in the notebooks of F. Scott Fitzgerald, who (while at a party in Long Island) noticed "a curious little man." While he initially identifies the man as "an aristocrat, . . . extol[ling] the very rich . . . in an upper-class Boston accent," Fitzgerald is later "stunned to see the same man speaking with the kitchen help." He now has a "coarse" accent and presents himself as a democrat. In these introductory scenes, the "problem" of Zelig is neatly tied to the problem of a society artificially yet increasingly stratified along lines of wealth and privilege, lines that spread outward in all directions, demarcating a vast array of codified communities functioning as so many niche markets. While providing the illusion of choice and individuality, these communities (of race, of class, of culture) insist upon any number of fixed standards of identity. Yet, and as we saw in part I (while considering the problem of racial ambiguity), inclusion in any one of these communities invariably requires exclusion from another—*even as* the American democratic ideal espouses inclusion for all. Zelig thus displays "a personal trait in everybody's life" (Allen, *Allen on Allen* 141) insofar as he expresses the central anxiety of a society that has come to associate "inclusion" with marketability: the fear of being excluded, unmarketable, not worthy of consumption. As Zelig (while under hypnosis) tells Fletcher, "It's safe to be like the others . . . I want to be liked."

The irony, of course, is that when he is at his most "safe" and thus most marketable—when he is a fetishized personality capable of inspiring a dance craze (i.e., "the chameleon"), novelty clocks, games, and Hollywood films—his "existence is," as the narrator bemoans, "a nonexistence." He exists *only* as a commodity: he is "devoid of personality . . . a cipher, a nonperson, a performing freak." We see this ostensible loss of selfhood most obviously in those scenes after Zelig is taken into his half-sister's custody. Exploited as a type of sideshow act, Zelig's sole function is to exhibit his inexplicable "chameleonism"—his empathic and apparently autonomic response to those who surround him. Amid a group of Hasidic rabbis, Zelig instantly grows a beard and *payot*; in the presence of black jazz musicians, his skin darkens and his nose widens; among the French, he speaks passable French. People come from "all over the country"—and eventually the world—to see him "perform." Outside the farm of his sister's "dubious-looking lover," signs read "See the Living Chameleon" and "See Zelig Turn into You." And Zelig, being Zelig, "does not disappoint."[4] Thus Zelig's labor becomes the most alienating labor imaginable: he is repeatedly compelled to reenact his own self-effacement.

However, we should avoid the temptation to view the central irony here—that Zelig's fame and sense of communal acceptance comes at the cost of the self that seeks it—as simply or only a side effect of unfettered consumerism. While the film is obviously invested in a critique of commercial exploitation (including Allen's own), it ultimately ties that critique to a much larger (if more subtle) commentary on the ontological paradox that both defines and obstructs the American dream. This larger commentary is implicit in the narrator's claim that, at the height of his fame, Zelig is only a "cipher." When the narrator makes this observation, we are given footage of Zelig eating absently and alone at the end of a nondescript hallway. A person walks past the camera and thus Zelig, but this person is apparently unaware of Zelig. Moreover, the static nature of the shot suggests that the camera is idle, or without purpose; it has no particular subject. Without an audience, Zelig simply does not exist. He exists only in context; or rather, he *is* (only) context. He presents as a fiction only, a performance. What we get, then, is an inverse relationship between Zelig's stability as an individual and the rate at which he is consumed. America's desire to consume Zelig peaks the moment he (ostensibly) offers them nothing to consume. All they get is a reflection of themselves; as the sign promises, "See Zelig Turn *into You*" (my emphasis). Just as he lets his sister and her lover parade him across the country, Zelig allows America to *make of him* what they please. He resists offering anything of himself,[5] for he apparently has no self to offer. While this ability or willingness to dissolve in the face of the other is at first attractive to a majority of Americans, it is finally denounced as a symptom of terrifying corruption and immorality. This is hardly surprising. My desire to *be* Zelig—which is impossible to disentangle from my desire to see *Zelig become me*—surely signifies my own terrifying potential for transience, instability, moral corruption.

Without any signs of the "anguish" Sartre links to the "manifestation of freedom" (72), Zelig exposes and ostentatiously revels in the absence of essence (i.e., the "nothingness") that paradoxically makes identity possible; he is literarily and overtly "characterized by a constantly renewed obligation to remake the *Self* which designates the free being" (Sartre 72). For Sartre, of course, "Anguish ... is the recognition of a possibility as *my* possibility" (73). The problem (and what inexorably couples the experience of freedom with the feeling of anguish) is that "what I project as my future being is always nihilated and reduced to the rank of simple possibility because the future which I am remains out of my reach" (73). In other words, "Anguish is the fear of not finding myself at that [future] appointment [with my *true self*], of no longer even wishing to bring myself there" (73).⁶ Anguish is the feeling I experience upon discovering that my true self is imaginary, a lure always yet to come, a hallucinatory blip on the horizon, a mere *possibility*. Zelig displays no such anguish. His utterly empathic and passive selflessness suggests that he refuses to believe in or anticipate the possibility of a finally coherent or *immanent* self. It suggests that Zelig does not have what Lacan refers to as an "Ideal I," a fantasmatic reflection that I necessarily misrecognize as my essential and coherent self.⁷ Instead, he accepts and presents himself only as *possibility*. We might in fact read Zelig as Agamben reads Bartleby—as "pure, absolute potentiality" ("On Contingency" 254). Like Bartleby, Zelig confounds the theological (or essentialist) impulse "to drive all experience of possibility from the world" (248–49). At the very moment he promises freedom,⁸ the perpetual potential of the self, he threatens us with a "world in which nothing is compossible with anything else, where nothing 'exists rather than something'" (270).

The reflection Zelig's admirers initially hope to see in his transformations has a double resonance. On the one hand, such a reflection validates the satisfying possibility of effacing the other in favor of the self—the possibility of being victorious in the "life-and-death struggle" Hegel sees as prelude to a lord/bondsman dialectic (*Phenomenology* 114). My desire to impose such a reflection is a symptom of my egotism—the desire to confirm my sense of a concrete and absolute self capable of solipsistically determining the world. On the other hand, the very possibility of the reflection simultaneously implies my own instability or inconsistency, my own freedom (or potential) to *not* be me. This latter implication is precisely uncanny. In experiencing Zelig's transformations, I am necessarily confronted with the possibility that, if he can become me, I am not (nor will I ever be) truly my*self*. Thus, and while (or, perhaps, *because*) he displays none himself, Zelig inevitably provokes anguish in his audience: the response of the self when faced with its inability to be the imaginary ideal it pretends to be or hopes to become. At the same time, Zelig's willingness (or ability) to transform satisfies the egotism that defines the self's efforts to deny or repress this anguish, this freedom. Consequently, both Zelig (the man) and *Zelig* (the film) expose us (yet again) to America's profound conflict of desires: for both empathic fraternity and solipsistic selfhood. And, as do Melville and Dick, Allen suggests that either extreme must necessarily lead to the self's dissolution. The route of the chameleon can lead only to entropic ruin, the end of difference, the irresponsible abandonment of the self *in* the other. Yet the route of the egotist will largely lead to the same: the imposition of the one, solipsism, the totalitarian dream.

Empathy, Perversion, Fascism

This brings us back to the film's ostensible critique of consumer society, a critique that is ultimately and significantly paralleled by an equally vehement critique of fascism. By linking the problem of fascism's move to dominance in Europe with the problem of America's naïve acceptance of a market without restraint, the film entertains the possibility that neither one is the *cause* of Zelig's condition. Certainly, and as Irving Howe sagely quips in one of the film's interviews, Zelig's disease reflects "the nature of our civilization, the character of our times"; yet the film finally suggests that this "nature" and this "character" are merely the effects of an ontological crisis—a crisis that is inextricably linked to the frightening possibility of the self's utter and empathetic dissolution. Such a crisis transcends the various socioeconomic realities that expose and confirm it. Both fascism and capitalism are *effects* of the "disease" in question: the former sees the self overcoming its inherent lack and thus freedom by identifying absolutely with a fetishized authority; the latter sees the self "fixing" its terrifying potential via a process of identificatory consumption. While Zelig's version of the condition presents in an obvious and undeniable manner, the condition itself is in no way unusual. Zelig merely forces America to face the reality of a certain fundamental lack at the heart of *all* human identity. In this way, the film returns us (full circle) to the problem of passing.[9] As do the various problematic characters discussed in part I, Zelig threatens us with the possibility that our own apparently fixed identities are always also performances. America is certainly quick to embrace him as a spectacular gimmick, but the larger implications of his disease soon become impossible to accept or ignore. Just as essentialist groups like the Ku Klux Klan reject him as a "triple threat"—"a Jew who is able to transform himself into a negro or Indian"—America eventually and predictably comes to reject him as a potential catalyst for social instability and moral corruption. And his connection to a larger social anxiety (in America and on the continent) about the "transient" Jew becomes explicit. As a representative of the "Holy Family Christian Association" states (after Zelig is "cured" by Fletcher and it is revealed that he had multiple wives and fathered numerous children during his "chameleon" years), "America is a moral country. It is a God-fearing country. We don't condone scandals, scandals of fraud and polygamy. In keeping with a pure society, I say lynch[10] the little Hebe."

Zelig's chameleonism invokes the anti-Semitic fear of the "Jew" as a perpetual and dangerously unfixable "performer." As Iris Bruce notes (quoting

Derrida), "What is proper to the Jew is to have no property or essence. Jewish is not Jewish" (185). This pure potential represents the ultimate social fear (or desire): the impossibility of the coherent self. While this impossibility actually opens up the *possibility* of fraternal sympathy (as we see in Zelig's many transformations), it simultaneously suggests that such fraternity is not rooted in any essential bond, such as blood. Indeed, Žižek argues that "the 'Jew' is the means, for fascism, of taking into account, of representing its own impossibility: in its positive presence, it is only the embodiment of the ultimate impossibility of the totalitarian project—of its immanent limit.... [T]he 'Jew' is just the embodiment of a certain blockage—of the impossibility which prevents ... society from achieving its full identity as a closed homogenous totality" (*Sublime Object* 127). The "transient Jew" is to blame for society's impurity.[11] But, as Žižek is quick to note, the "Jew" (as source of social corruption) is actually and only "a paranoid construction" (126), a way of displacing a terrifying aspect I secretly know to be innate (to myself and my society) on to a potentially excisable (or consumable) other.

That Zelig does not suffer his "disease" alone is made most evident when the film gives us a glimpse at Fletcher's various efforts to treat him. She first manages to access the "real" Zelig by placing him under hypnosis. Once under, Zelig explains that he first began transforming after he was asked if he had read *Moby-Dick*. Zelig tells Fletcher that he "was ashamed to say [he] had never read it." Fletcher quickly interjects, "And you pretended?" In linking Zelig's much more spectacular transformations to such an innocuous event—one with which most viewers will likely empathize—the film suggests that Zelig's impulse (and ability) to conform largely mirrors our own. This suggestion becomes even more explicit when Fletcher finally decides to remove Zelig to a rural cabin (after, that is, the deaths of his sister and her lover leave him once again in the hands of the state). Here she sets up a not-so-hidden camera and begins her famous "White Room" sessions. While hypnosis continues to give her access to Zelig's ostensibly true self, she is unable to stop Zelig from becoming a psychoanalyst whenever he is not under hypnosis. During this time, she admits (in her diary) that "there is something very appealing about [Zelig]"; she also decides to "keep flexible, and play the situation by ear." And, indeed, in a remarkable display of chameleonesque "flexibility," she finally manages to "trick" Zelig. After asking "Dr. Zelig" if he could help her with a problem, she explains that she recently lied to a group of friends about having read *Moby-Dick*. She continues, stating that she "wants so badly to be liked, to be like other people." Clearly uncomfortable, Zelig points out that she's "a doctor [and] should know how to handle that." Fletcher's reply breaks Zelig completely: "I'm not an actual doctor. . . . I've been pretending to be a doctor to fit in with my friends. You see, *they're* doctors." The sudden inversion is apparently too much for Zelig, and he is forced to admit that he is not a doctor either, or anything else for that matter: "I'm nobody. I'm nothing. Catch me, I'm falling." From this point on, Fletcher builds Zelig's identity from the ground up. But we should be wary of overlooking the obvious here: Fletcher too is performing. Most obviously she is playing the role of Zelig, but this performance suggests (in turn) that even her role as a doctor is performed—or rather, that she is a *particular* kind of doctor *for* Zelig. Moreover, as Fletcher works to erect a finally coherent and stable Zelig, she (quite predictably) falls in love with *a* Zelig—a Zelig who has begun to express his own feelings of affection. Over footage of Fletcher smoking a cigarette, this love is confirmed by the voice of a contemporary-day Fletcher (whose interviews are cut into the documentary throughout): "I found that I had very strong feelings for him. I never thought I was attractive. I never had a real romance." Not coincidentally, the footage depicts a young Fletcher who appears as alone and as isolated as the Zelig we see (earlier) sitting alone and ignored at the end of an empty hallway. The composition of the two shots is in fact virtually identical. In both, the subject is positioned (inside) beside a glowing window segmented by vertical lines, or *bars*. Both subjects appear cut off from a larger social whole, unable to connect in any "real" sense. And if, in the former scene, Zelig is nothing but a "cipher," then (on some level) so too is Fletcher. Neither, it would seem, is capable of traversing the boundary between what is authentic and what is relationally performed, the effect of otherness.

In short, the film encourages us to entertain the possibility that Zelig's "disease" is omnipresent in America, that only via an act of "bad faith" can I hope to ignore my own display of symptoms. As Richard Wasson notes, the film repeatedly draws attention to the way in which its characters (like *or as* real historical personages) necessarily "[ape] the *gestes,* the motions, the facial expressions, the stances that conventionally signify power and authority" (83). The scene in which Fletcher draws attention to her own performance as a doctor is only the most obvious. But all such scenes highlight the way in which Zelig's "antics" have what Žižek would call a "perverse" effect on his American doctors and admirers: they expose and undermine the illusion of an essence to which we all necessarily cling. And significantly, as Žižek claims, "The position of the pervert is uncannily close to that of the analyst" (*Tarrying* 71), for the pervert (like the analyst, *like* Zelig), "literarily 'steals the kernel of our being,' the *object small a,* the secret treasure, *agalma,* what we consider most precious in ourselves, denouncing it as a mere semblance. Lacan defines the *object small a* as the fantasmatic 'stuff of the I,' as that which confers on the $, on the fissure in the symbolic order, on the ontological void that we call 'subject,' the ontological consistency of a 'person,' the semblance of a fullness of being . . .'" (48). It is perhaps hardly surprising, then, that Zelig (while in the role of analyst) compels Fletcher to denounce her identity *as analyst.* He even effectively exposes the entirety of the "White Room" sessions as fictional. Given his past transformations, his dramatic "breakdown" before Fletcher (whom he has finally convinced to "play along") can be read as just another performance, another transformation. Such a reading is encouraged when, during the first of their sessions, Zelig waves and smiles at the "hidden" camera.[12] By opening himself up to Fletcher's analysis (and, in turn, her eventual reconstruction of his identity), Zelig offers himself as the perfect object of her desire: a convalescing patient who is also a potential lover. At the same time, he exposes Fletcher (as he necessarily does everyone else) to the terrifying possibility that he is not the only one playing a role.

But Zelig only *plays* at being an analyst; given his endless and ultimately unethical play (in the "White Room" sessions and throughout), he is certainly more of a pervert than an analyst. Like the Lacanian analyst, who (according to Žižek) "functions as *objet a* for the analysand, . . . as a kind of blank screen onto which the analysand projects his or her fantasies . . . [,] the pervert's ultimate fantasy is to be a perfect servant of his other's (partner's) fantasies, to offer himself as an instrument of the *other's* Will-to-Enjoy" (*Tarrying* 71). However, "the pervert [only] confirms the subject's fantasy, whereas the analyst induces him or her to 'traverse' it, to gain a minimal distance toward it, by way of rendering visible the void (the lack in the Other) covered by the fantasy-scenario" (72). That said, and while he is markedly similar, Zelig is obviously not the pervert Žižek has in mind. His ostentatious transformations—his impossible flexibility— necessarily "confirms the other's fantasy" while also exposing that fantasy *as fantasy,* as performance, as fiction. At the same time, and unlike the Lacanian analyst—who helps us (as Žižek repeatedly implies) "to experience how this negative, disruptive power, menacing our identity is simultaneously a positive condition of it" (*Sublime Object* 176)—Zelig merely revels in and thus endorses dissolution, the entropic decay of society, the schizophrenic (á la postmodern) breakdown of self and other, essence and performance, reality and fiction. He is always in as much "bad faith" as those who abjectly fear him, for "the position of the masochist pervert is ultimately an attempt to elude . . . [the] uncertainty [which defines the subject], which is why it involves the loss of the status of the subject, i.e., a radical self-objectivization: the pervert *knows what he is for the Other,* since he posits himself as the object-instrument of the Other's *jouissance*" (Žižek, *Tarrying* 71). In other words, while Zelig certainly announces the traumatic yet essential uncertainty (or undecidability) of the self, he does so via a concerted effort to avoid facing that uncertainty. He thus provokes problematic responses. On the one hand, he encourages flight from ontological uncertainty via irresponsible and endless play, for (like the "pervert") his "universe is the universe of the pure symbolic order, of the signifier's game running its course, unencumbered by the Real of human finitude" (Žižek, *Ridiculous* 36). On the other hand, the threat implied by Zelig's ostentatious form of perversion compels deeper entrenchments of identity, the violent rejection of all that might expose the impossibility of finally apprehending myself.

The Fiction of the Real

Allen's film repeatedly implies that the opposed extremes of entropic empathy and abject egotism—implied (respectively) in the perverse performance of what the other desires and the sterile absolutism of bad faith—are responses to the same threat: the impossibility of "achieving my full identity with myself" (Žižek, *Sublime Object* 176). We see this convergence most obviously when Fletcher first presents her colleagues with an ostensibly "cured" Zelig. As contemporary-day Fletcher recalls, she was initially anxious about this first meeting; she "worried that if [Zelig] was with strong personalities he might lose his personality." Her fears, we learn, were unwarranted. The documentary presents us with footage of several professional-looking men exiting a car. As they are lead around the cabin grounds by Fletcher and Zelig, the narrator tells us that (initially) "Leonard Zelig seems calm and at ease. Despite the fact that he is surrounded by physicians, he does not turn into one." However, when "Dr. Henry Myerson comments innocently about the weather, saying that 'it is a nice day,' Zelig tells Dr. Myerson that he does not agree that it is a nice day. Dr. Myerson is taken aback at the firmness of Zelig's conviction. He points out that the sun is shining and that it is mild. Zelig, *trained* to voice his own personal feelings fearlessly, is too aggressive . . . and cannot brook any disagreement with his own views" (my emphasis). Over this narration, the footage continues to run. The group slowly travels away from the static camera; eventually, and in the distance, we see Zelig take off his jacket and push one of the doctors. Soon he is attacking the entire group with a rake. Apart from its obvious humor, the scene is remarkable on two accounts. (1) It suggests that, like his various chameleon identities, Zelig's "true" identity is determined solely by the other; it is "trained." (2) It suggests that Zelig's problem is not his chameleonism; it is, rather, a desperate need to avoid the perpetual uncertainty of who he is. The scene reinforces the film's overall suggestion that both the impulse toward empathic dissolution and the impulse toward egotistical solipsism function as an evasion of the self's *in*finite potential (to recall Levinas), an effort to circumvent the impossibility of realizing a finally immanent self. At the same time, and consequently, both extremes lead to the end of difference *as* the self's very possibility. In the former, the self is lost utterly to the other; in the latter, the self finally refuses any possible relation (to *an* other) that could provide it with definition. The two are merely different means to the same end. The former is marked by irresponsible passivity, while the latter is marked by violent aggression, the effort to consolidate the self by violently insisting that the other be (like) me *or not at all*.

In this way, the film neatly parallel's the problem of conformity with the problem of aggression. While the former problem is significantly more pronounced, the latter is highlighted in Zelig's violent response to opposition (in the scene just discussed) and then implicitly referenced during the climactic rally in Germany. In linking the aggression necessary to stabilize the ego with the rise of Nazism (and, by proxy, the impulse to efface the possibility of otherness), the film stresses both the necessity and the potential dangers of egotism *as aggression*. Or rather, it highlights the fact that aggression toward the other (out there) is a necessary and unavoidable response to the fundamental distance or boundary between me and the imaginary ideal to which I aspire. As Lacan puts it, largely echoing Hegel, "The structural effect of identification with the rival . . . can only be conceived of if the way is prepared for it by a primary identification that structures the subject as a rival with himself" ("Aggressivity" 22). Predicated upon a formative "mirror stage" and the self's first conception of its "Ideal I," aggression is essential to "a development of the ego" (25). And while we should not "delude . . . ourselves . . . into believing in some kind of pre-established harmony that would free of all aggressive induction in the subject the social conformisms made possible by the reduction of symptoms" (24), Allen's film finally suggests that the impulse toward extreme aggression and egotism is no less delusional (or unethical) than the impulse toward utter empathy and conformity. Since both are ultimately efforts to efface the otherness that necessarily corrupts (while making possible) the self, both must always also threaten the possibility of selfhood and therefore the possibility of taking a position with or against others.[13] Both are always a matter, in Levinasian terms, of evading my responsibility for the other. While these two extreme impulses—the impulse toward communal wholeness and fraternity and the impulse toward egotistical self-determination—largely define the American democratic ideal, both (at their respective extremes) shut down the possibility of a *relation* between the self and the other. Both function as a rejection of democracy, of any truly egalitarian state, of any true communion with the other.

This potential and problematic collapse of difference is reflected in the film's form. The film mirrors (while simultaneously mocking) the totalitarian or aesthetically aggressive efforts of a typical documentary film—the effort, that is, to *appear* as a coherent and unbiased presentation of the truth.[14] For instance, in the scenes leading up to the Munich rally (and the spectacular and impossible moment of reunion), the narrator tells us how Fletcher, after seeing a man who resembles Zelig (and thus Allen) in American newsreel footage of Hitler, traveled to Berlin and then Munich in search of her lost patient. In true documentary style this narration is presented in conjunction with ostensibly authentic images and archival footage—from what may or may not be stock footage of an ocean liner moving toward some distant horizon to images and footage of Hitler touring a Germany "deep in the throes of the depression." In these moments—when neither Farrow nor Allen appears on screen—the film could easily *pass* as a bona fide documentary. Were it not for the presence of Farrow and Allen in previous scenes, we would have little ground to question the authenticity of what we are shown. This ostensible authenticity is only further confirmed via the various contemporary interviews to which the film frequently cuts. Along with Saul Bellow, Susan Sontag, Irving Howe, and Bruno Bettelheim, we are shown clips from interviews with (among a host of others) John Morton Blum, Oswald Pohl, and Mike Geibell and Ted Bierbauer—the latter two being, as the film tells us, "formerly of the *New York Daily Mirror.*" Like any other documentary, *Zelig* gives us little reason to entertain the possibility that the people named in these interviews are not the people shown. At the same time, the film forces us to reassess the passive way in which we view such films. Once Allen appears on screen, few viewers are likely to mistake *Zelig* for a real documentary. And even if a viewer is not acutely familiar with Allen's famous face and acting style, the more ridiculous sight gags will undoubtedly demystify any residual confusion. At one point the narrator tells us that (in their initial effort to cure him), doctors subjected Zelig to an experimental drug. As a consequence, Zelig experiences "severe mood changes, and for several days will not come off the wall." This narration is paired with footage of Zelig literally walking up a hospital wall.

Such scenes have a troubling (because double) function. While they confirm our suspicion that the film is fake, they simultaneously mock our passive viewing habits, our willingness to yield to the authoritarian rhetoric of biographies and documentaries. The contemporary interviews are a case in point. In confirming our suspicion that the story presented is not real, the film forces us to question our initial assumptions about the interviewees presented. And the more we think we know, the more troubling the film becomes. If we recognize, say, Sontag and Bellow (who do, in fact, portray themselves), we must then make a guess about the rest: Is that really Howe? Or Bettelheim? Some viewers may even wonder if Bettelheim and Blum are real (whether they are being portrayed by actors or not). Few, after all, will buy the film's claim that Blum is the author of *Interpreting Zelig*; and interviewees like the contemporary Fletcher are obviously fictional. Alternatively, a viewer may know that an interviewee such as Oswald Pohl—a Nazi who rose to the rank of SS-Obergruppenführer—is "real" yet not know (or remember) that he was executed more than thirty years prior to the making of Allen's film. Simply put, the film works absurdly hard at trying *to pass* as an authentic documentary while simultaneously reminding us (at every step) that it is also pure fiction. In doing so, it exposes our typical passivity (or conformity) as viewers while simultaneously identifying the typical documentary as a largely unethical manipulation—what Kenneth Burke might call a dominant "terministic screen,"[15] or "mystification," a single presentation of the "facts" that encourages us to forget an almost infinite number of *other* "important ingredients of motivation" (*Rhetoric* 113).

And, of course, the film's refusal to pass (effectively) is paralleled by Zelig's (or, perhaps, Allen's) own inability to efface himself completely. For all his startling transformations—some of which we are shown on screen in "real time"—Zelig always remains (for both his and the film's audience) recognizably Zelig. This ineffaceable quality, this apparent symptom of an always residual yet immanent self, is a direct consequence of Allen's decision to play the title character. Not only are we given, as Stam and Shohat note, "a figure who is at once recognizably Woody Allen *and* recognizably black, Indian, Chinese" ("*Zelig* and Contemporary Theory" 213), we are given a type of cinematic "anchor." This anchor, as we've seen, has a dual function: it confirms the fictional nature of the film while simultaneously highlighting "the fundamental paradox of symbolic fictions [which necessarily] bring about the 'loss of reality' *and* provide the only possible access to reality" (Žižek, *Tarrying* 91). While confirming the absolute limit of the Real—neither Zelig nor Fletcher is real (since both are played by recognizable actors)—the film reminds us that such limits can only be approximated via fiction. What is "Real" (in any presentation of reality or in any performance of the self) is always only accessible via its fictional appearance. Žižek (again, following Hegel) puts it like this: "True, fictions are a semblance which occludes reality, but if we renounce fictions, reality itself dissolves" (91). The film, in this sense, critiques both the violent aggressivity of the absolutely true or egotistically dominant as well as its inverse: the postmodern confusion of fact and fiction, the schizophrenic collapse of self and other. At precisely the same time, it insists upon the necessity of both. While it is impossible to disentangle (finally) the self from the other, the real from the fictional, this impossibility does not imply that such distinctions do not exist. Nor does it imply that such distinctions should be abandoned. Like the film, I have a limit—a point at which I cannot be confused with any other.[16] To deny this limit is to refuse (like a chameleon) to gamble on an approximation of myself, to refuse risking a position *in relation*. Alternatively, to reject the possibility that my approximation of this limit is always necessarily a fiction is to require (like a dictator) the violent elimination of all that belies my fantasy.

At the Point Where We Began

Let's return to the climactic scene in "Munich." At the moment the ostensibly "real" Hitler turns to respond to the commotion caused by Zelig, the film cuts abruptly to a comparable scene from *The Changing Man*. In this scene, an actor playing Zelig stands vacantly near an obviously fictional Hitler speaking at an obviously fictional version of the rally. All around Zelig torches burn ominously; Hitler stands above him in an ostentatiously grand podium. As Fletcher waves from the audience, Zelig melodramatically "awakens" from his comatose state. Like the "real" Zelig, *this* Zelig soon waves back. Eventually and miraculously, Fletcher manages to move from the audience to the stage; there, she and Zelig embrace and kiss. The music (predictably) swells. Just as the music reaches its crescendo, the documentary cuts again—this time to contemporary-day Fletcher. She tells us that "it was nothing like it happened in the movie. When Leonard came down from the podium, they didn't know what to think." Then another cut, to an interview with Oswald Pohl. "We couldn't

THE CHAMELEON AND THE DICTATOR / 151

believe our eyes," Pohl states. "Hitler's speech was ruined." As they would in any documentary, these cuts function to buttress the apparent authenticity of the original footage. *This* is what Hollywood made of the event; but *this* is what "really" happened. While the parodic nature of the scene is surely humorous, its satiric function extends beyond the obvious. Even as they mock the conventions of the traditional documentary, the cuts "validate" the original footage. Of course Allen has obviously been "inserted," but (when juxtaposed against the Hollywood version) the footage of Hitler is obviously real. Right? The film lets us in on the joke at the very moment the joke is actually (and paradoxically) on us.

The point is this: the film (as a whole) quickly and overtly abandons its initial efforts to pass as an authentic documentary *even though* the majority of its individual scenes do not. As a result, Allen confirms the fictional nature of his film while stressing the impossibility of sustaining a clear distinction between what is real and what is not. Or, inversely, Allen insists upon a "Real" that necessarily limits *even as it is inevitably obscured by* its fictional approximation. The only thing that provides access to the Real—or rather, the only thing that ensures the possibility of the self—is the very thing that corrupts it, that leaves it always still to come. Only through fiction can the documentary present reality; only through performance can I *be* myself. It is the paradoxical absence of presence (of truth, of identity, of the Real, etc.) that makes the very thought of presence possible. I cannot know myself unless "I" am separated from "myself." To be myself (finally) *being myself* is to succumb to the death drive, "to return to the quiescence of the inorganic world" (Freud, *Beyond* 62)—or, in Hegelian terms, "the calm of simple universality" (*Phenomenology* 270). It is to cease being (conscious of) oneself, to *be* (finally) the Sartrean "in-itself," to *be* "like a rock." Or as Žižek puts it (quoting Wagner's *Parsifal*), "only the spear that smote you / can heal your wound" (*Tarrying* 92). And how else might we account for *Zelig*'s strange conclusion?

After Pohl laments the fact that Zelig "ruined" Hitler's speech, he explains that the "SS wanted to grab Zelig. But if they would have grabbed him, they probably would have tortured him or maybe even shot him. So in the confusion, Fletcher and Zelig got out the building and through a side door. They grabbed a car that sped away; and the car, and the SS after them, shot them . . ." At just this point—the point when Pohl's narrative is at its most absurd and most obviously at odds with Fletcher's claim that "it was nothing like that happened in the movie"—the film cuts to "rare German newsreel footage." This footage shows two figures (who may or may not be Fletcher and Zelig) getting into a German biplane and flying off. Contemporary-day Fletcher then tells us how (as a trained pilot) she managed to fly out of the German airfield but was too frightened to maintain her composure: "Something happened. I was frightened. I lost control. We went into a dive. Leonard was so terrified that he changed his personality. And before my eyes, because I was a pilot, he turned into one too." Then, over footage of a particularly acrobatic biplane, the narrator concludes the story: "Zelig, who had never flown before in his life, not only escapes the German pilots, but sets a record for flying nonstop across the Atlantic upside down."

In the end, Zelig returns to America a hero. But is he "cured"? Has he finally become *himself*? The answer is, apparently, yes *and* no. In the final frames of the film—and after we see Zelig and Fletcher happily married—we are provided (in typical documentary fashion) with a concluding intertitle. The text informs us that "Zelig's episodes of character change grew less and less frequent and eventually his malady disappeared altogether." There is a certain ambiguity to this claim; we are not told when or why his malady disappeared. The only thing we know with certainty is that it is gone when he dies. It's thus of some significance that he tells doctors on his "deathbed . . . [that] the only annoying thing about dying was that he had just begun reading *Moby Dick* and wanted to see how it came out." The implicit suggestion is that, even at the moment of death, Zelig's identity continues to be removed from (and thus *continually redefined by*) an anterior possibility of selfhood. It is, after all, the expectation that he had read *Moby-Dick* that initiated his dramatic transformations in the first place. In this sense, the final intertitle subtly recalls the short speech Zelig makes upon his heroic return to New York: "I've never flown before in my life. And it shows exactly what you can do if you're a total psychotic." Or rather, the intertitle confirms Saul Bellow's final assessment of the Zelig phenomenon: "Oh, the thing was paradoxical, because what enabled him to perform this astounding feat was his ability to transform himself. Therefore his sickness was also at the root of his salvation. And I think it is interesting to view the thing that way, that it was his very disorder that made a hero of him." If his transformations are indeed at "the root of his salvation"—if, in fact, and as the film ultimately seems to suggest, his "being" is utterly contingent upon a process of perpetual becoming—then we must assume that his "malady disappeared" only and necessarily in death.

That said, we should note that Zelig's final speech parallels an earlier speech—one which he makes immediately after Fletcher "cures" him (and before he flees to Germany). Speaking to the "kids" of America, Zelig extols the virtues of individualism: "Kids, you got to be yourself. You know you can't act like anybody else just because you think they have all the answers and you don't. You have to be your own man and learn to speak up and say what's on your mind. Now maybe they're not free to do that in foreign countries, but that's the American way." Zelig appears to be at his most naïve during this speech—and (paradoxically) at his most conformist. But just as the film refuses to resolve the tension between what is real and what is not (even as it continually highlights the fact that there *is* a difference), it also refuses to sustain a clear distinction between the individualism extolled in the first speech and the psychosis endorsed in the latter. The film never denies the possibility of the individual or the need for faith in that possibility. Zelig's metonymic conformity to Nazi ideology is proof enough of the film's appeal to individualism. However, the film also finally suggests that "psychosis" is the necessary and unavoidable pharmakon or supplement of the individual, of a being that is finally and *indivisibly* itself. In other words, and in the light of Derrida's early discussions of the pharmakon, psychosis in *Zelig* is both the cure and the disease, the very thing that makes possible what it necessarily forbids, that which corrupts my always *plastic* identity *so as* to give it shape (like the frame that gives a picture form).

The ethics of the film are not tied to the depiction or possibility of a finally cured or *fixed* Zelig, nor are they tied to the depiction or possibility of a man who is no one *and* everyone. They are, instead, to be found in Zelig's subtle move from a state of utter perversion to a state of anchored performance—at the point, that is, when Zelig seems capable of gambling on a *true* self while simultaneously accepting the fact that any such self can only be known or communicated via its (fictional) performance. At precisely this point, Zelig offers *without imposing* himself. It is tempting to add here that this is exactly what Allen seems intent on doing again and again in his films; he repeatedly *narrates* a public and largely consistent self while simultaneously maintaining the suggestion that his true self is never (and can never be) present. His more recent use of actors who perform their parts as if they are him is, perhaps, a telling sign of his careful and ethical negotiation of the public and the private, the fictional and the Real. (In the following chapters we will look at how a number of other American artists have attempted similar negotiations.) But what we need to note here is that *Zelig* endorses the type of democratic ethics that Derrida articulates long before he finally shifts his attention formally to issues of friendship and cosmopolitanism. In "Plato's Pharmacy"—or, more specifically, in the preface to his sustained discussion of the pharmakon, and while stressing the ethics of "reading"—Derrida insists that "the same foolishness, the same sterility, obtains in the 'not serious' as in the 'serious'" (64). Such a claim maps neatly onto Derrida's much later reapplication of an apocryphal quote from Aristotle: "O friends, there is no friend."[17] The suggestion in either is that the possibility of communication, the possibility of sharing the self or relating with the other, entails both commitment and play, *a gamble* that must simultaneously and necessarily hollow itself out. This gamble is precisely what *Zelig* (more so than either Melville's "Bartleby" or Dick's *Androids*) finally endorses. It is also the gamble we identified (in part I) as the mark of a distinctly *ethical* modernism. At the moment I present myself (like reality in a documentary) *in all seriousness*—at the moment I present myself *and* the other as absolute—I reject the possibility of a relation with, and an understanding of, that which is *not* me. I refuse *the risk* of confusing myself and the other; like Bartleby, I am friend to no one. Yet when I play the perverse fool, the constant performer, the empath and professed friend to all, I avoid making any commitment to what is potentially true. And without a commitment to the truth (of myself or the other), I am nothing like a friend.

Allen's solution to this dilemma is close (if not precisely equitable) to the cold and cruel justice Žižek valorizes. Such justice is an outright rejection of a Christian model of love, a model that sees the subject necessarily excluding all who cannot be recognized and loved "as thyself." The problem, as we saw in the preceding chapter, is that this effort to refuse (utterly) the "lure" of the face sanctions a certain irresponsibility, justifying an outright refusal to make oneself known, or accessible. It seems quite likely that (if we return to Derrida) a person who practices such justice might, "through 'methodological prudence,' 'norms of objectivity,' or 'safeguards of knowledge' . . . refrain from committing anything of himself" ("Pharmacy" 64). It is precisely this lack of "commitment" that *Zelig* cautions against, *just as* it cautions against the violence and the irresponsibility implicit in any effort to "love thy neighbor as thyself." The film suggests that we can only deal ethically with each other, that we can only be truly democratic, if an effort is made to *love* the other, to offer the self as distinct, to be "true." But such an effort is only possible via a performative act or fictional construct that necessarily implies its failure. In depicting Zelig's "disease" via an overt parody of the comforting yet false transparency of the documentary mode, Allen's film returns us to the possibility (touched upon in part I) of identifying and sustaining a form of narrative ethics. The task of the following chapters will be to delineate this form as fully as possible—that is, a form of narrative *giving* that openly negotiates the endless responsibility of literary invention, the ethical trauma of sustaining a *true* self that can only be known or related via the supplement, or frame, of discourse. It is from this trauma that, as *Zelig* suggests, both the egotist and the empath, the dictator and the chameleon, hope (melancholically) to escape. Surely this is why Zelig is far less troubling at his most perverse (when he is ultimately offering America a way out of this traumatic ordeal) than he is when he is neither "cured" nor "sick," neither purely real nor merely performed. This is when he is promptly and necessarily forgotten, promptly and necessarily repressed. This is when (if we can borrow Saul Bellow's phrasing in the film), he truly "touch[es] a nerve in people, perhaps in a way which they would prefer not to be touched."

PART III

BEING GIVEN

And since each of us, every one else, each other is infinitely other in its absolute singularity, inaccessible, solitary, transcendent, nonmanifest, originarily nonpresent to my ego . . . , then what can be said about Abraham's relation to God can be said about my relation without relation to every other (one) as every (bit) other [tout autre comme tout autre], in particular my relation to my neighbour or my loved ones who are as inaccessible to me, as secret, and as transcendent as Jahweh. Every other (in the sense of each other) is wholly other (absolutely other).

—JACQUES DERRIDA, *THE GIFT OF DEATH*

7 / The Autonarratives of Ernest Hemingway (and Others)

> *Now you must provide some answers*
> *For what you sell has not been received*
> —BOB DYLAN, "NOTHING WAS DELIVERED"

Autobiographical Touches

Could we not bring together (if not, on some level, summarize) the previous six chapters via a single question: If love entails touching—if love *is* touching—how might we effectively touch the other while giving (in turn) the self to be touched? The very question returns us to the paradox lurking at the heart of America's melancholic dream: that both the self and the other must remain (*by remaining at a distance*) in the moment of touching. Taken in its *most* stereotypically Christian sense, it is impossible to "love thy neighbor as thyself." No community could ever commune so purely, not even a community of the self—not, anyway, if any*one* were to remain as witness. As we saw in chapter 5, this is precisely the paradox that justifies Žižek's efforts to locate in the Judeo-Christian edict a gesture of enmity, an act of violence that privileges the law (and justice) over the imposition of imaginary understanding: "When the Old Testament enjoins you to love and respect your neighbor, this does not refer to your imaginary *semblable*/double, but to the neighbor qua traumatic Thing... Judaism opens up a tradition in which an alien traumatic kernel forever persists in my Neighbor—the Neighbor remains an inert, impenetrable, enigmatic presence that hystericizes me" ("Neighbors" 140–41). For this reason "the Jewish commandment which prohibits images of God is the obverse of the statement that relating to one's neighbor is the *only* terrain of religious practice, of where the divine dimension is present in our lives" (141). While we might take this to mean that Christianity—with its own version (or repetition) of "love thy neighbor"—begins to slip (backward) into a dependence upon the image or face of God, Žižek insist (à la Hegel) that Christianity finally sublates the absolute unknowability of God in Judaism by "asserting the identity of God and man—or, as it is said in John 4:12: 'No man has ever seen God; if we love one another, God abides in us and his love is perfected in us'" (141). "Love," in other words (and as Žižek reminds us), "*is* divine"—or, better, love is only ever *just* or *true* when it is love *of the divine*. But it is only the neighbor, and *never* God, who is here to be loved; God is discovered as—and *only as*—the divine monstrosity of the neighbor. If we love the neighbor truly, then we love God. In pointing us toward such a possibility, Žižek comes as close as he dares to a full understanding of the *in*finite in Levinas and, thus, the idea of "God in me" (Levinas, "God and Philosophy" 63). Žižek, after all, clarifies his central point by turning to a line from Levinas's *Difficult Freedom*: "Nothing is more opposed to a relation with the face [or an image of the other] than 'contact' with the Irrational and mystery" ("Neighbors" 141). But such a line does not imply, as Žižek seems to assume, that the face and the Irrational are mutually exclusive. It implies (instead)—especially when read alongside much of Levinas's other work—that the neighbor is *here* (to be loved) because the neighbor, unlike God (*sensu stricto*), *has a* face. And certainly no commandment prohibits the image of the neighbor. But Žižek must overlook the implications of such tacit permission if he is to arrive at his "radical" conclusion—that only the violent imposition of symbolic law can effectually lead us to an ethical encounter with the neighbor's faceless (and therefore divine) monstrosity.

In his effort to privilege the faceless and the monstrous, Žižek loses sight of the ethical necessity of the face-to-face encounter and the "imaginary lure" of identity. Nevertheless, as we've seen, we must take as seriously as possible his effort to reaffirm the necessity of a certain "ethical violence"—"the violent gesture of discarding, of establishing a difference, of drawing a line of separation" (Žižek, "Neighbors" 186). Such violence, for Žižek, paradoxically ensures the survival of the divine self or radically other. We lose ourselves the moment we assume that some *radical* act of "nonalienated spontaneity, self-expression, [or] self-realization" can free us from those "ethical injunctions that 'terrorize' us with the brutal imposition of their universality" (135). There is no autonomy except in the negative space delineated by the failures of the symbolic order—an assertion that certainly echoes Derrida's "Economimesis." Like Derrida, Žižek presents the fallacy of self-expression as the assumption that what is expressed can escape a certain necessary deficit, a certain abject remainder of disgust.[1] Žižek counters this fallacy—the fallacy of displaying *and then conflating with reality* "one's imaginary 'inner life'" (135n3)—by insisting that, "in true art, the artist has to undergo a radical *self*-objectivization[;] he has to die *in and for himself*, turn into a kind of living dead" (135). Rather than complaining about—and, in turn, trying to evade via endless acts of self-display (e.g., in "memoirs," on social media and reality TV, etc.)—the "violence" of the Other, the violence of imposed categories and law, we must undergo a "pitiless self-censorship of ourselves" (135). Only by submitting to such violence do I manage, paradoxically, to preserve (and even bear witness to) "the 'inner Thing' that haunts and drives" (135n3) me. That Thing is left to remain as the *negative* of law and of sense—of, that is, the very mediations that falsely define me and organize my world, the very mediations into which I am unwillingly yet necessarily "thrown" (140). I preserve my monstrous "potential" (if we recall Agamben) as an abjectionable nonobject of pure disgust, that which the Other is never given to consume: "Insofar as the subject occupies the place of the lack in the Other (symbolic order), it can perform separation (the operation which is the opposite of alienation), and suspend the reign of the big Other, in other words, to separate itself from it" (137). Ethics come into play when I perform this act while accepting the same limitation and vulnerability in the other: I cannot imagine away—that is, *make an image of*—the Thingness of my neighbor (whose reality, or identity, I nevertheless accept as only ever the mere imposition of law). Such a response to the other entails "fundamental forgiveness"; I cannot give so I cannot *reasonably expect* "a full answer to 'who are you?'" (138). To love *as thyself* is therefore to love what is traumatically absent.

If we wish to love—and by loving, touch—we must never reach out. Or rather, and if we are to accept Žižek at his extreme, silence becomes the sine qua non of ethics: an utter withdrawal, a "pitiless censorship," a Bartleby-like resistance to statements of motivation. Only by relating according to the "blind" parameters of the law can we relate ethically—for "this primordial exposure/dependency opens up the properly ethical relation of individuals who accept and respect each other's vulnerability and limitation" (Žižek, "Neighbors" 138). The "false" alternative is to assume (as the typically Foucaultian Butler does) that the "norms [of the Other] rule only insofar as they are practiced by subjects, and [that] the subject [can therefore] dispose[] . . . of a minimum of freedom to arrange itself with these norms, to subvert them, to (re)inscribe them in different modes, and so on" (137). But to assume this is to risk losing the *divine* lack of self to the constitutive framework of the Other—or even to slip into another form of postmodern perversity. Indeed, Žižek convincingly links such assumptions to popular forms of "psychotherapy" and the current tendency toward historical revisionism. We are increasingly encouraged to "rewrite" our stories as we see fit: childhood abuse is transformed into a memory of support and kindness; the precolonial is depicted as a lost utopia; Han Solo suddenly shoots second. Žižek's point is this: "What disappears in this total availability of the past to its subsequent retroactive rewriting are not primarily the 'hard facts,' but the Real of a traumatic encounter whose structuring role in the subject's psychic economy forever resists its symbolic rewriting" (136). The paradox is that every time we "imagine" ourselves as anterior to the symbolic we lose sight of what is Real(ly) outside the symbolic; and what we "imagine" necessarily gets lost within an economy of symbolic (re)writing, or sense making—that is, the language or desire of the Other. However, what Žižek fails to account for is the way in which an active engagement in "rewriting" the self can function, in its own way, as a radically "'suicidal' gesture" (140). Is this not Allen's point in *Zelig*? When I change my story at every turn, when I take on one face moments after appearing in another, I *also* say "No! to any positive element that I encounter" (140); I *also* "'cleanse the plate,' draw a line, exempt myself, step out of the symbolic" (140). What is the difference between saying "No!" to everything and saying "Yes" to everything? If the latter must be dismissed as feckless perversity, must we not strive to avoid the former as well? Are we not, in other words, back at the ethical Scylla and Charybdis of silence and cacophony, hegemony and perversity, egotism and empathy?

If we are to navigate through these waters, we will need to take a gamble on the face. We must risk communicating the imaginary. Surely we cannot preserve the Real by simply forgoing the imaginary. Lacan certainly never suggests that a "cleans[ing]" of the "imaginary lure" is possible—nor, for that matter, does Hegel (who holds to the necessity of enduring "the strenuous effort of the Notion" [*Phenomenology* 35]).[2] And is not the imaginary inherently tied to the uncanny, to the experience of a certain traumatic rupture? As we have seen, the uncanny can be taken as a profoundly ethical experience—*insofar as* it can be understood as the experience of recognizing or imposing a substitution (i.e., seeing a "*semblable/double*") while *simultaneously* being exposed to that traumatic Thing that can never be substituted. If this is indeed the case, surely we must risk (as Butler insists) an account of ourselves; and we must risk taking seriously the accounts of others. But this does not mean we should or must confuse our (re)writings with what is necessarily absent in them. Can a person *not* imagine and in turn speak of their Real childhood abuse in a way that preserves, and even gestures toward, its profoundly absent truth? Have we not already been witness, in foregoing chapters, to certain efficacious efforts to account for the self via acts of overt fictionality and therefore erasure?[3] Such efforts begin to proliferate in the modern era, when, as Caughie argues (and as we saw in chapter 3), "writing [becomes] a matter of effacing—not expressing—the self" (404). While Caughie would like to hold this "ethics of concealment" in direct opposition to "getting personal, breaking silence, coming out" (404), we have already seen that an act of truly *ethical* (or efficacious) concealment must entail a paradoxical (because sincere) commitment to *reveal* the self. We saw this in those texts that suggest the possibility of maintaining an "ethics of concealment" while (or by) "getting personal." Is this not, on some level, what Johnson is up to in his *Autobiography*? Or what Jolson is up to in *The Jazz Singer*? Or Larsen in *Passing*? Each of these texts offers us a fictional version of its author or star via narratives that grapple with the problem of identity and ethical self-expression in America. In the latter—the most "modernist" of the three—the potential of self-effacement clearly animates the plot even as its dangers are exposed and navigated via the rhetorical moves Larsen employs. We might say, too, that Melville (in "Bartleby") and Allen (in *Zelig*) do something similar—namely, employ a fictional narrative so as to expose *as absent* a central truth of the self. The problem is that, in these texts, little is actually risked in terms of self-exposure—in terms of gambling on a certain (imaginary) "ideal I." The literary scholar might tease out acts of autobiography and expressions of autobiographical ethics, but the texts are given merely as "fictions." While they have much to say and teach about an ethical relation to the intrusive other, they only marginally *put into practice* such an engagement.

Language of the Self

The line we are attempting to draw now (and in light of our consideration of the texts just mentioned) is the line that runs somewhere between those accounts of the self that would assume the possibility of some "New Age Gnostic . . . self-realization or self-fulfillment" (Žižek, "Neighbors" 140) or (via an act of outright negativity *or* perversely capricious acceptance) the futility of expressing anything anterior to the mandates of the Other. What immediately comes to mind are those texts that present themselves as autobiographies while strategically and *overtly* stretching the bounds of their veritability. Not surprisingly, one of the first and most overt examples of such writing in America appears in the modern era—in Henry Miller's *Tropic of Cancer* (1934). The novel/memoir openly plays with the line between the self/author and its fictional construction. Miller, in fact, via the novel's epigraph, suggests that he is making good on an Emersonian prophecy: "These [romantic and predictable] novels will give way, by and by, to diaries or autobiographies—captivating books, if only a man knew how to choose among what he calls his experiences that which is really his experience, and how to record truth truly."[4] Miller seems to take up Emerson's "challenge" by refusing to choose, by making truth itself a matter or consequence of distortion—of, that is, heteroglot polyphony. As Anaïs Nin asserts in her 1934 preface to the novel/memoir, Miller "restore[s] our appetite for fundamental realities . . . [by engaging] a continual oscillation between extremes, with bare sketches that taste like brass and leave the full flavor of emptiness" (xxxi). What would Žižek think of this? Is Miller just some proto–New Age gnostic? On the one hand, it is difficult (if not absurd) to associate Henry Miller with John Gray (the author of *Men Are from Mars, Women Are from Venus* and the object of much Žižekian ridicule in the essay we've been discussing). On the other, Miller is very much caught up in modernist nostalgia—the desire to get beyond the restrictions of language and to speak truly. This is why, as Nin gleans, *Tropic of Cancer* is so concerned with the body and with acts of pleasure and pain. Miller "can't get it out of [his] mind what a discrepancy there is between ideas and living. A permanent dislocation, though we try to cover the two with a bright awning. And it won't go. Ideas have to be wedded to action; if there is no sex, no vitality in them, there is no action. . . . Ideas are related to living: liver ideas, kidney ideas, interstitial ideas, etc." (Miller 242). But Miller's effort "to get off the gold standard of literature" (243) leads him into dangerous territory—insofar, that is, as it risks running afoul of the violent ethics Žižek mandates. As James Decker puts it, Miller "strives to maintain a unity between art and artist and to recreate *the aura of immediate experience*" (75; my emphasis). So as to circumvent "the preimposed conventions and rules" of traditional narrative forms, Miller deploys "interior monologues to create a more transparent relationship between author and narrator . . . [and to] reveal[] . . . that the supraself[5] wants a text composed of blood rather than abstractions" (75).

In celebrating Miller's technical achievement, Decker highlights (also) Miller's tendency to stumble across the ethical limits of modern polyphony, or "novelistic discourse." Rather than narrating an "inner Thing" that is only ever "given" *in absentia*, Miller tends to align a distortion of language/symbolic law with the Thing that traumatically refuses it. He attempts, in other words, to provide an *image* of disgust. Such a narrative act is surely akin to Hegel's "symbolic art"—art that struggles to locate the divine in grotesque distortions of reality. Unable to find its satisfactory articulation in any of the forms to which it is ascribed, "the Idea [comes to] exaggerate[] natural shapes and the phenomena of reality itself into indefiniteness and extravagance; it staggers round in them, it bubbles and ferments in them, does violence to them, distorts and stretches them unnaturally.... For the Idea is here still more or less indeterminate and unshapable" (Hegel, *Aesthetics* 76). The extreme risk of these distorted forms is, obviously, a type of cacophony, or utter incomprehensibility, in which the mode of representation is brought into jarring "harmony" with an unknowable Thing. But even a more manageable or understandable modality of the polyphonic—what Kant might associate with "poetic genius"[6]—can lack ethical efficacy *insofar* as it tends to be invested with the claim that it *is* a finally *natural* mimetic act. And so (again) "What disappears ... [is a] Real ... whose structuring role in the subject's psychic economy forever resists its symbolic rewriting" (Žižek, "Neighbors" 136). We are given a mere image of God that necessarily eviscerates *any trace of the divine*. If, then, we are to write or to speak the *divine* self—as an act of ethical or democratic violence—a more naïve form of narrative is perhaps necessary, one that would not depend, because *it would not need to depend*, on overt acts of linguistic dissolution or obfuscation. Such acts, after all, tend merely to expose a law of (mimetic) diminishing returns, the futility of struggling toward anything *like* a synthesis of what cannot be said and what can. But synthesis is not what is needed here, nor is a perversely postmodern insistence upon unconstrained simulation. What is needed is an act of sublation—a narrative form that sublates (i.e., negates so as to hold to) the unsaid *in* the said, that (re)presents the divine in the portraiture of its absence.

But let's be clear: this is not to suggest that modern novelistic practice is simply incapable of such sublation (for at its most efficacious it surely opens us to its possibility); it is to suggest, rather, that the order of the ethical day is to sustain the *infinite* or divinely unknowable in or *through* its formal articulations—and *not* to struggle for synthesis via the overwhelming richness of the polyphonic text. To do so would necessitate engaging in (what Tilottama Rajan calls) "autonarrative" forms—those forms of autobiography that make overt *yet overtly sincere* gestures toward the necessity of self-construction.[7] Miller's *Tropic of Cancer* could be defined as such; the problem is that Miller often deploys autonarrative techniques so as to overcome the always "asymptotical"[8] relationship between an "imaginary lure" (or inner self) and its apprehensibility *by* the Other. At its most radically ethical, though, an autonarrative would gamble on a sincere and relatable face (or point of engaged and responsible contact) while sustaining and touching upon an *in*finite plasticity that utterly escapes ossification in *any* given form. Autonarratives thus have the *potential* to sublate the self—if, that is, they engage in or enact a type of neoromantic "autoplasticity." The precise distinction between these two terms ("autonarrative" and "autoplasticity") will become clearer as we go—especially when, in the following chapters, we begin to follow more rigorously a distinctly Hegelian thread. This thread will lead us, also, to Hegel's understanding of romantic art as a negation of symbolic art's negation in classical sculpture—that is, romantic art *as* "a negation of the negation." But let's remain focused, for now, on the potential and the potential dangers of the simply auto*narrative* form. And because it largely moves between a modern desire to relocate the (authentic) self in linguistic innovation and a postmodern tendency to refuse the possibility of a self *anterior to* its linguistic construction, Hemingway's posthumously published memoir, *A Moveable Feast* (1964), is a particularly useful point of reference.

The Moveable Self

Rajan defines "autonarration" as "a larger (post)romantic intergenre that . . . locates ideology within a fictional rewriting of personal experience" (149). The goal of autonarrative is therefore to perform "the transposition of personal experience into fiction [that] recognizes . . . experience as discursively constructed" (150). While Rajan uses an overtly fictional text as her example—Mary Hays's *Memoirs of Emma Courtney* (which we might associate more readily with *fictional* American texts like Larsen's *Passing* or Johnson's *Autobiography*)—her definition of autonarration becomes all the more salient (in our current discussion of American ethics, love, and democratic relations) if we apply it to those texts that fully admit to an autobiographical impulse. We might say tentatively that the more overtly or irresponsibly fictional an autonarrative becomes the less ethical or *loving* it can be (as, that is, an expression of the self)—*even if,* and at the same time, the opposite (i.e., a melancholic intimation of autobiographical authenticity) must be viewed as no less inimical.

What is then striking about Hemingway's memoir—as an effort to recount his time as an expatriate in Paris during the bohemian 1920s—is its willingness to present as a traditional autobiography (narrated by a symbolically coherent and verifiable "I") while simultaneously opening up the possibility that it "may be," as Hemingway asserts in the preface, "regarded as fiction."[9] Faced with Hemingway's often subtle tendency to confuse the fictional with the verifiably "real," critics have typically struggled to reestablish a clear boundary between what is true and what is not, as if the task were simply to know when, why, and to what extent Hemingway is lying.[10] If, though, we are to look past the face Hemingway gives (and in turn accept his ostensible invitation to "love" the monstrosity that "glimmers through the fissures"), we must avoid succumbing to a hysterical fixation on the "problem" of historical validity—or what Žižek calls the "hard facts." The accuracy of Hemingway's account of the past is surely less significant than the efficacy of his effort (via that account) to delimit the constitutive absence at its heart—the *infinite* space carved out for an "I" *prior to its narration*. By gesturing toward its own inaccuracies (while nevertheless grounding those inaccuracies as potentially telling renditions of the past), Hemingway's text often functions as a willful reconstruction of self that intimates a desire for, yet the impossibility of, complete self-recognition. It announces the fact that the self is only ever *at a distance*, only ever in its moment of com-pearance, that it *is* always in a process of *notional* re-formation. The ethical efficacy of Hemingway's autonarrative is thus tied to its willingness to gamble on a coherent and verifiable self while simultaneously resisting bad faith, or the possibility that a subject can ever be aligned with its "imaginary lure."

More specifically, Hemingway's claim (in the preface) that the work "may be regarded as fiction" is justified, most obviously, whenever the text draws our attention to its own literariness, or narrative "reconstructedness." Consider Hemingway's first "sketch" of, and conversation with, Gertrude Stein (in the chapter "Miss Stein Instructs"). The scene borders on the absurd. After explaining that he had allowed Stein to read one of his short stories, "Up in Michigan," Hemingway tells us that she found it to be "good" but *"inaccrochable"* (15). He then proceeds to record *verbatim* (for dialogue in A Moveable Feast is always presented, à la traditional autobiography, verbatim) Stein's diatribe on "inaccrochable work" and his own defense of his apparent "inaccrochability":

> "But you don't get the point at all," she said. "You mustn't write anything that is *inaccrochable*. There is no point in it. It's wrong and it's silly."
>
> She herself wanted to be published in the *Atlantic Monthly,* she told me, and she would be. She told me that I was not a good

enough writer to be published there or in the *Saturday Evening Post* but that I might be some new sort of writer in my own way but the first thing to remember was not to write stories that were *inaccrochable*. I did not argue about this nor try to explain again what I was trying to do about conversation. (15)

Even more than do the obviously contrived moments of dialogue that precede and follow it, this episode forces the reader to recognize the fact that conversation in *A Moveable Feast* precisely mirrors what Hemingway "was trying to do about conversation." While representing Stein as ridiculously obtuse and stubborn, this passage self-reflexively draws attention to the fact that *A Moveable Feast* is, itself, the work of a fiction writer, a writer whose main goal is to avoid "writ[ing] elaborately, or like someone introducing or presenting something" (12). It is somewhat difficult to imagine that Gertrude Stein spoke in the same staccato fashion as every other character in a Hemingway novel: "It's good" (15); "But it is *inaccrochable*" (15); "It's wrong and it's silly" (15); etc. Unlike Miller, Hemingway makes no attempt to *seem* immediate or, for that matter, honest. He does not dwell on, or attempt to deny, the impossibility of apprehending the past in full; he simply embraces the necessity of fictional reconstruction, representing his memoir as the type of text the critic (Hal) in a later chapter ("Birth of a New School") would consider to be "too stark, too stripped, too lean, too sinewy" (96). Coupled with the episodic and fragmentary nature of the text—the memoir/novel consists of a series of "sketches" or temporally disconnected chapters[11]—the undeniably "Hemingwayesque" style makes it almost impossible to approach the text as an accurate, or nonfictional, depiction of the "Paris movement." Faced with its ostentatious style and disorienting form, a reader is compelled to accept the possibility that *everything* must be questioned, from the annoying and pretentious behavior of Ford Madox Ford to Fitzgerald's apparent naïveté about the size of his penis.

Following Jill Rubenstein, we might then say that Hemingway largely overcomes "the unavoidable lack of detachment and objectivity" implicit in the autobiographical project by "enlisting it in his service" (239)—the suggestion being that Hemingway strategically employs an aloft attitude so as to position himself as a certain "type" of writer. *A Moveable Feast* becomes, through its reconstruction of a young and still (somewhat) naïve Hemingway, a text that propounds "the supremacy of art, the need for loneliness in its creation, and the beauty of the simple, uncluttered life" (Rubenstein 239). Hemingway *fashions himself* as an artist who remains true to his art, who does not allow friendship or a sense of responsibility to others to interfere with his abilities as a writer. This *image* is repeatedly stressed, or reconstructed, throughout the text, but it is also reflected in his willingness (at the time of writing) to reconstruct his relationships with other expatriates as tenuous, volatile, and finally of little importance. After describing "the way it ended with Gertrude Stein," Hemingway is quick to point out that he and Stein "were getting to be better friends than [he] *could ever wish to be*" (117; my emphasis). Likewise, Hemingway never suggests that he was, in any way, invested in his friendship with F. Scott Fitzgerald. Although Hemingway dedicates a large portion of the text to him, the descriptions of Fitzgerald are almost always deprecatory. He often intimates that Fitzgerald's "fall" was directly linked to his inability to remain, as Hemingway does, aloft. Fitzgerald is *too* attached, particularly to his wife, Zelda. "Zelda wants to destroy you" (191), Hemingway tells Fitzgerald in one of the later "sketches." In Hemingway's eyes, Fitzgerald's attachment to Zelda is a sign of artistic weakness—if not, simply, impotence. Even Hemingway's seemingly nostalgic reconstruction of his breakup with his first wife, Elizabeth Hadley Richardson, functions to (re)present a writer who, although having once faltered, has learned to avoid the dangerous influence of others (like, in the end, the duplicitous "pilot fish" and "the rich").

There is, of course, something melancholic (or even *melancholically perverse*) about the vitriolic nature of such accounts—especially since they ostensibly serve the goal of *realizing* a certain singular vision of Hemingway's persona, a certain *imago*. We should not forget that Hemingway reportedly described his memoir as "biography by *remate*."[12] Since the Spanish *remate* can be translated as "to end" (by killing, or *re*killing), this assertion opens up the possibility that *A Moveable Feast* is little more than an effort to deploy proto-postmodern (or late existential) assumptions about discursive play so as to justify negative and finalizing accounts (or biographies) of others. Hemingway presents his accounts or "sketches" as fictions—but in doing so he often leaves us with the suggestion that these fictions imply truths that no "hard fact" is likely to convey *as well*. Is this not the logic behind any number of modern and (post)modern aesthetic movements—from impressionism and primitivism to cubism (all of which we might in turn associate with Hegel's definition of symbolic art)? Insofar as Hemingway's memoir can be aligned with such implicitly nostalgic efforts, it can be viewed as no less naïve and imposing than (say) McBride's *The Color of Water*. It functions "to lynch" both the self and those others whose stasis (or death) is necessary for the stabilization of the "I" in question. *In this sense,* a critic like Jacqueline Vaught Brogan is correct to see in *A Moveable Feast* a nostalgic desire for what Kierkegaard calls "repetition"—the *complete* (re)apprehension of a past event. Insofar as it *is* a "biography by *remate*," *A Moveable Feast* is Hemingway's futile (if not tragic) attempt to assert, in its totality, an impossible idealization of a past self: his innocence as a writer and his "sacred and unblemished love with Hadley" (Brogan 10). And yet, or at the same time, we might say (as Rubenstein does)—and especially if we maintain a focus on Hemingway's obvious and concerted effort to highlight the constructed nature of his recollections (e.g., his use of artificial yet verbatim dialogue, his use of repetition, symbolism, and allusion)—that this problematic and often nostalgic "sense of moral superiority serves the larger conception of *A Moveable Feast*" (Rubenstein 240). Hemingway consciously employs "the inevitable autobiographical bias . . . as part of the 'degree of alchemy' that transforms memory into art" (240)—or perhaps *art into memory*. While a memoirist like McBride tends to assume and in turn offer the illusion of an *authentic* reconstruction of the past (and the self—even to the point of a racial *essence*), Hemingway consistently and strategically undermines and ameliorates his vitriolic "sketches" by signaling again and again that they are always only repositionable frames—or, if we recall our brief discussion of Kenneth Burke in chapter 6, "terministic screens."

A Feast of Screens

Burke claims that "even something so 'objectively there' as behavior must be observed through one or another kind of *terministic screen*, that directs the attention in keeping with its nature" (*Symbolic* 49). The implication is that "we must use terministic screens, since we can't say anything without the use of terms; whatever terms we use, they necessarily constitute a corresponding kind of screen; and any such screen necessarily directs the attention to one field rather than another" (50). Here Burke (writing in 1966, but extending ideas he introduced in the late 1940s and early 1950s) anticipates the major concerns of poststructuralism—*as well as* (then) Levinas's more specific interest in the problem of delimiting themes, or the schematism of the "said." However, the concept of "screens" applies somewhat more readily to Hemingway's memoir—as the text functions as a collation of various discreet accounts (or "sketches"). Presented back to back, these accounts emerge as a series of accurate *yet always also contingent* portraits—of Hemingway as a young author, of other famous writers working in the same place and time, of the specific events that defined the function of writing during the "Paris movement."

As Burke suggests (and as Lacan has intimated since his earliest seminars), a given screen can become an "ultimate term," or hegemonic "mystification"—a symbolic imposition that directs many diverse and opposed voices into a single unified direction. But Hemingway tends to imply the possibility (which Burke also considers) that it is always possible to demystify a given screen via the application of another *no less mystifying* screen.[13] At, then, its most ethical (or ethically autonarrative), *A Moveable Feast* manages two distinct tasks. On the one hand, it functions to demystify the Hemingway that has been constructed by scholars, the public, and other writers of the period. This would be its function as a "biography as *remate*." On the other, it offers us (re)mystifications of Hemingway's life that simultaneously draw our attention toward the very process of (de/re)mystification it undergoes. It offers us a series of ironically positioned screens. While often and explicitly unrelated (temporally or thematically), each sketch is offered as no less valid *or* delimiting than any other. The discontinuity or disjuncture between one section and another implicates a space that is always still anterior to any one frame—a certain "proximity" (in Levinas's sense of the term). Take, for instance, the discontinuity between chapter 9 and chapter 10. The former ("Ford Madox Ford and the Devil's Disciple") details an absurd conversation between Ford and Hemingway about the nature of "cads" and the process of "cutting" someone down and then ends abruptly with Hemingway accidentally *or* intentionally confusing Hilaire Belloc with Aleister Crowley.[14] What follows ("Birth of a New School") begins with a non-sequitur description of Hemingway's writing materials, his process, and the various impediments to that process. Each chapter therefore works to give us *a* Hemingway, or *a* face (an *idealization*), we can know *while announcing* that the face (or mystification, or image) before us is only ever supplementary to what it obscures or corrupts, that Hemingway is always *also* other to those (re)constructions we are given to understand in the symbolic, or according to the Other.

To a certain extent, then, the Burkean screen (as we see it deployed in Hemingway) anticipates most overtly Julia Kristeva's notion of the "phenotext"—that is, "a structure (which can be generated, in generative grammar's sense); it obeys rules of communication and presupposes a subject of enunciation and an addressee" (87). Always itself a form of mystification, a given phenotext can "function *without* reintroducing within the sign the instinctual nucleus that would have disarticulated it, pluralized it, and imbued it with non-sense" (91; my emphasis). Such closure is, for Kristeva, in direct opposition to poetic or revolutionary language; it is the type of closure we see in, say, a traditional autobiography, or particularity beguiling documentaries (e.g., those parodied in *Zelig*). While Hemingway does not engage in the type of poetic language Kristeva tends to valorize (and which informs, also, Rajan's specific definition of "autonarration"), his tendency to deploy overtly constructed language while offering us a series of noncontiguous *yet interrelated* screens provides an echo of the prelinguistic "*process*" Kristeva identifies as the "genotext" of poetic language. *A Moveable Feast* leads us to see that Hemingway's "self-representation in the text is something quite different from [his] presence, and [that he] enters the text neither as an absolute ego nor as the mature and completed subject referred to by Wayne Booth as the implied author, but as a subject-in-process represented through a figure of the self" (Rajan 159).

As Rajan describes it, the genotext is that part of a text which "exists partly as an intertext or connective zone between the biographical and diegetic worlds, which is to say that it consists of the possibilities released by the negation of the various scripts into which the subject has been or could be written" (165). Evident in various syntactical disruptions, semantic slips, or extralinguistic rhythms, the genotext works as a type of bridge between the phenotext and the semiotic *chora*—that which "precedes evidence, verisimilitude, spatiality, and temporality. Our discourse—all discourse—moves with and against the *chora* in the sense that it simultaneously depends upon and refuses it. Although the *chora* can be designated and regulated, it can never be definitively posited" (Kristeva 26). What we might cautiously think of as another expression of the Levinasian *in*finite (or even the Hegelian "family"), the *chora* is associated with DNA, RNA, genes, biological drives, etc. It can undergo an "ordering," but it necessarily refuses to be "ordered" by (symbolic) law. Even more significant (given the discussion above) is Kristeva's insistence that the always indecipherable, or unplaceable, vocalization of the *chora* (or "agitated body") is necessarily and initially "projected . . . onto [a] facing *imago*" (46); this imaginary projection of the *chora* (and thus its separation from the subject who perceives it at a distance) makes way for the sign, for representation, for communication. We might in fact say it makes possible a coherent face *to face*. The task of "art" is to expose what is always still beyond or agitating this representation of coherence, to "disturb the transparency of the signifying chain . . . and move . . . [us] toward the instinctual, material, and social process the text covers" (101). But to do so, Kristeva insists, the artist must endure the "difficulty of maintaining the symbolic function under the assault of negativity" (69). For no transgression is possible in the absence of the law transgressed. An outright absence of law would entail, as Kristeva suggests, a type of schizophrenia, a complete lack of coherence or point of relation.

The problem is that Kristeva's poetic language is hardly discernable from Bakhtin's heteroglossia. At its best, a privileging of "poetic language" mandates a balancing act between the comprehensible and the incomprehensible. At its most troubling, it mandates that which Kristeva implicitly warns against: schizophrenic cacophony. And of course Kristeva celebrates only the most modern of modernists: "Only certain literary texts of the avant-garde (Mallarmé, Joyce) manage to cover the infinity of the process, that is, reach the semiotic *chora*, which modifies linguistic structures" (88). Kristeva sees in these exemplary texts a markedly effective "explosion of the semiotic in the symbolic" (69)—an explosion she then contrasts with Hegel's "negation of negation, an *Aufhebung* that would suppress the contradiction generated by the thetic [or identificatory separation] and establish in its place an ideal positivity, the restorer of pre-symbolic immediacy" (69). Kristeva's goal here is to identify "poetic language" as a way of evading two extremes: (1) the illusion of synthetic immediacy (which Kristeva attributes to the Hegelian *Aufhebung*) and (2) an inverse tendency to utterly "foreclose the thetic phase" and undermine the possibility of "symbolic function" (69). "Art" must transgress the symbolic and disrupt the thetic boundary that makes the symbolic possible, but it must not "relinquish the thetic even while pulverizing it through the negativity of transgression. Indeed, this is the only means of transgressing the thetic" (69). Kristeva clearly insists (like Žižek) that only in the symbolic is the semiotic to be touched, or experienced.[15] Yet Leon S. Roudiez (in his introduction to Kristeva's *Revolution*) is certainly correct to associate Kristeva's poetic language with those texts "in which language becomes partly unintelligible; that is, an unmediated physical presence" (5).[16] Kristeva, in other words, never gets us too far beyond a text like Miller's—which is primarily interested in effecting (through language) an "unmediated physical presence." But such a goal merely tends toward an assumption of synthesis, an illusory aligning of linguistic practice with that which is only ever extralinguistic, or anterior to symbolic organization, or law. Might we not in fact say that modern poetic language is innately prone to effecting (at, especially, its Joycean/Mallarméan extremes) the type of synthetic immediacy Kristeva associates with Hegel? In the face of these faceless texts we are problematically led to assume the arrival of a presence that is categorically impossible, or only possible when it fails to arrive, when it is allowed to keep coming.

Again, this is not to deny the often efficacious manner in which modern polyphony—in, especially, the form of the modern heteroglot novel—directs our attention toward that which cannot be said. The point here is that, to do so, a text cannot simply depend upon the cacophonous and the impenetrable. Instead, and if we read Hegel as Žižek or Catherine Malabou does (and *not* as Kristeva does), what is necessary is *in fact* a form of "romantic" sublation, a certain negation of the negation. At its most radical, the Hegelian *Aufhebung* in no way entails an effort toward final synthesis, or "pre-symbolic immediacy." Nor is it a matter of "pulverizing" the thetic. It is, rather (and in specifically aesthetic terms), a matter of asserting, "even if in a higher way, . . . that difference and opposition of the two sides which in symbolic art remained unconquered" (Hegel, *Aesthetics* 79). It is a matter of "tarrying with the negative" (*Phenomenology* 19), of perpetually *facing up to* that "which remains after all its content [is] 'subjectivized'" (Žižek, *Tarrying* 21). To do so is most certainly to allow for the "*Aufhebung* of the semiotic in the symbolic" (Kristeva 51)—if we take the Hegelian *Aufhebung* in its most radical sense. By negating an overt negation of the Kristevean semiotic, a text might retain its inescapable complicity with the symbolic realm of law and communication while returning us (in a manner that is likely more akin to metafiction than modern polyphony) to that which has been necessarily refused, or masked. We are given a symbolically coherent face, one that we could locate in reality (or the "realm of the truth"), while at the same time this overt refusal or false masking of the semiotic is negated via the implication that something is missing, that something cannot be said. This is not an effort to say that *Thing* by means of a linguistic breakdown; it is an effort to retain it as the constitutive negative of what *is* said. After all, for Hegel (as Žižek repeatedly suggests), the *Thing* emerges only in our failure to give it form. It is what all possible—or *possibly correct*—versions lack; yet, for this very reason, it is the "transcendental object" of their unification: "What at first appeared to be an epistemological obstacle turns out to be the very index of the fact that we have 'touched the Truth'; we are in the heart of the 'Thing-in-itself' *by the very trait which appeared to bar our access to it.* The implication, of course, is that this 'Thing-in-itself' is already mutilated, split, marked by a radical lack, structured around an antagonistic kernel" (Žižek, *Sublime Object* 177).

The Burkean concept of a screen is, for this reason, particularly useful—especially in the way it allows us to account for the autonarrative potential of a text like Hemingway's. Rather than offering us a phenotext that is somehow *authenticated* by the distortions and confusions of an explosive genotext, Hemingway provides a series of ostentatiously transparent screens. Each screen is largely contained and coherent in itself. However, the overtness of their artificiality—along with the dissociative nature of their organization (as loosely connected "chapters" or "sketches")—tends to negate the loss or negation necessitated by the effort to give (a) form. The "non-linguistic" portion of the text that "the reader senses in the *form* taken by the content" (Rajan 165) is *given* in the implication that an infinite number of *other* terministic directions, or screens, have been necessarily denied, or suppressed. These other screens, or mystifications, could be anything, from another writer's portrayal of Hemingway to what we might consider to be the "real" life story (or history) of Hemingway. This series of closures simultaneously undoes their pretense to closure by opening us to the fact that another *equally valid* (en)closure is always also possible. What matters is that the "plasticity" (Hegel) or "motility" (Kristeva) of this "inner" Thing—this *infinite*, this semiotic—is not given to ossify, that it is not lost to the fixed form of its appearance, or presentation. This is surely what happens when textual or linguistic distortion is given in the place of motility—just as it is surely what happens when the delimiting fact of *a* motility is abandoned in favor of perverse irresponsibility, or the unconstrained play of the symbolic. Could we not in fact hazard the claim that a genotext is simply impossible, a mere illusion of what allows us to see by blocking our view? Autonarrative sublation (as an act of "autoplasticity") is, therefore—if we recall our discussions in part II—a matter of giving oneself to be eaten *well*. This entails giving what is *ready made* to be consumed while (at the same time) effecting a certain amount of disgust, a certain echo of what *would* make a meal complete or *completely satisfying*.

At its best, *A Moveable Feast* functions as just that: a moveable feast—a feast (of Hemingway, of Paris in the twenties, of other writers and the conditions of modern writing) that is always in an*other* place, or never contained in any one preparation. Each sketch can be likened to *a* (satisfying, or hospitable) meal that is always and also an hors d'oeuvre—that is, what implies by asserting itself as always distinct from a larger, never complete, object of consumption. These hors d'oeuvres gesture toward while preserving an object of desire. The absent whole emerges only as that which is always other to the sum of its constituent parts—like the *experience* of a multicourse dinner. The text gives its "semiotic motility" as a kind of "*also*, or the *universal medium* in which the many properties subsist apart from one another, without touching or cancelling one another; and when so taken, the Thing [or essential, *motile* whole] is perceived as what is true" (Hegel, *Phenomenology* 73). Hemingway gestures toward this form of giving when he recounts the moment Hadley told him that "memory is hunger" (57). While playing on this metaphor, Renza suggests that "Hemingway . . . defines writing as a desirable and perpetually reproducible concrete project in and for itself—as a metaphorical version of *hunger,* which quite clearly constitutes the 'central image' and dominant trope of *A Moveable Feast*" (664). At the same time, Renza takes hunger to mean (also) a "desire *to* write truly, or, the same thing, to represent things in a way that stimulates [Hemingway's] desire to be with their concrete thereness" (665). The implication is that the "perpetually *reproducible* concrete project" of writing remains fettered to a "desire to write *truly.*" Hunger in *A Moveable Feast* thus signals a desire (for the self) that is satisfied by remaining insatiate. As Rajan puts it, "[Desire] is the power of the negative in experience, as well as the reflexivity of a consciousness that must know itself partly as an other and as existing for another" (155). Hemingway negotiates this hunger by engaging (and drawing our attention to) what Sartre refers to as "a constantly renewed obligation to remake the *Self*" (72). Just as "there is never any ending to Paris" (Hemingway 211) there is never any ending to Hemingway. Every screen in *A Moveable Feast* is offered (only) as an*other* form, an*other* possible that preserves while opening us to the motility or potential or *plasticity* it fails to grasp. At its most ethical, the memoir gives itself to be eaten while encouraging us to eat well.

What Is Essential, Perhaps

That said, Hemingway's memoir often seems tempted by the allure of *post*modern perversity. While there are certainly moments when the text seems overtly melancholic in its effort to concretize an idealized self, it tends (at other times) toward a complete evisceration of anything *like* constitutive motility—in that it tends to imply the possibility of remaking the self in *whatever* manner is most beneficial. That the memoir has a tendency to swing from one extreme to the other is hardly surprising; as we have seen in previous chapters, both extremes signal an abject refusal to endure responsibility. For the most part, though, Hemingway's memoir largely signals the possibility of navigating through such extremes, of giving *by letting slip* an autobiographical subject. The point is that autonarrative forms are always likely to forgo the ethics of perpetual sublation in favor of authentic textual distortions or the seduction of a perverse universe (in which any account is equally permissible or valid). To succeed, the autonarrative act must perpetually endure the undecidable, or the gamble of a *certain* "perhaps."

As Derrida suggests in *Politics of Friendship,* Nietzsche's strategic overuse of the term "perhaps" functions to preserve truth in the moment of its (false) utterance. "Perhaps" implies a willingness to gamble in the moment of doubt, to endure the undecidable. The possibility of friendship—as, that is, the possibility of understanding, or giving the self to be understood by, the other—entails a *certain* "perhaps" (its echo or implication). On the one hand, a conditional "perhaps" promises that the statement in which it is lodged (like a ghost) could be true absolutely and without doubt; on the other, it defers and delays the possibility of any such certainty. The "perhaps" promises and forbids a narrative telos, an ideal future (of self-apprehension) to come: "There will come, *perhaps;* there will occur, perhaps, the event of that which arrives (*und vielleicht kommt*), and this will be the hour of joy, an hour of birth but also of resurrection" (Derrida, *Politics* 28). We might, in this sense (and if we recall our discussion of Nancy in chapter 5), associate the echo of the "perhaps" with "the movement, the delay, and the incompletion of being born." The "perhaps" withholds its promise that a future (self)—as *an always motile ghost*—will finally manifest itself. We might even say (in this particular context) that it promises while frustrating the possibility that the obligation to "remake the self" will no longer need to be "renewed." It signals a form of sincerity or accountability that is nevertheless haunted by the impossibility of absolute verification or the durability of a given choice from one moment to the next. We must *choose* a "screen" as well as the specific imago we aim to give. And yet, given the infinite number of choices or configurations possible, no decision could ever "provide itself with the infinite information and the unlimited knowledge that could . . . justify it" (Derrida, *Force of Law* 255). We can never make a finally correct choice—for no screen could ever *be* what it screens and no imago is ever what we imagine it to be. However, it is always possible to make a *better* choice—a better choice "perhaps." The gamble of the "perhaps" preserves the accountable self, the inescapabilty of a grounding (if always plastic) Real, by refusing *both* the melancholic need to assume its fixity or purity *and* the perverse tendency to embrace its unknowability as an excuse for always unimpeachable deceptions (i.e., feckless acts of "make-believe"). If Hemingway's various sketches/screens work to give their always absent subject in a loving way, they do so because they are imbued with a certain "perhaps"—the echo of which is generated by its self-referential artificiality and sustained in its various spaces of dis-jointure.

Perhaps, though, a better (or at least more explicit) example of the "perhaps" can be found in Derrida's own attempt at autonarrative, his 1980 *Envois* (a sincere parody of the epistolary novel that recounts two years in Derrida's life). Spanning 3 June 1977 to 30 August 1979, the various letters or posts (or "cards" as he calls them in the initial entry) develop

Derrida's various theoretical concepts (especially his focus at the time on the relationship between Socrates and Plato, Freud and psychoanalysis, Lacan's seminar on Poe, etc.) while also recounting to an unnamed addressee, or "love," his travels between and experiences at various speaking engagements and academic meetings. Interactions with verifiable colleagues—Jonathan Culler, J. Hillis Miller, etc.—are described in detail, as are encounters with often brash and arrogant graduate students. Even the specifics of sleeping arrangements are mentioned. There is little about the work that seems contrived, or outwardly false. We get what certainly seems like two years of Derrida's *real* life—as an academic, a friend, and a lover. The content or subject of the work therefore justifies the feeling of guilt Derrida expresses throughout. As he tells his "love" at the outset—a "love" who may stand in for the reader *in general,* Derrida's wife (Marguerite Aucouturier), his mistress (Sylviane Agacinski), or someone even more secret—"I am ashamed of underlining, of wanting to be intelligible and convincing (as if for others, finally), I am ashamed of saying it in everyday language, of saying it, therefore, of writing, of signifying anything at all in your direction" (*Envois* 7–8). At the very moment he is ashamed to say it (in "everyday language," in the language of the Other, or according to the laws of "common usage"), Derrida fully admits to and implies the necessity of a motivating desire to be understood *in truth,* to be apprehended finally and at last. He desires that his letters reach their target, enter into circulation, be returnable. The letters, as posts, clearly function to imply the location of their sending, a place/subject that can be addressed in (re)turn, a "unique destination, unique you understand me, unnameable and invisible" (10). And it is this lure, this terrible but absolutely necessary desire, that keeps Derrida writing—or rather, *running to no end:* "I run, I run to bring them news which must remain secret" (8).

But in expressing his guilt—along with the impossibility of fulfilling his unavoidable, if not ethically mandated, desire[17]—Derrida distances himself from, or *from within,* the intelligibility he engages by necessity. The sense we get is that the secret (self) Derrida would like to disclose can only be preserved in its absence; yet, and at the same time, such preservation could never be known without paradoxically risking some element of loss in "everyday language." Either loss is, however, problematic. The latter form gives the illusion of understanding, of a perfect "substitution"; it encourages or even breeds a *"bad* reader"—that reader who is "in a hurry to be determined, decided upon deciding (in order to annul, in other words to bring back to oneself . . . to expect (oneself))" (*Envois* 4). Such a reader aims only to take what they already know, or understand, what they bring "prepackaged" to the text; they read nothing but the language of the Other. They refuse to endure what they cannot see, or take into account. And yet a tendency toward silence in no way forestalls the possibility of a bad reader. And no reader is good enough to read nothing. A writer, or (in this case) a memoirist, must therefore remain accountable for *something*. Does not Derrida, after all, and at the very outset of his career, accuse Plato of a reckless lack of accountability—a lack of accountability buttressed by an extreme tendency toward logocentrism? In the conclusion to "Plato's Pharmacy" (which, itself, is almost too fragmentary and elusive to be accountable), Derrida slips into a passage from Plato's Second Letter (to Dionysus)—a letter that concerns Plato's paradoxical *lack* of publications. Given our concerns here, it's worth quoting in full:

> ... Consider these facts and take care lest you sometime come to repent of having now unwisely published your views. It is a very great safeguard to learn by heart instead of writing ... *to mē graphein all'ekmanthanein*. ... It is impossible for what is written not to be disclosed. That is the reason why I have never written anything about these things ... *oud'estin sungramma Platōnos ouden oud'estai*, and why there is not and will not be any written work of Plato's own. What are now called his ... *Sōkratous estin kalou kai neou gegonotos* ... are the work of Socrates embellished and modernized. Farewell and believe. Read this letter now at once many times and burn it ... (qtd. in Derrida, "Plato's Pharmacy" 170)

And while Derrida clearly resists the impulse to write nothing *of himself*, to publish nothing that is by and about him—he even assures us (if somewhat backhandedly) that he (i.e., the signatory "Jacques Derrida") "assume[s] without detour the responsibility for these *envois*, for what remains, or no longer remains" (*Envois* 6)—the advice in Plato's letter (which may *or may not*, in fact, be by Plato) clearly haunts his efforts.

A central concern, or mystery, running throughout *Envois* concerns a strange postcard Derrida was led to discover by Culler and Cynthia Chase. The postcard, which appears on the cover of *The Postcard* (in which *Envois* is housed), and which is again reproduced within *Envois*, depicts Socrates at a desk writing; Plato, standing behind him, appears to dictate. As Derrida says, "What a couple. *Socrates* turns his *back* to plato [sic], who has made him write whatever he wanted while pretending to receive it from him" (12). This incongruity is mentioned and theorized again and again throughout. It serves as a type of leitmotif, a metaphorical echo of the central task Derrida undertakes—to not lose himself in what he writes while also refusing to refuse such a loss. His goal is to remain, unlike Plato, wholly accountable for what he writes even if what he writes is necessarily and always (the) other—in the sense that, as Levinas might say, communication necessarily entails a "substitution" for what is other (to me, to my motile truth). While the desire that animates and ensures the effort of communication is "the wish . . . to triumph over distancing" (27), the very possibility of communication *is* distance: "You understand, within every sign already, every mark or every trait, there is distancing, the post, what there has to be so that it is legible for another, another than you or me . . . The condition for it to arrive is that it ends up and even that it begins by not arriving" (29). If we recall our discussion of economimesis in chapter 3, we might say that Derrida struggles—while always also reflecting upon that struggle—to sustain disgust within that which is wholly palatable. He resolves, after all, to "leave all kinds of references, names of persons and of places, authentifiable dates, identifiable events" (177). These references, these facts, will compel us (at least at first) to assume we have located the subject we seek. As Derrida assures his lover, "They rush in with eyes closed, finally believing to be there and to find us there when by means of a switch point I will send them elsewhere to see if we are there, with a stroke of the pen or the *grattoir* I will make everything derail,[18] not at every instant, that would be too convenient, but occasionally and according to a rule that I will never give, even were I to know it one day" (177). Like Hemingway, Derrida signals his secret. And yet he keeps it. We are told what we shouldn't know—that what we *can* verify is only a lure, an evasion. But we are told, too, that the pattern or cipher of displacements (which even Derrida does not or cannot know) is impossible to decipher. Not everything is an evasion—for "that would be too convenient"; it would lead to a (bad) reading program, a consistent and prepackaged strategy. We are instead forced to endure what is missing, what intrudes upon the form that obstructs it, what never arrives.

Derrida articulates this paradoxical strategy best in those moments he redeploys Plato's call for fire. As he tells us in his ostensibly nondiegetic preface to the *actual* envois, "You might consider [the following letters], if you really wish to, as remainders of a recently destroyed correspondence. Destroyed by fire or by that which figuratively takes its place, more certain of leaving nothing out of the reach of what I like to call the tongue of fire, not even cinders if cinders there are [*s'il y a là cendre*]" (3). What we get is not the correspondence itself; we get, instead, its remainders, or "the preface to a book [Derrida has] *not* written" (3; my emphasis). These coherent or palatable remainders are not just anything, and they are necessary if the subject in question is to signal (or give) what they are not, what they must necessarily fail to contain: "For the totally incinerated *envois* could not be indicated by any mark" (5). To write himself Derrida must therefore undergo a "rigorous principle of destruction" (176). And such a principle must remain perpetually undecidable. At every turn Derrida reminds his lover—whom we are increasingly lead to read as *also* himself, his *own* other[19]—that he must decide what to keep (and therefore "doom to loss by publishing it" [176]) and what to "burn" (and thus preserve in silence, in absolute secrecy): "What will we burn, what will we keep (in order to broil it *better* still)?" (176; my emphasis). Loss cannot be avoided if something true is to be given. Had his love, as Derrida requests at the outset, burnt everything, "nothing would have arrived" (23). But that nothing would have been "something ineffaceable" (23). For this reason, and as Derrida fully admits, the request to "burn" was always also a request to "save." And so "nothing has arrived because you wanted to preserve (and therefore to lose), which in effect formed the sense of order coming from behind my voice, you remember, so many years ago, in my first 'true' letter: 'burn everything'" (23). The paradox is that whatever remains—"if there is any[thing] that remains"—in the wake of any such conflagration "is us, is for us, who do not belong to the card. We are the card, if you will, and as such, accountable, but they will seek in vain, they will never find us in it" (176–77). To burn is to keep through absolute loss—while the alternative is to lose through preservation, or forms of coherence. The desire for the purifying or cleansing effect of fire is no less melancholic than the desire for complete and transparent authority. The effect of an always ineffectual fire must, then, be signaled in an always failed account (or posted "card"), what remains outside the flame (if nevertheless showing a bit of char) and thus accountable. In other words, and long before he rigorously articulates an ethics of giving (in works like "Eating Well" and *The Gift of Death*), Derrida struggles in *Envois* to maintain accountability while or by undermining the illusion of authority. He works to give himself in truth—by giving that which signals a constitutive failure to give, or arrive. To do so he must constantly renegotiate the undecidable, the effort of choosing one screen and burning down another, of remaining haunted by the "perhaps." As he suggests throughout, he is no less accountable for what he does *not* say than for what he does.

The possibility of public expression that animates the autobiographical act is a dangerous logocentric lure; but it is no less mendacious than a desire for purification, the temptation toward silence and the threat of paralysis. The latter is a move (also) toward absolute apprehension, the end of all possible promises, the end of all contact *because the end of all separation*. It promises the secret revealed by promising to preserve the secret from the inevitable corruption of the decision-making process, from the ordeal of the undecidable. Is this not, also, the danger of cleansing the imaginary lure? Regardless, the purity of a fire that leaves no living trace (like, perhaps, the fire of a lynching) signals the end of all decisions, all autonarrative or interpretive gestures. It is the end of love. It is the end of eating. As does the impulse to speak and to be understood *finally*, the refusal to seek or leave a trace moves us toward silence and death. Suicide and the death drive are, for this reason, common points of reference throughout *Envois*. The only ethical alternative to either is the gamble—and to gamble is to endure the "perhaps," spectrality itself. Autonarratives like Hemingway's and Derrida's signal the possibility of just such a gamble. They gamble on what is *perhaps* the truth, what is perhaps a real and accurate portraiture. In stressing the impossibility of exorcising the "perhaps" from such a portraiture (whether subtly or overtly) they compel us to see what remains invisible, or lost to the purifying fire of silence. They sublate what is true;[20] by relinquishing their grip they manage to touch upon their respective subjects. What we see is this: in the act of trying to account for the self we must yield to and reject the impossibility of arriving (secret self intact). This is the only way of preserving the possibility of an autoplastic act in the face of (on the one hand) melancholic certainty and (on the other) feckless perversity. This is the only way to "touch on the untouchable" (Derrida, *On Touching* 18)—to give *by preserving* God (in me).

8 / The Divinely Unshareable Self: From Edward Albee to Larry David

> *Well I'm sittin' in church in an old wooden chair*
> *I knew nobody would look for me there*
> —BOB DYLAN, "MARCHIN' TO THE CITY"

Communicating in the Zoo

The possibility of an ethical relation entails the paradox of giving while simultaneously preserving what is divine in me. This is surely what Derrida means when, in *Politics of Friendship*, he insists that "the specter must be respected" (288). It is surely also, then, the only way to "eat well." But the problem of eating is the problem of relating to *any* other (human or otherwise). Or rather, if we are to take seriously the Levinasian idea of "God in me" (and thus the *in*finite divinity of otherness), we must move beyond Levinas by radically decoupling divinity and humanity. What is divine, what is *in*finite, is necessarily inhuman (even if it is also always *in*-human). Humanity is merely a forward-facing—that is, imaginary, or thematic—access point, a recognizable and empathy-inducing appearance. If otherness is, by definition, *in*finite, then *all* forms of otherness are equally other and equally withdrawn. The implications are twofold: (1) if all otherness is equally other, then the other human with whom I am faced must be taken as no less foreign than any other "thing" (be it a nonhuman animal or a stone); (2) the world of nonhuman "things" must be negotiated with the same care we afford our encounters with other humans. While we are obviously most concerned here with the former, the latter brings us into the uncertain and often bewildering territory of "object-oriented ontology" and "speculative realism." We will need to spend some time traversing this territory, for better or worse. By way of an approach, let's linger on the possibility of relating that which is divinely *in*human. If we are to learn (finally) to share *by sublating* our *in*finite divinity—and, in turn, endure and respect the other's—we must first accept its inherent affinity to the *least* human of things. To a certain extent, we entertained this possibility in chapter 5 when we discussed Dick's take on androids and animals in *Do Androids Dream of Electric Sheep?* But we have yet to determine how an ability to embrace this radical affinity might affect or even forestall an autobiographical impulse. The effort to make such a determination will lead us back to Dick and his own efforts to relate his *in*finite self through the overt artifice of (science) fiction. However, a more useful starting point is surely Edward Albee's famous "two-hander," *The Zoo Story*.

First performed in 1959, *The Zoo Story* plays out an autobiographical impulse to its extreme, negotiating in turn the paradox of making known that which necessarily exceeds the knowable. At the same time, and by exposing us to the ethical limits of existential absurdism, the play exemplifies an American shift out of modernism. Like Hemingway, Albee employs overtly postmodern or metafictional tropes so as to comment upon—and then move beyond—a modern tendency toward silence as an act of ontological preservation. This is the very tendency John Barth associates with Beckett: "For Beckett . . . to cease to create altogether would be fairly meaningful: his crowning work; his 'last word.' What a convenient corner to paint yourself into" (68). This problem of writing toward silence—of, that is, preserving the infinite (truth or meaning) by saying nothing—is, as we have seen, the perfect obverse of modernism's tendency toward dialogic cacophony. The effect is the same, as is the impulse. But Albee's proto-postmodern play does not simply overturn this impulse. It pits the hopelessness of the modern project against a perverse denial of authenticity; the apparent impossibility of authentic communication against a feckless submission to the arbitrariness of repositionable frames, or discursive contexts. If the play is about anything, it is about the possibility of communicating (if only, and finally, through physical violence) the "Infinite in me" (Levinas, "God and Philosophy" 63). The play exposes the utter necessity of sincerely relating as *and to* the divinely other while exposing us to the dangers of both modern *and* postmodern withdrawal. And since it exposes us to this necessity by conflating human and nonhuman relations, it leads us (also) to see that the *in*finitely other is always and necessarily an *in*human Thing, that all things (human and nonhuman) must be negotiated as equally and radically other.

When the play opens, Jerry, a mysterious stranger, suddenly and unexpectedly invades the isolation of a seemingly mundane father, husband, and publisher (Peter) who is sitting quietly on a bench in Central Park.

After telling Peter that he has "been to the zoo" (12), and then asking him a series of ostensibly random questions about his family—after, that is, repeatedly frustrating the norms of communication and utterly "bewilder[ing]" (17) Peter—Jerry explains that he "[doesn't] talk to many people" (19), but that "every once in a while [he] like[s] to talk to somebody, really *talk*; like[s] to get to know somebody, know all about him" (19). This impulse toward authentic communication is frustrated by Peter's contrary desire to "make sense out of things," to "bring order," to "pigeonhole" (25). The account Jerry wishes to give and the thematizing "norms" through which Peter translates that account are, in other words, wholly incompatible. The play thus seems intent on enacting, at least initially, a futile effort to communicate. Jerry's acute sense of this futility becomes evident when he "predicts" the details of the event he has initiated: "I'll start walking around in a little while, and eventually I'll sit down. (*Recalling*) Wait until you see the expression on *his* face" (22; my emphasis).¹ On the one hand, this distinctly metatheatrical—or postmodern—moment confirms the scripted nature of Peter and Jerry's relationship; it necessarily relies upon and is bounded by certain norms of understanding and behavior. On the other, it implies a fundamental rift between the Jerry who speaks (here) and the Jerry who will, in the end (after impaling himself on a knife he has manipulated Peter into wielding), lie dead on the stage; for the expression Peter (and, by extension, the audience) is to witness will appear on *"his"* face—on *that* Jerry's face.² The implication is this: if Peter is to understand Jerry, he must first understand that the object with which (or with whom) he is being compelled to commune is, perhaps even in death, a moving target. Any given set of normative frames are utterly inadequate for the task. It is precisely this truth that seems to account for Jerry's strange relationship to frames in general. As he tells Peter, while cataloging the various "oddities" that fill his depressingly minimalist apartment, he has "two picture frames, both empty" (27). When Peter asks why he doesn't place a picture of his "parents . . . perhaps . . . [or] a girlfriend" (28) in the frames, Jerry launches into an extended account of his miserable childhood and inadequate parents. He claims to be "broken up" about the fact that their "particular vaudeville act is playing the cloud circuit now" (28) and wonders how he could "look at them, all neat and framed" (28). While suggesting that his parents might not be *worth* framing, Jerry clearly intimates (at the same time) that the act of framing is always itself inadequate, a betrayal of the truth. It's too neat, too reductive. Whatever might appear in the frame would only be *a* face, never *the* face—never the *in*finitely plastic truth. A frame is just another "pigeonhole," another device for bringing "order." Or rather, and as we saw in our discussion of Larsen's *Passing* (in chapter 2), the frame always threatens to overtake the Thing it reveals or presents in relief.

The inevitable failure of framing therefore foregrounds Jerry's efforts to remain true to (while sharing) his own *in*finite opacity—what Butler associates with the self's radical distance from the various gestures or articulations that produce the illusion of access, or transparency. These are illusions to which Peter has long since succumbed. Jerry's various intrusions—which tend to come as frustrating manipulations or parodies of the norms he attacks—constantly remind Peter (as they remind us) that the opacity of the self is always absolute and always no different than the opacity of any *other* with whom a self might relate. We exist, Jerry seems intent on demonstrating, in (or *as*) a zoo of utterly incommensurable objects—human, nonhuman animal, or otherwise. There is, however paradoxical it may sound, no difference. This conflation of human communication with *any* other ritual of relating is most explicit during Jerry's "Story of Jerry and the Dog" (36). The story, which "has something to do with how sometimes it's necessary to go a long distance out of the way in order to come back a short distance correctly" (36), functions to demonstrate that a true act of relation entails a radically paradoxical gesture of indifference, of connecting *through* withdrawal or the imposition of distance. Or if we recall Levinas, the story points to the necessity of sustaining a radical "difference with respect to the other as non-indifference" (*Otherwise* 58). It is only "In the non-indifference to a neighbor [or, we might say here, "Thing"], where proximity is never close enough, [that] the difference between me and the other, and the undeclinability of the subject are not effaced, as they are in the situation in which the relationship of the one with the other is understood to be reciprocal" (138). Jerry confirms the necessity of such nonindifference by exposing the inadequacy of behavioral "norms" while simultaneously describing and employing forms of misdirection that have the potential to disrupt expectation, or the inertia of ritualized communication. More specifically, the story—which concerns a vicious black dog that, every day, stands between Jerry and the entrance to his apartment complex—interrupts or disrupts Jerry's efforts to "really talk" to Peter. Yet, at precisely the same time, the story metonymically comments upon this very effort.

Jerry explains that he tried desperately to understand (so as to forestall) the dog's apparent cruelty, its endless attempts to bite him whenever he came home. In the end, he decides to "kill the dog with kindness, and if that doesn't work . . . just kill him" (37). Significantly, either approach will result in (a type of) death. Either Jerry will manage to "connect" with the animal (and thus reduce it via some facile gesture of anthropomorphism and empathy), or he will simply eliminate its inexplicability altogether (via an absolute and egotistical imposition of the self). But the dog resists both tactics. Jerry feeds him fresh hamburgers, yet the dog's enmity persists; Jerry feeds him a poisoned hamburger, yet the dog lives. This dual failure justifies Jerry's earlier and somewhat humorous claim that "you can't say 'a dog I know' without sounding funny" (39). You just can't *know* a dog. Yet, Jerry insists, the dog is his friend. This friendship is realized when, after a poison-induced sickness, the dog faces off once again with Jerry: "During that twenty seconds or two hours that [they] looked into each other's face, [they] made contact" (41). As Jerry explains, "[He] had tried to love, and [he] had tried to kill, and both had been unsuccessful by themselves" (42). Now, though, the dog and Jerry appear to relate without any impulse toward understanding; their face-to-face opens them to what is beyond the face. Or rather, and as a direct consequence of Jerry's sincere effort to *face* the dog, they approach each other in the spirit of (what Žižek understands to be) justice: an abject refusal to treat the other as anything but a "faceless monster." Jerry puts it like this: "Whenever the dog and I see each other we both stop where we are. We regard each other with a mixture of sadness and suspicion, and then we feign indifference. We walk past each other safely; we have an understanding. It's very sad, but you'll have to admit that it is an understanding. We made many attempts at contact, and we had failed. The dog has returned to garbage, and I to solitary but free passage" (43). This "sad" realization (or understanding) is particularly significant since, for Jerry, it is in no way limited to human/animal relations; such relations simply open us up to *it*:

> I hoped . . . and I don't really know why I expected the dog to understand anything, much less my motivations . . . I hoped that the dog would understand.
> (*Peter seems to be hypnotized*)
> It's just . . . it's just that . . . (*Jerry is abnormally tense, now*) . . . it's just that if you can't deal with people, you have to make a start somewhere. WITH ANIMALS! (*Much faster now, and like a conspirator*) Don't you see? A person has to have some way of dealing with SOMETHING. If not with people . . . if not with people . . . SOMETHING. With a bed, with a cockroach, with a mirror (42)

At this point, Jerry proceeds to articulate a litany of "starting points"—all of which ostensibly belong to a vast network of objects (inanimate or otherwise) that, while remaining perpetually withdrawn (or utterly unfathomable), relate to his own opaque core. That this litany ultimately ends with "God" is telling; each of the objects mentioned (from the vicious black dog and the cockroach to "oily wet streets" [42]) is accorded the same ontological status as that which is categorically anterior to all human perception—the *in*finitely divine. Any sincere effort "to understand and just possibly be understood" (43) demands that I attend to and endure the utterly *in*human (whether that inhuman be *in*-human or "in" anything else with which or with whom I might find myself *in relation*).

Realism's Detour

Albee's play anticipates and negotiates some of the more troubling ethical implications lurking at the core of the recent realist revival—associated most prominently with actor-network theory, object-oriented ontology (OOO), and speculative realism. According to the various theorists behind these movements, the problem with philosophy (especially with the advent of phenomenology and idealism in the eighteenth century) is a tendency toward what they call (following Quentin Meillassoux) "correlationism." As Timothy Morton explains in *Hyperobjects: Philosophy and Ecology after the End of the World*, correlationism is "the notion that philosophy can only talk within a narrow bandwidth, restricted to the human-world correlate: meaning is only possible between a human mind and what it thinks, its 'objects,' flimsy and tenuous as they are" (9).[3] In other words, as Todd McGowan has pointed out, the neorealist movement tends to position itself in direct opposition to Kant, for it is Kant who most rigorously exposes a fundamental fissure between phenomena and noumena. All we can know is what *we* (as humans) *know*, or how we perceive what we know. The Thing "in-itself" is forever beyond apprehension. There is, as any number of neorealists are inclined to point out, something problematically anthropocentric about such a view. Proponents of OOO and speculative realism (like Morton) therefore insist that we must begin "finding out real things about real things" (15). But this is no easy task.

For Morton, this task has become all that more pressing in an era of "hyperobjects"—an era in which we are increasingly faced with the "reality" of objects that "massively outscale us" (12). An "object" like global warming, for instance, is staggeringly immense in time and space. And yet, as Morton notes, it cannot be ignored even if it cannot be fully grasped by human perception or regulated by human behavior. Such "hyperobjects have magnified [the] weirdness of things for our inspection: things are themselves, but we can't point to them directly" (12). Morton's basic point is a good one—especially as it relates to the current relationship between reckless human behavior and the "reality" of a world that is every day becoming too volatile to predict or control: faced with a world of things being *and doing* things regardless of human will, humans must confront the troubling consequences of the Anthropocene. The problem with Morton's argument—insofar as it is based on the central tenants of OOO and speculative realism—is that it tends to eat its Kantian cake and disregard it too. While Morton insists that he is interested in "real entities whose primordial reality is withdrawn from humans" (15), he simultaneously (and within the same paragraph) claims the ability to say "real things about real things" (15). Unlike the rest of us, it would seem, the speculative realist has the uncanny ability to see and *to recognize* that which is anterior to the biases of human perception; such a theorist can say (with a sense of certainty that would surely seem anthropocentric or arrogant coming for an eighteenth-century philosopher) that "a hammer '*wants*' to be held a certain way. A forest path *issues* directives to my body to walk at a particular pace, listen for animals, avoid obstacles. A cigarette butt *demands* that I put it out" (141; my emphasis). Is the coincidence here not startling? Who knew hammers and paths and cigarettes had such (human) interests? What luck that the human concepts (or themes) of "wanting," "issuing," "demanding," etc., can be applied so accurately to things "whose primordial reality is [utterly] withdrawn."[4] Speculative realists want, quite justifiably, to return us to a world of things, a world that exists whether or not humans are present to perceive it or engage it; but, in doing so, they find themselves contradicting their most basic assertion—that *every* object is equally withdrawn from every other (humans included). As McGowan puts it, "Speculative realists are not speculative enough and accept an empirical account of objects. Some aspect of the object is simply there and has an identity distinct from what surrounds it. But on the other hand, they are too speculative and assert unsupported philosophical claims about the true nature of reality" (107). Either way, the neorealist escapes the hermetic seal of Kant's phenomenological box by simply assuming a position outside it.

Even more than Morton, Levi Bryant attempts to effect just such as escape. Bryant even drops the pretense of speculation, engaging instead in what he calls a "realist ontology." Such an ontology opposes the claims of contemporary (or, we are given to assume, postmodern) theorists, from Lacan to Foucault to Derrida—theorists who "treat[] the beings that populate the world as an effect of the signifier" (35). Poststructuralism is merely the apotheosis of a correlationist trajectory, the direct descendant of phenomenology and idealism. As such, it must be viewed as yet another "ontotheology with the human in the place of God" (40). Morton suggests something similar when he asserts that "the emerging ecological age gets the idea that 'there is no metalanguage' much more powerfully and nakedly than postmodernism ever did" (4). This is because the emergent wave of neorealists *finally* understands that "there are real things for sure, just not as we know them or knew them, so some metaphors are better than others" (4). While neither Morton nor Bryant is willing to assert what precisely gives us as humans the ability to effectively judge one metaphor as more efficacious than another, the fact that there are "real things for sure" signals (for Bryant) the possibility of a radical "*democracy* of objects or actants where all objects are on equal ontological footing" (39). In such a democracy, "humans [would] no longer [be] monarchs of being but ... instead *among* beings, *entangled* in beings, and *implicated* in other beings" (40). We must learn to forgo the assumption that the social is merely a web of human interactions impacting an indifferent world; we must learn, instead, to account for all the varied objects involved as participants and thus "mediators" of whatever social formation we might wish to understand. The social or the human is never a priori—or, at least, never any more a priori than anything else. This promise or possibility of "a democracy of objects" is (for Bryant) inextricably tied to the promise or possibility of a new and radical ethical order, an order in which "priority" (of humans over animals, of humans over nature, of humans over machines) is no longer thinkable. Yet Bryant (like Morton) is curiously reticent or unclear about the practical implications of such a schema.

This reticence is clearly tied to the problem McGowan highlights—the problem of "access." Like Morton, Bryant is clear (if also inconsistent) about the fact that "the object-oriented ontologist is not claiming that we have access to beings, that they are given, or that our perception is identical to the way the world is, but that the existence of substance is a necessary premise for a whole slew of our practices to be intelligible" (65). Yet if access is not assumed (in one way or another), how does the ontological realist differ from the Kantian who, in Bryant's terms, "[holds] that in addition to phenomena (beings for-us) things-in-themselves exist" (37)? Or how does the ontological realist differ from the Lacanian who (like Žižek) insists that the symbolic is forever encumbered by the "inertia of the Real"? Bryant clearly struggles to maintain a clear distinction, repeatedly insisting that ontological realism opposes (postmodern) correlationsim *as well as* "the [modernist] thesis that objects are constituted by their relations" (26; my emphasis). Objects, he insists, are forever "withdrawn from [such] relations" (26). On the one hand, Bryant's ontological realist wants to circumnavigate the tendency toward anthropocentrism (or, perhaps, and in light of our discussions in part II, unethical "empathy") by insisting that any object I may apprehend remains forever withdrawn from that apprehension, forever itself *being itself*. On the other hand, the ontological realist is "committed to the thesis that it is possible to know something of beings independent of their being-for-thought" (37). Implied here is the absurd assumption that it is possible to know something without thinking it. The object-oriented ontologist must reject access at the very moment she or he must claim some vague form of it. We can only sustain a democracy of objects if we treat all objects as equally inaccessible, yet the possibility of deprioritizing certain modes of being entails dismantling the "correlationist" assumption that the self can only ever translate *and thus impose itself upon* a perpetually inaccessible network of objects.

This is obviously a dangerous game, as it must necessarily run the risk of deploying a type of "back door" anthropocentrism (which we certainly hear opening and closing in the work of Morton). Bryant, after all, finds himself suggesting that the world must exist in a certain concrete manner because "a whole slew of *our [human]* practices" are "intelligible"—a claim that most certainly recalls Nietzsche's caustic assertion that "when someone hides something behind a bush and looks for it again in the same place and finds it there as well, there is not much to praise in such seeking and finding" ("On Truth and Lies" 85). In short, and if we shift (slightly) the emphasis of McGowan's observations, the project of neorealism (speculative or ontological) finds itself being swallowed by the Charybdis of entropic empathy whenever it's not being overtaken by the Scylla of solipsistic correlationism. But what is the alternative? Neorealists like Morton and Bryant are certainly correct to challenge the comforting perversity of postmodern self-reflexivity (at least at its most corrosive extreme). And we certainly cannot hope to resecure the authentic via "modern" acts of overt distortion or irresponsible silence. Perhaps, then, and as paradoxical as it might sound, the best—if not *only* course—is to locate the truth of otherness in our failure to apprehend it. But this would entail, as McGowan points out (following Žižek), a radical return to idealism itself—Hegel's specifically.

As McGowan notes, and as we have already started to surmise in previous chapters, "Hegel . . . extends speculation beyond the subject to objects in themselves. In doing so, he . . . brings transcendentalism and realism together in an inseparable knot.... Our inability to think the world as a whole, as recounted in Kant's first antinomy, informs us that the being of the world itself is contradictory" (106). This is not to suggest that, for Hegel, "thought and being are identical" (106); it is to suggest, instead, that objects are no more self-identical than the subjects that perceive them; for "if objects were self-identical, we could never have gained the capacity for speaking about them, and the fact that we do speak about them—a fact that testifies to the subject's self-division—testifies to their self-division at the same time" (107). Does this not imply that all objects are always already (in some sense) subjects? For Hegel the "subject ... is nothing but the very gap which separates phenomena from the Thing, the abyss beyond phenomena conceived in its negative mode, i.e., the purely negative gesture of limiting phenomena without providing any positive content which would fill out the space beyond the limit" (Žižek, *Tarrying* 21). Read through Hegel, then—or, at least, a contemporary Žižekian or Malabouian Hegel—object-oriented ontology misses or intentionally avoids the struggle of a radically *subject*-oriented ontology, or a form of "transcendentalism ... that enables us to grasp the failure of correlation by making evident how the self-contradictory structure of the subject causes it to infect the object and vice versa" (McGowan 107). I can only know the other "through the distortion of [my] subjectivity" (107), but that distortion signals the fact of a Real encounter. This brings us back to the idea of the narrative gamble, or the necessity of an effort toward the totalization or complete apprehension of the other—and, in turn, the *total* giving of the self. We cannot simply assert that neither is accessible, that all objects are withdrawn and in-themselves, and then make bewildering assertions about their *true* reality. In the act of the narrative gamble, though—which transcends the innate futility of its effort *while remaining haunted* by the ghost of a "perhaps" (as we saw in chapter 7)—I grasp the other by signaling a constitutive absence that necessarily slips away. In this sense, what we began calling acts of autoplasticity (in the previous chapter) achieve a type of ethical success by perpetually exposing and enduring a revelatory failure; the divine content is given (only) as a negative to the form that frames it. The advocates of neorealism largely fail to see and to endure the necessity of such an act because they assume "a teleological rather than a plastic Hegel" (McGowan 114).

Nevertheless, our detour through neorealism—and its various efforts to abandon *while maintaining* the possibility of "access"—effectively confirms our assumption that an ethical relationship with the other entails risking sincere judgments about the other; it reminds us that we must gamble upon which objects we can (or must) impose ourselves upon, and which objects we can (or should) endure without any gesture toward empathy or knowing. But these necessary judgments cannot be justified by appealing to the possibility of some hollow and vague form of pseudoaccess. While Bryant assures us that "all objects [humans included] translate one another [and] the objects that are translated are irreducible to their translations" (18), we must never forget that any act of translation is always also a form of "consumption"—an act of taking in *or relating to* other objects. Every act of translation must therefore entail an effort to "eat well"—which, of course, implies choosing what to eat and what not to eat (plants, humans, nonhuman animals). I must, at every turn, endure an "obligation to protect the other's otherness" (Derrida, "Eating Well" 276). Such an obligation is always as much an obligation to the other as it is to myself. For only in the face of the other's profound or opaque otherness is my perpetual articulation of selfhood possible. It is only in relation, and through the thematics of a face (of imagined coherence) that I am known—if always and perpetually *mis*given. I must, in the simplest sense, eat to live. But to do so in the "*most giving* way" (to recall Derrida's phrasing) entails "learn[ing]," as Bruno Latour suggests, "to *feed* off uncertainties, instead of deciding in advance what the furniture of the world should look like" (115; my emphasis).

It is precisely this lesson that Jerry attempts to teach (or perhaps accept) in *The Zoo Story*. His understanding of the dog—who, significantly, he relates to by feeding—stands in metonymically for his understanding of anything else: Peter or God, himself, etc. All are equally distant from yet equally before him. Yet Jerry's effort to intrude upon Peter's (ontological) isolation signals his desire and compulsion to "understand and to be understood"—and, in turn, one must assume, to gamble on what or who he is willing to privilege and what or who he is not. Significantly, too, Jerry demands less of Peter than he gives of himself (i.e., his very life by the end). He may certainly be accused of going too far, of losing the self in the face of the other (which must always imply, also, its inverse), but his effort signals the possibility of an effectively autoplastic act: since we can only impose upon the unknowable other before us, our best bet is to provide an accessible yet sincere account of the self. The nature and necessity of "play" should not be overlooked here. As a "two-hander," *The Zoo Story* is fundamentally a face to face, a sustained depiction of two individuals "compearing." Jerry self-reflexively manipulates Peter (and, in turn, the audience) by telling a series of autobiographical stories; in exposing Peter (and us) to the performative nature of these stories—the fact that they are necessarily staged—Jerry struggles to penetrate the self-effacing tools (i.e., codes, norms, themes) he must employ if he is to be understood. He endures so as to awaken a responsibility to otherness: I cannot *simply* remain faceless, as Žižek would like; I cannot abandon my responsibility by perpetually excusing myself as a faceless monster, even if (at the same time) I cannot demand that the monstrous other put on a face I recognize. I can and must gamble on an account of an always *imagined* self if I am to relate to, *or decide upon my relation to,* the other. This does not mean that I should "perversely" liquidate myself in the performative norms or themes that might produce an illusion of empathy, nor does it mean that I must maintain my eternal opacity or secret by refusing or evading (through cacophony or silence) all "false" gestures toward commonality, or sense. For indeed, as Judith Butler suggests, "An ability to affirm what is contingent and incoherent in oneself may allow one to affirm others who may or may not 'mirror' one's own constitution" (*Giving an Account* 41). What, in short, we see—in the light of neorealism's various contradictory moves—is this: the possibility of an ethical relationship hangs upon the possibility of a type of two-sided performance. On the one hand, we must gamble on a sincere articulation of the self, a recognizable (if imaginary) face, an identifiable position *in relation to* others.[5] On the other, we must signal or sublate (in the moment of this sincere expression) a constitutive negative, a perpetually generative or motile opacity, an *in*finite plasticity.

The Revelation of Dick

Even more overtly than Albee, Dick anticipates the assumptions (as well as the ethical roadblocks that obstruct the progress) of the current realist revival. Especially in those novels he produced in the 1960s—just as, that is, the postmodern dissolution of categorical absolutes was gaining momentum—Dick tends to depict worlds that are no longer capable of sustaining the illusion of ontological difference.[6] As a result, his characters frequently find themselves moving toward or assuming a type of hegemonic and anthropocentric egotism (or solipsism) that is only nominally opposed to its opposite—an inability or unwillingness to dissociate the self from an external world of things. While this troubling conflation of extremes is presented as an overtly ethical dilemma in *Do Androids Dream,* it is not until *VALIS*—one of his last novels (published in 1981) and one of his most theological—that Dick seems to provide his clearest response to the world's profound inaccessibility.[7] Set primarily in a contemporary and realistic Orange County, *VALIS* tells the story of Horselover Fat, a fictionalized version of Dick. Fat (like Dick) has suffered a number of emotional losses and claims (like Dick) to have been invaded by God in the form of a pink beam of light transmitted by an alien satellite called VALIS (a Vast Active Living Intelligence System). In other words, the novel articulates a complex and often contradictory theology, one that Dick developed and problematized himself over the course of almost twenty years. I will not attempt to relate the full details of this theology here.[8] At its heart, though, is a specific Heraclitian "insight": "The nature of things is in the habit of concealing itself," and so "Latent structure is master of obvious structure" (*VALIS* 36). This insight echoes any number of Dick's earlier efforts to theorize the complex relationship between the self, the world of other things (and persons), and an ideologically occluded reality.

As Lawrence Sutin notes, the bulk of Dick's writing is haunted by the assumption that all individuals must endure an ongoing "battle between the sheltered individual ("*idios kosmos*," or personal consciousness) and the external world ("*koinos kosmos*," or shared social consciousness)" (48)—the two categories of existence Dick articulates in "Schizophrenia & *The Book of Changes*" (1965). In this essay, the *idios kosmos* is clearly associated with a type of primary narcissism—insofar as this personal world of pure solipsism can, for humans, remain long after the moment of birth. We are, Dick assumes, "able to some degree to remain not thoroughly born" (175). Nevertheless, we are (sooner or later) faced with "the shared world" (175)—the *koinos kosmos,* the exterior world of law and opposition, of relational resistance to the ego's pure enjoyment. Dick here clearly anticipates Derrida's understanding of the "subjectile" ("Eating Well" 275),[9] of subjectivity as that which perpetually enters the world by being cut off from itself *as* other. For Dick, schizophrenia marks the problematic end of this ongoing and necessary process. Rather than a withdrawal into the self, Dick's schizophrenic experiences an utter loss of the self to that which opposes it. This is the type of schizophrenia that afflicts Isidore in *Do Androids Dream,* and it marks the end of an ontological "birthing process" just as surely as pure solipsism might. Dickian schizophrenia is, therefore, the end of destiny (i.e., a self "to come") because it is (paradoxically) the complete manifestation of destiny, the self's conclusion in *or by* the world. The problem, as Dick notes, is that this final manifestation of destiny "would be a greater loss than gain.... To understand the future totally would be to have it now. Try that, and see how it feels. Because once the future is gone, the possibility of free effective action of any kind is abolished" ("Schizophrenia" 181).[10] Hegel, of course, says something similar: "Spirit necessarily appears in Time, and it appears in Time just so long as it has not *grasped* its pure Notion, i.e. has not annulled Time" (*Phenomenology* 487). In Dick, however, this utter loss of the self to the shared symbolic strata of reality, this entropic moment of pure empathy, this dissolution of time itself, is clearly positioned as the obverse conclusion of the Freudian death drive—with the other side (as we have seen) being complete restitution in "the quiescence of the inorganic world" (Freud, *Beyond* 62). Both are defined by the loss of selfhood. A desire for either signals a profound refusal to endure what is uncanny, or asymptotically other.

Surely this is why, for Dick, "The nature of things is in the habit of concealing itself"; only through a type of withdrawal, or a form of concealment, can the self sustain its otherness and thus the very possibility of its authentic expression. Surely, too, this is why a biographer must, as Sutin notes on numerous occasions, contend with any number of "Phildickian inaccuracies and omissions" if he or she is to grasp an "essence [that] is true" (86). Dick, after all, once told a lover that the preservation of a "unique center of consciousness . . . [requires] a series of false-front personalities which we [can] shine in the faces of the people we meet to try to dazzle them" (letter to Mary, qtd. in Sutin 61). Dick's 1972 speech "The Android and the Human" says much the same. After articulating what he sees as the mechanization of human behavior and thought, Dick begins to praise the unpredictability of youth: "There are kids *now* who cannot be unplugged because no electric cord links them to any external power sources. Their hearts beat with an interior, private meaning. Their energy . . . comes from a stubborn, almost absurdly perverse refusal to be 'shucked'; that is, to be taken in by the slogans, the ideology—in fact, by any and all ideology itself, of whatever sort—that would reduce them to instruments of abstract causes, however 'good'" (188). This particular brand of "kids" evades "Androidization" because they never "allow [themselves] to become a means, or to be pounded down, manipulated, made into a means without . . . knowledge or consent" (191).[11] They "rebel[] not out of theoretical, ideological considerations, but only out of what might be called pure selfishness" (192). Dick thus struggles to demonstrate that the self must remain selfish if it is to survive its translation through the Other—or if, that is, it is to maintain its potential to be born. But such preservation comes with its own risks—as Dick's first semiautobiographical novel (*A Scanner Darkly* [1977]) makes apparent. The youth Dick praises in his 1972 speech are depicted in *A Scanner* as utterly lost to their own fantasies and idiosyncrasies. For the most part, in fact, the drug-addled characters that populate *A Scanner* (including Dick's own avatar, Bob Arctor) are paralyzed by their refusal to commit to (and thus be translated by) the norms of conventional society. Their potential to be born is certainly preserved, but the security of the womb proves too comforting to forsake in the name of change or action. Nevertheless, the book itself (as a concealed yet sincere account of Dick's most painful years) demonstrates the possibility of sustaining a selfish act of communion—a form of concealment that simultaneously "grasps" or "carries over" that which is preserved.

In *VALIS,* this possibility of a "disclosure or revelation . . . [that] is in fact concealment" (Hegel, *Phenomenology* 487) is directly related to the possibility and significance of a "theophany"—that is, "an in-breaking of God, an in-breaking which amounts to an invasion of our world" (Dick, *VALIS* 37). Yet the book is less about the reality (or lack thereof) of a divine entity called VALIS than it is about Dick's ability to relate the divine nature of his most intimate self, experiences, and beliefs—all of which he cannot help but question. Dick is careful to stress the "fictional" nature of the events depicted by stressing their absurdity. Indeed, the characters eventually find and view a film called *Valis,* which seems to justify Fat's must improbable claims. They then seek out and eventually meet the director: a Bowie-esque rock star (Eric Lampton) whose two-year-old daughter (Sophia) is the messiah—the bodily incarnation of VALIS. While many of the events in *VALIS* can be mapped onto "real" events in Dick's life, the film described (as well as Lampton and his messianic daughter) are offered as overt canards.

The absurdity of the plot is simultaneously compounded *and* undermined by the novel's unstable narrative perspective. The novel opens in the third person, clearly limited by Fat's point of view. However, before the introductory chapter ends, Dick intrudes as a first-person narrator, telling us that "[he is] Horselover Fat": "I am writing this in the third person to gain much-needed objectivity" (3). For the rest of the chapter, Dick reminds us of this conflation of identity by repeatedly "forgetting" to replace "I" with "Fat." For instance, while telling us about the funeral service for Gloria Knudson (a friend of Fat's who committed suicide), Dick "accidently" (yet intentionally) reverts to the first person: "The night before, Bob and I—I mean, Bob and Horselover Fat—drove to Oakland to see the movie *Patton*" (5). We are thus led to assume that the events described are true; only Fat is fictional. Or maybe not. Only a few lines earlier, Dick simultaneously asserts the story's veracity while denying it: "I am by profession, a science fiction writer. I deal in fantasies. My life is a fantasy. Nonetheless, Gloria Knudson lies in a box in Modesto, California" (5). This assertion—which opposes the fantasy of Dick's life with the absolute truth of Knudson's death—leads us to accept the fact that, if the novel is to provide a truth, that truth must be given as fiction. Even Knudson must be, at best, a fictionalized version of a "real" person—no matter how affective her death may have been. Things get more complicated once the initial chapter concludes. When the novel proper begins, Dick no longer tries to confuse Fat and Dick. Instead, he simply tells his own story in first person—that is, as the science-fiction writer Philip K. Dick, who happens to be friends with a man named Horselover Fat. In doing so, Dick strategically recounts while *or by* displacing much of his own biography. Dick's famous hallucination (*or authentic experience*) of a theophany becomes Fat's, including his "encounter" with the pink beam of light, his subsequent anamnesis, and the massive "exegesis" these experiences informed. The result is an autonarrative form that largely implies (in Julia Kristeva's terms) an extralinguistic genotext that determines, while being necessarily occluded by, a seemingly transparent phenotext. Or, more accurately (and given our discussion of Kristeva in the preceding chapter), Dick offers his account of the self as *nothing but phenotext,* as a necessary distortion of what cannot be said (if it is to remain true). He provides an authentic *and loving* account of himself by sublating that self through the mask of its narrativization, or coherent form. The novel's overt fictionality points to what is missing so as to "grasp" or point us toward the shadow of its absence.

Neoromantic Metafiction

To a large degree, *VALIS* (or Dick) behaves like one of Morton's hyperobjects. As Morton insists, "Objects [and not *just* hyperobjects] are hypocrites" (152). He makes this point by briefly considering lines from Gerard Manley Hopkins's "As kingfishers catch fire, dragonflies draw flames." Like an object—and, it would seem, *especially like* a hyperobject—Hopkins's "richly knotted vocabulary hides and tells the truth at the same time" (Morton 152). For Morton, Hopkins's complex phrasing exposes us to the fact that "you can only 'go yourself' if you are not yourself. You must be not-yourself at the same time as being yourself. When a thing cries, 'What I do is me,' the thing is saying 'This sentence is false'; 'I am lying'" (152). What we should take from this, Morton claims, is the fact that "the piercing blue note that the object sends out is both major and minor, a perfect photograph and an opaque mask, a femme fatale behind whose eyes is a depth of mystery or a blank void, or not even nothing. Doom" (152–53). Morton, though, fails to see the Hegelian implications of such a claim. While leading us to see (à la Hegel) that there is an "irreducible dissonance between my idea and the zone [*emitted* by an object]" (144), Morton insists on misreading Hegelian dialectics as a process of establishing an "A = A of immediacy" (145). What he misses is the fact that immediacy in Hegel never occurs without its negative, without its constitutive impossibility. Hegel, like Hopkins, largely disrupts the distinction between what is human and what is not—even if, at times, it might *seem* otherwise. In other words, Morton's point becomes that much more useful when its most Hegelian implications are extracted: if "the hyperobject is a liar" (153)—or if *all* (other) "objects are hypocrites"—then surely any effort to relate entails the possibility of sustaining our own "piercing blue note." Our only chance of preserving *and sharing* the other's subjec*tility* is by preserving *and sharing* our own. The alternative, as Dick frequently demonstrates, is extreme egotism and (or *as*) extreme empathy. It is precisely these conflating extremes that Dick manages to navigate via the autoplasticity of his final novels.

By the end of *VALIS*, the reality of God or aliens or the possibility of mapping a Vast Active Living Intelligence System remains wholly undecidable (simultaneously absurd and entirely possible). Dick finally seems to suggest that, in such a complex and ever-shifting network of occluded objects—a network that is clearly signified by the concept of VALIS itself[12]—all he can account for is himself, his own interpretation of that self and its experiences. The narrative structure functions to transpose the possibility of a theophany onto the possibility of relating the self. This function is first signaled when Dick invades the text immediately after the third-person narrator asserts that "one of God's greatest mercies is that he keeps us perpetually occluded" (3). But it becomes overt when Fat and Dick (and their two closest friends, Kevin and David) finally meet the messianic Sophia. The two-year-old messiah angrily points at Dick and chastises him for attempting suicide. Dick, though, quickly assures her that *he* did nothing of the sort: "It was Horselover Fat" (210). In this moment, Dick overtly displaces responsibility for his own behavior, his own doubt and his own confusion. But Sophia's response wholly refuses his efforts: "Phil, Kevin, and David. Three of you. There are no more" (210). And when Dick turns to "to speak to Fat—[he sees] no one. . . . Fat was gone. Nothing remained of him" (210). On one level, Fat's sudden disappearance is hardly surprising. It is anticipated in the preface when Dick overtly confuses his pronouns, and again when Eric Lampton rejects Dick's claim (made over the phone) that "the information [from VALIS] was fired at [his] friend Horselover Fat" (185). As Lampton notes, "That's you. 'Philip' means 'Horselover' in Greek, lover of horses. 'Fat' is the German translation of 'Dick.' So you've translated your name" (185). In such moments, Dick (as persona *and* author) is careful to remind us that he and Fat are analogues, or two sides of the same coin. Yet Fat's *actual* disappearance remains utterly bewildering and disruptive. His actual presence in the novel is frequently validated, and the plot largely depends upon this validation. His friends speak and refer to him as an independent entity, and he clearly lives a life that is distinct from Dick's. Consequently, this moment of profound healing, or closure—this *true* encounter with divinity, this realization of destiny *as* the future made present, this autobiographical admission that Dick (himself) attempted suicide and believes in the very theology his persona has thus far ridiculed—is given as a suture that cannot hold. The novel cannot hold itself together if Fat is merely Dick's hallucination. Divine revelation—as, that is, the experience of self-fulfillment—is possible *only* in the face of its impossibility. A few days later, and after fully convincing Dick that "[she] will not fail [him]" (223), Sophia is tragically and *accidently* killed, and Fat immediately reappears. A certain healing wound, or split, is by necessity reasserted:[13] Dick begins to suspect that "there is no savior" and Fat convinces himself that "St. Sophia is going to be born again" (242). In the end, Fat decides to travel the world in search of the next manifestation of VALIS, while Dick (who has come to accept that Fat is actually searching for "[him]self") begins to act on his own suspicion that "the divine intrudes where you least expect it" (254): "My search kept me at home; I sat before the TV set in my living room. I sat; I waited; I watched; I kept myself awake. As we had been told, originally, long ago, to do; I kept my commission" (255). But if Fat's search is, finally, for "[him]self," than so too must be Dick's. It is for himself that he waits. Unlike Fat, though, Dick seems to realize that he can only ever intrude in those places he is least expected—in the ephemeral norms and reductive impositions (or thematics) of a fictionalized world, or novel.

Of course, the larger implication is that Dick's commission must be our commission as well. Just as Dick must learn to endure divinity's constitutive delay—which, by the end of the novel, clearly signifies a willingness to endure what Sartre refers to as the "anguish . . . of being my own future, in the mode of not-being" (68)—we must find a way to take the overtly fictional nature of the novel as a type of deferred arrival. The novel asks that we endure a divine invasion,[14] an invasion that occludes or withholds the very thing (i.e., Dick) it presents in all sincerity; it struggles to give sense to, while maintaining the opacity of, "the hidden, concealed, secret or unknown god" (*VALIS* 35)—what, following Lacan, Žižek typically refers to as "agalma." In a world of faceless monsters, we must gamble on those faces or phenomenological surfaces that bring self and other into contact; but to do so ethically, we must resist abandoning the *in*finite other to those surfaces. To account for the self is to *invade* the form that would make such an account relatable. A true account entails the violent negation of what is negated. By opening us to a constitutive and motile absence at the heart of what gives him coherent and accessible form, Dick employs while simultaneously canceling the norms that necessarily occlude (or negate) his *in*finite otherness—his *in*humanity, his divinity, his plasticity. Like Albee's Jerry (a messianic avatar himself), Dick's *in*humanity "[comes] unto" (Albee 61) us by means of a violent diremption, the dehiscence of what binds Dick's mimetic form to its *in*finite ideal. In this moment of diremption, the form paradoxically "grasps" its content by signaling its inevitable cancelation or deferment; it "picks up" what it "annuls" (as does, of course, the Hegelian *Aufhebung*). Dick's book enacts a divine invasion that can be supported, or not. It is up to us, as it is to Peter. Likewise, it is up to us to gamble on a reciprocal invasion—to relate to this other that is (as Dick's translation of *koine* Greek suggests of God) "no where" *and* "now here."

The specifically Hegelian nature of this revelatory concealment becomes particularly apparent if we compare it to the metafictions of postmodernism. An autoplastic act must surely entail certain self-reflexive gestures. In the absence of self-reflexivity we risk succumbing to the illusion of fixed immediacy, or final apprehension. We risk losing the very self we wish to give. But the self-reflexivity of the autoplastic account is in no way the same as the self-reflexivity of the perversely postmodern. It does not simply *absent* the subject—assuring us (in turn) that the self is only ever an effect of the discursive frames that make it known. The type of metafiction we see in *VALIS* is, in this sense, less postmodern than (what we began to call in the previous chapter) "neoromantic." To a certain extent, *VALIS* represents one of the first overt moves beyond or *through* postmodernism. As Christopher Palmer suggests, *VALIS* struggles to employ the overtly fictional so as to "den[y] its fictionality" (236). But this "denial" is not simply "a sign of its realism" (236). Instead, Dick resists succumbing to the inescapability of simulacrum, to the inertia of the symbolic, by refusing to construct "a fake . . . presented as a reality" (236). Instead, he "disconcerts" us (according to Palmer) by constructing his autobiographical novel as "a not-fake" (236).[15] In doing so, he effectively sublates the typically "symbolic" nature of both modern and postmodern aesthetics—if, that is, we take "symbolic" to mean (as Hegel does) those forms of art that wholly refuse the illusion of mimetic accuracy or closure by ostentatiously embracing "indefiniteness and extravagance" (*Aesthetics* 76).

While, in modernism, this impulse toward "distortion"—toward streams of consciousness, cubism, primitivism, nonlinear storytelling, or any of the various styles Mark C. Taylor might associate with modern "disfiguration"[16]—is still motivated by a desire to "elevate... phenomenal appearance to the Idea by the diffuseness, immensity, and splendor of the formations deployed" (Hegel, *Aesthetics* 76), it finally exhausts itself in postmodernism; "indefiniteness and extravagance" become mere parody (or pastiche), pessimistic extremes that hollow out the possibility of a subject. Nevertheless, both modernism *and* postmodernism function to repudiate the problematic naïveté of what we might call (by continuing to redeploy Hegel's terms) "classical" forms—those artistic efforts that would claim the "adequate embodiment of the Idea in the shape peculiarly appropriate to the Idea itself in its essential nature" (77). For Hegel, of course, "classical" refers specifically to the beguiling perfection of Greek and Roman sculpture (which problematically assumes the immediacy of spiritual truth in its given form), but we can relocate a classical impulse in any number of subsequent movements: from the social realism of the nineteenth century to the documentary films of the twentieth. The experimental forms of both modernism and postmodernism are, in this sense, a strenuous response to persistent modes of classicism. The problem is that these largely oppositional or overtly antithetical forms frequently slip (backward) toward the abject skepticism of the symbolic—which, in Hegel, predates the classical. These forms risk negating the subject altogether—in cacophony, silence, or the vagaries of perverse textual play. A text like *VALIS* manages something else. As does romantic art for Hegel, the autoplasticity of *VALIS* effects a sublative return to the symbolic *through the classical*; its ideal of an autobiographical self is finally exposed *as* the failure to expose it. By forgoing the evasive polyphony of modernism (and cautiously redeploying the self-reflexive tendencies of postmodernism), the novel exposes and endures a fundamental discrepancy between form and content. As a result, it "throws us into the 'thing itself'" (Žižek, *Tarrying* 242n19), overcoming a symbolic tendency toward irresponsible withdrawal.

VALIS exemplifies the ethical implications of a subtle sublative shift in emphasis and heralds the possibility of an autobiographical expression that moves beyond both the modern and the postmodern symbolic. We can certainly find examples of similar efforts in both modernism and postmodernism—and, obviously (if we follow Hegel), in aesthetic movements that predate both. In the contemporary moment, however, the ethical promise of neoromantic autoplasticity is most fully realized in those works that strive to overcome the hegemony of the postmodern *at its extreme*. To track the full potential of this shift we must then look more closely at the way in which the self-reflexivity of high postmodernism is sustained *yet repudiated* in more recent (and ethically grounded) texts—those texts we might associate with a "post-postmodern" moment.[17] And nowhere is a shift in the function of self-reflexive technique more apparent than in the shift from the irresponsible metafiction of *Seinfeld* (1989), which places us in a world where everything is a game and everyone is solipsistically self-motivated, to the oddly sincere self-reflexivity of *Curb Your Enthusiasm* (2000), which constantly implicates an *in*finite absence at the heart of its fictional forms.

Curb Your Divinity

In season 7 of Larry David's HBO series, *Curb Your Enthusiasm* (which aired in 2009), Larry agrees to write and produce a *Seinfeld* reunion special with Jerry Seinfeld so as to cast his estranged wife, Cheryl (Cheryl Hines), as George Costanza's ex-wife and (thus hopefully) win her back. While negotiating (and, of course, simultaneously causing) a number of complications, Larry manages to implement his plan, and production goes forward as the season progresses. In episode 9, Larry finds himself standing beside Julia Louis-Dreyfus (who played Elaine Benes on *Seinfeld*) while looking upon the resurrected sets of Jerry's apartment and Monk's café—the two primary sets in *Seinfeld*'s nine-year run. Julia is quick to comment on the uncanny nature of the scene: "It's like going back in time, or never leaving the past, *or something*" (my emphasis).

It's virtually impossible to determine if, in any particular episode of *Curb Your Enthusiasm,* a line is scripted or improvised. Although David writes a guiding story for each episode, a story that ostensibly describes central plot points and character interactions, the show is primarily improvised. Scripted or not, Julia's remark functions metonymically as a commentary on the entire season—a season that reduplicates the metafictional regress that defined numerous *Seinfeld* episodes, particularly those episodes (in season 4) after Jerry is approached by NBC to create a sitcom based on his stand-up comedy routine. Instead of George (who is famously based on David) and Jerry discussing ideas for such a show—ideas, moreover, that are derived from previous episodes of *Seinfeld* (such as "The Chinese Restaurant" in season 2)—we get (in *Curb*) Jerry and the "real" Larry discussing ideas based on previous episodes of *Curb.* Most significantly, Jerry and Larry self-reflexively refer to the season 6 episode in which Cheryl finally decides to leave Larry because he's more worried about the TiVo guy than her phone call from a plummeting aircraft. The TiVo episode, in fact, becomes the central plot point of the *Seinfeld* reunion show as well as the basis for Larry's argument that Cheryl should play Amanda (i.e., George's ex-wife). "I think," Larry tells Jerry in episode 6, "that you want to go with an unknown for this part." He goes on to insist that an "unknown" will help viewers to "believe that it is real." And Cheryl is a particularly great "unknown" because (in terms of the TiVo-guy plot) "that happened to [him], *with Cheryl*" (my emphasis). Jerry, though, is unconvinced: "What's real got to do with what we do?" Would Nixon, Jerry wonders, be the best person to play Nixon in *Frost/Nixon*?

This argument is repeated and stressed in episode 8. After watching Cheryl audition for the role (by reenacting, almost word for word, the original TiVo scene), Larry asserts that her rendition is "perfect" because "she lived [the] part." But Jerry is again confused by Larry's insistence on verisimilitude: "Who cares who was on the plane? It's not a real plane. It's not a real show. It's not a real story." When the actual scene is filmed, Jerry insists, "They're gonna cut the plane in half. It's not even gonna be a whole plane." There is, in other words, nothing *real* going on here. The self-reflexive nature of the scene is blatantly corrosive, as Jerry's referent is utterly unstable. Which plane, which show, which story is *not* real? Is he talking about *Curb* or the *Seinfeld* reunion? Did a "real" TiVo guy have any part to play in David's "real" divorce from Laurie Lennard—which, significantly, ended a short time before Cheryl left Larry in *Curb*? The entire season thus repeats those moments in *Seinfeld* when the line between the show's real creation and its fictional re-creation (*in Seinfeld*) are absurdly confused. Or rather, viewing season 7 of *Curb* is "like going back in time, or never leaving the past, *or something*." But what marks this ambiguous "or something"? What, if anything, signals a difference between *Curb* and its postmodern predecessor? Given our discussion of *VALIS* and metafiction, we might say this difference—this "something"—is merely a matter of emphasis, the mark of a certain "shift" in intent. Such a shift is signaled by Larry's various appeals to verisimilitude as well as *Curb*'s tendency toward cinema verité or documentary style (e.g., handheld camera work, improvisation, actors playing themselves, etc.). If this is indeed the case, we are nevertheless left to wonder about the precise effect of this shift, this overt reduplication of the very devices we have come to associate with postmodernism's perverse irresponsibility.

Seinfeld (which ran from 1989 to 1998) was surely the watershed mark of canonical postmodernism, the broadest *because most populist* rotation of its relatively brief historical spiral. At its most basic, *Seinfeld* is an ostentatiously solipsistic TV à clef, the key to which is provided (or at least *intimated*) in episode 3 of season 4, "The Pitch." After George suggests (while referring to *and on the heels of* a random conversation at Monk's) that "*this* should be the show," Jerry attempts to clarify the idea: "So on the show there's a character named George Costanza?" "Yeah," George piquantly insists, "you base a character on me ... There's something wrong with that? *I'm* a character. People are always saying to me, 'You know, you're quite a character.'" In the end, Jerry and George decide that the show will focus on Jerry and George and their friends (Elaine and Kramer) and that it will be about "nothing"—nothing, that is, but *their* everyday (real) experiences. In other words, the show they make (*in the show*) will be the show we are watching—once removed. Yet nothing about the show (*in the show*) will be real. What they are discussing is merely a simulation of a simulation, after all. This moment of infinite regress functions to exemplify "the signifier's game running its course" (Žižek, *Ridiculous* 36). We are reminded that Jerry Seinfeld *is* Jerry Seinfeld in *Seinfeld* and that the scene depicted mirrors a *real* conversation between David and Seinfeld; but the self-reflexivity of the moment (along with the obviously fictionalized Jerry who speaks) finally and effectively throws into question the possibility of a *real* Jerry Seinfeld anterior to his performance. Likewise, George *is* indeed "a character"—a character who simply implies (or reflects back) David's own status as another interpellated subject, another player effected and defined by his position in an intersubjective network.

The easy point to make here is that *Curb* is different because it is more inclined to privilege the (possibility of the) real. The show constantly risks effacing the line that separates the fictional Larry and the real David[18]— Larry's separation and then divorce from Cheryl and David's *actual* divorce from Lennard being only the most obvious point of conflation. The fictional Larry thus always seems bound to—*even as* he is presented as an infinitely pliable, or fictional, expression of—an anterior self. Larry (like any of the other characters who play themselves in the show) incessantly gestures toward, and thus sustains *by never becoming,* the real he necessarily effaces.[19] The "real" David remains *essentially* absent or a negative of his potential fulfillment, or destiny—an entity that is always *before* (temporally behind *and* in front of) Larry. Or rather, Larry sustains the Hegelian *notion* of David insofar as *he* "necessarily appears in Time, and [he] appears in Time just so long as [he] has not grasped [his] pure Notion, i.e. has not annulled Time" (*Phenomenology* 487).

This will make more sense if we begin to think of *Curb*'s metafictional repetitions as a series of temporal (or momentary) "deployments." Such deployments are, if we follow Malabou, distinctly Hegelian. Consider, as Malabou does (in her efforts to privilege the concept of plasticity in Hegel's system), the following passage from Hegel's *Philosophy of Mind*: "And so in spirit every character under which it appears is a stage in a process of specification and development, a step forward (*Vorwärtsgehen*) towards its goal (*seinem Ziele*), in order to make itself into, and to realize in itself, what it implicitly is" (qtd. in Malabou 19). In *Curb*, the deployment of representation toward its end—like, in this particular instance, the representation of a failed or failing marriage, of jealousy and unintentional acts of estrangement—is clearly tied to the essential plasticity of that end (which is always also its point of origin). These representations or repetitions entail, by implication, the possibility of a temporalization that maintains a future to come—a future, for instance, when the trauma or inexplicability of the *in*human other is finally reformed, understood and thus *cast* aside. Since, according to Malabou, Hegel's "God 'transplants (*verstzt*) himself into the world of time' . . . and thus appears in time before himself" (119), temporalization is the very possibility of representation, "the becoming accidental of essence" (119). Representation is the articulation or repetition of what "sees (itself) coming" (118)—that is, "the process through which individual subjectivity *repeats* the movements of the divine alienation" (112; my emphasis). In autoplastic works like *Curb* and *VALIS*, this coming into being of what "sees (itself) coming" promises but does not entail "the final banishment of all temporality and the advent of the spirit's [*or self's*] unchanging and indifferent present" (128). Instead, the sublative nature of these works *perpetually* opens us to "the time which lies ahead" (128), the plasticity of which results in or makes possible a perpetual series of momentary reformations.

In *Seinfeld*, though—and in the larger tradition of postmodern metafiction—this sense of distance is constantly at risk, or simply denied; "the horizon of a pure and absolute future" no longer seems possible or efficacious because the emphasis falls on its status as simulacrum. History comes to an end (as Dick fears it might); space and time collapse in on themselves. And so, while the metafictional repetitions of *Seinfeld* largely effect a sense of endless and vertiginous refractions—functioning, ultimately, to expose the manner in which the thing repeated was always already a repetition—*Curb*'s repetitions provoke an awareness of their inevitable failure *as repetitions*. This failure opens us to what is lost in, or effaced by, the moment of repetition *as* the necessary act of representation. *Curb* constantly asserts its verisimilitude—by overtly and consistently paralleling David's real life (e.g., his move from New York to LA, his friendship with Ted Danson, his divorce, etc.)—while simultaneously *and just as consistently* undermining it. For instance, early on in season 7 (and unbeknownst to Larry), Jerry invites Meg Ryan to play the role of Amanda in the *Seinfeld* reunion show. She eventually turns it down, and it is then offered to a character *played by* Elizabeth Shue. Inexplicably, Shue (unlike Ryan) does not play a version of herself; she plays a character named Virginia. In such moments, the show manages to adhere to some sense of an authentic "Thing" while simultaneously embracing the necessity of a fiction that can mediate it. We are exposed to the irreconcilable difference between an *in*human other "to come" and the representational play that gives it momentary form. At precisely the same time, this perpetual fissure—this diremptive "limit," this point of "mediation in virtue of which something and other each *both is and is not*" (Hegel, *Logic* 99)—is presented as the essential space of aesthetic and ethical responsibility, an always dehiscing seam that links truth and representation absolutely *even as* it precludes the ossification of the *in*finite *in* representation.

The suggestion is this: the fluidity of the *in*human self can only be expressed in those forms of representation that work sincerely to apprehend it while simultaneously opening us to *and forcing us to endure* what is always "leftover," or in excess of a given form, what always and necessarily escapes *while acquiescing to* that form. This is precisely what *Curb* seems intent on demonstrating: how, in Hegel's terms, "an individual cannot know what he [really] is until he has made himself a reality" (*Phenomenology* 240). And "to make oneself a reality" is, in Hegel, to act—to perform or to represent oneself—in full accordance with a plastic "end" that motivates *even as it is effected by* such action, or *acting*. The *in*finite self is what "in being laid hold of flees, or . . . has already flown" (131). It finds its "confirmation" only by "overcoming *and* enjoying the existence alien to it" (132; my emphasis). There is certainly little sense in contemporary metafictional works like *Curb* that we can lay hold of the real, yet we are constantly given to understand that the experience of failing to do so necessarily *entails* the very Thing that is lost. In the "appearance" put forth in any given episode of *Curb,* we are given to understand that "the inner [as ultimate or final referent] is no doubt a *visible* invisible, but it is not tied to this [one] appearance: it can be manifested just as well in another way, just as another inner can be manifested in the same appearance" (190–91). This is not to suggest that the show warrants the addition (or appearance) of "any old thing" (Derrida, "Plato's Pharmacy" 64); it struggles instead to "hold on to the original content of its essence" (Hegel, *Phenomenology* 239) and thus endures the "strenuous effort of the Notion" (35).

More simply: a work of reified postmodernism (like *Seinfeld*) largely abandons the *in*finite to its fictional representation(s), while a work like *Curb* struggles to *sublate* it. Neither allows us to assume that we have somehow escaped the fictional. Works like *Curb* do not simply return us to the illusion of an *accessible* real anterior to its fictional representations; they do not return us to the aesthetic totalitarianism of the traditional documentary mode or social/psychological realism—those aesthetic modes that in their own way effectively circumvent, or refuse to endure, the difference between referent and representation, real and symbolic. This is why the "classical" extremes of realism are no different—or no less perverse (in a strictly Žižekian sense)—than the extremes of modern and postmodern distortion. At either pole the *notion* of the *in*human is abandoned entirely to the form(s) in which it is given. While realism ostensibly denies this loss—offering the sense that "everything is revealed, and nothing obscure or inward is left over any more" (Hegel, *Aesthetics* 604)—postmodernism insists upon it. The paradox, of course, is that postmodernism's "symbolic" corrosion of mimetic unity, like the self-assured narratives of "classical" realism, finally collapses the difference between symbol and referent. This is why, in *Seinfeld*, the subject finally disappears altogether; it no longer "persists *sublime* above [the] multiplicity of shapes which do not correspond with it" (77). Like all opposites in Hegel, the classical and the symbolic are really no different.[20] The only way to navigate past these obverse extremes is to endure what refuses apprehension.

And indeed: the autoplasticity of a work like *Curb* (or *VALIS*) renews the efficacy of postmodernism's symbolic tendencies even as it negates (or undoes) them. Is this not the reason why Larry *denies* a "shift" in his aesthetic even as the very nature of *Curb* clearly undermines any such denial? In episode 3 of season 7, Jerry asks Larry why he is suddenly amenable to the idea of a reunion show. As Jerry notes, such shows have never lived up to Larry's "aesthetic standards." Such shows require, it would seem, too much self-certainty, too much sincerity, the sense that art is about more than ironic self-effacement. If Larry is willing to do the show, Jerry insists, there's been some sort of "shift." But Larry refuses the suggestion: "No shift." And Larry is right, of course. He only wants to do the show so as to manipulate Cheryl. But this effort at manipulation finally undermines the manner in which the show ostensibly conflates David's real life with its fictional representation. The absurdity that ensues implies the *in*finitely plastic referent it elides. Rather than fixating on the primacy of the signifier, on simply exposing the symbolic production of reality, *Curb* (unlike *Seinfeld*) shifts our attention to a plastic self (or Real) that is effaced *even* *as it effects* the form of its representation. In the reunion show, George wins only to lose Amanda again. In *Curb*, Larry wins only to lose Cheryl again. The connection to David's own divorce in the wake of Lennard's apparent infidelity cannot be denied—especially in light of Larry's absurd paranoia that Cheryl and Jason Alexander are having an affair. Yet the actual truth of David's relationship with Lennard remains absent, "a *visible* invisible." This does not mean that, as viewers, we can discover the "truth" and then compare it to its fictional representation. (There is surely even less truth to be had outside *Curb*.) The absence of the truth is instead implicated in its representation, or reduplication on screen. George's story is clearly not Larry's, yet something about Larry's cannot be effaced from George's. A certain "inertia of the Real" holds the two representations together. Rather than effacing the referent—of implicating it as *only* an effect of representation—the metafiction of *Curb* (like the metafiction of *VALIS*) confirms it *by absenting it*. Larry *is* David even as his performance of David gestures toward (or constantly insists upon) an insurmountable diremption. It is, then, *perhaps* David (and not Larry) who describes his plan to deal with the NBC executive in charge of the reunion show: "I'll go," David says, "somewhere between begrudging and sincere."

9 / Bob Dylan's Autoplasticity

> *It's you and you only I been thinking about*
> *But you can't see in and it's hard lookin' out*
> *I'm twenty miles out of town in cold irons bound*
> —BOB DYLAN, "COLD IRONS BOUND"

Plastic Vanity

Bob Dylan, too, is "quite a character." Viewed at a distance—and therefore as a whole consisting of innumerable and often contradictory parts—Dylan's body of work traverses the very course that links *Seinfeld*'s "The Pitch" to the seventh season of David's *Curb Your Enthusiasm*. I do not mean (especially) to be blithe: such a comparison is not as random or as forced as it might appear. In 2003—one year before releasing the first (and thus far *only*) volume of his autobiography (*Chronicles*)—Dylan produced and starred in a film he cowrote with Larry Charles (who, after working as a writer on *Seinfeld*, went on to direct numerous episodes of *Curb*). The star-studded (yet largely panned) film—*Masked and Anonymous* (which Charles also directed)—has Dylan playing Jack Fate, an old and washed-up folk/country artist. The film is set in an overtly fantasmatic America, one that echoes elements from any number of Dylan songs (e.g., the mythic Latin America evoked in "One More Cup of Coffee," "Isis," and "Señor"; the postapocalyptic landscape of "A Hard Rain's A-Gonna Fall," "All along the Watchtower," and "Ain't Talkin'"; and the absurdist tableaus of "Desperation Row" and "Tombstone Blues," etc.). Violent revolutionaries and equally violent counterrevolutionaries populate the landscape as the stoic Fate makes his way from an unnamed gulag-type prison to an unnamed city. He has been freed by his old manager, Uncle Sweetheart (John Goodman), so that he might headline a benefit concert for "the real victims of this revolution." Sweetheart, though, has little concern for these "real victims"; he simply needs money to pay off some debts. The film opens with a montage of "real" footage (depicting all manner of natural disasters and warlike activities). This montage eventually transforms into footage of an impoverished yet clearly staged street. Played over the whole is a Japanese version of Dylan's "My Back Pages," a version that begins and ends with the voice of a "preacher" playing on the radio. As the montage sequence ends, and right before the camera finally locates Sweetheart (who occupies an office in the "Midas Judas Building"), the preacher can be heard condemning a "false" Christianity: "The false Christianity you subscribe to is nothing more than the cult of the virgin. People, it's time to evaluate and reflect on your lives. God has turned his back on this nation. Think about it. What did Martin Luther King get out of the whole thing? A Boulevard?" For this reason alone, the preacher suggests, he'd "swear on the Bible." It's "a book," after all, "of treachery and murder and genocide." This strange admonishment of Christian moral certitude foregrounds the introduction of Sweetheart.

After a point-of-view shot leads us into an elevator, we find Sweetheart attempting to talk his way out of an imminent beating. Ostentatiously framed by two foregrounded bodies (carefully positioned to the left and right of the screen), he sits at his desk. He tells the two men—presumably the same two men whose perspective carried us up the elevator on their way to "shake down" Sweetheart—that they are "about to make a hideous choice": "You two are pitiable figures weeping with blood, and it's gonna be your own blood. Are you aware, gentlemen, that this is all a play?" The answer, apparently, is no. Or they don't care. They simply want to know if he's "got the money or not." In a final effort to avoid the inevitable, Sweetheart switches gears, claiming (suddenly) to "understand [that the two men] are not accustomed to staring in the face of God." Bewildered by these apparent non sequiturs, one of the men asks Sweetheart why he is still talking. Sweetheart's explanation seems to encapsulate the film as a whole—or rather, Dylan as its ostensible raison d'être: "As long as I keep talking I know I am still alive." The apparent yet largely farcical tension here—between the absolutes of life *as* the divine and the vagaries of performance, play and language—becomes even more pronounced when the next scene begins. After the two men finally fall upon Sweetheart, a dissolve leads to a series of establishing shots that take us out of Sweetheart's office and into what appears to be a large soundstage filled with garishly decorated trailers and circus-like props. This transition is accompanied by the voice of Nina Veronica (Jessica Lange)—a TV producer working with Sweetheart—as she tells two apparent "backers" that "[she's] not going to debate semantics." "Look," she insists, "it's real. It's beyond phenomena. They're shooting and killing." However, when the backers ask what "they are fighting about," her response is wholly dismissive: "I don't know what they're fighting about." What she *does* know is that the only way to get rock stars on television is to give them "a cause" or "an award."

These opening scenes draw our attention (à la postmodernism) to the utterly selfish and constructed nature of social engagement and revolutionary protest, the complete impossibility of effective communion or cultural change. The film, after all, is a pastiche of artificiality and simulacra[1]—what Charles calls "a post-apocalyptic, sci-fi, film noir, spaghetti western, musical comedy" (qtd. in Sounes 457). The star power of the cast—including Dylan's own—amplifies this sense of performativity. Each scene tends to play out as much between actors as between characters. And each scene appears overtly staged, another tableau in a series of tableaus. For instance, after Fate is released from jail, he walks with methodical "style" down a flight of stairs and alongside a graffiti-covered building. He finally stops beside a man named Prospero (Cheech Marin) who sits on the building's steps. Dylan *as Fate* carefully lifts one leg onto the step and arranges himself in the overtly artificial stance of a cinematic hero, his suit bag thrown casually over his shoulder. Both men look off into the distance as they discuss the fact that Fate is "leaving town." After noting that "nothing ever really is [by choice]," Prospero asks Fate, "Where [he's] headed?" Fate nods to the left and says, "That way." Prospero is positive yet absurdly indifferent: "That's a good direction. I've done that a lot. One of my favorites. You know what else is good? That way." He then points to the right. While r*eplay*ing or recontextualizing lyrics from Dylan's "Can't Wait"—"Night or day, it doesn't matter where I go anymore, I just go"[2]—the scene exemplifies while simultaneously undermining (via its ostentatiously parodic construction) a tendency toward abject fatalism. *This* is simply the way the stage has been set. Choice is an illusion effected by coercive market forces or God. *This* is all a play and life is only ever "actual" in the moment of its performance.

From this perspective, the film functions as pure and vacuous spectacle—an unforgivable "vanity production" (as Roger Ebert claims). There is no denying this: the problem of vanity lurks at the film's heart—as it lurks (or arguably defines) Dylan's entire career. But something else seems to be happening here, for the vanity in question is evident only insofar as it is also undermined, or negated. In the same respect, the moral vacuity of the film (its revelry in form, its apparent confirmation of Sweetheart's assertion that it's all "a play," its ostensible valorization of an indifferent Dylan/

Fate who might go left *or* right, etc.) is paradoxically given *or structured* to signal a commitment to (its) content, or what is "beyond phenomena": the real, the *in*finite, Dylan himself. We might in fact hazard the suggestion (even this early on) that the film *as* Dylan allows us to "stare into the face of God" by carving out (in or *through* "play") the absence of an *in*finitely plastic absolute. Or, in strictly Hegelian terms, we come to see the actor *because of* (not in spite of) a mask.[3] We are provided with what we might term a *concealatory* revelation, an experience of concealment *and* conciliation (with or through the language of the other/Other). This is not the mysterious suggestion of a "beyond" we get in acts of stringent and elitist obfuscation. It is an act of radically democratic friendship. But we should move slowly here.

Given the structure of the film, Fate (as *both* Dylan *and* the Hegelian concept for an uncontrollable and alien force) is finally presented as the effect of what he/it determines. As in the state of Hegel's "absolute knowledge," though, the two (Fate and the self *or* Fate and Dylan) remain distinct even as their difference is negated via the recognition or suggestion that such difference constitutes the (absent) whole. As Hegel asserts, "The disclosure or revelation which substance has in . . . consciousness is in fact concealment, for substance is still *self-less being* and what is disclosed to it is only the certainty of itself" (*Phenomenology* 487). What is revealed is never the self *finally*—or *finally fixed*. Such a revelation would be an illusion of Hegelian stoicism, or simplistic "picture thinking." In recognizing myself as "not there"—while simultaneously recognizing myself as that which recognizes—I retain *while becoming certain of* my *in*finite self. *I am* precisely and only my "own restless process of superseding [my]self, or *negativity*" (491). This "negation of the negation" is of course the very process we saw both Dick and David playing out. For Dylan, like Dick (like Hegel), it is a process that cannot be divorced from the potential for divine revelation. Like any number of Dylan songs, *Masked and Anonymous* draws out this connection, both literally and figuratively. Sweetheart even defends Fate's star power by asking Veronica if "Jesus [has] to walk on water twice to make a point." The line parodies the ridiculous nature of Dylan's often obsessive fan base while simultaneously clueing us into the film's specific process, or "movement" (as Hegel would say), a process that exemplifies the manner in which, since at least the midsixties, Dylan has struggled to conceal himself *as* God—in so far as he has struggled to sustain, share, and present to himself "God-in-me." Dylan's entire project can be defined as an ongoing "placing of the Infinite [self] in thought, but wholly other than thought, which is structured as a comprehension of the *cogitatum* [that is thought] by a *cogitatio* [who does the thinking]" (Levinas, "God and Philosophy" 63). What could be *more* vain? But this is a strategic and radical vanity, a vanity that is sure to frustrate those "thug-like" viewers who would demand anything like a simple "pay off." It is (if we follow Levinas alongside, or as already anticipated in, Hegel) a radically true or *sublated* form of vanity, a profoundly *auto*plastic vanity that sustains the *in*finite malleability of the self via its *concealatory* destructions—the effects of *plastique*.⁴ The infinite is given (vainly) to be thought *even as* its thinking "causes the 'formal reality' of the *cogitatio* to break apart" (63). In giving the self to be thought through *and in the moment of* an explosive breakup, the autoplastic (or radically vain) foments my responsibility for the *in*finite other.

Ebert's critique of *Masked and Anonymous* is, therefore, telling. After calling the film a "vanity production," he laments that he "[doesn't] have any idea what to think of [Dylan]. He has so long since disappeared into his persona that there is little received sense of the person there." In saying this, Ebert touches upon the very paradox we're attempting to track. If Dylan is inaccessible, how can we justify calling his work vain? *Whose* vanity are we talking about? Ebert senses the problem, as he finds himself (in the end) transposing the *egotistical* vanity he perceives onto the film's cast and crew: "The vanity belongs perhaps to those who flattered their own by working with him, by assuming (in the face of all they had learned during hard days of honest labor on a multitude of pictures) that his genius would somehow redeem a screenplay that could never have seemed other than what it was, incoherent raving juvenile meanderings." What Ebert seems to miss is the possibility that the vanity he perceives is the effect of *both* vacuity *and* presence—or rather, and by implication, *neither* vacuity *nor* presence. Strictly speaking, what is "vain" is empty, hollowed out, abandoned. While Ebert clearly uses the term in its popular sense (to denote the peak of egotism, the abject insistence upon oneself and one's thoughts above all else), his inability to disentangle his feelings about Dylan's vain artistic absence from his feelings about the film's egotistical vanity exemplifies a tension in the term itself. Unable to resolve this tension in a satisfactory manner, Ebert's critique cannot help but open us to the possibility that the film, like any number of Dylan's songs or performances or interviews or books, sustains a disconcerting relation(ship), an encounter of (ghostly or plastic) proximity: a distance that connects, or a representation that gives while refusing to efface.

And Ebert certainly seems disconcerted. After mocking a scene in which a character named Pagan Lace (Penélope Cruz) tells a Pope John

Paul II impersonator and a Gandhi impersonator that she loves Fate's lyrics because "they are not precise—they are completely open to interpretation," Ebert asserts that he "[feels] it ungenerous to have the answer but wrap it in enigmas." Given his transparency and honesty, Woody Guthrie is (according to Ebert) a far greater artist than Dylan. To prove his point, Ebert abruptly shifts gears to praise a documentary about Ramblin' Jack Elliot (Aiyana Elliott's *The Ballad of Ramblin' Jack*)—which tracks Dylan's efforts to usurp the legacy of both Elliot and Guthrie. At the peak of his frustration with Dylan and Dylan's film, Ebert takes (melancholic) refuge in the most conventional of documentaries and the illusion of accessing a subject in the absence *of vanity*. Simultaneously, he positions *Masked and Anonymous* as a *type of* documentary, but a type of autobiographical documentary that is somehow and simultaneously hollow *and* full of (it)self—or rather, an autobiographical text that "knows [or presents] not only itself [or its subject] but also the negative of itself, or its limit" (Hegel, *Phenomenology* 492). It is in precisely this sense that the film *and* Dylan can be viewed as "tarrying with the negative" (which is, as Žižek insists, the very activity that defines "absolute knowing").[5] More simply, and in terms of its autobiographical function, *Masked and Anonymous* sustains a paradoxical relationship between the artificiality of its performative modes and the possibility of grasping the authentic.[6] Fate is and *is not* Dylan—just as the various "stars" are never (entirely) lost to the characters they play. Nevertheless, and by implication, everyone in the film is already a "character." Dylan *as Fate* moves through a world of Hollywood types and Hollywood scenes—all false, all constructed, all performed. Everyone is at play and, like Dylan (as Stephan Scobie would insist), "masked"—forever countersigning for the performative nature of their ostensibly authentic signatures.[7] In this sense, the film is most clearly anticipated by two of Dylan's more noteworthy songs—"Brownsville Girl" ("Something about that movie though, well I just can't get it out of my head / But I can't remember why I was in it or what part I was supposed to play") and "Things Have Changed" ("This place ain't doing me any good / I'm in the wrong town, I should be in Hollywood").

By implying and drawing together these connections, *Masked and Anonymous* struggles to articulate or reimagine Dylan's larger project, a project that constantly risks losing *so as to locate* Dylan within what Roland Barthes famously calls a "ready-formed dictionary" ("Death" 146). Dylan's entire body of work could be defined, after all, as "a tissue of citations, resulting from the thousand sources of culture" (146). Even his early "protest" (or overtly "folk") songs are structured around traces of plagiarism.[8] "Blowin' in the Wind" "borrows" its melody from the Negro spiritual "No More Auction Block," and "A Hard Rain's A-Gonna Fall" is an overt reworking of the medieval ballad "Lord Randall." Dylan's "quotations" are in fact too numerous and too varied to track with any sense of certainty or finality: from lyrics that repeat dialogue from *Star Trek*[9] and passages from Junichi Saga's *Confessions of a Yakuza*[10] to whole passages (in *Chronicles*) lifted from the work of Jack London.[11] There is little doubt that, as Scobie suggests, Dylan is engaged in a form of trickster-like play that is (on some level) distinctly poststructural/postmodern, a "denial of the self" or "the silencing of a voice" (69). Dylan seems intent on reminding us (again and again) that "what we see and hear on the stage in front of us is not the singer but his alias, not the person but his name" (63). Still, not even Scobie can shake the sense that something authentic is (also) *in play*, that Dylan is "simultaneously delivering his presence and standing back from it" (63). What Scobie (and others) tend to miss is the possibility that Dylan is "delivering his presence" *by* "standing back from it"—that, in other words, Dylan is never simply "denying any possibility that he is really there" (63). By sustaining an *in*finite self, Dylan perpetually gives that self (*in the finite*) to be shared but *not* effaced (or unethically consumed). He is perpetually given because he is "not there" to be effaced, or lost. But this in no way means that the form of the giving can or will be "any old thing" (to recall Derrida), that right is always *just as good* as left. (Fate *decides* to follow fate and go left, after all.) The plastic potential of the momentary form of expression is infinite *yet limited*—limited, that is, by the intentions of its Real (if *in*finite) subject. Such giving entails perpetual acts of responsibility or decision making, *not* (what we have come to understand as) perversity.

Disclosing the Invisible

It should come as no surprise that Dylan frequently returns to the theme and image of the specter; these returns are most certainly part and parcel of his larger tendency to enclose himself in a network of quotations or masks—or rather, what we might think of as (in light of previous chapters) overtly thematizing "norms." But, as we have seen, the theme of the ghost opens up the possibility of an enclosing that is also a radically democratic act of disclosing. The possibility of a ghost is the possibility of an enclosed disclosure, a secret sustained via its utterance, or a "relation without relation" (as Derrida would say). Only a ghost can be a friend, or a lover who loves justly—with or *as* a certain *spirit* of enmity, a certain curtailing of attraction or a desire to know (and thus a certain frustration of proximity).

Let's take a moment to consider what is likely Dylan's most famous handling of spectrality: "Visions of Johanna." According to Scobie, this song most fully embodies Dylan's engagement with the ghostly "paradox of presence and absence" (75)[12]—as even the title points us toward that which is not there, or that which is finally uncontainable (like a "handful of rain"). The theme suggested in the title carries on throughout; things that are ostensibly present tend also to be absent: "Lights flicker from the opposite loft" and "The country music station plays soft / But there's nothing, really nothing to turn off." Even the speaker (like, more overtly, the speaker in "Tangled Up in Blue") is uncertain of his "location" in the song. Pronouns slip and shift. The suggestion we get (on at least one level) is that "Louise" is his make-do replacement for the absent yet clearly preferable "Johanna," yet the only thing to "turn off" is "Louise and *her* lover so entwined / *And* these visions of Johanna that conquer *my* mind" (my emphasis). The speaker, it would seem, is not himself when he's with Louise, for he is actually with Johanna *in thought*. As with everyone else, he is not entirely present. Everyone is "stranded," or disconnected from the other—*even if* they are doing their "best to deny it." And yet Johanna is somehow sustained as a result of her absence, an absence that is apparently unique insofar as the speaker has not been asked or compelled to "defy it" (which is, of course, the very thing Louise asks him—or rather "you"—to do with *her* rain).

Insofar as she represents a problematic replacement for Johanna, Louise can be contrasted with any number of female heroines in Dylan's songs—heroines who withstand or refuse systematic and finalizing apprehension. In, for instance, the ironically titled "She Belongs to Me," the Christlike (yet always disguised)[13] subject has "no place to fall / She never stumbles / The law can't touch her at all"; and while "You will start out standing / Proud to steal her anything she sees . . . [,] / You will wind up peeking through her keyhole / Down upon your knees." Louise, on the other hand, is problematically transparent: "Louise, she's all right, she's just near / She's delicate and seems like the mirror / But she just makes it all too concise and too clear / That Johanna's not here." Louise insists too overtly on her presence, her contemporaneousness. This suggestion is stressed in one of the song's alternative takes, as Dylan sings slightly different lines: "Louise, she's all right, she's just *too* near / Like silk, she seems like the mirror" (my emphasis).[14] In this version the theme and problem of proximity cannot be overlooked. *Because* Louise is "too near" she "seems like the mirror." Her nearness threatens a type of entropy—the entropy we associated with extreme forms of empathy in part II—and therefore a dissolution of the self in its mirrored image. For this reason, it would seem, "the ghost of 'lectricity howls in the bones of her face / Where these visions of Johanna have now taken *my* place" (my emphasis). The implication is that "these visions of Johanna" take the singer's "place" (and *not* Louise's) in or *as* the "ghost of 'lectricity." Even as Louise's abject concision and clarity threatens to dissolve the distinction between self and other, the singer is sustained by a ghostly portraiture of Johanna that finally overtakes Louise's vacuous mirroring (or irresponsible and masochistic reflection of the singer *as other*).

Whatever connection the singer and Johanna have—whatever the desire that sustains the singer—is predicated upon absence. Like the ideal friend in Dylan's "All I Really Want to Do" (which predates "Visions of Johanna" and, therefore, Dylan's 1965 turn to rock and more overt games of *intentional* misdirection), Johanna's coherence *as other* is sustained by the singer's refusal or inability to know or to have. Sustained as an unfixable "vison" (or even, perhaps, what Hegel calls a "notion"), Johanna's ghostliness frustrates the melancholic desire to "displace," "define," "confine," etc.[15] While the song itself often seems intensely melancholic—for the singer longs to *have* Johanna, to make her vision a reality *at last*—its melancholia is ultimately refused: the longing is sustained *as longing* and melancholia is traded for skepticism. We might in fact suggest (if only tentatively in this brief space) that Dylan tends to move through (and even, at times, mix together) the various cycles of consciousness Hegel outlines in his *Phenomenology,* and which he sees as necessarily sustained, as integral parts, within the *movement* of absolute knowledge.[16] Is there not a certain sense of (late modern) stoicism in Dylan's "folk" period; a certain sense of (postmodern) skepticism at Newport and then afterward (including Dylan's almost complete withdrawal from the public in 1966, following his mystery-shrouded motorcycle accident);[17] a certain sense of the "unhappy consciousness" in Dylan's gospel years—which, of course, are marked by Dylan's sincere turn toward an "unattainable *beyond* which, in being laid hold of, flees, or rather has already flown" (Hegel, *Phenomenology* 131)? Whether we can draw such easy parallels or not, in all instances or movements of Dylan's career we see an effort to accept *and surmount* the fact that "where[ever] that [absolute or infinite] 'other' is sought, it cannot be found, for it is supposed to be just a *beyond,* something that can *not* be found" (131).

The problem and promise of the ghost for Dylan is therefore always also the problem and promise of the double, of the self *as* infinite other.

Dylan's songs have a tendency to turn in on themselves; the often absent other to whom the singer speaks tends to implicate or interrogate the singer's own otherness. The problem of apprehending the other in the moment of address becomes the problem of expressing (or *laying hold of*) one's own otherness (while also somehow sustaining it as an unattainable, an *in*finite, beyond). In "Visions of Johanna" this theme of (spectral) doubles is evident in the problematic mirroring Louise induces and Johanna frustrates or resists. But even in earlier works, like the ostensibly antiwar "John Brown," the loss of the other entails the inability to preserve the self. After explaining to his idealistic mother how he finally came to see that the "[enemy's] face looked just like [his]," John Brown (whose "face [is] all shot up" and whose "hand [is] all shot off") goes on to stress the oddly paralyzing nature of his revelation: "I couldn't help but think, through the thunder rolling and stink / That I was just a puppet in a play / And through the roar and smoke, this string is finally broke / And a cannonball blew my eyes away." This moment of self-revelation is cast as a moment of ontological collapse; Brown is left blind and bereft of a coherent self—he is "all shot up." Even the (ideological and interpellative) strings of the Other come untethered. While the song obviously repudiates a distinctly melancholic (and war-buttressing) desire to sustain communities of pure inclusion/exclusion, it resists *also* a naïve endorsement of entropic empathy.

We can therefore trace a direct line between a "protest" song like "John Brown" and a later song like the intensely personal "Where Are You Tonight? (Journey through Dark Heat)"—a song in which distance and absence is overtly tied to the possibility *and* the impossibility of communication (or the potential resolution of a type of *double* trauma). In the opening verse, themes of accessibility and proximity are inextricably linked: "There's a long-distance train rolling through the rain / Tears on the letter I write / There's a woman I long to touch and I miss her so much / But she's drifting like a satellite." As the song progresses, the refrain shifts from the interrogative ("Where are you to night?") to the conditional ("If I could just find you tonight") and then, in the final line of the song, back to the interrogative. The song thereby sustains the sense of an ongoing quest (for the other) as well as the possibility of a culminating and redemptive act of unity—signaled most overtly when the singer refers to a "white diamond gloom on the dark side of this room / And a pathway that leads up to the stars." Yet (and like any number of Dylan songs that never seem to end)[18] every apparent moment of conclusion is frustrated by the implication that there is still more to come. While, in the final verse, the singer begins by celebrating the fact that "there's a new day at dawn and [he's] finally arrived," he immediately and paradoxically slips back into the conditional: "*If* I'm there in the morning, baby, you'll know I've survived" (my emphasis). On the one hand, the singer has already (in some sense) arrived/survived; on the other, his survival (from the perspective of the other) remains contingent upon his *potential* arrival—an arrival always yet to come.

The speaker's survival entails the frustrating preservation of a type of secret, some *Thing* that always frustrates a conclusive arrival or moment of communion: "I can't believe it, I can't believe I'm alive / But *without you* it just doesn't seem right" (my emphasis). If, however, survival entails the ongoing possibility of an arrival, then the inverse must also be true: the speaker's secret survival makes possible his arrival. He must remain alive (by staying secret) if he is to *continue arriving* as other, as (to recall Nancy) *l'intrus*. Such a reading is encouraged earlier in the song when the singer asserts that "the truth was obscure, too profound and too pure / To live it you have to explode." The problem of knowing an obscure and profound truth is tied (in the end) to the problem of the self's arrival/survival—which entails (as we've seen) a committed expression within the "'formal reality' of the cogitatio" (Levinas, "God and Philosophy" 63). The song confuses the problem of finding and knowing the other with the problem of relating the self *in truth*. This conflation becomes overt when the singer suddenly evokes the image of the double: "I fought with my twin, that enemy within / 'Til both of us fell by the way." The ostensibly negative consequences of this battle suggest that the self, like *or as* the other to whom the singer addresses his tear-stained letter, cannot be rejected as unknowable or forced to become the same. At the same time, the purity of the truth should never be abandoned to the finite resources of a common language. The other must remain addressable; but the task of addressing and being addressed entails risking (while never losing) the self within the circulation of common terms. There may be no way to "*tell*" (even to ourselves) what "[our] private thoughts [are]"—but this does not mean there isn't "some way of finding them out."

This brings us back to Dylan's autobiographical impulse—especially since "Where Are You Tonight?" appears to be one of Dylan's more intensely personal songs. At the moment the song outlines a generic relationship between a lover and a longed-for other—opening listeners to the possibility of a profoundly ethical moment of communication (i.e., the discovery and sustainment of an "invisible self")—it outlines (while obviously fictionalizing and symbolizing) Dylan's specific relationship with his first wife, Sara Lownds. In doing both—and not just or overtly the latter—the song outlines a relationship between Dylan and his listener. The song withdraws the possibility of a finally autobiographical gesture or moment of identifiable arrival so as to make that very gesture in all sincerity. Dylan's self is laid out for us—but only because it is laid out for us as an always "invisible self." The self to come—like Dylan's heart in "Highlands"—preserves its in*f*inite and plastic anteriority to the present even as that anteriority is grasped (or *sublated*) as anterior *in* the (con)temporary.[19]

Being Not *There*

Dylan's impulse to lay bare an invisible self is most obviously addressed in (and surely the motivation behind) Todd Haynes's antibiopic, *I'm Not There* (2007). The film, which uses six different actors to play characterizations of Dylan (at various stages in his career)—Arthur, the "Poet" (Ben Whishaw); Jack and Pastor John, the "Prophet" (Christian Bale); Billy, the "Outlaw" (Richard Gere); Woody, the "Fake" (Marcus Carl Franklin); and Robbie, the "Star of Electricity" (Heath Ledger). The sixth is "Jude" (Cate Blanchett). Jude is never given a "title," but s/he may or may not be the "Ghost"—as it is Jude's corpse that we see in the opening sequence while the narrator (Kris Kristofferson) loosely quotes from Dylan's stream of consciousness novel, *Tarantula* (1971): "Even the ghost was more than one person."[20] Before we see this body/ghost, we are presented with a point-of-view shot (in grainy black and white, or cinema verité style). The cacophonous sound of a band tuning up seems to be coming from somewhere down a long hallway, a hallway through which an unidentified man is beckoning us to move. As the sound grows louder, we are lead through a door marked "stage" and up several flights of stairs. The roar of a crowd overtakes the sound of instruments, and blinding floodlights flare on the camera lens as we arrive on stage from behind a giant American flag.[21] Haynes then suddenly cuts to a close-up of a foot starting a motorcycle and then of a hand pulling a clutch. Another cut takes us to an extreme long shot of a highway running (in the distance) across the screen. The motorcycle emerges from the left and moves past the frame on the right as the title slowly appears on the screen, undergoing a series of permutations—"I," then "I he," "I'm her," "not her," "not here"—before settling on "I'm Not There" (which is, of course, the title of a relatively obscure Dylan song). The next cut takes us to Jude's corpse—who, we are lead to assume, has died in a motorcycle accident. As an autopsy begins, Kristofferson's narration takes over: "There he lies. God rest his soul and his rudeness. A devouring public can now share the remains of his sickness, and his phone numbers. There he lay . . . Poet, Prophet, Outlaw, Fake. Star of Electricity." As each characterization is named, an image of the corresponding actor is displayed. Eventually—after several more obscure images (and the sound of Arthur telling us that a "poem is like a naked person. . . . But a song is something that walks all by itself")[22]—the credit sequence begins: a montage of (more) grainy black-and-white images accompanied by the nondiegetic sound of "Stuck Inside of Mobile with the Memphis Blues Again" (as sung *by* Dylan).

In short, Haynes's film employs and parodies various aspects of documentary filmmaking—employing the type of ostensibly "raw" (or unplanned) footage that we see in cinema verité films like D. A. Pennebaker's *Don't Look Back* (1966) as well as the cuts to modern-day (and color) interviews we see in more popular forms of documentary (e.g., Martin Scorsese's *No Direction Home: Bob Dylan* [2005]). In many respects, *I'm Not There* takes its cue from Allen's *Zelig*. But even more than does *Zelig*, Haynes's film clearly aligns the *apparent* honesty and objectivity of documentary technique with the overtly fictionalizing tendencies of the typical biopic—which invariably loses its subject within a romanticized and always singular (meta)narrative. We are never given to assume or realize that this coherence is necessarily misleading. Films like Clint Eastwood's *Bird* (1988), Taylor Hackford's *Ray* (2004), or James Mangold's *Walk the Line* (2005)—to name just a few—impose upon the viewer a hegemonic version of their respective subjects, never frustrating that version or exposing viewers to a Derridean crucible of undecidability that necessarily haunts any *particular* (or seemingly singular) narrative form. Haynes interrogates the assumptions of such films while suggesting that documentaries are no less constructed or artificial. Either leaves us with a false (because simplified and fixed) sense of knowing.[23] In typical postmodern fashion, Haynes's film exposes the impossibility of sustaining or legitimizing any particular (meta)narrative—by, that is, parodying documentary and biopic form while constantly re-presenting Dylan from "another point of view." But even at its most ostentatiously postmodern (e.g., when Robbie makes his appearance as the actor who became famous playing Jack in a biopic), a certain remnant (or *revenant*) of authenticity haunts Haynes's film. This sense of authenticity is signaled most clearly, as Ian Garwood suggests, via Haynes's use of Dylan's *actual* voice in the nondiegetic soundtrack.[24] Through a careful consideration of the songs Haynes employs and strategically manipulates (as well as the various scenes those songs accompany), Garwood works to demonstrate that Haynes's film "adopts the not-quite-there aesthetic of [postmodern] pastiche" while simultaneously maintain or exposing "'the real within': the *voice* of Bob Dylan" (21; my emphasis).

But we need to be careful here. In suggesting (as Harwood seems to) that Haynes's film finally locates Dylan's "romantic" genius as somehow outside of, or always beyond, any effort to express it, we find ourselves moving backward toward a problematic "certainty of self that aims to be absolute" (Hegel, *Phenomenology* 455). I am therefore more interested in the way Haynes's film uses (or, at the very least, *struggles to use*) Dylan's voice to signal a final *sublation* of Dylan. Our understanding of Dylan is effected because of—not *in spite of*—the film's protean characterizations. Haynes's film seems far more engaged in masquerade than (what we might think of as *cinematic*) transvestitism. As we saw in chapter 1—through Johnston's analysis of blackface in Crosland's *The Jazz Singer*—transvestitism simply reifies the distinction between the mask and the masked, while masquerade confuses the possibility of making or sustaining a distinction. Haynes's investment in or celebration of the latter is reflected (metonymically) in the figures of Jude (who is played by a woman) and Woody (who is played by a black boy). While it is certainly possible to suggest that both characters function to expose a tendency toward transvestitism (sexual and racial) on Dylan's part, doing so would entail overlooking the fact that Haynes carefully frustrates any suggestion of "disguise." On the surface, Woody does not *pretend* to be black. If he is pretending to be anything, he is pretending to be a "white" folk singer—namely, Woody Guthrie. But then again (and as we have seen), the possibility of passing as the one necessarily implies the artificiality of the other. Or rather, Dylan's black musical heritage is *given* to be just as authentic as his *performed* "whiteness." Likewise, we are never encouraged to assume that Jude is a woman pretending to be a man. Jude's apparent performance of masculinity is simply frustrated by the overt possibility that it entails the suppression of his *no less* performative femininity. Dylan is thus disclosed *within* these momentary performatives because they simultaneously imply the impossibility of finally reducing him to one or another.[25] As a result, these performative modes coalesce into a *notional* whole that simultaneously sustains the difference of its constituent parts. Dylan's voice signals—even as it is finally associated with, or *a part of*—this *infinite* whole.

At the same time—and through its use of Woody and Jude as masquerading *forms*—Haynes's film positions Dylan within a larger American context, one that points to the larger implications of both voice and racial masquerade (or the more radical implications of blackface) in his work.

Dylan's authentic (or individual) voice is, of course, always and *always overtly* performed. The voice we hear on *The Times They Are A-Changin'* is not the same voice we hear on *Blonde on Blonde,* and the voice on the latter is significantly different (again) from the voice on *Nashville Skyline.* And even after encouraging listeners to assume that the gravelly voice they hear on *Time Out of Mind* through to *Tempest* is the voice age has finally (and *truly*) left him, Dylan frustrates that assumption by releasing an album of smoothly sung Sinatra songs (*Shadows in the Night*). Like the constituent parts of Haynes's film, the difference that defines these voices simultaneously holds them (or Dylan) together as a plastic and unfixable whole — a whole that is, moreover, contained within these various parts. Or, if we can borrow Hegel's phrasing, Dylan's authentic voice, by "gathering and holding together all these moments within itself, . . . advances within this total wealth of its actual Spirit, and all its particular moments take and receive in common into themselves the like determinateness of the whole" (*Phenomenology* 414). Dylan's shifting (yet unified) voice implies a "knowledge of oneself in the externalization of oneself; the being that is *the movement* of retaining self-identity in its otherness" (459; my emphasis). This movement, this externalization, is precisely that which defines (what I am calling) *autoplasticity,* the radically democratic implications of which are signaled by Haynes's negotiation of *both* Dylan's authenticity and the promise of (racial) masquerade in America — the promise *and the problem* with which we began in chapter 1. Dylan certainly seems to encourage this negotiation, as the line we can trace between *The Jazz Singer* and *I'm Not There* is already anticipated in *Masked and Anonymous.* For this reason alone — though there are certainly others — we might view *I'm Not There* as a simple redux of *Masked and Anonymous.*

Voicing the Ghost

Midway through *Masked and Anonymous,* Sweetheart brings Fate to the stage on which he is to perform. He tells Fate that (according to legend) "some famous star of the Jazz Age was 'disfigured' right here on this stage during a live show." Sweetheart, though, cannot remember the name of the performer, so Fate offers (inexplicably) "Stagger Lee?" Sweetheart immediately dismisses the suggestion and the two move on. As Sweetheart and Fate walk out of frame, the camera slowly zooms in to two crew members (Christian Slater and Chris Penn) loitering near the stage. Slater's character launches into a harangue about the fact that "there is really only two races — workers and bosses. That's it." This scene sets up a latter scene in which Fate meets Oscar Vogel (Ed Harris)—the ghost of a blackface minstrel from the "Jazz Age." When he finally meets Vogel, Fate is "hiding" backstage. Dylan *as Fate* can be heard singing (in the background) lines from "Dirt Road Blues": "If I can't find my baby, I'm gonna run away and hide." These specific lines are obviously apropos, but so is the song as a whole. The singer of "Dirt Road Blues" claims that he's "been praying for salvation." The problem is that this salvation entails a profound and difficult (if not impossible) moment of liberation: "Gon' walk down that dirt road until my eyes begin to bleed / 'Til there's nothing left to see, 'til the chains have been shattered and I've been freed." Blindness once again comes to denote a type of entropic recognition, and salvation (in turn) is positioned in opposition to the burden of the double, or other. The singer finds himself "Lookin' *at* [his] shadow" even as he is "looking *for* the sunny side of love" (my emphasis). We are thus led to assume that, in the unfettered purity of sunlight, his shadow will finally dissipate altogether. The singer, though, seems to realize that such a state of satisfaction would entail withdrawing completely from the face of the other/Other: "Gon' walk on down that dirt road 'til I'm right beside the sun / Gon' walk on down until I'm right beside the sun / I'm gonna have to put up a barrier to keep myself away from everyone." Significantly, Fate's effort to attain this ideal of solitude is interrupted by the appearance of Vogel.

After descending from somewhere in the rafters, Vogel sits on a step next to Fate. He carries a banjo and wears a standard minstrel suit and is in standard minstrel blackface. "Hello, Jack," he says. "Do you know me?" Fate responds by admitting that Vogel "look[s] familiar." At this point, as Murray Leeder notes, the film's indebtedness to *The Jazz Singer* becomes overt. The two films suddenly seem to fall "in line"—*as if* the ghostly figure of *The Jazz Singer* has arrived along with Vogel. Just as Fate is encouraged to recognize something familiar in Vogel, the viewer is encouraged to recognize something familiar in the film. A "shadow" perhaps? Leeder, of course, identifies a number of connections—including the fact that "both [films] are backstage musicals about musicians using the stage name 'Jack' who are fictionalized versions of the stars who perform them" (187). Leeder also points out that both "Jacks" are struggling, at base, against a domineering father figure. The Jack of *The Jazz Singer* is cast out by his father for singing jazz, and the Jack of *Masked and Anonymous* is imprisoned after sleeping with his father's mistress. And while *The Jazz Singer* associates cultural law with the father *as* local cantor, the father in *Masked and Anonymous* is (more simply) the fascist president of America.

As it does in *The Jazz Singer*, the figure of the father in *Masked and Anonymous* stands in for the hegemony of law and tradition—"The Law of the Father," Lacan's Other. When Fate recalls his dalliance with the mistress, he notes (in voiceover) that, "in [his] father's world, you do not take what is his." At one time, however, Fate felt he could break this rule. Fate tells us that he had originally conceived of the affair with his father's mistress as an act of rebellion: "I thought I was doing it for my mother. I thought I was doing it for my country." But he realizes now that his reasons were simply selfish: "Ultimately I knew I was doing it for me." He concludes his reminiscence by stating (somewhat obliquely) that, "in the end, it's the strongest arm that stretches the bow." In these scenes, the film's "problem" becomes (at least on one level) the same problem we see play out in *The Jazz Singer*—the problem of reconciling the tension between family and nation, mother and father, self and Other. Fate laments his selfishness in the very moment he associates it with a break from "tradition," or hegemonic paternal law. The "pleasure of *enjoying his individuality*... passes away [into] his own self-consciousness as a citizen of his nation" (Hegel, *Phenomenology* 276–77). (It's worth noting, too, that the mistress is played by Angela Basset, and so the affair breaks the "rules" of both family *and* race.) Like Jack in *The Jazz Singer*, Fate finds himself vacillating between and finally confusing "that [self] which belongs to the divine law" and that self which stoically "holds to human law" (280). Paradoxically, either "self" acts in response to a type of fate, a force beyond control. This paradox is signaled or anticipated in Dylan's "Gotta Serve Somebody." As the singer states, "You're gonna have to serve somebody/ Well, it may be the devil or it may be the Lord/ But you're gonna have to serve somebody."[26] While obviously echoing Hegel's lord/bondsman "dialectic," these lines imply two ostensibly opposed "truths": *every individual* is fated to serve the generically human ("somebody") *and* the unknowably divine ("the devil or ... the Lord," the *in*human). But if "it's the strongest arm that stretches the bow"—*if* the rule of human law (in the form of ideology, or the symbolic) determines my fate, if there really are only "workers and bosses"—how am I to serve, also, that which is divine and therefore truly "virtuous"? Via a somewhat circuitous route, then—or via a series of embedded implications—Vogel's ghostly arrival is indicative of a desire, as Leeder puts it, to "resolve the paradox of authenticity and inauthenticity" (185). And yet, as he is *both* ghost *and* blackface minstrel, Vogel's arrival ties the possibility of such a resolution (in, that is, the specific context of America's identity politics) to the paradox of racial authenticity *as* racial performance. As Leeder notes, the film makes this connection overt when

Fate momentarily allows us to confuse Vogel with Stagger Lee—the black man who, after being hanged for the murder of Billy Lyons in 1895, became the subject of a famous and frequently adapted "folk song."

The very moment Vogel arrives on scene—the very moment the specter of *The Jazz Singer* (and therefore Al Jolson) is evoked—we are faced with the specter of Dylan's own Jewish identity, and (in turn) the suggestion that Dylan has masked himself in the "blackface" of black musical forms so as to (paradoxically) "whiten up." As a born-again Christian, Dylan is tied (like Jakie/Jack in *The Jazz Singer*) to the legacy of the Marrano; Vogel's haunting presence therefore signals (at least initially) a desire for absolution, a longing for Kol Nidre. But we should not forget that, in *The Jazz Singer*, blackface functions less to "whiten" Jakie/Jack than it does to signal the persistence of his (Jewish) "virtue"—as if, in fact, his opaque or infinite otherness can only be expressed in *or as* the mediating point that differentiates its finite performance (as blackness) from its always *in*finite truth. This is what Hegel might call a diremptive point of mediation, or a vanishing mediator. Or rather, *The Jazz Singer* finally suggests that the (authentic) Jewishness mandated by the father is no less performative than the (authentic) blackness mandated by the jazz community; *but* it is only through such performance (when performed as *a condition* of an always plastic self) that the "service" mandated by the Other can "service" also a virtuous "beyond," or *form of* divinity. Such a performance would be autoplastic. In bringing with him the ghost of *The Jazz Singer*, Vogel therefore arrives to inform or remind Fate that he cannot escape his performative mask(s) *if* he is to maintain, also, his virtue (or voice)—for which race (in this case, Jewishness) merely serves as a type of "stand in." In terms, then, of Dylan's own Jewishness, *or* blackness, his gender or his faith, etc.—to forgo the burden of his shadow, or ghostly double, would entail forgoing his responsibility to the other.

And it is precisely about responsibility that Vogel speaks. He explains that, as one of the president's "favorite performers"—and therefore as an artist with a "forum"—he was compelled to "[speak] out" against corruption and violence. Even though he was "disfigured" (and his apparent murder disguised as an "accident," or even a "suicide"), he assures Fate that it is "not what goes in the mouth but what comes out."[27] Fate, though, seems unaffected or utterly indifferent. "Well," he says, "I've got to get back to the stage." Faced with this apparent indifference, Vogel merely smiles. He then reminds Fate that "the whole world's a stage." The scene therefore ends by foregrounding the impossibility of forgoing a culturally constructed mask—or escaping the fact that "this is all a play." But Fate's line reminds us, also, that his encounter with Vogel has occurred "backstage," in a space anterior to performance—the space, after all, where Fate went to hide. This, we are given to understand, *is* the space of the ghost; if all the world's a stage, the performances it mandates must allow themselves to be haunted by that which remains always irreducible to its performance. Indeed, after descending from the scaffolding, Fate looks back to see a "black" janitor standing in the space Vogel had momentarily occupied, and we are reminded again of the suggestion that even something as authentic as race is always only the effect of our service to (or domination by) the Other. It is therefore significant that, in the next scene, Fate is back on stage singing "Cold Irons Bound." This song continues to play as the film moves toward its finale—the president/father finally dies, a new reign of terror is initiated by his surrogate son (played by Mickey Rourke), and the benefit concert is aborted. In the aftermath of these events, Uncle Sweetheart (after forcing Pagan Lace to drink alcohol) gets into a fight with Tom Friend (Jeff Bridges), an intrusive journalist and Lace's boyfriend. After Friend begins strangling Sweetheart to death, Fate and his sycophantic friend, Bobby Cupid (Luke Wilson), come to the rescue. In the end, and after Friend turns a gun on both Fate and Sweetheart, Cupid murders Friend with the neck of a broken guitar. When the authorities arrive, and after urging Cupid to run, Fate takes the "fall" for the murder. In the final scenes of the film, Fate is therefore headed back to prison. He is literally "twenty miles out of town in cold irons bound."

Tied to the film's final long take of an impassive Fate (shot in close-up) traveling toward his destiny—as well as his decision to endure the crucible of the undecidable and decide (with no real sense of "right" or "justification") who to befriend and who to save—the lyrics of "Cold Irons Bound" function to register the film's *as Dylan's* commitment to remaining both distant *and* bound (in all senses of the word—i.e., tangled up, limited, connected, directed, purposeful, etc.). As the singer in "Cold Iron Bounds" states, "It's almost like, almost like I don't exist." But it is—and *must remain*—only "almost *like.*" As Fate muses in his final voiceover, "Sometimes it's not enough to know the meaning of things. Sometimes we have to know what things don't mean as well, like what does it mean to not know what the person you love is capable of?" We are thus encouraged to view the film (*and Dylan*) as we should a lover—by, that is, remaining open to that which cannot be known in any voice we might recognize (but which has been given in the performance it necessarily disrupts *and* holds together). Is this not the *only* way to "serve somebody"—truly and democratically? The central paradox of "Gotta Serve Somebody"—its insistence that we must serve the human (or temporary) *and* the divine (or infinite)—is *sublated* by the implication that this insistence is *actually* a call to serve (or take responsibility for) the *in*finite other, or "God in me." This implication becomes overt the moment Dylan turns to the intensely personal. After supplying a list of "intimate" names for himself (including "Bobby" and "Zimmy"), the singer concludes: "You may call me anything but no matter what you say / You're gonna have to serve somebody." In saying this, the singer leads us to understand that the affectation of friendship in no way absolves our responsibility for the other's (divine) otherness. This responsibility always entails the trauma of a decision—both giving and interpretative. For whatever faces us "may be the devil *or* it may be the Lord" (my emphasis). In other words, the other's otherness is the otherness of the ghost, a ghost that can never be exorcised/conjured. No name, no act of language or representation, can hold it. *And yet* this ghost can *only* be respected in and through the figure of the mask *as mask* (racial or otherwise). If the mask is given *to be* the ghost made present: conjuration. If the mask is given as just another instance of perverse play (utterly devoid of a haunting presence): exorcism. In the former, the infinite mutability of the plastic is ossified; in the latter, its potential solidity *or destiny* is dissolved. Or, if we return to Hegel (while considering, also, Dylan's bewildering conversion to Christianity), the former leads us to the "cult of the Virgin"—or faith in a purity uncontaminated by its supplemental forms, the white marble of classical statuary or the melancholic blindness of biography, the documentary or biopic. In the latter, we are left with the inverse: abject faithlessness. At either pole, nothing is shared.

Auto(teleio)plasticity

Respect for the specter—respect, that is, for the other (friend) to come, or the secret to be revealed: this is precisely what Derrida associates with the term "lovance," or "love in friendship" (*Politics* 69). As Derrida states (while circling around the paradox of "knowing" Zarathustra in Nietzsche's *Thus Spoke Zarathustra*), "All things and all beings to be loved belong to spectrality" (288). Even as its tentative outline—its allusive suggestiveness, its *potential*—compels me toward a time (to come) when its ghostliness no longer intrudes upon (my) sense, a specter (as *l'intrus*) refuses to arrive in the present. What is ghostly is precisely "out of joint"—the disruption of a contemporary (moment), or of *contemporaries*: "For . . . [the contemporary] would be an unprecedented time [or, could we say subject?]; a time [or subject?] which, reserving itself in the unique, would remain without relation to any other, without attraction or repulsion, nor living analogy" (76). This is precisely the final resting place of a Bartleby or a Clare—just as it is paradoxically the desire of the melancholic. The ghost, therefore, is the possibility of "living analogy," of an act of thematizing communication (as opposed, that is, to what we might call the melancholic illusion of *contemporaneous communion*). For Derrida, as we saw in chapter 7, a just and loving friendship necessarily entails the "crucible of undecidability"—the responsibility to speak in the face of, or despite the impossibility of circumscribing, a ghostly "perhaps." Such an act of responsibility (for the self and or *as* the other) occurs as an instance of "auto-teleiopoetics" (32)—which implies both the productive movement (*poesis*) toward the self's messianic end (*telos*) *and* the persistence of a productive and therefore traversable distance from that end/other (*tele*). We might even say that teleiopoesis entails being, always, "cold irons bound"—insofar as it is a radically plastic act of self-revelation. It gives *a form of destruction,* a (con)temporary connection that reveals its reliance upon—and therefore the innate *allegiance of*—distance. It is an act of re-covering *in time* a ghostly presence.[28]

But surely *poesis* implies too strongly an act of making, of making (even) from scratch? The theme of plasticity is surely more suited to the theme of the specter—in that it makes us think less of *poesis* than of *mimesis,* of returns and *re*formations. The autoplastic frustrates the possibility of the autopoetic—which, in literary terms, would entail a making out of nothing and therefore a self that is only ever its fictional and perverse constructions. Such a conception wholly eschews responsibility; it is the very apotheosis of what we might call postmodern. In contrast, the autoplastic, or the auto(teleio)plastic, carries over the infinite possibility of self-making while retaining—while in fact *insisting upon*—an obligation to that which precedes and remains always beyond the activity that makes it present. We are given in relation, in the (con)temporary moments of our representations—but we must not forget that some *Thing* is being given, some *Thing* in(the)finite. Is this not what Levinas means when he asserts that "the 'birth' of being in the questioning where the cognitive subject stands would thus refer to a *before the questioning,* to the anarchy of responsibility, as it were on this side of all birth" (*Otherwise* 26)? *This* other "*before the questioning*" is precisely what we are responsible for—responsible for accepting *and* responsible for giving. Such accepting and such giving is what necessitates consciousness—that is, "a transparency and a veiling of the fugitive and the unstable in an allusion, a divination incapable of objectification, but aspiring to objectification and thus a consciousness—and thus consciousness of being" (25). The autoplastic effects this consciousness by giving the other in *the moment* of its explosive withdrawal, by signaling the fact that this very withdrawal is a constituent part of the *in*finite whole *being* given. We are given the whole because we are given to see its constituent absence. The autoplastic mandates and sustains the obligation of adaptation in the face of what is adapted, or re*de*formed. What is plastic "sees (itself) coming" (if we recall Malabou's reading of Hegel); its nature is to give its end or its *destiny (telos)* as a matter of distance *(tele)*. The autoplastic is *always already,* then, the auto*teleio*plastic, a (con)temporalization that disrupts or disturbs (so as *to preserve*) our understanding of what is *finally* present in its representation.

And it is, I am suggesting, precisely this activity that defines Dylan's career. Dylan has always been emphatic about the fact that he sees himself coming. Appeals to destiny can be found throughout his work.[29] But these appeals are always peculiar, or peculiarly plastic in nature. As he says in his extended interview for Scorsese's *No Direction Home,* "I had ambitions to set out and find like an odyssey of going home somewhere. I set out to find this home that I'd left a while back. . . . And I couldn't remember exactly where it was, but I was on my way there. And encountering what I encountered on the way, was how I envisioned it all. I didn't really have any ambition at all. I was born very far from where I was supposed to be." On the one hand, Dylan points toward his ambition and a distinctly modern brand of autonomy; what is to happen is exactly what he envisions it to be. On the other hand, what he envisions (as always yet) to come is a home (or self and family) he has never known. He therefore finds himself being born—or rather, he experiences the (perpetual) "incompletion of being born"[30]—where he isn't *supposed to be.* And it is *in this sense* that he doesn't "really have any ambition at all." This brings us finally, and by way of a conclusion, to Dylan's *Chronicles*—wherein Dylan most overtly and most carefully negotiates the task of locating himself as *or at* a distance (but also as a destiny). As he says early on, "I'd come from a long ways off and had started from a long ways down. But now destiny was about to manifest itself" (22).

Chronicles is *lovingly* sincere because it is *lovingly* playful. Dylan articulates a coherent and utterly relatable picture of himself. But this clarity or transparency is also beguiling. Through it we see only opacity. Whole passages are, as I've already noted, effectively plagiarized (yet carefully worked into the whole and thus unrecognizable as such), and facts are offered as absolute even though their veracity is questionable at best. Dylan maintains his "honesty" by reminding us (again and again) that we can expect no less. At the outset, in fact, he recounts (in impossible detail) one of his first interviews, telling us that the journalist tried "to get [him] to cough up some facts, like [he] was supposed to give them to him straight and square" (7). Midway through the book—and while recounting the time period between the recording of *Nashville Skyline* (1969) and *Blood on the Tracks* (1975)—he becomes even more overt about his inclination to falsify the "truth." He tells us that he "went to Jerusalem, got [himself] photographed at the Western Wall wearing a skullcap." This led to people claiming he was a Zionist—which, he claims, "helped a little." He then explains that he recorded "what *appeared to be* a country western album and *made sure* it sounded pretty bridled and housebroken" (my emphasis). He notes, too, that he "used a different voice." He even claims to have "started a rumor" that he was "quitting music and going to college"; this rumor lead to the press painting him as a man "on some eternal search" or as someone "suffering some kind of internal torment." This is, he suggests, precisely what *he* wanted: "It all sounded good to me." He ends the section (after implying that *Self Portrait* [1970] was intentionally ill-conceived) by revealing the "truth" about *Blood on the Tracks,* an album that most assume is almost entirely autobiographical (as it certainly *seems* to reflect upon Dylan's troubled marriage to Sara Lownds). "Eventually," he insists, "I would even record an entire album based on Chekov short stories— critics thought it was autobiographical—that was fine" (122). We are left to wonder which stories he might have used. The larger problem, though, is how—after having been told the "truth" about Dylan's lifetime of lies and manipulations—we are to take *this* ostensible truth? Nevertheless, in these moments (as in those more playful moments when he'll tell us of some ridiculous lyric he'd *almost* used on a recording),[31] the truth is left to flicker on the page, finally merging with (or becoming an effect of) its endless *disruptions.* Only in our awareness of the lies that structure it can we be privy to the truth. As regards *Blood on the Tracks,* its connection to a series of Chekov tales finally signals the specific nature of its autobiographical form. What we see of Dylan *in* that album—for, as he finally admits, "The stuff [he] write[s] does come from an autobiographical place" (199)—is also and necessarily an effect of his acquiescence to the language of the Other, to a "ready-formed dictionary." Over the course of the book we are given a sense of how Dylan works to preserve his "own *form* of certainty" (123; my emphasis)—but also, and paradoxically (as the release of every album and then the publication of *Chronicles* attests)—share it.

Dylan makes it clear that the purity of truth is the very thing that obstructs the possibility of self-expression; he does so by comparing himself to Oedipus (and returning us, yet again, to the theme of blindness and dictatorial fathers): "Oedipus went looking for the truth and when he found it, it ruined him. . . . So much for the truth. I was gonna talk out of both sides of my mouth and what you heard depended on which side you were standing. If I ever did stumble on any truth, I was gonna sit on it and keep it down" (126–27). Dylan resolves to forgo the "truth" in favor of sustaining (via an endless series of lies and carefully manipulated constructions) his own "form of certainty." This entails, he suggests, learning how to "freeze-fram[e] his image, [or] . . . suggest only shadows of [his] possible self" (140). Lurking at the heart of this lifelong project is a line by Arthur Rimbaud: "'I is someone else.' When I read those words the bells went off. It made perfect sense. I wished someone would have mentioned that to me earlier" (288). Significantly, this "revelation" comes at the end of the book—even though it occurs during Dylan's first years in New York (the early sixties). We are therefore led to see the manner in which the book itself exemplifies the paradoxical play of distance *and* immediacy that Dylan seems to be endorsing—the effort to "freeze-frame" and thus sustain (*in* shadows) a form of otherness. Indeed, Dylan manages to maintain a sense of immediacy throughout—often employing a past progressive tense (especially at the start of new chapters and sections). The final chapter, for instance, begins with Dylan telling us that "the moon was rising behind the Chrysler Building" (225). At this point, he has jumped backward from events in the late eighties to events in the early sixties. The sense of immediacy he effects—the sense that he is writing in the moment of an event and not simply recalling it—intensifies the book's theme of destiny; his past self suddenly seems capable of knowing what is to come. In the end, we get an almost vertiginous sense of Dylan as simultaneously present and *to come,* as if he is both the moment of narration and that which necessarily disrupts it from the outside. More specifically (and in light of the above), Dylan presents himself (only) as a type of *notional* whole, always present yet always in flux. In this precise manner the book exploits the possibility of going "way beyond metaphor" (285)—of giving a form of self that does not simply or only stand in for that which is absent.

While eschewing any sense of Sartrean anguish, Dylan leads us to accept the fact that, as Hegel puts it, "The movement of a being that is, consists partly in becoming an other than itself, and thus becoming its own immanent content" (*Phenomenology* 32). The suggestion (in both Hegel and Dylan) is that the self is sustained, or realized, through an endless process of self-projection, of self-othering. In Dylan's work we see (again and again) how this fact entails the very possibility of *being given*—and, therefore, the possibility of fomenting and sustaining a democracy of the incommensurable. Dylan provides, in other words, the "account" Judith Butler imagines: "That there is no final or adequate narrative reconstruction of the prehistory of the speaking 'I' does not mean we cannot narrate it; it only means that at the moment we narrate we become speculative philosophers or fiction writers" (*Giving an Account* 78). As an act of autoplasticity, such an account responds to the other, but it does so (finally and adequately) "without responding." By balancing both the naïve claims of transparent autobiography (e.g., McBride's memoir) and the perverse vagaries of the postmodern subject (e.g., Clare or Zelig), Dylan offers his various self-articulations as fictions *so as* to overcome their fictionality. Only *in* fiction *as fiction* can the self represent itself (in all sincerity) as that which remains incomplete, or "out of joint." Or rather, in giving himself as that which "sees (itself) coming," Dylan opens us to the possibility that the work of democracy—the work of sharing and accepting what is equally *in*finite, of respecting and being respected (in the mode of the specter)—*is* nothing other than "the strenuous effort of the Notion" (Hegel, *Phenomenology* 35). And if this is indeed the case, what *is* democracy but "the goal of plasticity" (39)?

NOTES

Introduction

1. As John Fagg argues, both "[Stephan] Crane and Bellows occupy a position on the cusp of period change. While their works relate to the nineteenth-century practices they stem from and to the twentieth-century modernism they anticipate, they cannot be defined simply by these relationships. Crane and Bellows inhabited a moment marked by transitions, uncertainties, and possibilities, and produced works that draw on and at the same time critique earlier modes of expression, and that hint at the extremity of later modernist strategies while suggesting that a popular, less esoteric, modernism may have been possible" (3). As we will see, this possibility of less "extreme" forms of modernism has significant ethical implications—especially as it relates to both modern and postmodern efforts to relate the self while *or by* preserving otherness. What I come to call autoplasticity in the following chapters could, at least in part, be defined as the ethical potential of "less esoteric" forms of modernism.

2. As Jennie A. Kassanoff puts it (referring to American thinkers such as Edward Bellamy, Ralph Waldo Emerson, and William Dean Howells), "To be subject to an interdependent democratic norm in the US is therefore to be dissociated from either divine causality or metaphysical essence" (664). Faced with the increasingly overt impossibility of sustaining or articulating a purely independent and divinely mandated self, America began to fear "a contagion of disability that seemed the result of socioeconomic and technological change" (662).

3. Marianne Doezema makes much of the connection between the terrifying victories of Jack Johnson and the subject of Bellows's painting. As Doezema suggests, Bellows's painting—originally titled *A Nigger and a White Man*—highlights the sense that (at the beginning of the twentieth century) "it was incumbent upon white Americans collectively, as a race, to reaffirm their dominance over all inferiors, before it was too late" (108). The increasingly futile effort to reaffirm such dominance was, though, never *no less* a matter of sustaining a host of other hierarchical distinctions—especially those

separating the human and the nonhuman. If African Americans were akin to animals yet no less human than (white) European Americans, how could one preserve a clear line between the human and the nonhuman animal? Moreover, how could one consistently and rigorously articulate a uniquely American identity?

4. In *The Knock Out*, three bodies meet in an overtly triangular shape: above the body of a fighter lying on the mat, a referee holds back a victorious opponent. To the left of the image (and at the level of the mat) the fallen fighter's foot touches the foot of the victor; at the top (and exactly in line with the midsection of the fallen fighter), the hand of the referee pushes against a raised glove; to the left (and, again, at the level of the mat), the referee's foot meets the tip of an outstretched arm.

5. Unless essential to the meaning of the quote, initial capitalization in quotations has been silently altered to fit the syntax of the surrounding sentence.

6. Notably, this problem of mandated and disabling codes is one of the reasons the *New York Times* resisted the bout between Johnson and Jeffries: "It is not well that the two races should meet in *formally arranged* and widely advertised competition" (qtd. in Doezema 107; my emphasis).

7. For more on the possibility that Bellows was influenced by Goya, see Eleanor M. Tufts, "Bellows and Goya." Tufts deals specifically with *Both Members*—its "triangular build-up of figures" (363) and its distinctly Goyaesque crowd of spectators. Surprisingly, though, Tufts does not consider the potential influence (and implications) of *Disparate matrimonial*.

8. The etching is also known as *Disparate desordenado*, or "Disorderly Madness."

9. Might we not in fact view Bellows's painting—especially its depiction of a desperate, complicit, and dissolving crowd—as an uncannily prescient vision of a Trump rally?

1 / Melancholics and Specters

1. My use of "melancholia" follows from and plays off Freud's in "Mourning and Melancholia" (discussed more fully in the following paragraphs). Ultimately, though, I retain little more than Freud's sense of melancholia as a desperate effort to hold on to an ideal that "reality testing" has *or would* show to be lost or impossible.

2. Consider, for instance, Hegel's discussion of a Thing's absoluteness in the "Perception" section of *Phenomenology of Spirit*: "It is only a *Thing*, or a One that exists on its own account, in so far as it does not stand in this relation to others; for this relation establishes rather its continuity with others, and for it to be connected with others is to cease to exist on its own account. It is just through the *absolute character* of the Thing and its opposition that it *relates* itself to *others*, and is essentially only this relating. The relation, however, is the negation of its self-subsistence, and it is really the essential property of the Thing that is its undoing" (75–76). Here Hegel is anticipating his more famous discussion of the lord and bondsman, as well as (then) his concept of the "unhappy consciousness"—i.e., that consciousness which perceives only to lament its inability to be only itself. However, in this earlier section, Hegel most clearly outlines the problem and necessity of ontological *relation*—especially as a thinker like Nancy conceives it. Indeed, my own example of whiteness versus blackness is anticipated (and thus supported) by Hegel's description of a salt molecule: "*It is* white, *also* cubical, and *also* tart, and so on. But *in so far* as it is white, it is not cubical, and *in so far* as it is cubical and also white, it is not tart, and so on" (73). I return to Hegel toward the end of this chapter, but with somewhat different concerns in mind. Hegelian dialectics also play an important role in part III.

3. See, especially, "Plato's Pharmacy" in *Dissemination*. Derrida ties supplementarity to the Greek term *pharmakon*, which can be translated "as both 'remedy' and 'poison'" (70) and which "properly consists in a certain inconsistency, a certain impropriety, this nonidentity-with-itself always allowing it to be turned against itself" (119). The importance and unavoidability of supplementarity is at the root of Derrida's entire oeuvre—his conception of *différance*, for instance—though it seems to return most prominently in *The Truth in Painting* (via the concept of the "parergon," or frame).

4. Throughout this chapter, and much of part I, I use the capital O other as Nancy tends to use it—which is to say I am not (here) referring to the Lacanian notion of a "Big Other." Instead, the capital denotes the perception of the other as immanent, or absolute: "The other becomes the Other according to the mode of desire or hatred. Making the other divine (together with our voluntary servitude) or making it evil (together with its exclusion or extermination) is that part of curiosity no longer interested in dis-position and co-appearance, but rather has become the desire for the Position itself. The desire is the desire to fix the origin, or *to give the origin to itself*, once and for all, and in one place for all, that is, always outside the world. This is why such desire is a desire for murder" (Nancy, "Being Singular" 20).

5. Does this not, after all, explain the melancholic's willingness to risk his or her own life (via starvation or inactivity)? As Freud frequently suggests, the demands of the death drive entail a certain return to primary narcissism: I would rather die (as I truly am, or as I am *supposed* to be) than face the change or experience of mutability that threatens my current position. The melancholic desire for death, then (tied, as it is, to a state of primary narcissism), can thus be understood as the desire for the immanent self. See note 4.

6. Derrida's most sustained discussion of spectrality can be found in *Specters of Marx: The State of the Debt, the Work of Mourning, and the New International*. However, his later *Politics of Friendship* is also grounded in an analysis of spectrality. In the latter, Derrida's emphasis is far more aligned with my discussion of racial ambiguity in this chapter and throughout. In *Politics*, Derrida suggests that true friendship or community can only be experienced as the acceptance of the specter, the friend who is neither friend nor enemy (yet both). As Derrida puts it, "All phenomena of friendship, all things and all beings to be loved, belong to spectrality. 'It is necessary to love' means: the spectres, they are to be loved; the spectre must be respected (we know that Mary Shelley brought our attention to the anagram that makes the spectre in respect become visible again)" (288).

7. A few notable precursors are Mark Twain's *The Tragedy of Pudd'nhead Wilson* (1894) and various works by Charles Chesnutt—though *The House behind the Cedars* (1900) is likely the most relevant here. That said, Johnson's novel stands out insofar as its plot hinges upon the representation of a racially charged society that is utterly incapable of discovering the (racial) "truth."

8. Along similar lines, consider Ella Shohat's and Robert Stam's discussion of stereotypes in cinema. While, for the marginalized, such stereotypes confirm (and hold in place) "some presumed negative essence . . . [,] [s]ocially empowered groups need not be unduly concerned about 'distortions and stereotypes,' since even occasionally negative images form part of a wide spectrum of representations" ("Stereotype, Realism" 183). However, and given the discussion above, the larger problem is this: either "role" (empowered or marginalized) is sustained by the stereotypes in question, and persistent inconsistencies or ambiguities necessarily threaten the desire to deny or efface the difference between stereotype and reality—that is, the desire to assume such roles are innate, or immanent.

9. On racial ambiguity and passing as a subversion of essentialist conceptions of race in America, see (for instance) Wendy Doniger, *The Woman Who Pretended to Be Who She Was: Myths of Self-Imitation;* Gayle Wald, *Crossing the Line: Racial Passing in Twentieth-Century U.S. Literature and Culture;* and Elaine K. Ginsberg's introduction to *Passing and the Fictions of Identity.* On Johnson's novel, more specifically, as an example of subversive passing fiction, see (for instance) Neil Brooks, "On Becoming an Ex-Man: Postmodern Irony and the Extinguishing of Certainties in *The Autobiography of an Ex-Colored Man*"; or Kathleen Pfeiffer, "Individualism, Success, and American Identity in *The Autobiography of an Ex-Colored Man.*"

10. In Derrida's phrasing, a ghost is always a matter of "repetition *and* first time" (*Specters* 10). In other words, the freedom of the ghost can be defined as the paradoxical freedom of perpetually repeating, or becoming, the self *for the first time.* Nancy puts it like this: "No one begins *to be* free, but freedom *is* the beginning and endlessly remains the beginning" (*Freedom* 77).

11. "Hauntology" is, of course, Derrida's coinage. See *Specters of Marx,* specifically.

12. For Sartre, "bad faith" entails convincing myself that "*I am* my essence in the mode of being of the in-itself" (81). For a more extended discussion see *Being and Nothingness* (specifically part I, chapter 2).

13. The rise of American nativism in the early twentieth century is, of course, intimately tied to a racializing of musical forms. As Marco Katz Montiel notes, "Commentators on *afrocubanismo* and the Harlem Renaissance . . . persistently isolated elements that reaffirmed exotic preconceptions of blacks as unalterably alien, reified blacks as primitives in a pre-civilized state, or, at the very least, legitimized the treatment of blacks as second-class citizens. Musical demarcations served these purposes well, with widely disseminated depictions of popular musical artists possessing magnificent albeit uncontrollable capacities fit for nightclubs but unsuitable on concert stages" (72).

14. In highlighting the repetitive nature of ragtime, Bruce Bamhart makes a similar point. However, Bamhart suggests that the benefactor ultimately "envisions an art unattached to and untainted by the conditions of its making, free to circulate beyond the bounds of race and nation. In this construction, art bears none of the responsibility to community that is so important to both Johnson and the narrator" (555). My point, though, is that—rather than simply "binding [music] to the dictates of capital" (555)—the benefactor intimates that music is only ever an effect of relation, that our responsibility to music (and thus community) is to accept music as necessarily transnational and transracial. As Salim Washington suggests, the narrator's great failure is his inability to accept his benefactor's conception of art, for (in the end) the narrator's music "is merely the soundtrack to the life of a petty capitalist. His music does not utilize the breakthroughs in conception that he experienced through the coupling of European and African American musical practices, and does not aspire to Johnson's own rendering of the artistic marriage between orality and literacy. There is no American synthesis, just as there is no abandonment of the binary opposition between blackness and whiteness in the protagonist's mind" (254).

15. Steven Wandler views the narrator's remorse at the end as a commentary on his need "to transform ontological luck into epistemic luck by retroactively reformulating the events of his life not as contingent experiences that form his identity, but instead as lucky occurrences that simply help 'truly' to see and understand his 'real' identity" (580).

16. The act is now famous for further developing the xenophobic implications of its 1917 predecessor—specifically its reduction of general immigration quotas and its outright exclusion of Asians. The act, in other words, functioned to further stress (by reinforcing) the *inherent* "whiteness" of American citizenry.

17. Or as Walter Benn Michaels puts it, "Family is the essential form of nativist identity" (11). For Michaels, though, modern American texts from the twenties onward are almost entirely complicit with such nativism, echoing its assumptions by valorizing the purity of bloodlines and employing linguistic practices that aim to *naturalize* the arbitrary relationship between signifier and signified—or, that is, to make real "the linguistic fantasy of the word becoming the thing" (5). However, as we'll see (especially in chapter 3), such a portrayal of modernism must necessarily overlook its ability and tendency (also) to critique such efforts.

18. As is common in Hollywood film (even today), *The Jazz Singer*'s "classical" score is distinctly romantic. As such, it is both narrative and nationalist in nature—the latter trait being particularly noteworthy (given the nationalistic tendencies that parallel the development of American cinema). Moreover, and while it is likely too much of an imposition to insist upon its significance, it is worth noting (given the above discussion) that the film employs, as part of its formal score, Tchaikovsky's Sérénade mélancolique, op. 26.

19. Of course, in Hegel, the obdurately virtuous consciousness comes to the (selfish and paradoxical) conclusion that "the way of the world" is wholly defined by individual self-promotion and gain—and thus antithetical to (its) virtue. The point, it would seem, is that individualism merely (re)asserts itself the moment it is "virtuously" sacrificed to the *true* universal. In the end, stoic virtue unravels as simple arrogance justified by groundless and individualistic appeals to what is *immanently* true. The virtuous self fails to see that individuality is only to be realized in external existence, negation, or the negotiation of communal reality as such. See *Phenomenology,* especially §394.

20. This is, Hegel seems to suggest, the best (if not the only) explanation for a misogynistic patriarchy: "Since community only gets an existence through its interference with the happiness of the Family, and by dissolving [individual] self-consciousness into the universal, it creates for itself in what it suppresses and what is at the same time essential to it an internal enemy—womankind in general" (*Phenomenology* 288).

21. Hegel, of course, distinguishes ethics (as culturally constructed) with morality (as innate and self-conscious); thus, while a discussion of "the ethical order" opens his section titled "Spirit" (in *Phenomenology*), a discussion of "Morality" closes it.

22. I am, of course, referring here to the Hegelian *Aufhebung*—what we might think of as an overcoming (or negating) of negation. The self is "sublated" insofar as it is preserved in the moment of its negation, or loss. The negative thus remains as an integral part of what is preserved, or carried over. The use of the term here anticipates a more detailed discussion of Hegelian dialectics in part III.

23. Another way of thinking about this, as Hegel shows later on in *Phenomenology,* is that the morality of the self can only actualize itself via its dissemblance in the ethical world of culture; and yet, as Hegel insists, "The scornful rejection of that dissemblance would be itself the first expression of hypocrisy" (383).

24. Johnston is referring, specifically, to Doane's "Film and the Masquerade: Theorizing the Female Spectator."

25. See Rogin's *Blackface, White Noise: Jewish Immigrants in the Hollywood Melting Pot.*

26. Johnston notes "that the deployment of blackface in [Crosland's] film is far more ambiguous than in *The Birth of a Nation,* where it functions to distinguish between black and white viewers" ("Construction" 386). In *Birth of a Nation,* as Johnston explains, black characters are portrayed by white actors in blackface. Those characters are, in turn, "duped" by white spies who present themselves (within the film's narrative) as black. The white audience confirms its whiteness the moment it "gets" what the black characters fail to see. The implication is this: while a black audience would be fooled by such a performance, a white audience is not. That said, we should not overlook the more simple fact that Griffith used white actors to portray black characters because he wanted to minimize the amount of "black blood" (qtd. in Stokes 87) on the set. The scene in question is therefore a simple necessity; without it, a white racist audience might very well mistake whites for blacks.

27. It's worth noting, along with Johnston, that this scene can be viewed as Jack's "coming out scene" ("Construction" 386)—as it is the first scene in the film in which we see Jack discussing his Jewish identity with Mary. The problem with such a reading is that there is nothing in the scene to suggest that Mary does not already know that Jack is, or once was, Jakie. And yet Johnston is correct to highlight Jack's obvious efforts to distance himself from his Jewish identity.

2 / Promising Intrusion in Nella Larsen's *Passing*

1. It is worth noting that critics of the text have a tendency to do the same. Cheryl Wall, for example, argues that Irene and Clare "demonstrate the price *black women* pay for their acquiescence and, ultimately, the high cost of rebellion" (131; my emphasis). Likewise, Merrill Horton, in summarizing the novel's plot, describes Irene and Clare as two women "who are black by birth and by culture, but whose light skin allows them to 'pass for white'" (31). And, more recently, Cherene Sherrard-Johnson, while demonstrating the ways in which "Larsen strikes at the core of what constitutes whiteness to reveal it as a performance" (852), persists (perhaps unconsciously) in maintaining the belief that Clare and Irene are *actually* black. While discussing the scene at the Drayton, in which Irene is unable to "detect" Clare, Sherrard-Johnson notes that "Larsen undermines the premise that only African Americans can authenticate the performance of blackness or whiteness" (853)—thus suggesting that the scene's relevance (albeit subversive) is tied to Irene's innate racial identity.

2. For an extended consideration of doubling and "uncanny mirroring" (146) in the novel, see Johanna M. Wagner's "In Place of Clare Kendry: A Gothic Reading of Race and Sexuality in Nella Larsen's *Passing*."

3. See chapter 1.

4. This is, of course, to a certain extent, Judith Butler's reading of the scene. See her influential "Passing, Queering." I return to this reading in the final section of this chapter.

5. "Saying" and "said" are recurrent concepts in Levinas's work. While "saying" is tied (for Levinas) to the possibility of a preoriginal language (or an "otherwise than being"), the very possibility of saying entails the necessity of the thematizing or reductive "said": "Being, its cognition and the said in which it shows itself signify in a saying which, relative to being, forms an exception; but it is in the said that both this exception and the birth of cognition [la naissance de la connaissance] show themselves" (*Otherwise* 6). While I merely introduce it here, this is a problem that runs throughout the following chapters.

6. As Kathleen Pfeiffer suggests, we must not overlook just how "literally Clare's self, her body, is connected to written text" (140).

7. I use postmodernism here as Henderson seems to mean it—i.e., in its most conical (and therefore limited) sense. In other words, "postmodern" denotes (here, or *for now*) an abject insistence upon "indeterminacy," the willful and persistent corrosion of stable referents. Taken as a whole, and as I point out in *The Passing of Postmodernism*, postmodernism was never so nihilistic, or simplistic. For now, though, and following Henderson, the term is useful in that it effectively denotes a specific "attitude"—one that we see in Clare and (to a certain degree) the novel itself.

8. After all, passing narratives (like *Passing*) traditionally depict, or are read as depicting, the story of the "tragic mulatto." As Teresa Zackodnik notes, "Passing narratives have been largely understood to be assimilationist in nature and intent" (47). Simply, passing tends to be viewed as the tragic and immoral act of a person who is attempting to escape their "blackness." And, of course, much of the criticism on passing and passing narratives has been responsible for perpetuating the idea that the passing mulatto is necessarily "tragic." For an insightful discussion of the negative critical responses to characters like Clare, see Martha J. Cutter, "Sliding Significations: Passing as a Narrative and textual Strategy in Nella Larsen's Fiction," specifically p. 76. Often, though, the inverse approach is equally problematic; for when the promise of passing is celebrated or endorsed, the threat of its more extreme implications is often ignored, or overlooked. I discuss a number these "positive" readings in the following sections—many of them excellent and compelling efforts to position Larsen's text as an antiessentialist (or "postmodern") novel. For now, though, consider as representative instances the work of Jonathan Little and Gayle Wald. Little, in fact, lays the foundation for much of the more recent criticism on *Passing* (and passing) by focusing on Larsen's strategic use of irony and her construction of Irene as a woman dangerously obsessed with maintaining rigid boundaries of community and self. Likewise, yet more broadly, Wald explores the high "stakes" of identity construction and appropriation while highlighting the way in which the act of passing exposes identity as "historically pliable and multiply articulated" (24). The problem is that critics like Wald and Little fail to negotiate the ethical problem of (Clare's) *finally* incommunicable invisibility.

9. I mean "perversity" here as Žižek tends to employ the term—as irresponsible revelry in performance and the endlessly mutable expectations of an intersubjective order. I discuss Žižek's understanding of perversity more fully in part II, especially chapter 6.

10. Although I do not have the space to explore the full implications (and evidence) of Clare's homoerotic desire for Irene, the issue has already been dealt with by several critics. While we might read much of this criticism, along with Carr, as "paranoid" in its desire to get to the bottom of the text's various "symptoms," the idea that the text explores homoerotic desire remains (as even Carr seems to admit) a valid one. See, for instance, David L. Blackmore, "'That Unreasonable Restless Feeling'"; Deborah McDowell, "'That Nameless . . . Shameful Impulse'", Judith Butler, "Passing, Queering"; and Corinne Blackmer, "The Veils of Law."

11. Arguably, Clare's easy interaction with Irene's friends is due to the fact that Clare views herself as black and is, therefore, not passing (or "performing") when in the presence of other "blacks." However, as Claudia Tate points out, "Clare does not seem to be seeking out Blacks in order to regain a sense of racial pride and solidarity. She is merely looking for excitement, and Irene's active social life provides her with precisely that" (142).

12. Whether or not Clare actually has an affair with Brian is, of course, beside the point; *passing* as heterosexual necessarily implies the performative nature of both heterosexuality *and* homosexuality.

13. See chapter 1.

14. For a more detailed take on the relationship between postmodernism and perversity (as Žižek tends to employ the term) see my *The Passing of Postmodernism* (chapter 3).

15. This is, of course, a phrase that Lacan employs while laying the groundwork for his seminar on Poe's "The Purloined Letter." Via his reading of Poe's story, Lacan explores the virtually inescapable and largely imperceptible inertia of a prevailing intersubjective—i.e., "symbolic"—order. I discuss this concept more fully in chapter 4.

16. See Sullivan's "Nella Larsen's *Passing* and the Fading Subject."

3 / Articulations of Ambiguity

1. Williams, of course, identifies New York as "the City of Emigrés and Exiles" (34) par excellence.

2. How, too, if we follow Williams, do we prevent "the painfully acquired techniques of significant *dis*connection [from being] relocated . . . as the merely technical modes of advertising and the commercial cinema" (35)? How, in other words (if we can extend the implications of Williams's concern), do we maintain strangeness and disconnection without accidently fixing it in its thematization or making it a marketable (and easy to consume) cliché?

3. Both "poststructuralist" thinkers (like poststructuralists *in general*) turn to distinctly modern texts to make their points about the subversive nature of nonhegemonic or nonreductive writing. Andreas Huyssen tracks this tendency in *After the Great Divide*—see specifically 208–9.

4. In using this phrase Caughie is referring to Sissela Bok's *Secrets: On the Ethics of Concealment and Revelation*.

5. This is Caughie's central point. It is possible, she notes, "to see passing and the anxieties it arouses, as well as the border crossings (both literal and imaginative) that at once enable and express it, as the peculiar identification at the heart of modernism — and not just in the sense that the androgyne and the mulatto served as cultural icons of the modernist generation" (387). In saying this, Caughie is elaborating on the claims of Henry Louis Gates Jr.—whom she quotes: "'The Thematic elements of passing,' Gates writes, 'fragmentation, alienation, liminality, self-fashioning—echo the great themes of modernism'" (387). See Gates's 1996 *New Yorker* article, "White Like Me," 75.

6. In the interview I cite to supplement my discussion of "Economimesis," Derrida aligns himself with Levinas while also outlining the problem of Levinas's problematic humanism: "Lévinas, more than anyone else, has emphasized the sovereign inaccessibility of the other. The other can never be understood as presence, but only with concepts like traces and exteriority. He has completely broken with the phenomenological metaphysics of presence—the other can never be understood in a theoretical act, but only by means of ethical responsibility: *I take responsibility for the other*. But this responsibility applies only to the other *human being*—Lévinas' humanism is based on an exclusion of the animal, just as in Heidegger. The biblical commandment 'Thou shalt not kill' applies to humans, but leaves out animals" (Derrida, "Interview"). We will need to deal with this problem of "animal sacrifice" in part II. For now, let me stress that my own (re)deployment of Levinas's work—especially his concept of the *in*finite other—is an effort to think of the

other as *any* other (human or otherwise). This is, I hope, most clear in chapters 5 and 8. *Every*thing in the world that is not me is equally other—what I must therefore learn and forever struggle to consume *ethically*. There are no *naturalizable* sacrifices. Or rather, all sacrifice must remain undecidable.

7. Nancy, as we've seen, argues that relation entails freedom because relation is the very impossibility of a fixed identity. Like or as the Derridean supplement, relation corrupts and ultimately prohibits the very identity it allows (if only for a passing moment) to emerge, to share itself, to "com-pear."

8. Derrida here is following Freud's assertion that mourning entails an act of consumptive idealization. See "Economimesis" 23n3.

9. As Derrida puts it, "nothing is inedible in Hegel's infinite metabolism" (Derrida, "Interview").

10. See chapter 1.

11. Surely it is a mistake to insist, as Michaels does, that a majority of modern American texts (in the twenties and thirties) condone incestual and sterile practices (both linguistic and physical) so as to further the "nativist project of racializing [and thus nationalizing] the American" (13). While it is certainly possible to show (as Michaels does in his introductory reading of Faulkner's *The Sound and the Fury*) that American modernism tends to concern itself with familial bonds and the failure of language, we must be careful to parse what is articulated and what is implied. Especially in Faulkner. Quentin's appeals to incest are surely Quentin's, not Faulkner's—just as Benjy's desire for material and concrete signs is problematized via the very narrative strategies Faulkner employs. This is not to suggest, however, that modernism *never* succumbs to the impulses that motivate nativism and nationalism.

12. That Faulkner's style changes from largely obfuscating and politically ungrounded "poetic and imagist prose" (Dimitri, 12) to something that can "confront social-political issues in a way that ordinary readers ... are able to recognize" (13) is a point that has garnered a fair amount of critical consensus. Dimitri, after all, is largely paraphrasing and developing claims made (some time ago) by Joseph Gold (in *William Faulkner, A Study in Humanism*), Judith Bryant Wittenberg (in *Faulkner: The Transfiguration of Biography*), and Wesley Morris and Barbara Alverson Morris (in *Reading Faulkner*).

13. As Masami Sugimori puts it, "Through the dilemma Chick encounters as an 'in-between' white male adolescent, Faulkner demonstrates the difficulty of developing discursive freedom into substantial resistance and of avoiding the constant and penetrative working of ideological recruitment" (68).

14. This moment therefore anticipates (or announces) the various images of twins and doubles Doreen Fowler identifies.

15. Sugimori makes much of this "insight"—along with Habersham's role as a marginalized subject at "the edge of town." See, specifically, 64–66. In doing so, Sugimori offers a nuanced reading of Faulkner's deployment of (Bakhtinian) heteroglot language as it relates (also) to Lucas's subversive "silence"—a reading that certainly anticipates and supports my own.

16. Truth is, of course, for Lacan, a matter of economy. The letter in Poe's story is "lost" because the queen and then the minister have pulled it out of circulation, out of symbolic sense (or law). The letter, for this reason, is transformed into an object of pure disgust (as Derrida would define it)—an object that has no value and cannot be reassimilated into the order of truth. A massive debt is exposed, yet the minister refuses to account for

it. As Lacan states, the minster is presented as immoral because "he suspends the power conferred on him by the letter in indeterminacy, he gives it no symbolic meaning, all he plays on is the fact [of] this mirage" (200). And while Dupin also sees through and manipulates the veil of law, his morality is signaled when, after stealing the letter back, he returns it to the police (or to symbolic authority) for a fixed fee. Dupin thus reestablishes sense even as he exposes its innate contingency. Might we not begin to think of such an economics as the ethics of democratic indeterminacy, or democratic intrusions?

17. As one of Lacan's participants asserts (in the seminar that precedes the famous seminar on Poe's story), "*a law that's discovered is no longer a law*" (*Seminar* 189).

18. Even in spite of his overt masculinity and claims to "manhood," Lucas seems to effect a confusion of gender norms. As Doreen Fowler suggests, "Lucas Beauchamp is a father whose authority is not defined by an Oedipal threat" (797). Fowler supports her claim by appealing to similar arguments in the work of Richard C. Moreland ("Faulkner's Continuing Education") and Minrose C. Gwin (*The Feminine and Faulkner*). Along these same lines, we can view Faulkner's antimasculinist language acts as representative of something *like* Hélène Cixous's "*écriture féminine*" ("The Laugh of the Medusa")—or even the poststructuralist ideal of *écriture* more generally. By extension, we can say something similar about the forms of autoplasticity I begin defining in part III. Nevertheless, as we have already begun to see, the ideal forms of poststructuralism (like those of modernism and postmodernism) must be approached with some hesitation.

19. "The Fire and the Hearth" is, however, based on two *earlier* stories, "A Point of Law" and "Gold Is Not Always." For one of the earliest discussions of Faulkner's various revisions, see Marvin Klotz, "Procrustean Revision in Faulkner's *Go Down, Moses*" (specifically 10–13).

20. Lucas's ability to sustain his passing state makes him the dialectic counterpoint to Joe Christmas in *Light in August*. Joe, one of Faulkner's most tragic figures, thinks he *might* be black (even though he looks white). Neither Joe nor the community through which he "passes" seems capable of enduring this ambiguity. The novel concludes when a lynch mob, believing he has murdered a white woman, chases and finally kills Joe. Once Joe is cornered behind a table in the house of an old minister, the leader of the mob (Grimm) proceeds to "empt[y] [his] automatic's magazine into the table" (464). Gun no longer of use, Grimm falls on Joe with a knife: "When [the rest of the mob] saw what Grimm was doing one of the men gave a choked cry and stumbled back into the wall and began to vomit. Then Grimm sprang back, flinging behind him the bloody butcher knife. 'Now you'll let white women alone, even in hell,' he said" (464). While Joe is barely conscious in these final moments, his reaction to the event of his own castration is striking: "For a long moment he looked up at them with peaceful and unfathomable and unbearable eyes" (464). Highlighted is a certain problematic desire for the reassuring *fixity* of death—tied, especially, as it is in the scene, to a literal act of "fixing" (as one "fixes" a dog). In death—and by way of a sterilizing lynching—Joe is *finally* black. Grimm, whose name is inextricably tied to death, comes, after all, to be the figurehead of certainty and order in the novel; he seems to be "served by certitude, the blind and untroubled faith in the rightness and infallibility of his actions" (459). His selfhood, his purpose, is never in doubt. He *presumes* to move, like Kant's genius, with "blind obedience to whatever Player move[s] him on the Board" (462).

21. Lucas's "troublesome" nature affects both characters (in Faulkner's novels) and critics (of those novels). One might indeed engage in a useful and extended study on the

history of "Lucas criticism." While I will not attempt such a thing here, suffice it to say that critics have traditionally "struggled" with Lucas far more than they have struggled with a character like Clare. Even as late as the mid-1980s, critics like Sandra D. Milloy find themselves suggesting that, because Lucas seemingly identifies with his white McCaslin heritage, "he cuts himself off from his brother and refuses to become involved in the general heart of man" (404–5). Likewise, in the early 1990s, critics like Keith Clark find themselves wondering "why . . . Faulkner find[s] it necessary not only to turn Lucas into an imitation *white* man, but also to place him at odds with the people with whom he shares the common bond of race" (68).

22. This is, essentially, Fowler's position.

23. While quoting Isaiah Berlin's *Four Essays on Liberty,* Dimitri suggests that Ike McCaslin practices a type of "self-abnegation [which] consists of the retreat into the self when the 'external world has proved exceptionally arid, cruel or unjust'" (16). This is, as Dimitri and Berlin note, a form of stoicism. Following Hegel, then, we might very well link it to the withdrawal mandated by the "law of the heart" and its paradoxical opposition to the "way of the world" (or the law of all *other* hearts). See chapter 1. That said, we should perhaps note here (also) that, as even Berlin suggests, positive liberty necessarily runs the risk of becoming an excuse for domination: "Once I take this view, I am in a position to ignore the actual wishes of men or societies, to bully, oppress, torture them in the name, and on behalf, of their 'real' selves, in the secure knowledge that whatever is the true goal of man (happiness, performance of duty, wisdom, a just society, self-fulfillment) must be identical with his freedom—the free choice of his 'true,' albeit often submerged and inarticulate, self" (133). There is surely something comparable here to the manner in which Hegel finally undoes the dialectical opposition of "virtue" (which would abandon individuality in favor of the universal good) and "the way of the world" (which consists only of self-interested individuals). Perhaps even more significantly, though, Berlin's comments clearly evoke the illusory (and dangerously hierarchizing) "freedom" Kant defines—an *imposed* freedom (of race or gender or whatever) that is justified via (necessarily constructed) appeals to universal naturalness.

24. Sugimori seems to suggest something similar when he claims that "Lucas's effort to buy himself out of the ideologically defined 'dependent nigger' category paradoxically involves looking at himself reflected in an 'ordering' mirror" (71).

25. *Tar Baby* is one of Morrison's earlier novels—her fourth, specifically.

26. As Duvall points out, "Son's sexual violation of Jadine is startling in two ways: first, for the way that critics have commented upon this key scene without noticing the sexual violation; and second, for the way that Morrison's own less-than-candid remarks on her novel have helped to conceal the rape" (334–35). Duvall, of course, tries to ameliorate the implications of the rape—the possibility that Morrison may even be somehow endorsing it—by reading in it a metaphor for the way in which "Morrison . . . has been violated metaphorically by the white corporate publishing world" (333). But this argument surely fails to account fully for the fact that the rape "is rhetorically constructed to deny the reader's awareness of the violence" (332–33).

4 / Touching Herman Melville's "Bartleby" (and Other Zombie Narratives)

1. In the first episode of AMC's televised adaptation, director and creator Frank Darabont wisely choose to highlight these frames, offering viewers an ostentatious "hero shot." In doing so, Darabont seemed intent on exposing the "fantasy" elements of

Kirkman's narrative. Indeed, the "reality" of the first season is significantly ambiguous, as Darabont stresses the fact that the show concerns a cuckolded man who has quite inexplicably survived a zombie apocalypse while lying comatose in a hospital. In this way, the series initially seemed to follow in the footsteps of any number of Hitchcock films, such as *Rear Window, The Man Who Knew Too Much,* or *North by Northwest*—films that present (while implicitly critiquing) the "fantasy" of a largely emasculated man and, in turn, the fantasy induced by a temporarily disrupted phallogocentric symbolic order.

2. Also the publication date of Philip K Dick's *Do Android's Dream of Electric Sheep?* (discussed in chapter 5).

3. What, then, is so interesting about Marc Forster's film adaptation is the fact that (despite its wanton indifference to the novel's actual plot) the film clearly replicates the novel's basic "fantasy." Forster's adaptation of Brooks's novel opens with the disintegration of an ideal American family. During the initial outbreak of the zombie infection, the family in question is enjoying breakfast. Cued by an ambiguous report concerning the imposition of martial law (in some other country), one of the "girls" asks her father (Brad Pitt) if he misses his old job (at, we eventually learn, the UN). Pitt's character (the cinematic version of Brooks's unnamed narrator), responds by asserting that "[he] like[s] his new job" (as full-time caregiver). Upon hearing this, the mother of the family looks wistfully and lovingly at her husband. But her look also expresses understanding: he *does* miss his old job! In terms of the film's narrative logic, a zombie apocalypse is precisely what he needs: a way to return (without any feelings of guilt) to his natural role as unfettered man and hero.

4. See chapter 1 and chapter 3.

5. A useful digression might be to compare the zombie and a character like Bartleby (or even the Nexus 6 android discussed in the following chapter) to the Derridean concept of the "pharmakeus"—"a being that no 'logic' can confine within a noncontradictory definition, an individual of the demonic species, neither god nor man, neither immortal nor mortal, neither living nor dead" (Derrida, "Pharmacy" 117).

6. "Quisling" is, of course, a reference to Vidkun Quisling, the Norwegian officer who collaborated with the Nazis and served as prime minister of Norway from 1942 to 1945. In *World War Z* the term seems to imply both "traitor" and "performer"—or, as I suggest above, "passer."

7. In this sense, as we'll see in chapter 6, Woody Allen's *Zelig*—a Jewish "chameleon" who finds himself "passing" as a Nazi soldier—is the ultimate quisling.

8. See chapters 1 and 2, especially.

9. Or, in Hegelian terms, "virtue" comes head to head with "the law of the heart." See chapter 1.

10. I deal with all three theorists (in varying detail) below.

11. The narrator describes Bartleby as a "ghost" (or undead entity) on numerous occasions: "Like a very ghost" (25), "the apparition of Bartleby" (26), "his mildly cadaverous reply" (30), "the apparition in my room" (38), "this man, or rather ghost" (38), etc.

12. Deleuze refers to Bartleby as "the man without references" (74), a description justified by the narrator's claim that Bartleby "seemed alone, absolutely alone in the universe. A bit of wreckage in the mid Atlantic" (32).

13. I use this term in a strictly Sartrean sense.

14. My point is that Bartleby's refusal to fulfill the narrator's "natural expectancy" violently disrupts such an order, exposing and undermining the artificial (or *un*natural) laws by which it is necessarily governed.

15. As the narrator insists, Bartleby is "*violently* unreasonable" (22; my emphasis).

16. As Freud repeatedly suggests, the "uncanny is in reality nothing new or alien, but something which is familiar and old-established in the mind and which has become alienated from it only through the process of repression" ("Uncanny" 241).

17. "Incontinent" is, of course, a derivative of the Latin *contineo,* meaning "to hold," or "keep together."

18. And yet Bartleby hardly seems interested in sustaining his apparent spectrality, as spectrality would entail sustaining a state of inclusion and exclusion, communion and egotism. Bartleby's self-willed exclusion might very well effect a sense of spectrality, but it ultimately speaks to his desire for utter and solipsistic independence—the culmination of which is not *un*dead ghostliness but death itself.

19. Matteson points to this fact when, briefly, he discusses Melville's conflation of pity and consumption. While referring to the scene in which the narrator first resolves to treat Bartleby well—a decision that will, the narrator assumes, "prove a sweet morsel for [his] conscience" (24)—Matteson highlights the fact that the narrator's "charity becomes an almost parasitic act, enabling the lawyer's soul to savor the juicy satisfaction of relieving another's misfortune" (47). In this sense, the narrator's ability to *feed off* of— or rather, *empathize with*—Bartleby requires, paradoxically, his distance (or difference) from Bartleby.

20. There is, for instance, no indication that the narrator overindulges in ginger nuts (as do his employees). More to the point, the narrator is never directly linked to food—as are (obviously) Turkey, Nippers, and Ginger Nut.

21. As Thomas Cousineau argues in his own critique of Deleuze's reading of "Bartleby," there is a "fundamentally mimetic relationship between [Melville's] two principal characters" (119), a relationship that Deleuze overlooks, or willfully ignores. For Cousineau, this relationship highlights Melville's critique of the American desire for an ideal community that cannot be reconciled with the exclusionary tactics upon which such communities are necessarily predicated. The story does not, then, offer Bartleby as the doctor for a sick America; instead, it exposes the inevitability of exclusionary (or competitive) tactics in community formation. The problem with Cousineau's reading is that Bartleby is yet again cast as the tragically necessary martyr.

22. As Deleuze notes, Bartleby is "someone who is born to and stays in a particular place, while the attorney necessarily fills the function of the traitor condemned to flight. Whenever the attorney invokes philanthropy, charity, or friendship, his protestations are shot through with an obscure guilt . . . sending [him] fleeing" (76).

23. At his most desperate, the narrator restrains himself "by recalling the divine injunction: 'A new commandment give I unto you, that ye love one another'" (36). He is, here, recalling John 13:34 (as translated in the Geneva Bible). I employ, though, the phrasing from Mark 12:31 (which appears in both the Geneva and the King James version, and which repeats Leviticus 19:18) so as to highlight the suggestion of empathy latent in John (and to anticipate my reading of "Mercerism" in Philip K. Dick's *Do Androids Dream of Electric Sheep?*). As Christ goes on to state, "*as I* have loved you, that ye also love one another" (John 13:34; my emphasis). As in Leviticus and Mark, the injunction insists upon

an almost violent conformity, to be *as the other*, to love the neighbor (only) *as thyself*. This "divine injunction" can be read, therefore, as a push toward entropic homogeneity—and hence, to some degree, Freud's dismissal of the injunction in *Civilization and Its Discontents* (in favor of more properly and reasonably sublimated aggression). I deal with this problematic injunction more fully in the following chapter.

24. While he is certainly correct to assert that Bartleby's "formula" subversively sustains and celebrates his potentiality "to be" (something), Agamben fails to confront the implications of Bartleby's (irresponsible) refusal to risk himself by gambling upon that potentiality, to chance *being* (identified as something), to chance communion with others from a relatable position. Agamben's Bartleby ostensibly desires and promises a state of solipsistic islands, all of which would be "at home ... [where] there is only a 'rather' fully freed of all *ratio*, a preference and a potentiality that no longer function to assure the supremacy of Being over Nothing but exist, without reason, in the indifference between Being and Nothingness" (258–59). But if we read Bartleby's state of "indifference" as (much more problematically) a failure to gamble his self *in relation*, to risk *a position*, then we might better understand Badiou's assertion that Bartleby's various refusals are a "betrayal" of truth (400).

25. I'm referring to Žižek's "Neighbors and Other Monsters" (which I discuss at some length in the following chapters). It's worth noting, too, that Žižek offers his own take on Melville's story—in *The Parallax View* and then (again) in "Notes Towards a Politics of Bartleby: The Ignorance of Chicken." In both, Žižek celebrates Bartley's "I would prefer not" as the ultimate revolutionary move, the "gesture of a pure withdrawal" that "effectively chang[es] the basic coordinates of a constellation" ("Notes" 393). This shift of coordinates "opens up a new space outside the hegemonic position *and* its negation" (393)—or what Žižek is fond of calling the mere "obverse" of a given ideological trap. Žižek entertains the revolutionary power of saying "I would prefer not" to a host of social "duties"—duties that ultimately sustain prevailing socioeconomic structures: protesting against racial and sexual injustice, saving the environment, finding "inner peace," etc. In his extremely cursive reading of Melville's text, though, Žižek fails to account for the fact that Bartleby is largely the mere "obverse" of the narrator, that his radical withdrawal is (in the end) as feckless as the narrator's naïve participation. Dead and "huddled at the base of [a] wall," Bartleby offers us no access point to whatever "new space" he may have opened up. Indeed, Žižek repeats, again, his take on Bartleby in *Less than Nothing*—comparing Bartleby's withdrawal to the strategies employed by the Occupy movement (which, we should add, had little long-term effect). But here Žižek admits that "soon we will have to address the truly difficult questions—not about what we do not want, but about what we *do* want" (1007).

5 / Consuming Androids in the Work of Philip K. Dick

1. Scott *might* have read the novel. It seems no one knows for certain—though Dick (with good reason) assumed he hadn't. Peoples has admitted (with far more clarity) that he had not. For more specifics see the Greg Rickman article I cite throughout this section.

2. Spelled "Voight-Kampff" in the film/screenplay.

3. I refer here again to Derrida's phrasing in "Eating Well," discussed in chapter 4.

4. The concept of speciesism comes, of course, from Peter Singer's *Animal Liberation*, a sustained and impassioned critique of animal cruelty as an effect of the illogical yet pervasive tendency to privilege one form of life over another.

5. Examples of such rhetoric abound. But perhaps the most famous will serve as a satisfactory example:

> I still have a dream . . . deeply rooted in the American dream that one day this nation will rise up and live out the true meaning of its creed—we hold these truths to be self-evident, that all men are created equal.
>
> I have a dream that one day on the red hills of Georgia, sons of former slaves and the sons of former slave-owners will be able to sit down together at the table of brotherhood. (King 219)

And while, as Ursula K. Heise points out, most American science fiction simply perpetuates and expands upon the problematic ideal of fraternal sympathy—"cast[ing] the alien as a figure for class, racial, ethnic, national, or religious difference, with the implication that alienness is ultimately knowable and assimilable" (504)—I am arguing that Dick (like Melville) is interested in problematizing this "implication." In other words, Dick's theme of empathy (along with his obviously satiric conjectures about human/animal/android relations in a postapocalyptic world) in no way affirms, as Heise claims, an "authentic humanness . . . associated with biophilia" (506). Instead, Dick offers a critique of empathy that openly reconsiders a problematically persistent tendency in America's various efforts to make manifest its ideal democratic state.

6. In many ways, then, the android is akin to the contemporary zombie (discussed in chapter 4). However, while the zombie is ostensibly linked to empathic breakdowns and the homogeneous communal horde, the android is linked to abject egotism and the impossibility of empathy. The former has no sense of self, while the latter is *only* (a) self (with no ability to relate via empathy). This difference, though, simply (and once again) reaffirms the inevitable inversion (or mirroring) I am interested in tracking.

7. This is a problem that surely haunts the basic assumptions of object-oriented ontology and speculative realism. See chapter 8.

8. The novel, I am suggesting, is no more concerned with "reclaim[ing] the essence of humanity" (Sims 67) than it is with promoting "a community of the *post*human, in which human and machine commiserate and comaterialize vitally shaping one another's existences" (Galvan 414). Nor is it concerned with simply and finally "rejecting the speciesist discourse that attempts to construct hierarchies and divisions" (Vint 117).

9. See Freud's *Civilization and Its Discontents,* in which he argues that the injunction to "love thy neighbor as thyself" is ultimately an injunction to restrict and thus direct inward an essential human drive: aggression. The effort to restrict or deny this drive results in a hyperinflated superego that bombards the ego with untenable feelings of guilt. As I show in the final section of this chapter, Žižek "plays off" this argument in a manner that is particularly germane to an analysis of Dick's novel. Moreover, Freud's consideration of the destructive and aggressive desire to exclude (as it both compliments and opposes an empathic desire to belong) echoes his earlier conception of the death drive, a conception that informs my analysis of both Melville's "Bartleby" and Dick's *Do Androids Dream.*

10. Or, in Freud's terms, "the quiescence of the inorganic world" (Freud, *Beyond* 62).

11. Recall, too, our discussion of Hegel's effort to locate the possibility of individuality in community and the possibility of community in the individual. See chapter 1.

12. Hayles's excellent discussion of consumption in Dick's oeuvre and biography can be found in *How We Became Posthuman,* specifically chapter 7. As Hayles points out, a

large portion of Dick's novels deals (in one way or another) with the tension between consuming and being consumed.

13. I am referring here to Dick's discussion of schizophrenia in a letter to Patricia Warrick (as discussed by Hayles). The quotes (from Hayles) are thus descriptors of the different "schizophrenics" Dick describes: the "psychotic schizophrenic" and the "neurotic schizoid," respectively.

14. In "Nazism and *The High Castle*," Dick is unequivocal: "I am a nominalist. To me, there are only individual entities, not group entities such as race, blood, people, etc." (117). For Dick, being human has nothing to do with biology. It is merely a matter of *not* being dead, or *like* an indifferent machine. I discuss Dick's nominalist take on humanity and selfhood more fully in chapter 8.

15. For a detailed investigation of Dick's indictment *and* valorization of schizophrenia as an effect of late capitalism, see (again) Hayles's chapter on Dick in *How We Became Posthuman*.

16. We might say, recalling chapter 1 and anticipating much of part III, that such "universal knowledge" marks the possibility of sustaining and relating what is "God in us," or "Infinity in me" (Levinas, "God and Philosophy" 63).

17. Perhaps, though, we should write this as "*in*finite hospitality"—as this would more clearly link Derrida's mandate to a Levinasian conception of *in*finite otherness (as discussed in chapter 2).

18. We should note, as Deckard himself intimates, that "you shall only kill the killers" is no less undecidable than "thou shalt not kill"—an injunction that, as Derrida notes, "has never been understood within the Judeo-Christian tradition . . . as 'Thou shalt not put to death the living in general'" ("Eating Well" 279).

19. One might (and perhaps should) compare the treatment of the android in Dick's novel to the treatment of any number of racially (or sexually) ambiguous characters in American literature and film—such as those discussed in part I. In other words, a critic like Michelle Reid is wise to link Dick's androids to Leilani Nishime's concept of a "mulatto cyborg" (Reid 362).

20. I discuss Lacan's concept of the "Ideal I" more fully in the following chapter.

21. As Vint astutely notes, "The treatment of androids within the novel comments on our historical and current exploitation of animals, and also our exploitation of those humans who have been animalized in discourse, such as women, the working classes, and non-whites, particularly slaves" (114).

6 / The Chameleon and the Dictator in Woody Allen's *Zelig*

1. Both the scene and the narrator's description of it—"like a man emerging from a dream"—recalls or evokes Friedrich Nietzsche's account (in *The Birth of Tragedy*) of the Apollonian actor's emergence out of the Dionysian "whole" *and* Jean-Paul Sartre's account (discussed in chapter 4) of the various acts of negation he must perform while futilely searching for "Pierre" in a café. Both accounts (like Allen's inexplicable emergence) stress a certain violence or aggression that defines all articulations of identity— the act of cutting the self *off of* or *out from* an indifferent background of otherness. Both accounts also point us toward the necessarily artificial or fictional nature of individuality. Nietzsche, in particular, exposes the tension between a Dionysian and schizophrenic Real and the rational impositions of an Apollonian symbolic. And, as a close viewing of *Zelig*

confirms, Allen (like both Melville and Dick) exposes a similar tension: between extreme empathy (chameleonism) and extreme egotism (totalitarianism).

2. Scholars of the film necessarily "gamble" on one of these two options. Robert Stam and Ella Shohat, for instance, assume the former, suggesting that "the chameleonism of postsynchronization weds Hitler's recorded voice to the lip movements of a contemporary double made up to look like Hitler" ("*Zelig* and Contemporary Theory" 201). However, Sam B. Girgus describes a much different scene: "Just at this point of Hitler's rage, the film cuts swiftly to a Hollywood version of the event. Thus, Allen makes a parody of a Hollywood movie about Zelig within *Zelig*. This demonstrates that at the technical limit of one device—the integration of Allen and Farrow into *real documentary footage of Hitler and the Nazis*—Allen immediately can muster another technique that he used before and will use again, the film within the film" (93; my emphasis). Stam and Shohat ostensibly support their "assumption" via a footnote directing readers to a 1984 interview with Willis in *American Cinematographer*. But apart from admitting that there are only two matte shots in the entire film (which he refuses to identify), Willis makes few claims that might support Stam and Shohat's position. At one point, though, and while discussing the problem of merging the "look" of film without sound and the "look" of film with sound, he adds (somewhat ambiguously) that, "in the Hitler sequence, . . . you will see that when working on the Hitler side you have sound. When we are using footage from the audience perspective, we are undercranking and, in fact, that is exactly how the original footage looked." My argument does not require that I make a gamble of my own, so I will simply encourage viewers of Allen's film to compare the scene closely to footage of Hitler's first speech as chancellor of Germany (which he gave at the Berlin Sportpalast on 10 Feb. 1933).

3. This is a common reading of the film. According to Richard Wasson, "*Zelig* encloses itself in its own world of sign production; all significance, all meaning and therefore all change is produced in that realm" (93). Likewise, Robert Stam and Ella Shohat argue that the film "implicitly subverts, perhaps against its will, the very idea of originality and, by extension, the idea of the true autonomous self" ("*Zelig* and Contemporary Theory" 213). While I am not interested in denying the obviously postmodern proclivities of the film, I would like to stress the way in which the film also problematizes the potential irresponsibility of such proclivities. It is, in my reading, quite significant that (as Stam and Shohat put it) the film often "seems to fall back into the mystification of self and romance" (213).

4. It is worth noting that this overtly commercial exploitation merely replicates the self-motivated efforts of Zelig's doctors (including Fletcher, who eventually admits that she "started out trying to use Leonard to make [her] reputation"). As Iris Bruce puts it, "Everyone is busy defining Zelig, commodifying him, fitting him into categories, appropriating him either as an enemy or friend, devil or saint, or using him as an object for intellectual speculation" (175).

5. As the film frequently intimates, this refusal is profoundly unethical (if, at the same time, justified by the fact that any effort to offer the self is necessarily doomed to fail). From a certain perspective, then, Zelig can be (at least initially) viewed in the same way Derrida views Plato—as, that is, irresponsibly uncommitted. For, as Derrida stresses in his conclusion to "Plato's Pharmacy" (by citing one of Plato's apocryphal letters), "There is not . . . any written work of Plato's own" (170). Derrida's point is that Plato hides behind the fictional construct of his master; like Zelig, he refuses to commit anything of

himself. He refuses to risk *a* self (or position) that may be corrupted or dismissed by the other. The same, of course, can be said of Melville's Bartleby. I discuss Derrida's critique of Plato in chapter 7.

6. In many ways, Sartre simply reminds us of (while never getting too far beyond) Hegel's "unhappy consciousness."

7. In this sense, Zelig's "problem" does not, as Richard Feldstein argues, "originate . . . in the *meconnaisance* experienced when perceiving in his mirror image an other who reflects back a sense of permanence, substantiality, and identity" (157). Zelig's "problem," we might say (instead), is that he is utterly unable or unwilling to accept *as real* the imaginary realm of permanence. Lacan's introductory discussion of the "Ideal I" and the "Mirror Stage" occurs in "The Mirror Stage as Formative of the Function of the *I* in Psychoanalytic Experience."

8. As one interviewed man tells us, "I wish I could be Leonard Zelig, the changing man, and be different people, and maybe someday my wishes will come true" (*Zelig*).

9. A fact that is discussed by Shohat and Stam and then considered in much more detail by Ruth D. Johnston in "Ethnic and Discursive Drag in Woody Allen's *Zelig*."

10. The connection between "lynching" and "fixing" is worth recalling. See chapters 1 and 3.

11. We should recall here, too, the strange relationship between Jewish identity and the rise of blackface in the early twentieth century—with blackface often functioning as a way to stabilize the "whiteness" of the Jewish body. See chapter 1.

12. Fletcher admits that she is recording the sessions after Zelig comments on how bright the room is.

13. As Jean-Luc Nancy notes, "The logic of Nazi Germany was not only that of the extermination of the other, of the subhuman deemed exterior to the communion of blood and soil, but also, effectively, the logic of sacrifice aimed at all those in the 'Aryan' community who did not satisfy the criteria of *pure* immanence, so much that—it being obviously impossible to set a limit on such criteria—the suicide of the German nation itself might have represented a plausible extrapolation of the process" ("Inoperative" 12).

14. The film functions as both a dizzying simulacra or pastiche *and* a traditional parody, "lampoon[ing]," as Robert Stam and Ella Shohat assert, "all the hackneyed rhetorical procedures of the 'canonical' documentary: its ponderously knowing male narrators; its ritualistic talking heads; its quasi-comic redundancy (the image of Eudora writing in her diary is accompanied by the comment 'Eudora writes in her diary'); its frequent implausibilities (through what legerdemain did the documentarist manage to witness such an eminently private act as 'writing in one's diary'?); its suspect manipulation of stock footage (the commentary 'Eudora goes to Europe' is superimposed on a stock shot of an ocean liner—her liner? that trip?)" ("*Zelig* and Contemporary Theory" 200).

15. Burke introduces and develops the concept of the "terministic screen" in *Language as Symbolic Action*. However, the problem and necessity of "terministic screens" is clearly anticipated in Burke's earlier discussion (in *A Rhetoric of Motives*) of ideological "mystifications." I attend more fully to Burke in chapter 7.

16. For instance, Zelig cannot transform into a woman—a fact that clearly supports Žižek's (Lacanian) claim that "sexual difference is a Real that resist symbolization" ("Courtly Love" 108).

17. See Derrida's *Politics of Friendship*.

7 / The Autonarratives of Ernest Hemingway (and Others)

1. Significantly, Žižek finds himself wanting to do away with the disgusting at the very moment he seems most intent on chastising those who might find a way to refuse it. He asserts that "true art has *nothing whatsoever* to do with disgusting emotional exhibitionism" (135). The implication is that *true* art preserves the traumatic Thing so absolutely that it finally purifies itself of disgust, of any possibility of experiencing the Thing. The uncanny clash between what is *Heimlich* and what is *Unheimlich* is, it would seem, lost. As we saw in chapter 3, there is surely nothing disgusting about the *absolutely disgusting* (because it simply never crosses or even gets to our plate/threshold)—*just as* there is nothing disgusting about the perfectly palatable, or law abiding.

2. Lacan, of course, insists that "the function of the *imago* . . . is to establish a relation between the organism and its reality—or, as they say, between the *Innenwelt* and the *Umwelt*" ("Mirror Stage" 4). Thus "it is our *privilege* to see in outline and in our daily experiences and in the penumbra of symbolic efficacity" the omnifariously "veiled faces" of so many "*imagos*" (4; my emphasis).

3. We should not forget that Žižek often implies and even (ostensibly) celebrates just such a possibility—in, for instance, his advocacy of an "art of the ridiculous sublime." As we saw in chapter 6, Žižek insists (in *Tarrying with the Negative*) that "fictions are a semblance which occludes reality, but if we renounce fictions, reality itself dissolves" (91). Given such claims—along with his appeals to forms of ethically efficacious art—Žižek obviously assumes (on some level) that the self/artist can and must choose fictions that are *more* or *less* revelatory, *more* or *less* giving. And surely only *in* the imaginary could such a hierarchy find its grounding. We must *imagine* the Real if we are to occlude it to good effect—a fact that applies as much to the world "out there" as to the opaque/divine core "in me."

4. The epigraph is drawn from Emerson's *Journals,* the entry for "Jan.–Feb. 1841."

5. Decker employs the term "supraself" as a way of distinguishing between a nondiegetic Miller/author and his autonarrative (or diegetic) counterpart/construction.

6. See chapter 3.

7. The French have taken (occasionally) to calling such texts "autofiction." (See, especially, Gérard Genette, *Fiction and Diction.*) I prefer Rajan's emphasis on "narration" only insofar as it is more suggestive of an ongoing construction. It also implies an expression of self that is as fictional as it is ostensibly sincere.

8. "Asymptotical" is used here to echo Lacan's assertion (in "The Mirror Stage") that the Ideal I "situates the agency of the ego, before its social determination, in a fictional direction, which will always remain irreducible for the individual alone, or rather, which will only rejoin the coming-into-being (*le devenir*) of the subject asymptotically, whatever the success of the dialectical syntheses by which he must resolve as *I* his discordance with his own reality" (2).

9. The memoir's troubling lack of veracity has been well documented. As Gerry Brenner puts it (by way of justifying the necessity of *A Comprehensive Companion* to the text), Hemingway's memoir employs "irregularities and discontinuities that continually destabilize its narrative integrity, at times so abruptly blurring allegedly factual episodes that they take on the life of fictive vignettes" (xii). Or more pointedly, and in Jacqueline Tavernier-Courbin's terms, "There are clear factual errors in the book, some of which cannot have been anything but deliberate" (83).

10. Louis Renza highlights this tendency—especially as it relates to "Hemingway's often vengeful depictions of Stein, Fitzgerald, and other literary contemporaries" (662).

11. As Faith Norris points out, "On a first reading *A Moveable Feast* seems to have no structure at all: 'sketch' seems to follow 'sketch' for no visible reason; one feels that Hemingway has left us at a total chronological loss" (107–8).

12. Hemingway's last wife, Mary, recalls him saying this—after she noticed that the manuscript for *A Moveable Feast* was "not much about [Hemingway]"—in a 1964 article for the *New York Times Book Review*. What exactly Hemingway meant by this, and whether or not Mary heard him correctly, is considered at some length by Suzanne Del Gizzo. Del Gizzo even considers the possibility that Hemingway actually said "autobiography" (instead of "biography") and "*rebote*" (instead of "*remate*"). While Mary suggests that "*remate* idiomatically is used to mean a two-wall shot in jai alai," Del Gizzo points out that the term (more formally) "comes from the Spanish verb, *rematar*, which literally means 'to re-kill,' with the suggestion of 'to kill' coming from *matar*. *Remate* is frequently translated into English as 'to finish'" (122). *Rebote*, on the other hand, "is Spanish for 'ricochet or rebound'" (123). Regardless, and even if we take Mary at her word, we get the sense that Hemingway saw his memoir as (on some level) an effort to *re*spond to critics and fellow writers with a killing blow—one (moreover) that would function to fix things (or at least Hemingway) in place.

13. The concepts of "ultimate terms" and "mystification" are discussed at length in Kenneth Burke's *A Rhetoric of Motives*. Burke points to both Hegelianism and Marxism as examples of "mystifications," suggesting in turn that Marxism serves to "demystify" Hegelianism: "Formally, we might say that, whereas one can talk of generic, specific, or individual human motives, the treatment of 'ideas' in terms of class conflicts would place the stress upon specific motives. That is, instead of some generally human motive, such as 'the essence of mankind,' Marx stresses the specifically *class* nature of ideologies. And the imputing of universal or generic motives is then analyzed as a concealment of the specific motives (hence, as 'mystification')" (110).

14. Who, of course, only marginally resemble each other.

15. But unlike Žižek, Kristeva holds to the imaginary as integral to the possibility of a thetic break, or space of symbolic communication.

16. Roudiez is here quoting Susan Sontag's "Approaching Artaud."

17. Is it (perhaps) possible to associate the desire Derrida is negotiating here with the responsibility Levinas insists upon, a responsibility to respond to an other's accusation or persecution, an accusation "I" can never actually answer? I am held "hostage" by the demands of the other, by a call for substitution, or sense making. Through such substitution I enter discourse, the arena of symbolic exchange: "Substitution frees the subject of ennui, that is, from enchainment to itself, where the ego suffocates in itself due to the tautological way of identity" (*Otherwise* 124). And yet, at the same time, "In substitution my being that belongs to me and not to another is undone, and it is through this substitution that I am not 'another,' but me. The self in a being is exactly the not-being-able-to-slip-away-from an assignation that does not aim at any generality. There is no ipseity common to me and the others; 'me' is the exclusion from this possibility of comparison, as soon as comparison is set up" (127). For this reason, Levinas seems to be suggesting, "Subjectivity is being hostage" (127). I am compelled to answer, to respond to the other (in the language of the Other), but doing so entails entering a discourse that is wholly inimical to the "traumatic violence" of a "subject resting on itself" (127). What

I necessarily become is therefore "a substitution by a hostage expiating for the violence of the persecution itself" (127). But I preserve my self *because* I come to occupy, at a distance that is always apparent, the place of "a deposition, not a *conatus essendi*" (127). It is precisely this demand/desire for substitution that a character like Bartleby refuses.

18. Plato (in the postcard), Derrida surmises, "drives avoiding derailment" (*Envois* 17).

19. The lover to whom the letters are addressed is, after all, always *written by* those letters—e.g., "What impels me to write you all the time" (Derrida, *Envois* 10). This lover, too, "will always precede [Derrida]" (19). On a certain level, then, the work of the *envois* is to actualize the possibility that "one is finally going to be able to love oneself [*s'aimer*]" (21).

20. The suggestion here is that Derrida is always more Hegelian (even at the outset) than he might like us to know. But this is, perhaps, an argument for another time.

8 / The Divinely Unshareable Self

1. I am referring here to the 1960 publication of the play. In 2004, Albee added a "first act" to the play ("Homelife"). The published version of these two plays (or "acts")—*At Home at the Zoo*—does not include Jerry's overtly self-reflexive utterances. As a product of the twenty-first century (and therefore the shift out of postmodernism), *At Home at the Zoo* is perhaps Albee's attempt to stress *The Zoo Story*'s predisposition toward sincerity and realism. However, it seems reasonable to suggest that he may have gone too far, losing some of the more significant nuances of the play (as it was originally performed).

2. Such a reading may be somewhat counterintuitive, for it is easy to assume, as a critic like Lisa M. Siefker Bailey does, that "Jerry's 'you' addresses the theatre audience; [and that] Jerry's 'his' refers to Peter's face" (38). But Bailey's reading clearly ignores or overlooks Jerry's dying words to Peter: "And now you know what you'll see in your TV, and the face I told you about . . . you remember . . . the face I told you about . . . *my* face, *the face you see right now*" (60–61; my emphasis). Still, Bailey is certainly correct to suggest that Jerry intentionally manipulates fiction so as to "make meaningful contact with another human being" (32). But, in overemphasizing the metatheatrical qualities of the play (as she does when she assumes Jerry's "you" refers to the audience and not to Peter), Bailey runs the risk of suggesting that, for Jerry, the stories he tells are *all* that matter, that he can (like any reductively postmodern hero) simply produce or reform the truth by telling a convincing story. But Jerry's stories, in the end, function to forestall Peter's innate tendency to confuse the real with the expression or form of apparent sense. Peter is, after all, a publisher who spends his Sundays reading fiction in the park. He also blinds himself to his largely fictional life—which is defined by the various trappings of a "standardized" man. Rather than confirming then simply abandoning himself (also) to fiction, Jerry uses stories paradoxically to effect the violent intrusion of what forever exceeds its fictional frames.

3. Indeed, as Meillassoux insists, "It becomes . . . possible to say that every philosophy which disavows naïve realism has become a variant of correlationsism" (5).

4. Here Morton is following arguments Alphonso Lingis makes in *The Imperative*. While his effort to make claims about the "intentions" of a strictly unknowable world "out there" is clearly problematic, we should take seriously the point he is trying to make— that the human is always and necessarily caught up in a network of things. The human is no more "an agent" than is anything else. We see, though, a much better account of this worldly "network" in Bruno Latour's *Reassembling the Social: An Introduction to*

Actor-Network-Theory. Take, for instance, Latour's "sociological" account of scallop fishing: "Scallops *make* the fisherman *do* things just as the nets placed in the ocean lure the scallops into attaching themselves to the nets and just as data collectors bring together fishermen and scallops in oceanography" (107). A word like "make" certainly suggests a problematic lack of choice or play, but Latour's point is sound: even if "'things don't talk' [and] 'fish nets have no passion' . . . [,] we can state as the new default position before [a sociological] study starts that all the actors we are going to deploy might be *associated* in such a way that they *make others do things*" (107).

5. Consider, in this sense, Latour's suggestion that "translation" might take on the "somewhat more specialized meaning . . . [of] a relation that . . . induces two mediators into coexisting" (108)—a suggestion that clearly echoes Nancy's concept of "compearance" (as discussed in chapter 2).

6. *The Three Stigmata of Palmer Eldritch* (1965) and *Ubik* (1969) stand out in this regard.

7. As Christopher Palmer notes, *VALIS* signals yet another attempt on Dick's part "to restore 'thingness,' phenomenological substance, to humble objects" (232). However, I disagree with Palmer's suggestion that *VALIS* is less effective (in this regard) than Dick's previous works.

8. Various critics have done just this already. See, for instance, Gabriel McKee's *Pink Beams of Light from the God in the Gutter: The Science-Fictional Religion of Philip K. Dick*. As well, Dick outlines his theology—and its various conflicting assumptions—in his *Exegesis*, a type of journal he began writing after his own encounter (of 2-3-74) with a strange beam of pink light. Parts of the *Exegesis* are included in *VALIS*—but they are "masked" as elements lifted from Fat's "journal" (not Dick's).

9. See chapter 5.

10. It's worth recalling that, for Freud, the uncanny double functions as the specter of other possible futures: "But it is not only this latter material [of self-observation], offensive as it is to the criticism of the ego, which may be incorporated in the idea of a double. There are also all the unfulfilled but possible futures to which we still like to cling in phantasy, all the strivings of the ego which adverse external circumstances have crushed, and all our suppressed acts of volition which nourish in us the illusion of Free Will" ("Uncanny" 235).

11. Given the concerns of the next chapter, it might be useful to note that (just two years prior to Dick's speech) Bob Dylan released "The Man in Me" (on *New Morning*—his first ostensible "comeback" album). After speaking at length (and in third person) of a "man in me," the speaker in the song asserts that "the man in me will hide sometimes to keep from bein' seen / But that's just because he doesn't want to turn into some machine."

12. In an epigraph to the novel, VALIS is defined as "a perturbation in the reality field in which a spontaneous self-monitoring negentropic vortex is formed, tending progressively to subsume and incorporate its environment into arrangements of information. Characterized by quasi-consciousness, purpose, intelligence, growth and an armillary coherence." In other words, VALIS effects sense-making "arrangements" (or relations) while ensuring the ("negentropic") preservation of *ordered* difference. The deity VALIS is therefore reflected in the very structure of the novel *VALIS*—a structure that consists, according to Christopher Palmer, of an "intricate web of splits" (227).

13. This moment is anticipated in Dick's first effort to fictionalize his encounter with VALIS, in *Radio Free Albemuth* (which was written in 1976 but left unpublished until

1985). The first part of the novel is titled "Phil" and narrated by Philip K. Dick (i.e., a successful science-fiction writer). Dick tells the story of his best friend Nicholas Brady, who, like Horselover Fat, endured a life-changing encounter with VALIS. This first section ends with a detailed account of Nicholas trying to go to sleep next to his wife. At the very moment Dick's narrative seems too detailed to be realistic as a second-hand account, the section breaks off (midsentence) with an ellipsis. On the next page is a single word: "Nicholas." A new section then begins on the following page. This new section begins (itself) with an ellipsis and picks up (grammatically) exactly where the last section left off. Now, though, the narrator is Nick and not Phil: "his" wife becomes "my" wife and Dick becomes a third-person participant in Nick's story. Nevertheless, the narrative voice remains (disconcertingly) the same. Like *VALIS*, then, *Radio Free Albemuth* struggles to manage the possibility that an act of overt displacement is necessary if we are to relate the self *in all sincerity*.

14. *The Divine Invasion* (1981) is, of course, the title of the book that followed *VALIS*.

15. Umberto Rossi largely confirms this claim—even though his goal is (ostensibly) to undermine it. According to Rossi, "Dick's novel denies any simplistic concept of textuality as a playful and irresponsible game with narrative materials; it complicates our ideas about the relationship between fiction and nonfiction, between the author's life and works ... Dick's complex game of mirrors (some of them definitely dark) should help us to understand that the relationship between autobiographical reliability and fantastic invention is more complex than a binary opposition" (258). Rossi, however, goes on to conflate Dick's refusal to engage in "a playful and irresponsible game with narrative materials" with now canonical postmodern texts—e.g., Vonnegut's *Slaughterhouse-Five* (1969). As a result, he overlooks the subtle difference between postmodernism's often perverse emphasis on subjectivity as the effect of narrative play and a more neoromantic emphasis on the possibility of sublating subjectivity by strategically reengaging such play.

16. See Taylor, *Disfiguring: Art, Architecture, Religion*.

17. I consider the connection between plasticity and post-postmodernism in previous publications—see, for instance, "Toni Morrison's *Beloved* and the Rise of Historioplastic Metafiction." What I am terming here "autoplasticity" can be viewed as an autobiographical subcategory of what I call, in these articles, "historioplastic metafiction." While my position is that the post-postmodern is largely defined by a commitment to a type of Hegelian plasticity, I do not mean to suggest that autoplasticity or historioplastic metafiction are exclusive to the post-postmodern era. Autoplasticity, in particular, should be considered a neoromantic quality that defines any number of texts since Hegel's romantic period (which, of course, begins to wane in the years following the Reformation).

18. For this reason, Louise Brix Jacobsen calls *Curb* a work of "vitafiction"—i.e., a narrative mode that "subsumes [Genette's] autofiction because it includes both ... self-referential representations in print and other kinds of 'self-acting'" (256). For Jacobsen, the specifically "audiovisual mode of vitafiction demonstrates that it is not necessarily the creator of the work who plays himself or herself. The cast playing themselves in any form can be an instance of 'vitafiction'" (256). Jacobsen, though, fails to demonstrate how her concept of vitafiction applies to a narrative mode that is usefully distinct from the metafictional tendencies of postmodernism (or any other period). Indeed, what she terms "vitafiction" would apply to *any* instances of self-reflexivity or historiographic metafiction—instances in which the author represents himself/herself along with any number of other historical figures. Granted, Jacobsen's discussion of "vitafiction" allows

us to parse out those moments (in film and TV) when multiple characters "play" themselves (in ways that are beyond authorial control); but the function and effect of such self-performance and self-construction, as Jacobsen explains it, is already well anticipated and theorized in any number of critical responses to postmodernism and late capitalism.

19. It's worth noting, too, that such gestures also distinguish *Curb* from the various reality TV programs that began to proliferate in the early 2000s (i.e., those various hackneyed and irresponsible manifestations of residual postmodernism).

20. This is surely why, too, high modernism often seems to oscillate between the ostensibly "classical" style of a Hemingway and the largely "symbolic" style of a Miller.

9 / Bob Dylan's Autoplasticity

1. Indeed, the film credits "Sergei Petrov & Rene Fontaine" as its authors, and the script, which credits the same authors, asserts that the film is "based on the Short Story '*Los Vientos Del Destino*' by Enrique Morales." Petrov is ostensibly Dylan himself; Fontaine, Charles. And the short story—whose title we can translate as "The Winds of Fate" (while assuming that someone with strong "morale" in the face of such winds wrote it)—is likely a complete fabrication. That said, it is entirely possible that Dylan is the author and that the work simply remains unpublished. It's impossible to know. (I'm referring here to an online version of script, located on the Internet Archive—i.e., archive.org.)

2. Unless otherwise noted, all Dylan lyrics are taken from his official website, Bobdylan.com.

3. This defines (for Hegel) the shift, in religious art, from tragedy to comedy: "The actual self of the actor coincides with what he impersonates" (*Phenomenology* 452).

4. As Malabou notes, after moving through a number of "plastic" definitions, "Plasticity's range of meanings is not yet exhausted, and it continues to evolve with and in the language. *Plastic material* is a synthetic material which can take on different shapes and proprieties according to the functions intended. 'Plastic' on its own is an explosive material with a nitroglycerine and nitrocellulose base that can set off violent detonations. The plasticity of the word itself draws it to extremes, both to those concrete shapes in which form is crystallized (sculpture) and to the annihilation of all form (bomb)" (9). For a more robust discussion of Malabou's revival of plasticity in Hegel, see chapter 8.

5. In many respects, Andrew Motion's own review of the film anticipates this reading. The film, he states, "is revelatory—in the paradoxical sense that it allows Dylan to say some important things out loud, and to keep the silences, and retain the elements of mystery, which are essential to his genius." Motion even goes on to suggest that the film "gives us a good deal of truth about Dylan, but realises that in his case the best route to the truth is 'slant.'"

6. It is common for critics to draw attention to the odd disparity between Dylan's insistence upon authenticity and his ever-apparent tendency to lie and plagiarize. As Murray Leeder notes, while discussing the function of the ghost (Arthur Vogel) in *Masked and Anonymous*, "One obvious paradox is the way Dylan cultivates the aura of a benign trickster while simultaneously being obsessed with authenticity" (185). Likewise, Keith Nainby highlights the tension between criticism (like Scobie's or Aidan Day's) that presents Dylan as a postmodernist determined to expose himself as only ever a series of "multiple" constructions and criticism (like Mike Marqusee's), which sees in Dylan's work a "modernist" tendency toward authenticity. In confronting this tension, Nainby makes

the very interesting and nuanced suggestion (via a reading of "Tangled Up in Blue") that Dylan is constantly "mov[ing] through becoming 'withdrawn'" (301).

7. Scobie makes great use of Derrida in his discussion of Dylan's deployment of various "aliases," noting that, for Dylan (like Derrida), "each signature [or expression/construction of the self] calls out for a countersignature" (63)—i.e., a repetition that necessarily contaminates the purity or uniqueness of its originary moment so as to effect a sense of *validating* recognition. Scobie's argument is based largely on Derrida's "Signature Event Context" (in *Limited Inc*) and *Signéponge/Signsponge*.

8. Even Dylan's Nobel acceptance speech bears absurdly obvious marks of plagiarism. Dylan appears to have appropriated his "analysis" of *Moby-Dick* straight from *SparkNotes*. For a comparison of Dylan's speech and the online study guide, see Andrea Pitzer's "The Freewheelin' Bob Dylan" (at Slate.com).

9. See the epigraph to chapter 1 of this book. The quote is a slight alteration of lines from the *Star Trek* episode "The Squire of Gothos." After being asked (by Sulu) "how far [should they] go along with this charade?," Kirk advocates playing along: "Until we can think our way out."

10. Howard Sounes discusses Dylan's use of *Confessions* in some detail; see especially p. 449.

11. See Scott Warmuth's work of "Dylanology" in the *New Haven Review*, "Bob Charlatan: Deconstructing Dylan's *Chronicles: Volume One*." Warmuth locates all manner of "borrowed" phrasing in Dylan's book, but the ones taken from London are particularly striking.

12. Scobie locates and discusses numerous references to ghosts and specters in Dylan's work, reading them all through a largely "Derridean" filter (see, specifically, chapter 2). Oddly, though (and given the fact that his book was revised and republished in 2003), Scobie never addresses Derrida's seminal works on spectrality—*Specters of Marx* and *Politics of Friendship*, specifically. It is, perhaps, for this reason that Scobie largely fails to see in Dylan's ghosts a metaphor for democratic expression and responsibility.

13. "Christlike" yet "disguised" is implied via the praise and the gifts the speaker mandates: "Bow down to her on Sunday / Salute her when her birthday comes / For Halloween give her a trumpet / And for Christmas, buy her a drum."

14. This phrasing comes from "Visions of Johanna (Take 5, Rehearsal)" on disc 4 of *The Cutting Edge 1965–1966*.

15. These are all things the singer in "All I Really Want to Do" *doesn't* want to do. See, as well, the epigraph to chapter 4. It's worth noting that "All I Really Want to Do" largely replicates (so as to counter) the structure of "I Just Want to Make Love to You" (the blues standard written by Willie Dixon in 1954 and originally performed by Muddy Waters). While, in Dixon's version, the other's distinctiveness is finally negated by the demand for self-gratification (e.g., "I don't want you to be no slave / I don't want you to work all day / I don't want you to be true / I just want to make love to you"), the singer, in Dylan's version, disrupts the inertia toward reductive *acts of love* by sustaining a profoundly *indifferent* (or, we might say at this point, *notional*) mode of friendship.

16. As Hegel states, "These are the moments of which the reconciliation of Spirit with its own consciousness proper is composed; by themselves they are single and separate, and it is solely their spiritual unity that constitutes the power of this reconciliation. The last of these moments is, however, necessarily this unity itself" (*Phenomenology* 482).

17. Sounes discusses this "mysterious" incident in some detail—noting (as most do, even Dylan himself in *Chronicles* [114]) that "the accident gave Dylan an excuse to get out of numerous business commitments then threatening to overwhelm him" (219).

18. Long songs are a Dylan trademark. However, some of his songs (even some of his shorter songs) employ a type of structure that frustrates the expectations established by and for popular music (e.g., an intro, verses, a chorus, a bridge, an outro). As Nainby points out, a song like "Stuck Inside of Mobile with the Memphis Blues Again" employs a repetitive yet oddly unpredictable structure so as to highlight the problem of communicating the incommensurable (e.g., "The post office has been stolen / And the mailbox is locked"): "There is . . . no bridge either lyrically or musically to relieve the insistence of the long verse-and-refrain structure of 'Memphis Blues Again'" (295). The song thus "develop[s] an 'ironist' perspective" by deploying a form of secretive communication that can only ever tease the promise of satisfaction (or an end). Each time the song starts up again (after apparently ending), we find ourselves asking the very question the singer is forced to ponder: "Can this really be the end[?]" Dylan employs similar structures in various songs throughout his career—e.g., "Brownsville Girl," "Highlands," "Ain't Talking," etc. "Highlands" is particularly noteworthy, as it most overtly links this (type of) structure to the problem of autobiographical expression as self-realization. The singer—who "listen[s] to Neil Young," who's an "artist," who may or may not be "registered to vote"—tells us again and again that his "heart's in the Highlands." His arrival in the Highlands is, though, always yet to come: "There's a way to get there" but he'll have to go "one step at a time." After twenty stanzas (and over sixteen minutes of the same few chords), the singer finally confirms a type of *notional* victory: "Well, my heart's in the Highlands at the break of day / Over the hills and far away / There's a way to get there and I'll figure it out somehow / But I'm already there in my mind / And that's good enough for now." Ultimately, the song suggests that Dylan's "heart" *is* in the "Highlands"—that the very effort to describe (in all sincerity) his inability to arrive makes his arrival a reality. But such an inversion—or negation of a negation—surely goes beyond a merely "ironist perspective."

19. As we have seen, time (in Hegel) is integral to consciousness and knowing: "Time, therefore, appears as the destiny and necessity of Spirit that is not yet complete within itself. . . . [Time functions] to set in motion the *immediacy of the in-itself*, which is the form in which substance is present in consciousness; or conversely, to realize and reveal what is at first only *inward* (the in-itself being taken as what is *inward*), i.e. to vindicate it for Spirit's certainty of itself" (*Phenomenology* 487). But this surely does not mean, as commentators often assume, that Hegel seeks or foresees the *end of time*.

20. The actual lines (which Scobie discusses in some detail) run as follows: "bob dylan—killed by a discarded Oedipus / who turned / around / to investigate a ghost / & discovered that / the ghost too / was more than one person" (Dylan, *Tarantula* 102). Scobie's analysis appears on p. 76.

21. The suggestion being that the viewer is seeing through Dylan's eyes as he makes his way onto a stage (in London) during his 1965–1966 world tour—his first "electric" tour. One of the props on this tour was a giant American flag.

22. These are lines taken—and then inverted—from Dylan's liner notes for *Bringing It All Back Home*: "A song is anything that can walk by itself / i am called a songwriter. a poem is a naked person . . . some people say that i am a poet." Oddly—and perhaps by accident—Haynes's inversion of the lines implies a hierarchy (with songs reigning over poems); but such a hierarchy is not actually apparent in the original. In the liner notes,

Dylan seems to be suggesting that he is *both* a poet and a songwriter—his songs, therefore, "walk all by themselves" even though they are *intentionally* pure (or "naked"), or (perhaps) mandated by a singular author. The liner notes thus echo Bakhtin's distinction between novelistic and poetic discourse; Dylan, though, seems to view songs as a type of hybrid that balances both the "novelistic" and the "poetic" (or, if we recall Barthes, the "writerly" and the "readerly" [See Barthes's *S/Z*]). My point is that Dylan finally seems intent on overcoming the stark opposition both Bakhtin and Barthes embrace.

23. As Haynes notes in an interview with *Cineaste*, "This film ... [like all biopics] blends fact and fiction, but the difference is that you're in on the joke, you're invited to laugh at this process along with me and push the fiction one step further, so there's no question that it's a creative choice to make a point. Take the choice of making 'Woody' a little black kid who calls himself 'Woody Guthrie.' We all know that's not true to life. But you're forced to think about why that choice is being made—as opposed to the traditional biopic where you're not allowed to think about these choices because that would ruin the entire illusion" ("Many Faces" 20).

24. All the Dylan songs *within* the film's diegesis are, of course, covers.

25. For a more extended discussion of race and masculinity in Haynes's film—and thus the manner in which Dylan "performs" both—see John McCombe's "Minstrelsy, Masculinity, and 'Bob Dylan' as Text in *I'm Not There*."

26. One of the many verses, of course, includes the lines "You may be somebody's mistress, may be somebody's heir."

27. As Leeder points out, this line (which alludes to both Mark 7:15 and Matthew 15:11) is repeated by Jude in Haynes's film (190n4).

28. Malabou might, of course, disagree with this sense—or function of—plasticity, as she tends to oppose Derrida's assumption that all forms of recovery entail both loss and return.

29. Grant Maxwell has taken such appeals to mean that "for Dylan, the explanation for his art ... lie[s] in both future and past, both chicken and egg, both final and efficient causation. In his experience, one thing led to another, but events were led by 'an other,' Dylan's future self; a more literal translation of Rimbaud's phrase [to which Dylan refers in *Chronicles*] is 'I is an other,' which suggests that Dylan is never quite identical with himself, that his true self is somewhere out there in the hazy distance and he is passing through many partial incarnations eventually to become the fullness of the potentiality implicit in the processual concrescence that calls itself Bob Dylan" (161). What I am suggesting, though, is that Dylan can *never* "become the fullness of the potentiality implicit in the processual concrescence that calls itself Bob Dylan." But this should not lead us to assume that Dylan is "never quite identical with himself."

30. Recall the discussion of Nancy's take on birth in chapter 5.

31. For instance, he assures us that, for "Political World," he recorded (but decided not to include) the following verse: "We live in a political world. Flags flying into the breeze. Comes out of the blue—moves toward you—like a knife cutting through cheese" (*Chronicles* 166).

WORKS CITED

Agamben, Giorgio. "Bartleby, or On Contingency." *Potentialities: Collected Essays in Philosophy.* Trans. Daniel Heller-Roazen. Stanford, CA: Stanford UP, 1999. 243–71.
———. *The Coming Community.* Trans. Michael Hardt. Minneapolis: U of Minnesota P, 2007.
Albee, Edward. *The Zoo Story. Three Plays: The Zoo Story, The Death of Bessie Smith, The Sandbox.* New York: Coward-McCann, 1960. 11–62.
———. *At Home at the Zoo.* New York: Dramatists Play Service, 2008.
Allen, Woody. *Woody Allen on Woody Allen: In Conversation with Stig Björkman.* Rev. ed. Ed. Stig Björkman. London: Faber and Faber, 1995.
———, dir. *Zelig.* Perf. Woody Allen, Mia Farrow. Orion Pictures, 1983.
Badiou, Alain. *Logics of Worlds: Being and Event II.* Trans. Alberto Toscano. New York: Continuum, 2009.
Bailey, Lisa M. Siefker. "Absurdly American: Rediscovering the Representation of Violence in *The Zoo Story.*" *Edward Albee: A Case Book,* ed. Bruce Mann. New York: Routledge, 2004. 33–46.
Bakhtin, Mikhail. *The Dialogic Imagination: Four Essays.* Ed. Michael Holquist, trans. Caryl Emerson and Michael Holquist. Austin: U of Texas P, 1981.
Bamhart, Bruce. "Chronopolitics and Race, Rag-Time and Symphonic Time in *The Autobiography of an Ex-Colored Man.*" *African American Review* 40.3 (2006): 551–69.
Barnes, Elizabeth. "Fraternal Melancholies: Manhood and the Limits of Sympathy in Douglass and Melville." *Frederick Douglass and Herman Melville: Essays in Relation,* ed. Robert S. Levine and Samuel Otter. Chapel Hill: U of North Carolina P, 2008. 233–56.

Barth, John. "The Literature of Exhaustion." *The Friday Book: Essays and Other Nonfiction*. New York: Putnam, 1984. 62–76.

Barthes, Roland. "The Death of the Author." *Image-Music-Text*. Trans. Stephen Heath. New York: Hill and Wang, 1977. 142–48.

———. *S/Z*. Trans. Richard Miller. New York: Noonday, 1974.

Bellows, George. *Both Members of This Club*. 1909. Oil. National Gallery of Art, Washington, DC.

———. *The Knock Out*. 1907. Pastel and India ink. Crystal Bridges Museum of American Art, Bentonville, AR.

———. *Stag at Sharkey's*. 1909. Cleveland Museum of Art, Cleveland, OH.

Berlin, Isaiah. *Four Essays on Liberty*. Oxford: Oxford UP, 1969.

The Bible: Authorized King James Version. Oxford: Oxford UP, 1997.

Blackmer, Corinne. "The Veils of the Law: Race and Sexuality in Nella Larsen's *Passing*." *Race-ing Representation: Voice, History and Sexuality*, ed. Kostas Myrsiades and Linda Myrsiades. Lanham, MD: Rowman and Littlefield, 1998. 98–116.

Blackmore, David L. "'That Unreasonable Restless Feeling': The Homosexual Subtexts of Nella Larsen's *Passing*." *African American Review* 26.3 (1992): 475–84.

Blanchot, Maurice. *The Unavowable Community*. Trans. Pierre Joris. New York: Station Town, 1988.

Boynton, Sandra. *But Not the Hippopotamus*. New York: Little Simon, 1982.

Brenner, Gerry. *A Comprehensive Companion to Hemingway's "A Moveable Feast": Annotation to Interpretation*. Lewiston, NY: Mellen, 2000.

Brogan, Jacqueline Vaught. "'It's Only Interesting the First Time': Or, Hemingway as Kierkegaard." *North Dakota Quarterly* 64.3 (1997): 5–26.

Brooks, Max. *World War Z: An Oral History of the Zombie War*. New York: Three Rivers, 2007.

Brooks, Neil. "On Becoming an Ex-Man: Postmodern Irony and the Extinguishing of Certainties in *The Autobiography of an Ex-Colored Man*." *College Literature* 22.3 (1995): 17–29.

Bruce, Iris. "Mysterious Illness of Human Commodities in Woody Allen and Franz Kafka." *The Films of Woody Allen: Critical Essays*, ed. Charles P. Silet. Lanham, MD: Scarecrow, 2006. 171–97.

Bryant, Levi. *The Democracy of Objects*. Ann Arbor, MI: Open Humanities, 2011.

Burke, Kenneth. *Language as Symbolic Action: Essays on Life, Literature, Method*. Berkeley: U of California P, 1966.

———. *A Rhetoric of Motives*. 1950. Berkeley: U of California P, 1969.

Butler, Judith. "Critically Queer." *Bodies That Matter: On the Discursive Limits of "Sex."* New York: Routledge, 1993. 223–42.

———. *Giving an Account of Oneself*. Bronx, NY: Fordham UP, 2005.

———. "Passing, Queering: Nella Larsen's Psychoanalytic Challenge." *Bodies That Matter: On the Discursive Limits of "Sex."* New York: Routledge, 1993. 167–86.

Carr, Brian. "Paranoid Interpretation, Desire's Nonobject and Nella Larsen's *Passing*." *PMLA* 119.2 (2004): 282–95.

Caughie, Pamela L. "Passing as Modernism." *Modernism/modernity* 12.3 (2005): 385–406.

Charles, Larry, dir. *Masked and Anonymous*. Perf. Bob Dylan, John Goodman, Jessica Lange. Columbia Tristar, 2003.

Cheng, Anne Anlin. *The Melancholy of Race: Psychoanalysis, Assimilation, and Hidden Grief*. Oxford: Oxford UP, 2000.

Cixous, Hélène. "The Laugh of the Medusa." *Signs* 1.4 (1976): 875–93.

Clark, Keith. "Man on the Margin: Lucas Beauchamp and the Limitations of Space." *Faulkner Journal* 6.1 (1990): 67–79.

Cousineau, Thomas. "The Future of an Illusion: Melville's Deconstruction of Deleuze's A/Theology." *Deleuze and Religion*, ed. Mary Bryden. London: Routledge, 2001. 115–25.

Crosland, Alan, dir. *The Jazz Singer*. Perf. Al Jolsen, May McAvoy. Warner Bros., 1927.

Curb Your Enthusiasm. Created by Larry David. HBO, 2000–2017.

Cutter, Martha J. "Sliding Significations: Passing as a Narrative and Textual Strategy in Nella Larsen's Fiction." *Passing and the Fictions of Identity*, ed. Elaine K. Ginsberg. Durham, NC: Duke UP, 1996. 75–100.

Day, Aidan. *Jokerman: Reading the Lyrics of Bob Dylan*. Oxford: Basil Blackwell, 1988.

Decker, James. *Henry Miller and Narrative Form: Constructing the Self, Rejecting Modernity*. New York: Routledge, 2005.

Deleuze, Gilles. "Bartleby; or, The Formula." *Essays Critical and Clinical*. Trans. Daniel W. Smith and Michael A. Greco. Minneapolis: U of Minnesota P, 1997. 68–90.

Del Gizzo, Suzanne. "Redefining Remate: Hemingway's Professed Approach to Writing *A Moveable Feast*." *Hemingway Review* 28.2 (2009): 121–26.

Derrida, Jacques. "Eating Well, or the Calculation of the Subject." Trans. Peter Connor and Avital Ronell. *Points . . . Interviews, 1974–1994*, ed. Elisabeth Weber. Stanford, CA: Stanford UP, 1995.

———. "Economimesis." Trans. Richard Klein. *Diacritics* 11.2 (1981): 1–25.

———. *Envois*. *The Postcard: From Socrates to Freud and Beyond*. Trans. Alan Bass. Chicago: U of Chicago P, 1987. 1–256.

———. "Force of Law: The 'Mystical Foundation of Authority.'" *Acts of Religion*, trans. Mary Quaintance, ed. Gil Anidjar. New York: Routledge, 2002. 228–98.

———. *The Gift of Death*. Trans. David Willis. Chicago: U of Chicago P. 2008.

———. "An Interview with Jacques Derrida on the Limits of Digestion." By Daniel Birnbaum and Anders Olsson. Trans. Brian Manning Delaney. *e-flux* 2 (2009).

———. *On Touching—Jean-Luc Nancy*. Trans. Christine Irizarry. Stanford, CA: Stanford UP, 2005.

———. "Plato's Pharmacy." *Dissemination*. Trans. Barbara Johnson. Chicago: U of Chicago P, 1981. 61–171.

———. *Politics of Friendship*. Trans. George Collins. London: Verso, 1997.

———. "Signature Event Context." Trans. Samuel Weber and Jeffrey Mehlman. *Limited Inc*, ed. Gerald Graff. Evanston, IL: Northwestern UP, 1988.

———. *Signéponge/Signsponge*. Trans. Richard Rand. New York: Columbia UP, 1984.

———. *Specters of Marx: The State of the Debt, the Work of Mourning, and the New International.* Trans. Peggy Kamuf. New York: Routledge, 1994.
Dick, Philip K. "The Android and the Human." *The Shifting Realities of Philip K. Dick: Selected Literary and Philosophical Writings,* ed. Lawrence Sutin. New York: Vintage, 1995. 183–210.
———. *Do Androids Dream of Electric Sheep?* New York: Del Rey, 1996.
———. "Nazism and *The High Castle.*" *The Shifting Realities of Philip K. Dick: Selected Literary and Philosophical Writings,* ed. Lawrence Sutin. New York: Vintage, 1995. 112–17.
———. *Radio Free Albemuth.* New York: Vintage, 1998.
———. *A Scanner Darkly.* New York: Mariner, 2011.
———. "Schizophrenia & *The Book of Changes.*" *The Shifting Realities of Philip K. Dick: Selected Literary and Philosophical Writings,* ed. Lawrence Sutin. New York: Vintage, 1995. 175–82.
———. *The Three Stigmata of Palmer Eldritch.* New York: Mariner, 2011.
———. *Ubik.* New York: Mariner, 2012.
———. *VALIS.* New York: Mariner, 2011.
Dimitri, Carl, J. "*Go Down, Moses* and *Intruder in the Dust:* From Negative to Positive Liberty." *Faulkner Journal* 19.1 (2003): 11–26.
Doane, Mary Ann. "Film and the Masquerade: Theorizing the Female Spectator." *Femme Fatales: Feminism, Film Theory, and Psychoanalysis.* New York: Routledge, 1991. 17–32.
Doezema, Marianne. *George Bellows and Urban America.* New Haven, CT: Yale UP, 1992.
Doniger, Wendy. *The Woman Who Pretended to Be Who She Was: Myths of Self-Imitation.* Oxford: Oxford UP, 2005.
Duvall, John N. "Descent in the 'House of Chloe': Race, Rape, and Identity in Toni Morrison's *Tar Baby.*" *Contemporary Literature* 38.2 (1997): 325–49.
Dylan, Bob. "All I Really Want to Do." *Another Side of Bob Dylan.* Columbia, 1964.
———. Blowin' In The Wind." *The Freewheelin' Bob Dylan.* Columbia, 1963.
———. "Brownsville Girl." *Knocked Out Loaded.* Columbia, 1986.
———. "Can't Wait." *Time Out of Mind.* Columbia, 1997.
———. *Chronicles: Volume One.* New York: Simon and Schuster, 2004.
———. "Cold Irons Bound." *Time Out of Mind.* Columbia, 1997.
———. "Gotta Serve Somebody." *Slow Train Coming.* Columbia, 1979.
———. "A Hard Rain's A-Gonna Fall." *The Freewheelin' Bob Dylan.* Columbia, 1963.
———. "Highlands." *Time Out of Mind.* Columbia, 1997.
———. "It's All Right, Ma (I'm Only Bleeding)." *Bringing It All Back Home.* Columbia, 1965.
———. "John Brown." *The Bootleg Series,* vol. 9, *The Witmark Demos: 1962-1964.* Columbia, 2010.
———. "Like a Rolling Stone." *Highway 61 Revisited.* Columbia, 1965.
———. Liner Notes. *Bringing It All Back Home.* Columbia, 1965.

———. "Marchin' to the City." *The Bootleg Series,* vol. 8, *Tell Tale Signs.* Columbia, 2008.

———. "Scarlet Town." *Tempest.* Columbia, 2012.

———. "She Belongs to Me." *Bringing It All Back Home.* Columbia, 1965.

———. "Stuck Inside of Mobile with the Memphis Blues Again." *Blonde on Blonde.* Columbia, 1966.

———. "Tangled Up in Blue." *Blood on the Tracks.* Columbia, 1975.

———. *Tarantula.* 1971. New York: Scribner, 2004.

———. "Things Have Changed." *The Essential Bob Dylan.* Columbia, 2000.

———. "Tight Connection to My Heart (Has Anyone Seen My Love)." *Empire Burlesque.* Columbia, 1985.

———. "Visions of Johanna." *Blonde on Blonde.* Columbia, 1966.

———. "Visions of Johanna (Take 5, Rehearsal)." *The Bootleg Series,* vol. 12, *The Cutting Edge 1965–1966,* deluxe ed. Columbia, 2015.

———. "Where Are You Tonight? (Journey through Dark Heat)." *Street Legal.* Columbia, 1978.

Ebert, Roger. Review of *Masked and Anonymous,* dir. Larry Charles. *Chicago Sun-Times,* 15 Aug. 2003.

Emerson, Ralph Waldo. "Friendship." *Essays and Lectures,* ed. Joel Porte. New York: Library of America, 1983. 340–54.

———. *Selected Journals 1820–1842.* Ed. Lawrence Rosenwald. New York: Library of America, 2010.

Fagg, John. *On the Cusp: Stephan Crane, George Bellows, and Modernism.* Tuscaloosa: U of Alabama P, 2009.

Faulkner, William. *Intruder in the Dust.* New York: Vintage, 1991.

———. *Go Down, Moses.* New York: Vintage, 1991.

———. *Light in August.* New York: Vintage, 1991.

Feldstein, Richard. "The Dissolution of the Self in *Zelig.*" *Literature Film Quarterly* 13.3 (1985): 155–60.

Forster, Marc, dir. *World War Z.* Perf. Brad Pitt, Mireille Enos, Daniella Kertesz. Paramount, 2013.

Fowler, Doreen. "Beyond Oedipus: Lucas Beauchamp, Ned Barnett, and Faulkner's *Intruder in the Dust.*" *MFS* 53.4 (2007): 788–820.

Freud, Sigmund. *Beyond the Pleasure Principle.* Trans. James Strachey. *The Standard Edition of the Complete Works of Sigmund Freud,* vol. 18. New York: Vintage, 2001. 1–64.

———. *Civilization and Its Discontents.* Trans. Joan Riviere. *The Standard Edition of the Complete Works of Sigmund Freud,* vol. 21. New York: Vintage, 2001. 57–145.

———. "Mourning and Melancholia." Trans. Joan Riviere. *The Standard Edition of the Complete Works of Sigmund Freud,* vol. 14. New York: Vintage, 2001. 237–60.

———. "The 'Uncanny.'" Trans Alix Strachey. *The Standard Edition of the Complete Works of Sigmund Freud,* vol. 17. New York: Vintage, 2001. 217–56.

Galvan, Jill. "Entering the Posthuman Collective in Philip K. Dick's *Do Androids Dream of Electric Sheep?*" *Science Fiction Studies* 24 (1997): 413–29.

Garwood, Ian. "Great Art on a Jukebox: The Romantic(ized) Voice of Bob Dylan in *I'm Not There*." *Film International* 42.6 (2009): 6–22.

Gates, Henry Louis, Jr. "Talking Black: Critical Signs of the Times." *Loose Canons: Notes on the Cultural Wars*. New York: Oxford UP, 1992. 71–83.

———. "White Like Me." *New Yorker*, 17 June 1996, 66–81.

Genette, Gérard. *Fiction and Diction*. Trans. Catherine Porter. Ithaca, NY: Cornell UP, 1993.

Ginsberg, Elaine K. Introduction to *Passing and the Fictions of Identity*, ed. Elaine K. Ginsberg. Durham, NC: Duke UP, 1996. 1–18.

Girgus, Sam B. *The Films of Woody Allen*. Cambridge: Cambridge UP, 2002.

Gold, Joseph. *William Faulkner, A Study in Humanism: From Metaphor to Discourse*. Norman: U of Oklahoma P, 1966.

Goya, Francisco. *Disparate desordenado*. 1815–19. Etching. Museo del Prado, Madrid.

Gwin, Minrose C. *The Feminine and Faulkner: Reading (beyond) Sexual Difference*. Knoxville: U of Tennessee P, 1990.

Hayles, N. Katherine. *How We Became Posthuman: Virtual Bodies in Cybernetics, Literature, and Informatics*. Chicago: U of Chicago P, 1999.

Haynes, Todd, dir. *I'm Not There*. Perf. Christian Bale, Richard Gere, Cate Blanchet. Weinstein Company, 2007.

———. "The Many Faces of Bob Dylan: An Interview with Todd Haynes." *Cineaste* 33.1 (2007): 20–23.

Hegel, G. W. F. *Aesthetics: Lectures on Fine Art*. Vol. 1. Trans. T. M. Knox. Oxford: Clarendon, 1975.

———. *Encyclopedia of the Philosophical Sciences in Basic Outline*. Part I, *Science of Logic*. Trans. Klaus Brinkmann and Daniel O. Dahlstrom. Cambridge: Cambridge UP, 2015.

———. *Phenomenology of Spirit*. Trans. A. V. Miller. Oxford: Oxford UP, 1977.

———. *The Science of Logic*. Trans. and ed. George di Giovanni. Cambridge: Cambridge UP, 2010.

Heinert, Jennifer Lee Jordan. *Narrative Conventions and Race in the Novels of Toni Morrison*. New York: Routledge, 2008.

Heise, Ursula K. "The Android and the Animal." *PMLA* 124.2 (2009): 503–10.

Hemingway, Ernest. *A Moveable Feast*. New York: Simon and Schuster, 1992.

Hemingway, Mary. "The Making of the Book: A Chronicle and a Memoir." *New York Times Book Review*, 10 May 1964.

Henderson, Mae. Critical foreword to *Passing*, by Nella Larsen. 1929. New York: Modern Library, 2002. xvii–lxxiv.

Hitchcock, Alfred, dir. *The Man Who Knew Too Much*. Perf. James Stewart and Doris Day. Paramount, 1956.

———, dir. *North by Northwest*. Perf. Gary Grant and Eva Marie Saint. MGM, 1959.

———, dir. *Rear Window*. Perf. James Stewart and Grace Kelly. Paramount, 1954.

Hopkins, Gerard Manley. "As kingfishers catch fire, dragon flies draw flame." *The Poems of Gerard Manley Hopkins,* ed. W. H. Gardner and N. H. MacKenzie. London: Oxford UP, 1967. 90.

Horton, Merrill. "Blackness, Betrayal and Childhood: Race and Identity in Nella Larsen's *Passing.*" *CLA* 38.1 (1994): 31–45.

Huyssen, Andreas. *After the Great Divide.* Bloomington: Indiana UP, 1987.

Jacobsen, Louise Brix. "Vitafiction as a Mode of Self-Fashioning: The Case of Michael J. Fox in *Curb Your Enthusiasm.*" *Narrative* 23.3 (2015): 252–70.

Johnson, James Weldon. *The Autobiography of an Ex-Colored Man. The Essential Writings of James Weldon Johnson,* ed. Rudolph P. Byrd. New York: Modern Library, 2008. 29–148.

Johnston, Ruth D. "The Construction of Whiteness in *The Birth of a Nation* and *The Jazz Singer.*" *Quarterly Review of Film and Video* 28.5 (2011): 382–89.

———. "Ethnic and Discursive Drag in Woody Allen's *Zelig.*" *Quarterly Review of Film and Video* 24 (2007): 297–306.

Kassanoff, Jennie A. "Gilt Stricken: The Interdependencies of the Gilded Age." *American Literary History* 25.3 (2013): 660–71.

Katz Montiel, Marco. *Music and Identity in Twentieth-Century Literature from Our America: Noteworthy Protagonists.* New York: Palgrave, 2014.

King, Martin Luther, Jr. "I Have Dream." *A Testament of Hope: The Essential Writings and Speeches of Martin Luther King, Jr.,* ed. James M. Washington. New York: HarperCollins, 1991. 217–20.

Kirkman, Robert. *The Walking Dead.* Vol. 1, *Days Gone Bye.* Illustrated by Tony Moore. Berkeley: Image, 2006.

Klotz, Marvin. "Procrustean Revision in Faulkner's *Go Down, Moses.*" *American Literature* 37.1 (1965): 1–16.

Kristeva, Julia. *Revolution in Poetic Language.* Trans. Margaret Waller. New York: Columbia UP, 1985.

Lacan, Jacques. "Aggressivity in Psychoanalysis." *Ecrits: A Selection,* trans. Alan Sheridan. London: Routledge, 1977. 7–23.

———. "The Mirror Stage as Formative of the Function of the *I* in Psychoanalytic Experience." *Ecrits: A Selection,* trans. Alan Sheridan. London: Routledge, 1977. 1–6.

———. *The Seminar of Jacques Lacan.* Book 2, *The Ego in Freud's Theory and in the Technique of Psychoanalysis 1954–1955,* ed. Jacques-Alain Miller, trans. Sylvana Tomaselli. New York: Norton, 1991.

Larsen, Nella. *Passing. The Complete Fiction of Nella Larsen: "Passing," "Quicksand," and the Stories.* Ed. Charles Larson. New York: Anchor, 1992. 163–276.

Latour, Bruno. *Reassembling the Social: An Introduction to Actor-Network-Theory.* Oxford: Oxford UP, 2007.

Leeder, Murray. "Haunting and Minstrelsy in Bob Dylan's *Masked and Anonymous.*" *Journal of Popular Film and Television* 40.4 (2012): 181–91.

Levinas, Emmanuel. "God and Philosophy." *Of God Who Comes to Mind,* trans. Bettina Bergo. Stanford, CA: Stanford UP, 1998.

———. *Otherwise Than Being, or, Beyond Essence*. Trans. Alphonso Lingis. Pittsburgh: Duquesne UP, 1998.

Lingis, Alphonso. *The Imperative*. Bloomington: Indiana UP, 1998.

Little, Jonathan. "Nella Larsen's *Passing*: Irony and the Critics." *African American Review* 26.1 (1992): 173–82.

Lyotard, Jean-François. *The Postmodern Condition: A Report on Knowledge*. Trans. Geoff Bennington and Brian Massumi. Minneapolis: U of Minnesota P, 1984.

Malabou, Catherine. *The Future of Hegel: Plasticity, Temporality and Dialectic*. Trans. Lisbeth During. New York: Routledge, 2005.

Marqusee, Mike. *Wicked Messenger: Bob Dylan and the 1960s*. New York: Seven Stories, 2005.

Matteson, John. "'A New Race Has Sprung Up': Prudence, Social Consensus and the Law in 'Bartleby the Scrivener.'" *Leviathan: A Journal of Melville Studies* 10.1 (2008): 25–49.

Matthews, John T. "Whose America? Faulkner, Modernism, and National Identity." *Faulkner at 100: Retrospect and Prospect*, ed. Donald M. Kartiganer and Anne J. Abadie. Jackson: UP of Mississippi, 2000. 70–92.

Maxwell, Grant. "'An Extreme Sense of Destiny': Bob Dylan, Affect, and Final Causation." *Journal of Religion and Popular Culture* 25.1 (2013): 146–62.

McBride, James. *The Color of Water: A Black Man's Tribute to His White Mother*. 10th anniversary ed. New York: Riverhead, 2006.

McCombe, John. "Minstrelsy, Masculinity, and 'Bob Dylan' as Text in *I'm Not There*." *Post Script* 31.1 (2011): 12–25.

McDowell, Deborah E. "'That Nameless . . . Shameful Impulse': Sexuality in Nella Larsen's *Quicksand* and *Passing*." *Black Feminist Criticism and Critical Theory*, ed. Joe Weixlmann and Houston A. Baker. Greenwood, FL: Penkevill, 1988. 139–67.

McGowan, Todd. "On the Necessity of Contradiction: Hegel with the Speculative Realists." *Umbr(a)* (2013): 101–25.

Meillassoux, Quentin. *After Finitude: An Essay on the Necessity of Contingency*. London: Bloomsbury, 2009.

Melville, Herman. "Bartleby, the Scrivener: A Story of Wall-Street." *The Piazza Tales and Other Prose Pieces, 1839–1860*, ed. Harrison Hayford, Hershel Parker, and G. Thomas Tanselle. Evanston: Northwestern UP and the Newberry Library, 1987. 13–45.

Michaels, Walter Benn. *Our America: Nativism, Modernism, and Pluralism*. Durham, NC: Duke UP, 1995.

Miller, Henry. *Tropic of Cancer*. New York: Grove, 1994.

Milloy, Sandra D. "Faulkner's Lucas: An 'Arrogant, Intractable and Insolent' Old Man." *College Language Association Journal* 27.4 (1984): 393–405.

Mobley, Marilyn E. "Narrative Dilemma: Jadine as Cultural Orphan in Toni Morrison's *Tar Baby*." *Southern Review* 23.4 (1987): 761–70.

Moffitt, Letitia. "Finding the Door: Vision/Revision and Stereotype in Toni Morrison's *Tar Baby*." *Critique* 46.1 (2004): 12–26.

Moreland, Richard C. "Faulkner's Continuing Education: From Self-Reflection to Embarrassment." *Faulkner at 100: Retrospect and Prospect,* ed. Donald M. Kartiganer and Ann J. Abadie. Jackson: UP of Mississippi, 2000. 60–69.
Morris, Wesley, and Barbara Alverson Morris. *Reading Faulkner.* Madison: U of Wisconsin P, 1989.
Morrison, Toni. *Tar Baby.* New York: Vintage, 2004.
Morton, Timothy. *Hyperobjects: Philosophy and Ecology after the End of the World.* Minneapolis: U Minnesota P, 2013.
Motion, Andrew. "Masked and Anonymous." *Sony Classics.* Sony, 2003. 15 Aug. 2016.
Nainby, Keith. "Free, Stuck, Tangled: Bob Dylan, the 'Self' and the Performer's Critical Perspective." *Contemporary Theatre Review* 21.3 (2011): 286–301.
Nancy, Jean-Luc. "Being Singular Plural." *Being Singular Plural,* trans. Robert D. Richardson and Anne E. O'Bryne. Stanford, CA: Stanford UP, 2000. 1–100.
———. *The Experience of Freedom.* Trans. Bridget McDonald. Stanford, CA: Stanford UP, 1993.
———. "Identity and Trembling." Trans. Brian Holmes. *The Birth to Presence.* Stanford, CA: Stanford UP, 1993. 9–35.
———. "The Inoperative Community." Trans. Peter Conner. *The Inoperative Community,* ed. Peter Conner. Minneapolis: U Minnesota P, 1991. 1–42.
———. "L'Intrus." Trans. Susan Hanson. *New Centennial Review* 2.3 (Fall 2002): 1–14.
Nietzsche, Friedrich. *"The Birth of Tragedy" and "The Case of Wagner."* Trans. Walter Kaufmann. New York: Vintage, 1967.
———. "On Truth and Lies in a Nonmoral Sense." *Philosophy and Truth: Selections from Nietzsche's Notebooks of the Early 1870s,* ed. and trans. Daniel Breazeale. Atlantic Highlands, NJ: Humanities, 1979. 79–97.
Nin, Anaïs. Preface to *Tropic of Cancer,* by Henry Miller. New York: Grove, 1994. xxxi–xxxiii.
Norris, Faith G. "*A Moveable Feast* and *A Remembrance of Things Past:* Two Quests for Lost Time." *Hemingway in Our Time,* ed. Richard Astro and Jackson Benson. Corvallis: Oregon State UP, 1974. 99–111.
North, Michael. *Dialect of Modernism: Race, Language, and Twentieth-Century Literature.* New York: Oxford UP, 1994.
Oates, Joyce Carol. "George Bellows: The Boxing Paintings." *(Woman) Writer: Occasions and Opportunities.* New York: Obelisk, 1989. 294–301.
Palmer, Christopher. *Philip K. Dick: Exhilaration and Terror of the Postmodern.* Liverpool: Liverpool UP, 2003.
Pennebaker, D. A., dir. *Don't Look Back.* Pennebaker Films, 1967.
Petrov, Sergei, and Rene Fontaine. *Masked and Anonymous.* Filmscript, 2002. Archive.org.
Pfeiffer, Kathleen. "Individualism, Success, and American Identity in *The Autobiography of an Ex-Colored Man.*" *African American Review* 30.3 (1996): 403–19.
———. *Race Passing and American Individualism.* Amherst: U of Massachusetts P, 2002.

Pitzer, Andrea. "The Freewheelin' Bob Dylan." Slate.com, 13 June 2017.

Rajan, Tilottama. "Autonarration and Genotext in Mary Hays' *Memoirs of Emma Courtney.*" *Studies in Romanticism* 32.2 (1993): 149–76.

Reid, Michelle. "Rachel Writes Back: Racialised Androids and Replicant Texts." *Extrapolation* 49.3 (2008): 353–67.

Renza, Louis. "The Importance of Being Ernest." *South Atlantic Quarterly* 88.3 (1989): 661–89.

Rickman, Gregg. "Philip K. Dick on *Blade Runner:* 'They Did Sight Simulation on My Brain.'" *Retrofitting "Blade Runner": Issues in Ridley Scott's "Blade Runner" and Philip K. Dick's "Do Androids Dream of Electric Sheep?,"* ed. Judith B. Kerman. Madison: U of Wisconsin P, 1997. 103–9.

Rogin, Michael. *Blackface, White Noise: Jewish Immigrants in the Hollywood Melting Pot.* Berkeley: U of California P, 1996.

Romero, George A., dir. *Dawn of the Dead.* Perf. David Emge, Ken Foree, Scott H. Reiniger. United, 1979.

———, dir. *Night of the Living Dead.* Perf. Duane Jones, Judith O'Dea, Karl Hardman. Continental, 1968.

Rosenberg, Joel. "What You Ain't Heard Yet: The Languages of *The Jazz Singer.*" *Prooftexts* 22 (2002): 11–54.

Rossi, Umberto. "The Shunts in the Tale: The Narrative Architecture of Philip K. Dick's *VALIS.*" *Science Fiction Studies* 39 (2012): 243–61.

Roudiez, Leon S. Introduction to *Revolution in Poetic Language,* by Julia Kristeva. Trans. Margaret Waller. New York: Columbia UP, 1985. 1–12.

Rubenstein, Jill. "A Degree of Alchemy: *A Moveable Feast* as Literary Autobiography." *Fitzgerald-Hemingway Annual* (1973): 231–42.

Sartre, Jean-Paul. *Being and Nothingness.* Trans. Hazel E. Barnes. New York: Washington Square, 1956.

Scobie, Stephen. *Alias Bob Dylan: Revisited.* Calgary: Red Deer, 2003.

Scorsese, Martin, dir. *No Direction Home: Bob Dylan.* PBS, Vulcan Productions, BBC, 2005.

Scott, Ridley, dir. *Blade Runner.* Perf. Harrison Ford and Sean Young. Warner Bros., 1982.

Seinfeld. Created by Jerry Seinfeld and Larry David. Castle Rock Entertainment, 1989–98.

Sherrard-Johnson, Cherene. "'A Plea for Color': Nella Larsen's Iconography of the Mulatta." *American Literature* 76.4 (2004): 832–69.

Shohat, Ella, and Robert Stam. "Stereotype, Realism and the Struggle over Representation." *Unthinking Eurocentrism: Multiculturalism and the Media,* ed. Ella Shohat and Robert Stam. New York: Routledge, 1994. 178–219.

Sims, Christopher A. "The Dangers of Individualism and the Human Relationship to Technology in Philip K. Dick's *Do Androids Dream of Electric Sheep?*" *Science Fiction Studies* 36 (2009): 67–86.

Singer, Peter. *Animal Liberation.* 1975. New York: HarperCollins, 2002.

Sontag, Susan. "Approaching Artaud." *Under the Sign of Saturn: Essays.* London: Picador, 2002. 13–72.
Sounes, Howard. *Down the Highway: The Life of Bob Dylan.* New York: Grove, 2011.
"The Squire of Gothos." *Star Trek.* NBC. 22 June 1967.
Stam, Robert, and Ella Shohat. "*Zelig* and Contemporary Theory: Mediation on the Chameleon Text." *The Films of Woody Allen: Critical Essays,* ed. Charles P. Silet. Lanham, MD: Scarecrow, 2006. 198–216.
Stokes, London Melvyn. *D. W. Griffith's "The Birth of a Nation": A History of the Most Controversial Motion Picture of All Time.* Oxford: Oxford UP, 2007.
Sugimori, Masami. "Signifying, Ordering, and Containing the Chaos: Whiteness, Ideology, and Language in *Intruder in the Dust.*" *Faulkner Journal* 22.1–2 (2006): 54–79.
Sullivan, Neil. "Nella Larsen's *Passing* and the Fading Subject." *African American Review* 32.3 (1998): 373–86.
Sutin, Lawrence. *Divine Invasions: A Life of Philip K. Dick.* New York: Carroll and Graf, 2005.
Snyder, Zack, dir. *Dawn of the Dead.* Perf. Ving Rhames, Sarah Polley, Mekhi Phifer. Universal, 2004.
Tate, Claudia. "Nella Larsen's *Passing:* A Problem of Interpretation." *Black American Literature Forum* 14.4 (1980): 142–46.
Tavernier-Courbin, Jacqueline. *Ernest Hemingway's "A Moveable Feast": The Making of Myth.* Boston: Northeastern UP, 1991.
Taylor, Mark C. *Disfiguring: Art, Architecture, Religion.* Chicago: U of Chicago P, 1992.
Toth, Josh. *The Passing of Postmodernism: A Spectroanalysis of the Contemporary.* New York: SUNY, 2010.
———. "Toni Morrison's *Beloved* and the Rise of Historioplastic Metafiction." *Metamodernism: Historicity, Affect, and Depth after Postmodernism,* ed. Robin van den Akker, Alison Gibbons, and Timotheus Vermeulen. London: Rowman and Littlefield International, 2017. 40–53.
Traylor, Eleanor W. "The Fabulous World of Toni Morrison: *Tar Baby.*" *Critical Essays on Toni Morrison,* ed. Ellie Y. McKay. Boston: G. K. Hall, 1988. 135–49.
Tufts, Eleanor M. "Bellows and Goya." *Art Journal* 30.4 (1971): 362–68.
Vint, Sherryl. "Speciesism and Species Being in *Do Androids Dream of Electric Sheep?*" *Mosaic* 40.1 (2007): 111–26.
Wagner, Johanna M. "In Place of Clare Kendry: A Gothic Reading of Race and Sexuality in Nella Larsen's *Passing.*" *Callaloo* 34.1 (2011): 143–57.
Wald, Gayle. *Crossing the Line: Racial Passing in Twentieth-Century U.S. Literature and Culture.* Durham, NC: Duke UP, 2000.
Wall, Cheryl A. "Nella Larsen: Passing for What?" *Women of the Harlem Renaissance.* Bloomington: Indiana UP, 1995. 85–138
The Walking Dead. Created by Frank Darabont. AMC, 2010–.
Wandler, Steven. "'A Negro's Chance': Ontological Luck in *The Autobiography of an Ex-Colored Man.*" *African American Review* 42.3–4 (2008): 579–94.

Warmuth, Scott. "Bob Charlatan: Deconstructing Dylan's *Chronicles: Volume One*." *New Haven Review* 6 (2008): 70–83.
Washington, Salim. "Of Black Bards, Known and Unknown: Music as Racial Metaphor in James Weldon Johnson's *The Autobiography of an Ex-Colored Man*." *Callaloo* 25.1 (2002): 233–56.
Wasson, Richard. "The Contrary Politics of Postmodernism: Woody Allen's *Zelig* and Italo Calvino's *Marcovaldo*." *Ethics/Aesthetics: Post-Modern Positions*, ed. Robert Merrill. Washington, DC: Maisonneuve, 1988. 83–94.
Waters, Muddy. "Just Make Love to Me." Written by Willie Dixon. Vinyl single. Chess, 1954.
Williams, Raymond. *Politics of Modernism: Against the New Conformists*. 3rd ed. New York: Verso, 2007.
Willis, Gordon. "Gordon Willis, ASC, and *Zelig*." Interview by Michelle Bogre. *American Cinematographer* 65.4 (1984): 43ff.
Wittenberg, Judith Bryant. *Faulkner: The Transfiguration of Biography*. Lincoln: U of Nebraska P, 1979.
Zackodnik, Teresa. "Passing Transgressions and Authentic Identity in Jessie Fauset's *Plum Bun* and Nella Larsen's *Passing*." *Literature and Racial Ambiguity*, ed. Teresa Hubel and Neil Brooks. Amsterdam, NY: Rodopi, 2002. 45–69.
Žižek, Slavoj. *The Art of the Ridiculous Sublime: On David Lynch's "Lost Highway."* Seattle: U of Washington P, 2000.
———. "Courtly Love, or, Woman as Thing." *The Metastases of Enjoyment: On Women and Causality*. London: Verso, 1994. 89–112.
———. *Less Than Nothing: Hegel and the Shadow of Dialectical Materialism*. London: Verso, 2012.
———. "Neighbors and Other Monsters: A Plea for Ethical Violence." *The Neighbor: Three Inquires in Political Theology*. Chicago: U of Chicago P, 2005. 134–90.
———. "Notes Towards a Politics of Bartleby: The Ignorance of Chicken." *Comparative American Studies* 4.4 (2006): 375–94.
———. *The Parallax View*. Cambridge, MA: MIT, 2009.
———. *The Sublime Object of Ideology*. London: Verso, 1989.
———. *Tarrying with the Negative: Kant, Hegel, and the Critique of Ideology*. Durham, NC: Duke UP, 1993.

INDEX

actor-network theory, 188, 255–56n4
Agamben, Giorgio, 7, 99, 108, 141, 161, 248n24
aggressivity, 147, 150
Albee, Edward, *The Zoo Story*, 184, 188, 193–94, 201, 255n1
Allen, Woody. See *Zelig*
Anthropocene, 189
Ashcan realism, 1
autobiography, 21, 90, 163, 166–67, 171, 234; autonarrative forms of, 165; and metafiction, 201–3, 206, 209, 257nn17–18; modernist forms of, 163–65
Autobiography of an Ex-Colored Man, The (Johnson), 18–26, 28, 33, 36, 38, 45, 163, 166, 237n7, 238n14
autofiction, autonarration vs., 253n7, 257n18
autoplasticity, 8, 10, 21, 182, 192, 193, 199, 201–2, 206, 208, 214, 224, 227, 230–31, 234, 235n1, 244n18, 257n17; and autonarrative, 165–67, 171, 174–77, 182, 198, 253n5; auto-teleiopoetics vs., 230. See also plasticity

Badiou, Alain, 248n24
Bailey, Lisa M. Siefker, 255n2
Bakhtin, Mikhail, 29, 31, 54, 66, 243n15, 261n22. See also heteroglossia; modernism; polyphony
Bamhart, Bruce, 238n14

Barnes, Elizabeth, 103, 105
Barth, John, 184
Barthes, Roland, 64, 87, 215, 261; "The Death of the Author," 64
"Bartleby, the Scrivener" (Melville), 10, 61, 64, 93, 95, 99–110, 113–15, 117, 121, 123, 126, 138, 141, 154, 161, 163, 230, 246n5, 246nn11–12, 247nn14–15, 247nn18–19, 247nn21–22, 248nn24–25, 249n9, 251–52n5, 254–55n17
becoming, as mode of existing, 21, 43, 54, 96, 106, 152, 205, 233, 238n10. See also relation; spectrality
Bellows, George: *Both Members of This Club*, 1–4, 6, 8, 9, 10, 235n4, 236n7; *The Knock Out*, 4, 236n4; *Stag at Sharkey's*, 3. See also Johnson, Jack; modernism; realism
Berlin, Isaiah, and positive liberty, 90, 245n23. See also stoicism
Bible, 160, 247n23
biopic, as realism, 222, 229, 261n23
blackface, 26, 35–38, 63, 223, 225–27, 240n26, 252n11; and American-Jewish identity, 26, 28, 34–37, 142, 227, 240n26, 252n11. See also Crosland, Alan; Jolson, Al
Blackmer, Corinne, 241n10,
Blackmore, David L., 241n10
Blanchot, Maurice, 7, 10
Bok, Sissela, 242n4

boxing, 1, 3–7
Boynton, Sandra, *But Not the Hippopotamus*, 14–16
Brenner, Gerry, 253n9
Brogan, Jacqueline Vaught, 169–70
Brooks, Max, *World War Z: An Oral History of the Zombie War*, 93, 95–97, 246n3, 246n6
Brooks, Neil, 238n9
Bruce, Iris, 142, 251n4
Bryant, Levi, *The Democracy of Objects*, 189, 190–91, 193,
Burke, Kenneth: and mystification, 149, 171, 252n15, 254n13; and terministic screens, 149, 170, 174, 252n15
Butler, Judith: *Giving an Account of Oneself*, 60, 133, 194, 234; and passing, 49, 51, 61, 240n4, 241n10; and performativity, 50–51; and self-identical subject, 62, 186. *See also* norms

capitalism, 93–94, 112, 142, 250n15; late form of, 257n18
Carr, Brian, 47, 52, 241n10
Caughie, Pamela L., 64–65, 163, 242nn4–5
Charles, Larry, 210, 212, 258n1
Cheng, Anne Anlin, and racial melancholia, 14–17, 29, 90, 104
Chesnutt, Charles, 237n7
Christianity, 159–60, 211, 229
Cixous, Hélène, and *écriture feminine*, 244n18
Clark, Keith, 244–45n21
communism, 53
community, 9, 16, 52, 54, 77, 106, 124, 159, 237n6, 238n14, 239n20, 247n21, 249n8; democratic form of, 7, 10; individual vs., 19, 34, 36, 40, 45–46, 48–50, 52–54, 98, 241n8, 249n11; and myth of immanence, 16, 37, 69, 252n13; racially determined, 14–18, 21, 49, 52, 75, 82–83, 85, 244n20; and risk of entropy, 9, 14, 59, 90, 94, 96–97, 100, 106, 108, 112–20, 123, 126, 128, 130, 134, 138, 141, 145, 146, 191, 196, 217–19, 247n23
consumption, of the other, 9, 80, 89, 105, 109, 112–14, 122, 139, 142, 175, 193, 247n19, 249n12
correlationism, 188, 190–91, 255n3. *See also* speculative realism
Cousineau, Thomas, 257n21

Crosland, Alan: *The Jazz Singer*, 26–38, 44, 60, 68, 163, 223–27, 239n18; and Jewish identity, 26–28, 32, 34–37, 227, 240n27; melancholy in, 38
Cutter, Martha J., 241n8

David, Larry: *Curb Your Enthusiasm*, 203–6, 208–10; metafictional tendencies in, 203–6; and *Seinfeld*, 204–5, 210
Day, Aidan, 258n6,
Decker, James, 164, 253n5
deconstruction, 81, 94
Deleuze, Gilles, "Bartleby; or, The Formula," 99, 106–8, 246n12, 247nn21–22,
Del Gizzo, Suzanne, 254n12
democracy, 10, 100, 114, 234; to come, 106, 131; and communion, 68, 148; as egalitarian state, 2, 9, 15–16, 19, 148; as goal of plasticity, 234; of incommensurable, 10, 234; of objects, 190, 191
Derrida, Jacques, 7, 21, 113, 125, 142, 189, 216, 243n9, 250n17, 254n17; and carno-phallogocentrism, 122; and conjuration, 19, 69, 89, 229; and democracy, 68, 100, 131; and disgust, 65, 67, 68–69, 87, 180, 243n16; "Eating Well," 87, 108, 109, 113, 115, 121–23, 129, 130, 133, 134, 181, 193, 195, 248n3, 250n18; "Economimesis," 65–68, 160, 242n6, 243n8; and enjoyment, 66–67; *Envois*, 177–82, 255nn18–19; and ethics, 68, 113, 153, 181; *The Gift of Death*, 99, 108–9, 181, 259n7, 259n12; and hauntology, 31, 238n11; and lovance, 229; on Nietzsche, 176–77; and pathology of the community, 19, 84; and perhaps, 176–77, 182; and pharmakeus, 246n5; and pharmakon, 14, 153, 237n3; "Plato's Pharmacy," 153–54, 179, 207, 216, 237n3, 246n5, 251–52n5, 259n12; *Politics of Friendship*, 19, 45, 84, 120–21, 131, 176–77, 183, 229, 237n6, 252n17, 259n12; and secret, 178, 182, 229; *Specters of Marx*, 237n6, 238nn10–11, 259n12; and subjectiles, 109, 121, 195; and teleiopoetics, 230; and undecidability, 4, 129, 146, 222, 230. *See also* deconstruction; hospitality; signature, the; spectrality; supplementarity
Dick, Philip K.: "The Android and the Human," 196; *The Divine Invasion*, 257n14; *Do Androids Dream of Electric Sheep?*, 111–35, 138, 154, 184, 194–95, 246n2,

247n23, 248n1; "Nazism and *The High Castle*," 250n14; *Radio Free Albemuth*, 256–57n13; "Schizophrenia & *The Book of Changes*," 195; *The Three Stigmata of Palmer Eldritch*, 256n6; *Ubik*, 256n6; *VALIS*, 194–95, 197–202, 204, 206, 208–9, 256nn7–8, 256–57nn12–14
Dimitri, Carl J., 70, 72, 77, 80, 243n12, 245n23
Dionysian, Apollonian vs., 99, 250n1
diremption, as condition of self-consciousness, 201, 209
Doane, Mary Ann, 35, 239n24
Doezema, Marianne, 3, 4, 235n3, 236n6
Doniger, Wendy, 238n9
Duvall, John N., 84, 86, 245n26
Dylan, Bob: "All I Really Want to Do," 218, 259n15; "Ain't Talking," 260; "Blowin' in the Wind," 216; *Bringing It All Back Home*, 260n22; "Brownsville Girl," 215, 260n18; "Can't Wait," 212; *Chronicles*, 210, 216, 231–32, 259n11, 260n17, 261n29, 261n31; "Cold Irons Bound," 228; "Gotta Serve Somebody," 226, 228; "A Hard Rain's A-Gonna Fall," 210, 216; "Highlands," 221, 260n18; "John Brown," 219; *Masked and Anonymous* (Charles), 210, 213–15, 224–26, 258n6; "My Back Pages," 211; and *No Direction Home* (Scorsese), 222, 231; "She Belongs to Me," 217; "Stuck Inside of Mobile with the Memphis Blues Again," 222, 260n18; "Tangled Up in Blue," 217, 258–59n6; *Tarantula*, 221, 260n20; "Things Have Changed," 215; "Visions of Johanna," 217–19, 259n14; "Where Are You Tonight? (Journey Through Dark Heat)," 219–20

Ebert, Roger, 212, 214–15
egalitarianism, 7, 13, 15, 93, 96, 98, 100, 105, 113, 114, 121, 148. *See also* democracy
egotism, 9, 99, 107, 129, 133, 138, 141, 194, 214, 247n18, 250–51n1; bad faith of, 147; empathy vs., 105, 117, 124, 125, 146, 162, 199, 249n6; as monomania, 106
Emerson, Ralph Waldo, 99, 164, 235n2; "Friendship," 7
essence, 38, 87, 143, 144, 196, 206, 207, 235n2, 237n8, 249n8, 254n13; and racial purity, 24, 52–53, 74, 170; and selfhood, 33, 140, 145, 238n12. *See also* immanence

ethics: American, 166; of concealment, 64–65, 163; democratic, 68, 153, 165, 243–44n16; of the face, 133; Levinasian, 54, 60; masculine code of, 5; of the modern novel, 64–65; morality vs., 239n21; narrative, 9, 154; of passing, 65; of perpetual sublation, 176, 202; of reading, 153; violent, 115, 130–33, 160, 164, 165. *See also* silence
existentialism, 17, 20, 31, 101, 169, 184

face-to-face, the, 131–33, 160. *See also* Levinas, Emmanuel; Žižek, Slajov
Fagg, John, 235n1
fantasy, 6, 19, 22, 51–53, 93–94, 97–99, 145, 150, 197, 239n17, 245–46n1, 246n3; of the autonomous self, 94; of communion, 59; of essential norms, 61; of hierarchal absolutes, 24; ideological, 54; of immanence, 56, 62; melancholic, 13, 46; as nightmare, 95, 98; of pure inclusion, 2; of a stable social order, 56
Faulkner, William, 26, 31, 78, 81, 87, 96, 132, 243nn11–15, 244nn18–19, 244–45n21; *Go Down Moses*, 69, 75–76; *Intruder in the Dust*, 70–80, 87, 244–45n21; *Light in August*, 69, 244n20
Feldstein, Richard, 252n7
Fitzgerald, Scott F., 139, 168–69, 254n10
Fontaine, Rene, 258n1. *See also* Charles, Larry
Forster, Marc, *World War Z*, 246n3. *See also under* Brooks, Max
Fowler, Doreen, 77, 80, 243n14, 244n18, 245n22
frames: fictional, 255n2; of knowledge, 38; of identity, 40–41, 153; mediating, 8, 62, 201; performative, 68; thematizing, 44. *See also* Nancy, Jean-Luc: compearance; relation; supplementarity
fraternity, 20, 84, 98, 141, 143, 148. *See also* egalitarianism; empathy
freedom: ontological form of, 17, 20–25, 31, 42, 48, 51, 69, 77–80, 140–42, 238n10, 243n7; terror of, 51. *See also* Nancy, Jean-Luc
Freud, Sigmund, 16, 32, 102, 133, 178, 243n8, 247n16; *Civilization and Its Discontents*, 247n23, 249n9; and death drive, 151, 196, 237n5, 249nn9–10; and double, 42, 218, 220, 225, 256n10; and ego devel-

Freud, Sigmund (*continued*)
opment, 101; and Hegel, 32, 116; and Judeo-Christian ethics, 115, 130, 249n9; "Mourning and Melancholia," 17, 236n1; and pleasure principle, 107, 117, 133; and primary narcissism, 195, 237n5; and repetition compulsion, 7, 116. *See also* oedipal situation; psychoanalysis; uncanny, the

Galvan, Jill, 249n8
Garwood, Ian, 222
Gates, Henry Louis, Jr., 87, 242n5
Genette, Gérard, 253n7, 257n18
Ginsberg, Elaine K., 238n9
Girgus, Sam B., 251
Gold, Joseph, 243n12
Goya, Francisco, *Los disparates*, 5–6
great white hope, 7
Gwin, Minrose, 244n18

Hayles, N. Katherine, 117, 120, 249–50nn12–13, 250n15
Haynes, Todd, *I'm Not There*, 221–24, 260–61nn22–23, 261n25, 261n27
Hegel, G. W. F., 6, 8, 37–38, 130–31, 147, 150–51, 160, 175, 191–92, 198–99, 206, 208, 215, 223–24, 227, 229, 223, 231, 239nn20–21, 239n23, 249n11, 254n13, 257n17, 258nn3–4, 259n16; and absolute knowledge, 213; and alien existence, 130, 207, 213; and *Aufhebung*, 173–74, 201, 239n22; and classical art, 202; and conscience, 34–36, 96, 123, 218, 252n6; Derrida on, 68, 243n9, 255n20; and family vs. nation, 32–33, 226, 239n20; and God, 213; and human law vs. divine law, 116, 120, 226; and individuality, 34; and law of the heart, 33, 81, 245n23, 246n9; and law of all other hearts, 245n23; with Levinas, 172, 174; and lord/bondsman dialectic, 141, 226, 236n2; and maternal vs. paternal, 33, 116; and negation of the negation, 173, 213; and Notion, 162, 207, 234; and romantic art, 166, 174, 202, 257n17; and symbolic art, 165–66, 169, 174, 201; and third term, 4, 124; and Time, 195, 205, 260n19; and virtue, 207, 239n19, 245n23, 246n9. *See also* community; diremption; ethics; skepticism; stoicism; sublation
Heinert, 86
Heise, Ursula K., 249n5

Hemingway, Ernest, *A Moveable Feast*, 166–72, 174–76, 254nn11–12
Hemingway, Mary, 254n12
Henderson, Mae, 44, 55, 57, 241n7
heteroglossia, 30, 173; as heteroglot world, 31, 38; and novelistic style, 64. *See also* modernism; polyphony
Hitchcock, Alfred: *The Man Who Knew Too Much*, 245–46n1; *North by Northwest*, 245–46n1; *Rear Window*, 245–46n1
Hopkins, Gerard Manley, 198–99
Horton, Merrill, 240n1
hospitality, 123; infinite form of, 123, 129, 133, 250. *See also* Nancy, Jean Luc: *l'intrus*
Huyssen, Andreas, 242n3
hysteria, 3, 56, 62, 85; definition of, 58–59

identity, 2, 7, 10, 15, 17, 19–22, 26, 29, 35–36, 39–42, 48–51, 53–54, 56, 58, 61–62, 64–65, 72, 74–78, 80, 82–86, 89, 94, 97–98, 101–2, 104–5, 112–15, 120–21, 123, 129, 133, 135–36, 139–40, 142–47, 151–53, 160–61, 163, 189, 197, 224, 226–27, 235–36n3, 237n3, 238n15, 239n17, 240n27 (chap. 1), 240n1 (chap. 2), 241n8, 243n7, 250n1, 252n7, 252n11, 254n17. *See also* essence; frames; immanence; race; self
ideology, 9, 19, 51, 54, 81, 86–87, 153, 166, 195–96, 219, 226, 243n13, 245n24, 248n25, 252n15
imaginary, the, 131, 133, 141, 147, 160, 162, 166–67, 182, 252n7, 253n3, 254n15
immanence, 5, 7, 8, 13, 16–18, 35–37, 39, 43–44, 50, 52–53, 56, 59, 62–63, 67, 69, 116, 123, 252n13. *See also* Nancy, Jean-Luc; self
interpellation, 15, 18, 50, 51, 58, 205, 219

Jacobsen, Louise Brix, 257–58n18
jazz, 26–30, 32–34, 38, 68, 138–39, 227; as literary form, 25, 38; as model for identity, 22–23, 25, 36–37. *See also* modernism; polyphony
Jeffries, Jim, 3, 236n6. *See also* great white hope
Johnson, Jack, 3, 5, 235n3, 236n6
Johnson, James Weldon. See *Autobiography of an Ex-Colored Man, The*
Johnston, Ruth D., 35, 223, 239n24, 240n26, 247n27, 252n9
jouissance, 66, 146
Judaism, 27–28, 132, 159, 160

Kant, Immanuel: and genius, 74, 165, 244n20; and naturalization, 66; and object-oriented ontology, 183, 188, 192, 249n7; and poetics, 67
Kassanoff, Jennie A., 235n2
Katz Monteil, Marco, 238n13
King, Martin Luther, Jr., 211n5
Kirkman, Robert, *The Walking Dead*, 93–96, 245–46n1
Klotz, Marvin, 244n19
Kristeva, Julia, 172–73, 175, 198; and genotext vs. phenotext, 171–72, 198; and Hegelian negation, 174; and poetic language, 64, 172–73; and semiotic chora, 172–73; and symbolic, 172–74; and thetic, 174–75, 254n15

Lacan, Jacques, 28, 33, 46, 64, 138, 162, 171, 178, 189, 190, 200, 226, 237n4, 252n16, 253n2; and *das Ding*, 68; and dimension of truth, 74; and father, 77; and ideal I, 128, 141, 147, 250n20, 252–53nn7–8; "The Mirror Stage," 252–53nn7–8; and *objet petit a*, 145; on "The Purloined Letter," 57, 242n15, 243–44n6, 244n17; and symbolic inertia, 61. *See also* aggressivity; imaginary, the; Other, the; Real, the; self; symbolic, the
Larsen, Nella, 10, 44, 46–47, 55, 57–58, 62, 163, 166, 241n8. *See also Passing*
Latour, Bruno, 193, 255–56nn4–5
Leeder, Murray, 225–27, 258n6, 261n27
Levinas, Emmanuel, 43, 86, 147, 180, 186, 220, 254n17; and bad silence, 45; "Difficult Freedom," 160; and face, 131–33, 160; and God-in-me, 55, 160, 185, 213, 250n16; and humanism, 183, 242n6; and infinite, 54–55, 60, 160, 172, 184, 213–14, 250nn16–17; and play, 66, 184; and proximity, 42, 171, 187; and responsibility, 44–45, 148, 230, 254n17; and saying vs. the said, 132, 240n5; and substitution, 180; and thematization, 44–45, 51, 132, 170. *See also* hospitality
Lingis, Alphonso, 225n4
Little, Johnathan, 241n
lynching, 18–23, 35, 38, 68, 69, 73, 80, 182, 244, 252n9; as act of conjuration, 19, 69, 89, 229; as narrative act, 23–25, 28, 68, 69; as rape, 85
Lyotard, Jean-François, and self as post, 61

Malabou, Catherine, 174, 192, 206, 231, 258n4, 261n28
Marqusee, Mike, 258n6
Marxism, 254n13
Matteson, John, 98–99, 247n19
Matthews, John T., 26, 30
Maxwell, Grant, 261n29
McBride, James, *The Color of Water*, 87–90, 169–70, 234
McCombe, John, 261n25
McDowell, Deborah E., 241n10
McGowan, Todd, 188–92
Meillassoux, Quentin, 188, 255n3
Melville, Herman, *Moby-Dick*, 106, 143, 152, 259n8. *See also* "Bartleby, the Scrivener"
metafiction, 80, 174, 184, 201, 203–7, 209, 257nn17–18. *See also* autoplasticity; postmodernism; neoromantic
Michaels, Walter Benn, 239n17, 243n1
Miller, Henry, *Tropic of Cancer*, 164–65
Milloy, Sandra D., 244–45n21
Mobley, Marilyn E., 82–83, 86
modernism, 87, 157, 184, 235n1, 239n17, 242n5, 243n11, 258n20; and passing, 44, 64–65; postmodernism vs., 9, 64–65, 69, 86–87, 165–66, 169, 184, 190–91, 201–2, 208, 218, 235n1, 244n18. *See also* polyphony
Moffitt, Letitia, 82–83, 86
monolingualism, 96–97
monomania. *See* egotism
Moreland, Richard C., 244n18
Morris, Barbara Alverson, 243n12
Morris, Wesley, 243n12
Morrison, Toni, *Tar Baby*, 81–87, 245nn25–26
Morton, Timothy, *Hyperobjects*, 188–91, 198–99
Motion, Andrew, 258n5, 260n19

Nainby, Keith, 258–59n6, 260n18
Nancy, Jean-Luc, 17, 18, 21, 22, 38, 42, 54, 68, 85, 87, 108, 121, 236n2, 237n4, 238n10; and being alone, 3; and community, 37, 45, 53, 54, 69, 98, 252n13; and compearance, 59, 243n7, 256n5; and ecstasy, 53, 54; *The Experience of Freedom*, 20–21; and evil, 20, 31, 36; and identity as perpetual birth, 121, 177; "The Inoperative Community," 45, 52–53; with Levinas, 132; and *l'intrus*, 55, 68–69, 220; and Nazism, 252n13; and

280 / INDEX

Nancy, Jean-Luc (*continued*)
  presence as copresence, 13; and wickedness, 20–21; and withdrawal, 37, 69. *See also* Other, the; relation
narrative, 9, 10, 24, 25, 44, 55, 64, 81, 82, 86, 96, 151, 167, 197, 199, 208, 222, 234, 239n18, 240n26, 243n11, 257n13, 257n15, 257n18; ambiguity, 29; and disruption of convention, 164; of dominant culture, 87; ethics of, 9, 154, 163–65, 176–77; gamble, 192; integrity of, 253n9; modalities, 10; and norms, 9, 62; of passing, 18, 109, 241n8; voice, 60, 75, 80, 257n13; of zombies, 93–95, 98, 99, 246n1. *See also* autofiction; autoplasticity; ethics
nationalism, 8, 14, 17, 38, 239nn17–18, 243n11
nativism, 3, 26, 63–64, 238n13, 239n17, 243n11; racism, 38, 73, 113
neoromantic, 166, 257n15, 257n17; and metafiction, 201–2. *See also* Hegel, G. W. F.: and romantic art
Nietzsche, Friedrich, 176–77, 191, 229, 250n1; *The Birth of Tragedy*, 250. *See also* Dionysian
Nin, Anaïs, 164
norms, 59, 60, 62, 161, 194, 200, 201; behavioral, 61, 185; communal, 3, 9; of conventional society, 197; democratic, 235n2; discursive, 5; equalizing, 8; gender, 244n18; of objectivity, 154; performative, 59, 194; regulatory, 3; thematizing, 185–86
Norris, Faith G., 254
North, Michael, 30

Oates, Joyce Carol, 1, 5
object-oriented ontology (OOO), 183, 188–92, 249n7; subject-oriented ontology vs., 192. *See also* actor-network theory; speculative realism
oedipal situation, 32, 233, 244n18, 260n20
other. *See* self
Other, the: Lacanian concept of, 33, 52, 64, 79, 123, 145, 146, 161–62, 163, 166, 171, 178, 179, 196, 213, 219, 225–28, 232, 254n17; Nancyian concept of, 14–19, 68, 85, 116, 237n4

Palmer, Christopher, 201, 256n7, 256n12
paranoia, 39, 47, 49, 52, 55–56, 59–60, 209
passing, 48, 93, 109, 126, 142, 223, 246n7, 261n29; gender, 71; novelistic, 47–48, 54–60, 62, 65, 67–69, 241n8; racial, 18–25, 35, 46–51, 65, 69, 75, 93, 95, 238n9, 241n8, 242n5, 244n20; sexual, 48, 49, 241n10, 242n12. *See also* modernism; race: and racial ambiguity
Passing (Larsen), 39–62, 67, 85, 100, 186, 230, 241nn11–12
Pennebaker, D. A., *Don't Look Back,* 222
perversity, 56, 81, 89, 162, 182, 216; definition of, 241n9; and postmodernism, 60, 81, 89–90, 162, 176, 191, 242n14. *See also* hysteria; Žižek, Slavoj
Petrov, Sergei (pseudonym of Bob Dylan), 258n1
Pfeiffer, Kathleen, 238n9, 241n6
plasticity, 8, 23, 26, 153, 166, 176, 177, 185, 192, 194, 201, 207, 208, 213, 214, 216, 221, 224, 227, 229, 230–31, 257n17, 258n4, 261n28; Hegelian concept of, 175, 206, 234, 257n17
Poe, Edgar Allan, 57, 74, 99, 178; "The Purloined Letter," 242n15, 243–44nn16–17
polyphony, 29–31, 56, 63, 164, 174, 202; cacophony vs., 31, 34, 38, 44–45, 68, 80, 162, 165, 173–74, 184, 194, 202. *See also* silence
posthuman, 249n8
postmodernism, 44, 65, 86, 87, 89, 94, 190, 201–4, 208, 212, 241n7, 242n14, 244n18, 255n1, 257n15, 257–58nn17–19; and metafiction, 201. *See also* modernism; perversity
Pitzer, Andrea, 259n8
prudence, American forms of, 98–99, 154
psychoanalysis, 178

race: and black identity, 3–5, 14, 18–19, 21–24, 35, 36, 39–41, 44, 48, 50, 52, 63, 72, 73, 75–76, 81–89, 97, 223, 227, 240n26 (chap. 1), 240n1 (chap. 2), 241n11, 244n20; and debt, 76, 78–79, 86; disgust, 68, 70, 78, 80, 85, 87, 90; and Jewish identity, 26–28, 32, 34–37, 88–89, 136, 142–43, 227, 240n27, 246n7, 252n11; and melancholia, 8, 14–18, 20, 25, 29, 84, 104; and racial ambiguity, 9, 16–17, 21–22, 35, 50, 61, 63, 66, 70, 139, 237n6, 238n9; and racialization, 6, 15, 20, 68, 84, 87, 88, 104, 238n13, 243n11; and racism, 38, 73, 113. *See also* community; essence; immanence; lynching
Rajan, Tilottama, 165–66, 172, 175–76, 253n7
Real, the, 8, 23, 46–47, 51, 53, 89, 121, 138, 146, 151, 153, 162–63, 165, 177, 190, 192, 209, 216, 250–51n1, 252n16, 253n3

realism (aesthetic), 4, 8, 201, 255n1; Ashcan, 1; biopic as, 222, 229, 261n23; as classical, 202, 208; documentary, 208, 222, 229; nineteenth century social, 202, 208
Reid, Michelle, 259n19
relation: between blackness and whiteness, 3, 5, 13–14, 20–22, 36–38, 40, 41, 52–53, 75, 236n2; communal, 10, 13–14, 16–17, 37, 40, 43, 45, 52–53, 59–60, 69, 97, 116, 148, 238n14; as condition of identity, 2–3, 17, 41, 53, 101, 121, 123, 129, 243n7; corruptive nature of, 3, 8, 13–14, 16–17, 43; ethical, 8, 22, 62, 75, 161, 163, 183, 192, 194; as freedom, 20–23, 42, 67, 69, 80, 243n7; immanence vs., 5, 17, 36–37, 43, 53, 69, 116; as ineffaceable, 109, 121; melancholia vs., 8, 13–14, 16–17, 20, 23, 36–38, 45, 62, 108, 230; with negative, 5, 194; outside of, 17, 38, 53, 122; as performance, 31, 36–38, 97, 144, 194; as perpetual consumption, 109, 122; as proximity, 4, 43, 45, 53, 60, 186, 214, 216–17; without relation, 10, 216. *See also* face-to-face, the; jazz; supplementarity
religion: Christianity, 159–60, 211, 229; Judaism, 27–28, 132, 159, 160
Renza, Louis, 175–76, 254n10
Rickman, Gregg, 111–12, 248n5
Rogin, Michael, 35, 36
Romero, George A., *Dawn of the Dead*, 93; *Night of the Living Dead*, 94
Rosenberg, Joel, 27–29, 37–38
Rossi, Umberto, 257n15
Roudiez, Leon S., 173, 254
Rubenstein, Jill, 168, 170

Sartre, Jean-Paul, 20, 21, 101, 176, 246n13, 250n1, 252n6; and anguish, 140, 200, 233; and bad faith, 21, 52, 238n12; and in-itself, 106, 151. *See also* existentialism
Scobie, Stephen, 215–17, 258–59nn6–7, 259n12, 260n20
Scorsese, Martin, *No Direction Home: Bob Dylan*, 222, 231
Scott, Ridley, *Blade Runner*, 111–13, 248n1
Seinfeld, Jerry, 203–5
self: divine nature of, 33–34, 38, 160, 161, 165, 183, 200, 213, 226, 253n3; as other, 1, 5–6, 42, 96, 114, 124, 127, 130, 138, 145, 150, 218. *See also* relation
Sherrard-Johnson, Cherene, 240n1

Shohat, Ella, 149, 237n8, 251nn2–3, 252n9, 252n14
signature, the, 67, 215, 259n7; and countersigning, 259n7
silence, 26–29, 32, 34, 38, 44–45, 51, 65, 68–69, 75, 77, 179, 181–82, 191, 194, 202, 243n15, 258n5; as ethical act, 162–63, 184
Sims, Christopher A., 249n8
Singer, Peter, 248n4
skepticism, 202, 218
Snyder, Zack, *Dawn of the Dead*, 93
Sontag, Susan, 138, 148–49, 254n16
Sounes, Howard, 212, 259n10, 260n17
spectrality, 19, 89, 104, 182, 217, 229, 237n6, 247n18, 259n12. *See also* lynching: as act of conjuration
speculative realism, 183, 188–89, 249n7
Stam, Robert, 149, 237n8, 251nn2–3, 252n9, 252n14
Star Trek, 216, 259n9
stoicism, 77, 96, 213, 218, 226, 239n19, 245n23
Stokes, London Melvyn, 240n26
stranger, the, 19, 56, 64, 69, 107
subject, formation of the, 51, 167
sublation, 8, 34, 68, 165, 174–76, 223
Sugimori, Masami, 78, 243n13, 243n15, 245n24
Sullivan, Neil, 61–62, 242n16
supplementarity, 3, 5, 8, 13–14, 40, 43, 66–67, 90, 97, 122, 123, 124, 133, 138, 153, 155, 171, 229, 237n3, 242–43nn6–7
Sutin, Lawrence, 195–96
symbolic, the, 28, 46–47, 51–52, 54, 57, 59, 62, 71, 74, 79, 89, 100, 122, 131, 145–46, 160, 162, 171–75, 190, 196, 201–2, 208, 226, 242n15, 243–44n16
symptom, 2, 17, 19, 30, 41–42, 46–47, 50, 81, 122, 134, 137, 140–41, 144, 147, 149, 241n10

Tate, Claudia, 48–49, 241n11
Tavernier-Courbin, Jacqueline, 253n9
Taylor, Mark C., 202, 257n16
totalitarianism, 138, 141, 143, 148, 208, 250–51n1. *See also* egotism
Toth, Josh, *The Passing of Postmodernism*, 241n7, 242n14
Traylor, Eleanor W., 83
Trump, Donald, 7, 236n9
Tufts, Eleanor M., 236n7
Twain, Mark, *Pudd'nhead Wilson, and Other Tales*, 237n7

uncanny, the, 42, 47, 100–103, 105, 107, 114, 126–29, 132, 141, 162, 189, 196, 203, 240n2, 247n16, 253n1, 256n10

Vint, Sherryl, 126, 249n8, 250n21

Wagner, Johanna M., 240n2
Wagner, Richard, *Parsifal,* 151
Wald, Gayle, 238n9, 241n8
Wall, Cheryl A., 240n1
Wandler, Steven, 238n15
Warmuth, Scott, 259n11
Washington, Salim, 238n14,
Wasson, Richard, 144, 251n3
Waters, Muddy, "Just Make Love to Me," 259n15
Williams, Raymond, 64, 242nn1–2
Willis, Gordon, 137, 251n2
Wittenberg, Judith Bryant, 243n12

Zackodnik, Teresa, 241n8
Zelig (Allen), 114, 117, 136–55, 162, 163, 172, 222, 234, 246n7, 250–51nn1–5, 252nn7–9, 252n12, 252n14, 252n16

Žižek, Slavoj, 7, 46–47, 51–52, 56, 58, 81, 143, 144, 145, 146, 151, 163, 164, 167, 205, 215, 241n9, 242n14, 249n9, 254n15; and Christianity, 159–60; and ethical violence, 115, 130–32, 164; and God, 159–60, 165, 200; and Hegel, 174, 191, 192; and imaginary face, 131–33, 160–62, 194; and Judaism, 132, 160; and justice, 131, 154, 187; and law, 131–33, 160–61, 253n1; and Levinasian ethics, 131–32, 160–61; and love, 115, 130–32, 154, 160–62, 249n9; and necessity of fiction, 150; "Neighbors and Other Monsters," 248n25; and "Notes Towards a Politics of Bartleby," 248n25; *The Parallax View,* 248n25; and revisionism, 162; and Thing-in-itself, 174, 202. *See also* Lacan, Jacques

zombies: *Dawn of the Dead* (Romero), 93; *Dawn of the Dead* (Snyder), 93; *Night of the Living Dead* (Romero), 94; *The Walking Dead* (Kirkman), 93–96, 245–46n1; *World War Z* (Forster), 246n3; *World War Z: An Oral History of the Zombie War* (Brooks), 93, 95–97, 246n3, 246n6

Recent Books in the Series
Cultural Frames, Framing Culture

Rachel Hall
Wanted: The Outlaw in American Visual Culture

Stephanie L. Hawkins
American Iconographic: "National Geographic," Global Culture, and the Visual Imagination

Stephanie Harzewski
Chick Lit and Postfeminism

Samuel Chase Coale
Quirks of the Quantum: Postmodernism and Contemporary American Fiction

Eric Aronoff
Composing Cultures: Modernism, American Literary Studies, and the Problem of Culture

James J. Donahue
Failed Frontiersmen: White Men and Myth in the Post-Sixties American Historical Romance

Jinny Huh
The Arresting Eye: Race and the Anxiety of Detection

Ann Brigham
American Road Narratives: Reimagining Mobility in Literature and Film

Lauren S. Cardon
Fashion and Fiction: Self-Transformation in Twentieth-Century American Literature

Josh Toth
Stranger America: A Narrative Ethics of Exclusion

CPSIA information can be obtained
at www.ICGtesting.com
Printed in the USA
LVOW12s2011170518
577562LV00003B/499/P